SOCIAL PSYCHOLOGY AS POLITICAL ECONOMY

W. PETER ARCHIBALD

SOCIAL PSYCHOLOGY AS POLITICAL ECONOMY

W. Peter Archibald

Department of Sociology

McMaster University

McGRAW-HILL RYERSON LIMITED

Toronto Montreal New York St. Louis San Francisco Auckland
Beirut Bogotá Düsseldorf Johannesburg Lisbon London Lucerne
Madrid Mexico New Delhi Panama Paris Sãn Juan São Paulo
Singapore Sydney Tokyo

**SOCIAL PSYCHOLOGY AS
POLITICAL ECONOMY**

Copyright © McGraw-Hill Ryerson Limited, 1978. All rights reserved.
No part of this publication may be reproduced, stored in a retrieval system, or
transmitted, in any form, or by any means, electronic, mechanical, photo-
copying, recording, or otherwise, without the prior written permission of
McGraw-Hill Ryerson Limited.

ISBN 0-07-082347-2

1 2 3 4 5 6 7 8 9 0   D   7 6 5 4 3 2 1 0 9 8

Printed and bound in Canada

Canadian Cataloguing in Publication Data

Archibald, William Peter, 1943-
    Social psychology as political economy

(McGraw-Hill Ryerson series in Canadian sociology)

Bibliography: p.
Includes index.
ISBN 0-07-082347-2

1. Social psychology.   2. Political psychology.
I. Title.

HM251.A765   301.1   C77-001707-X

CONTENTS

Editor's Introduction

Acknowledgments

Preface

Editor's Introduction

As fields of intellectual inquiry become larger and better established, the questions they ask typically become smaller. In social psychology, a flood of careful experiments have poured their results into an ever fuller reservoir of knowledge; however, the student has waited in vain for a grand summation. Of late, the nonexperimenters in social psychology have provided even less. They have retreated from the practised intuition of symbolic interactionism to the skepticism of ethnomethodology and the nihilism of phenomenology!

Too many social psychologists have stopped asking those questions which have important answers: How does social inequality affect social behavior and self-conception? Is man naturally selfish and competitive or is he naturally cooperative? How is a person's view of the world a product of his place in that world?

Nevertheless, questions about the nature of man and how his supposedly immutable nature is shaped by the surrounding political economy never lost their appeal for one group—the Frankfurt School of so-called "critical theorists." Formed from the fusion of Marxist, Freudian, and "sociology of knowledge" traditions, critical theory began to win popularity in North America with the growing interest in the work of Herbert Marcuse in the late 1960s. Since that time, interest in critical sociology has spread throughout this continent—especially throughout Canada, where history and political economy have always enjoyed an important place in sociological studies owing to the influence of Harold Innis, S. D. Clark, and John Porter.

In this extremely ambitious book, Peter Archibald undertakes three main tasks. After specifying the kinds of questions modern social psychology either cannot or will not attempt to answer, he traces the development of social theory since the industrial revolution, placing his own critical perspective in relation to earlier formulations of "man in society." Functionalism, exchange theory, symbolic interactionism, Marxism, and psychoanalytic theory are among the approaches discussed. Finally, Professor Archibald applies his critical perspective to analyzing the processes by which "identities" are formed and maintained. Here in his examination of class, ethnicity, and national character, the author shows an acute insight into the Canadian situation.

Clearly and carefully argued and full of lively examples, *Social Psychology as Political Economy* is both a brilliant first step toward sociopsychological theorizing of the future and a good start toward understanding how social inequality affects our present thought and behavior.

Lorne Tepperman

ACKNOWLEDGMENTS

This labor of love and hate has benefited from a great many people.

To Reg Robson, who first sparked my interest in the philosophy and techniques of experimentation in social psychology, I shall always be grateful. Without the insistence of Eric Chester, Paul Gingrich, and others among my associates at the University of Michigan that comparative-quantitative methods more generally can make a worthwhile political contribution, I might never have attempted to bridge the gap within social psychology. Finally for these formative influences, my postdoctoral year at the Universität Bielefeld, West Germany, and the encouragement I received there from Rolf Klima, Lothar Hack, and others was decisive for the development of the view of alienation around which much of the present work revolves.

As for the manuscript itself, Jim Rinehart has been a constant source of support (as has John Gartrell) and a tough critic on the stratification issues of Chapter 8. Jim Curtis, Brian Milton, Rick Guscott, Harvey Krahn, and Irving Zeitlin gave helpful suggestions on some of the theory chapters of Part 2. Almost the entire department of anthropology at the University of Western Ontario seems to have given me comments on my foray into their discipline in Chapter 7, but special thanks should go to Jim Freedman and Martin Silverman. My painful attempt to make sense of the vast literature on women's studies owes much to suggestions from Phyllis Jensen, Dorothy Smith, Constantina Safilios-Rothschild, and Linda Moffat. Finally, I would like to thank Jim Curtis, Carl Cuneo, Linda Moffat, and Craig McKie for their help on Chapter 10. Needless to say, none of these commentators should be held responsible for any shortcomings in the final product.

For the technical production of the manuscript I would like to thank my typists: Judy Smith, Barb Rand, and Alexis Archibald, and my patient editors: Herb Hilderley, Lorne Tepperman, Jane Abramowitz, and Tim Griffin. My wife Alexis shared in some of the excitement of the project, but probably more in its pain, typing portions of the manuscript under duress when deadlines loomed large and funds small, and generally holding the rest of the world off while I struggled with my own as well as others' alienation.

PREFACE

The only sociological approach to social psychology which has been taken at all seriously, by North American academics at least, is what is now known as "Symbolic Interactionism." As I shall later argue in Chapter 6, this is understandable but lamentable. Understandable, because its focus upon freely acting individuals in "negotiated inter-action" and failure to come to grips with conflict and coercion is very flattering to the American society which has spawned it; lamentable, because, as we shall see in Part 3, our capitalist socie-ties do not deserve this naïvely laudatory image.

The present work falls within the rubric of "radical" or "critical" social science; however, from the beginning I should like to dis-tinguish it from some of the characteristics which have sometimes been associated with these labels. Chief among these is a certain arrogance, an air of near-religious purity which disdains all main-stream social science as "bourgeois" and therefore second-rate.

In contrast to such narrowly one-sided approaches, this text is designed as a serious double debate with the mainstream. One side of the debate is with those who prefer a psychological over a sociological approach to social psychology. Thus in Part 1, I try to demonstrate how much of mainstream social psychology is psy-chologically biased, offering, in a very general way at that point, a series of sociologically oriented alternative assumptions. In Part 2, I attempt to show, by reconstructing the debates among social theorists, that much of sociological theory was in fact formulated as an alternative to psychological theory. Finally, in the examination of a number of related empirical topics in Part 3 the importance of a sociological perspective is again emphasized. I hope that this thrust of the book will prove useful not only to sociological social psychologists who wish to entertain more than a Symbolic-Inter-actionist approach to social psychology, but also to psychologists who would like their students to be aware of the various sociologi-cal approaches.

The other side of the debate is with mainstream sociological social psychologists. In Parts 2 and 3, I have tried to present and empiric-ally evaluate the major approaches. In order to facilitate these com-parisons I have looked at their "political-economic" aspects defined in the weakest sense; that is, what they have had to say about how individuals relate to the "political" and "economic" aspects of society as colloquially defined. I make no pretense to having been "unbiased" in these comparisons; rather, my own preference for a "political-economic" approach in the stronger sense of the term[1] has obviously affected my presentation of the other approaches. How-ever, I think I can honestly say that I have at least been fairer to non-Marxian approaches than their adherents have typically been to the Marxian.

Cutting across both of these bridges with the mainstream is a more eclectic methodological approach than one typically finds either in the mainstream or among Marxists. Thus whereas many texts insinuate—if not proclaim—that experimentation and quantification is the only correct way of doing social psychology, I have made liberal use of such more "discursive" materials as historical studies, participant observations, and autobiographies. Whereas many Symbolic Interactionists as well as Marxists have summarily rejected experimental and survey data, I have also made extensive use of these potential sources of knowledge.[2]

Finally, the reader will note that although this book appears in a Canadian sociology series, I have refrained from using any such title as "Social Psychology in Canada." I have attempted to make use of Canadian material wherever possible. This has meant, among other things, qualifications to some of the generalizations about class, status, and power (Chapter 8) and differences in emphasis in discussions of race and ethnic relations (Chapter 9) from American texts. Yet there is still a paucity of Canadian studies on many of the issues taken up, and general theoretical relevance rather than national origin has been the major criterion for inclusion. For this reason the book is not intended to be only for Canadians.

Interestingly, however, my theoretical orientation has led me in certain directions which have thus far not found their way into Canadian texts. For example, whereas the topic of Canadian national character is taken up in existing texts, there is no mention of what has recently come to be popularly known as Margaret Atwood's (1972) "colonization" thesis. Here this topic is related to those in the chapter on race, ethnicity, and sex, particularly through the theorizing of Frantz Fanon (see Chapter 3).

W. Peter Archibald

---

[1] For Adam Smith, David Ricardo, and other "classical economists" as well as for Marx, the term referred to the study of the sources and distribution of wealth and the various ways in which they relate to other aspects of a society's structure (see Lichtheim, 1965:170-191). Among contemporary Marxists the term often refers to Marxist theory alone.

[2] Criticism of quantitative methods by Marxists has by now almost become orthodoxy. See, for example, Lukács (1971), Marcuse (1964), and Shaw (1975). My own position is that such a stance is unnecessary, nor was it intended by Marx (see Hansen, 1967; Easton, 1970; Archibald, 1976b).

1

INTRODUCTION

1
THE IMPORTANCE OF A CRITICAL SOCIOLOGICAL APPROACH

Most social psychology texts begin by focusing upon the presumed general characteristics of an individual's psychology, upon "human nature." We are usually first told about the perceptual apparatus of humans and how, given a host of filtering, organizing, or distorting bases, they perceive other people. Next is a discussion of "beliefs, attitudes, and values" (in fact, there seems to have been more research into attitudes than any other concept in social psychology), leading eventually to attitudes toward other people ("interpersonal attraction"), "social influence," and the more complicated topics of group structure and social roles. The assumptions behind this approach are presumably these:

(1) The social emanates from, or is built into, the psychological. More specifically, what individuals do socially is ultimately a reflection of what they "want" to do individually, such that the major task of social science is to discover what they want. Among philosophers the issue of the relative explanatory importance of what the individual wants and other sources, including social sources, of his or her activity has usually been referred to as that of *"voluntarism"* versus *"determinism."*

(2) People are usually more or less conscious of what they want, such that one can, for example, discover what they want by having them answer questions about their beliefs, attitudes, and values. Their social behavior can then be predicted and explained by their attitudes or general states of consciousness. The issue here is one of *"idealism"* (i.e., "ideas rule the world") versus *"materialism"* (physical or "material" events are more important).

That there must be a great deal of truth to the image of humans as constructing and distorting reality as they see fit seems clear if we observe social psychologists themselves, for these presumptions have been remarkably resilient in the face of a great deal of contradictory evidence — evidence obtained, interestingly enough, by mainstream social psychologists themselves. Let us first look at the history of discoveries of social influence, discoveries which seem to have tickled social psychologists and the general public precisely because they contradict prevailing presumptions.

SOCIAL INFLUENCE: DOING WHAT WE SHOULDN'T AND NOT DOING WHAT WE SHOULD

As early as the 1920s, for example, Floyd Allport (1924) discovered that the mere presence of others led his experimental subjects to considerably modify their judgments of weights, odors, and the like. Later in the 1940s Solomon Asch (1960) mercilessly confronted subjects with a clear choice among vertical lines (one was obviously much longer than the other two), with up to eight other subjects who swore that the middle length line was the longest. About a third of the subjects' judgments conformed to those of the majority, even though these latter judgments were clearly wrong! Some subjects later insisted that the middle line really *was* the longest, although a majority either simply expressed doubts about their own initial judgments or admitted that they simply did not want to appear different.

In the 1970s, 50 years after the first of these studies was undertaken, we still seem to be startled by the results of similar studies in the 1960s. For example, following the murder of Kitty Genovese on a New York street in broad daylight, during which none of 38 witnesses even telephoned the police, Bibb Latané and his associates (Latané and Darley, 1968; Darley and Latané, 1968; Latané and Rodin, 1969) simulated some of the major features of such "bystander emergencies" in the laboratory. The results were clear and striking: the *more* people present, the *less* likely subjects were to intervene! In another set of simulations, this time of the conditions which presumably existed in Nazi Germany, Stanley Milgram (1963; 1965a) had his subjects believe they were administering electric shocks to someone who claimed to have a heart condition, and who vigorously protested receiving the (alleged) shocks. Although the only visible pressure upon subjects to continue to shock the "victim" was the experimenter's insistence that the nature of the experiment required the subject to continue, approximately two-thirds of the subjects went "all the way." This meant believing that they were delivering shocks marked "Danger XXX" on the shock generator even after the "victim" had earlier refused to cooperate on the experimental task on the grounds that he feared for his life!

Although it seems reasonable to assume that Latané's bystanders *wanted* to help the victims, just as Milgram's subjects did *not* want to hurt their victims, what subjects wanted, and this is often true for studies of the effects of attitudes upon behavior more generally (Mischel, 1968; Wicker, 1969), was not the major determinant of their actual behavior. Rather, *whether they acted upon their attitudes appears to have depended upon the social circumstances under which they acted.* In the experiments by Allport, Asch, and Latané one assumes that the mitigating social circumstances are these: we do not normally expect to receive support for our actions from strangers in our society, even when we know that our actions would be proper in terms of popular morality. Instead, we fear "looking foolish" in front of others, such that the more of "them" there are, the less likely we are to act on our attitudes and intentions. Some of the comments of Latané's subjects support such an interpretation. Similarly, when subjects were faced with friends rather than strangers, they were as likely to intervene as if they were alone.

In the Milgram experiments the crucial circumstance is presumably the similarity between the subject-experimenter relationship in the laboratory to other relationships with power figures the subject had had in the past—at work, and so on. Under these other circumstances, disobedience, if not impossible, had at least been extremely costly, and there may well have been a generalization of learning from these past experiences to those of the laboratory. Hence, when the experimenter was not in the same room with the subject obedience dramatically decreased. Similarly, the importance of support from others is evident in the fact that when subjects were in the presence of others who defied the experimenter, they were much more likely to defy him themselves.

In summary, the results of social influence studies should lead us to question the individualistic starting point of mainstream, and especially psychological, social psychology, and the voluntaristic and idealistic assumptions about human nature which are behind it. This is not to suggest that we therefore become Skinnerian "Behaviorists" (see Chapter 2) and presume that humans are passively conformist *by nature*. Rather, the point is that social circumstances in our society apparently make them so, and that these circumstances appear to be especially inequalities in power and a lack of social support from others.

Given that this is the case, it might well make sense to reorient social psychology and start, not with the presumed psychology of allegedly independently acting individuals, but with the way in which power and support relationships in our society are typically structured. Typically, however, social psychologists have reacted to the fact that so many people in our society act immorally or amorally by attempting to explain it away as a methodological artifact, or by making a modified voluntaristic/idealistic argument that blames the individual rather than the structure of our society.

The methodological defense has usually taken one or more of several forms. One is the argument that we simply have not been able to measure attitudes well enough; if we did, so this argument goes, attitudes would predict behavior better.[1] There turns out to be some truth to this argument, but certainly not enough to dismiss the inconsistencies in attitude and behavior in experiments such as Milgram's. Another suggestion is that we should be measuring not general attitudes, but attitudes toward situations (Rokeach, 1968). If we asked white people how they would feel about signing a petition for open housing, for example, we could better predict their behavior than if we simply asked them how they felt about black people. Again, we gain *something* through such a procedure, but it is not clear that asking people whether they would do this or that is measuring an important attitude or simply asking them to predict how they would act under those circumstances.

The second set of arguments represents an attempt to protect voluntaristic/idealistic assumptions about attitudes and individuals' freedom of movement in a different way. One argument is that we have not measured *enough* attitudes. If we can capture an individual's entire attitude *structure,* so this argument goes, we can then demonstrate that attitudes explain behavior well. The most preferred explanation for Milgram's results, for example, is that subjects regarded the experimenter as a true authority figure; that is, as someone with a legitimate *right* to give them orders. This attempt to attribute subjects' conformity to their attitudes toward the experimenter is undoubtedly not completely off base, yet there are many results which simply cannot be explained by this argument. For example, it is unlikely that the experimenter's legitimacy would decrease simply because he was out of the room, yet obedience *did* decrease under these conditions. Similarly, while one might expect the experimenter's legitimacy to increase when an accomplice sided with him, obedience did *not* significantly increase at that point.[2]

A second, related argument is that individuals have simply not learned to act on their attitudes (Ehrlich, 1969; Abelson, 1972). The problem here is that this argument presumes a benign environment, that *others* who are present *want* individuals to act on their attitudes. This may well be the case in the bystander emergency case, but it is certainly not in Milgram's. Similarly, the insinuation that individuals have "failed" to learn to act on their attitudes can just as legitimately be recast as *others* have "failed" to *teach* them. The explanatory problem then becomes how to explain *their* behavior.

Given these considerations, we might also explain the failure of so many social psychologists to come to grips with the evidence against their voluntaristic/idealistic assumptions.[3] Certainly they cannot claim that others have not tried to teach them. In 1934, for example, Richard LaPiere reported that almost all of the American hotel and restaurant managers approached accepted a Chinese couple on their premises, although most of them later claimed that they would not. His conclusion was prophetic: "It would seem far more worthwhile to make a shrewd guess regarding what is essential than to accurately measure that which is likely to prove irrelevant" (LaPiere, 1934:31). But for that matter, our popular culture has long been replete with similar warnings: "Actions speak louder than words"; or "You can't judge a book by its cover"; and so on.

One important reason for the persistence of these assumptions among social psychologists may be that it is simply more convenient for them to continue to use the survey questionnaire. This method is reasonably useful for getting at attitudes and intentions, but poor for analyzing actual social situations and the pressures that individuals confront in them.

A second source may lie with the privileged social class position of social psychologists relative to most of the general public. It is of course debatable that social scientists have a great deal of freedom of movement in absolute terms. For example, during the student strike at Columbia University in 1968, professors who believed in the students' cause did not necessarily support it behaviorally. Rather, such support was only provided if professors saw more than half of their colleagues agreeing with them (Cole and Adamsons, 1969). On the other hand, professors clearly have much more freedom of movement than, for example, most blue-collar workers; and, as shown in Chapter 8, this freedom is reflected in psychological differences between these two categories of individuals. It may be that this relatively greater freedom and a certain psychological peculiarity prevents their totally understanding the standpoint of their subjects.

There is a third, and, one suspects, even more important explanation for the failure of social psychologists to reorient to the discipline. However, before considering it I would like to examine a second tradition of research whose results have implications similar to those we have been discussing.

BECOMING WHAT WE DO: THE ATTITUDINAL CONCOMITANTS OF BEHAVIOR

In the early 1950s a host of experiments were conducted where subjects were required to argue publicly for positions which contradicted their attitudes. Herbert Kelman (1953), for example, induced children to write in favour of comic books which they did not find interesting, King and Janis (1956) enticed male college students to claim that the U.S. draft requirements should be increased from two to three years, and Frances Culbertson (1957) had whites argue in favour of racial integration. In these and other studies subjects' attitudes tended to change in the direction of the position they had taken publicly.

A more recent set of studies is particularly interesting because the attitudes in question were those toward subjects themselves, or what is variously referred to as "self-evaluation" or "self-esteem." In a study by Kenneth Gergen (see Gergen, 1968), for example, subjects were given a mock job interview and subtly pressured to ingratiate themselves with the interviewer; that is, the interviewer smiled or nodded her head when the subject rated herself positively and displayed mild disapproval when she referred to herself negatively. The results indicated not only that subjects rated themselves more positively than they had previously, but that these higher self-evaluations persisted after subjects were later told to simply rate themselves honestly without the interviewer present!

The results of these studies suggest that the attitudes of individuals in our society may be as much, and perhaps even more, "consequences" as "causes" of their behavior. Again, one might think that this fact would embarrass social psychologists into modifying their voluntaristic/idealistic assumptions about human nature, yet the dominant tendency has been to try and interpret the results in voluntaristic/idealistic terms. King and Janis, for example, suggested that their subjects came to accept their counter-attitudinal argument because they felt satisfied with their performance to the point where the argument itself took on pleasurable connotations. Other researchers then countered that the attitude change process is less rational than rationalizing, with subjects bringing their attitudes in line with their overt behavior because they would otherwise feel too uncomfortable living with the knowledge that they had been so personally inconsistent.

Although this particular issue has sparked a long-standing tradition of experimentation and debate, it is not necessary to take it up here.[4] Rather, for present purposes it is significant to note that such explanations have been much more popular than other, more social explanations. In general terms, such explanations would place individuals' *interpretations* of their own behavior as well as the behavior itself *under the influence of others.*

In this regard, we do know that internally generated pressures are not necessary to produce behavior-attitude or attitude-attitude consistency; instead, such pressures may be either absent (Bem, 1967)[5] or derived from the exigencies of having to act (Zajonc, 1960; Jones and Gerard, 1967:180–181). They may also be imposed upon one by others, in that, as Jones and Gerard (1967) and Gergen (1968) suggest, others often pressure us to be consistent—to "practice what we preach" and preach and practice consistently over time—in order to make us predictable. On the other hand, Erving Goffman (1959) notes that in many of our everyday activities we are one kind of person in one situation and a very different person in another with relatively little concern about personal inauthenticity. (Gergen's subjects, for example, did not feel that they had been dishonest.)

Again, these considerations highlight the importance of the way in which our relationships with others are structured. Thus, our ability to be inconsistent presumably arises from the fact that the "roles" we play tend to be segregated in time and space (Goffman, 1967). However, when different aspects of ourselves are organized within the same role and under the purview of the same others, pressures toward consistency can be intense. This is presumably the explanation for the results of a study by Seymour Lieberman (1956). After he had measured the attitudes of shopfloor workers in a home-appliance factory toward management and the union, some of these workers were promoted to foremen whereas others were elected as shop stewards in the union. He then found that those who had become foremen became much more promanagement and antiunion than those who remained shopfloor workers, whereas those who had become stewards changed in the opposite direction. Even more striking is what happened after a subsequent recession when many of the foremen again became shopfloor workers—they lost their promanagement outlook!

In this latter case one assumes that the conflicts of interest which characterize union-management relations foster strong ingroup pres-

sures toward conformity which lead individuals to bring their attitudes into line with their role-related behavior changes. On the other
hand, the conflict of interest underlying relations with others in the
outgroup may actually require personal inconsistency: we misrepre-
sent our true feelings about the automobile we are selling, and winning at sports requires deception. Similarly, to reflect upon the
Gergen experiment, how likely would we be to get a job if we presented ourselves honestly rather than in more or less glowing terms?

We can summarize the implications of the present section as follows: that specific attitudes are as likely to follow as precede an
individual's behavior argues against the voluntaristic/idealistic assumptions of mainstream social psychologists. Although the tendency
for us to bring our attitudes into line with our behavior can undoubtedly be partly attributed to internal psychological processes, external
pressures from others, themselves contingent upon the way in which
our relationships with particular others are structured, are probably
at least equally as important.

The results of several different traditions of research therefore
point to the need for an approach which (1) is not dependent upon
voluntaristic/idealistic assumptions about human nature, and (2)
provides an adequate account of the social structure of our society.
Most mainstream approaches, I maintain, do not meet either of
these two conditions. Indeed, *their conceptions of social structure
are themselves based on voluntaristic/idealistic assumptions,* and
this provides the third and major reason for the reluctance of most
social psychologists to face up to and incorporate the contradictory
findings we have been discussing.

THE ORGANIZATION OF WHAT WE DO: DOES "IT" REFLECT US, OR DO WE REFLECT "IT"?

What would a conception of social structure based upon voluntaristic and idealistic assumptions about human nature look like? A
safe bet would be the "Social Contract" conception of Hobbes,
Locke, or Rousseau, for here society is claimed to reflect the more
or less conscious wills of its individual members. Such a conception
is in fact the most popular one among social psychologists, especially
within psychology, but also sociology.

Jones and Gerard (1967), for example, rely heavily upon a study
by Thibaut and Faucheux (1965) where Parisian schoolboys played

a game under two sets of independently manipulated conditions. Although one player always had the power to receive more of the winnings than his opponent, the potential difference in winnings was either large or small, and the number of points available to the low-power player if he left rather than remained in the relationship was either large or small.

Thibaut and Faucheux reasoned that the low-power person would be particularly concerned to get some assurance that he would get more than the minimum number of points when the difference in potential earnings was large, while the high-power person would be particularly concerned to ensure that the low-power person did not leave the situation altogether when he had the greater chance of doing so. These assumptions seem to make sense of the results; that is, while all subjects were given the opportunity to establish either or both of two norms—that the low-power player get a certain number of points or that he agree not to leave the game, those playing the game when there was both a high potential difference in winnings and a high likelihood that the low-power player would leave if he did not receive an adequate number of points were much more likely to agree to contracts involving these two rules.

First, however, note that it is misleading to imply that the Social Contract models all of the crucial social circumstances in the experiment itself. Rather, the high-power player's privileged position is nonnegotiable because it is fixed by the experimenter's partisan intervention. While the "contractual" outcome is at least "second best" for the high-power player, since it still maintains his relative advantage, it is really only "least worst" for the low-power player, and hence is much less likely to be voluntarily or contractually agreed to by him.

Second, it is still worse to claim, as both Jones and Gerard (1967:651–653) and Secord and Backman (1974:xv, 399–400) do, that the conditions surrounding such small-scale laboratory groups can serve as *the* model for relationships between employers and employees and other large-scale structural phenomena. In fact, neither employers nor employees are likely to have this much freedom to maneuver. For example, given the present state of the economy most "outside offers" have been eradicated.

Another perennial favorite among social psychologists is a research program by Robert Bales and his associates (1958). After observing small groups of individuals who had met for the first time in action, he suggested that such groups face two major problems: (1) they must get the group task accomplished, but (2) in the course of deciding what is to be done some members may be less influential than others and thus dissatisfied with the outcome. As a consequence, they must be "cooled out"; that is, they must be accorded approval and induced to accept the most preferred solution to the group task. However, making good suggestions may take so much effort that a person who does so cannot also do the cooling out. Alternatively, it may be that making good task suggestions entails a certain singlemindedness of purpose that makes being nice difficult. Thus, the two abilities usually tend to develop in different individuals rather than within the same person.

If this argument is correct, one might expect that two different roles would develop, making task suggestions and being nice to others, and that these roles would tend to be filled by separate individuals (i.e., segregated). Although on occasion they found "great men or women," Bales and his associates usually found this role differentiation; that is, one member tended to become the "task" and another the "socioemotional" leader.

Note again the importance of the initial, constraining conditions of the experiment: had the experimenters not chosen subjects of similar social status and power outside the laboratory and instructed them to come to a group consensus, they might not have obtained a social structure quite as "freely formed" and consensual as it appears to have been. Similarly, one certainly should not imply that, for example, employer-employee and a host of other real-world relations can be characterized by a similar consensus of goals and absence of fundamental conflicts of interest.

The upshot of these considerations would seem to be this: *however well contractual/consensual conditions may apply to certain small groups, they are by no means the only bases for the emergence and continued functioning of social structure.* Rather, the pattern of interaction which constitutes an institution or other social structure can also be *imposed* on one party to the relationship by another. Another interesting possibility is that a pattern will emerge and persist through the intentions of neither one nor both parties, but through a process of evolution which is largely unrecognized and unintended by everyone.

Interestingly, given social psychologists' propensity to study social organization through laboratory experimentation, a good case can be made that such processes have already been demonstrated with these methods. Mustafer Sherif (1935), for example, had his subjects attempt to estimate how far a pinpoint of light in an otherwise completely dark room moved. Actually, any movement perceived was totally illusory, since the light was stationary and only seemed to move because there were no reference points with which to localize the light in space. However, subjects tended to establish their own range of judgments anyway, and when they heard other subjects giving their estimates they tended to change their own in the direction of a group norm or average judgment. By providing a reference point, this norm, once established, may well have reduced subjects' uncertainty and made them feel more comfortable. On the other hand, since they did not appear to have deliberately attempted to influence each others' judgments, and since many subjects did not appear to be aware that a norm was being established, they probably did not intend the group norm that appeared.[6]

Jacobs and Campbell (1961) later demonstrated that a similar process could be the basis for aspects of a society's culture. They had three accomplices say that the light moved between 15 and 16 inches, considerably more than most subjects estimated. They then systematically replaced the accomplices with naive subjects until there were no more of the former left in the group. Although the norm was completely arbitrary, and although none of the naive subjects had participated in its initial formation, or even officially agreed with it, its effects remained as many as four or five generations after the last stooge had been removed!

RETROSPECTUS AND PROSPECTUS

An adequate theory of social psychology should help us recognize and explain power and support relationships rather than simply rely upon voluntaristic/idealistic assumptions about human nature. It should also provide an account of social structure which does not depend upon such assumptions; this means that it must be capable of explaining the existence, persistence, and change of institutions based upon coercion as well as consensus, upon the unintended as well as intended consequences of social interaction.

What the various answers by sociological social psychologists are and where they have come from is the subject matter of the chapters of Part 2.

Notes

[1]See especially Campbell (1963), Tittle and Hill (1967), and the review by Liska (1974).

[2]Some experiments do show an increase in the predictability of behavior from attitudes when more attitudes are taken into account. On the other hand, even the best results (Norman, 1973, for example, explained 21.2 percent of the variation in behavior) hardly warrant modifying the conclusion that when situational pressures contravene an individual's attitudes, attitudes usually lose out.

[3]Not all social psychologists, of course, have failed here. For an approach which takes account of situational pressures as well as behavioral intentions, see the work of Martin Fishbein and his colleagues (Ajzen and Fishbein, 1970).

[4]For reviews of this debate see Jones and Gerard (1967) and Fishbein and Ajzen (1975).

[5]This is not to suggest that Bem's account does everything he claims it can. See Note 4.

[6]In fairness to Jones and Gerard, it is important to note that they seem to come halfway round to admitting that social organization can occur unintentionally:

> It has perhaps not been sufficiently stressed that the course of normative growth and development in a group is often implicit. It *may* happen that the members of the group actually sit down together and make out a set of explicit ground rules they propose to follow, conduct a vote, codfiy the rules as by-laws, and so on. But at least as often norms develop through [a] trial-and-error process. . . . Perhaps by chance, perhaps because of appropriate transfer from other relationships, perhaps through the give-and-take of rather subtle exchanges of social reinforcement, silent understandings may develop that govern the judgments of each group member concerning the right and wrong ways to behave [Jones and Gerard, 1967:653; reprinted by permission of John Wiley & Sons Inc.].

2

MAJOR
SOCIOLOGICAL
APPROACHES
TO SOCIAL
PSYCHOLOGY

2

CLASSICAL POLITICAL ECONOMY AND MODERN EXCHANGE THEORY

> Human ingenuity does not exist as a collective—it comes in small, compact parcels called individuals. All of man's progress is the result of a small number of great individuals. The rest of us have been pulled out of the cave on their-coattails. . . . Capitalism—laissez-faire capitalism—is the only moral politico-economic system because it is the only one in keeping with man's nature, the only system that faces up to the reality of our existence . . . [Letter to the London Free Press, September 30, 1975].

The 17th and 18th centuries were times of profound social change for Western Europe. Out of the feudal economy of the Middle Ages had come mercantilism and colonialism, and with them came new classes of merchants, financiers, and eventually industrialists. These "middle" or "bourgeois" classes (i.e., midway between the feudal aristocracy and the peasantry) were not long in complaining about their lot, for while they were central to the rise of cities, industries, and markets for manufactured goods, their political rights and influence lagged far behind this economic prominence. They argued that those contributing so much to trade and commerce through hard work, those capable of acquiring and maintaining wealth through their own individual effort, were capable of governing themselves and should have as much influence as the landed gentry whose wealth derived solely from inheritance. Among the events which followed this dissatisfaction were none less than England's "Glorious Revolution" of the late 1600s and the American and French Revolutions of the 1700s.[1]

It should come as no surprise that changes as extensive as these greatly affected social theorizing. Thus whereas earlier conceptions of human nature had stressed sacrifice and allegiance to tradition and authority, the new ones were more likely to emphasize the naturalness of self-interest and a desire for individual freedom. Also not surprisingly, these ideas were first given prominence in England, the country where the above-mentioned social trends were most advanced. Here we shall examine the social psychological aspects in the theorizing of three early thinkers whose ideas have had a very great impact upon subsequent social psychologists.

BENTHAM'S UTILITARIANISM AND SMITH'S "PROPENSITY TO TRUCK, BARTER, AND EXCHANGE"

The core of Jeremy Bentham's (1748–1832) conception of human nature was disarmingly simple: an individual will act in a certain way if the consequences of doing so are pleasurable and refrain from doing so if the consequences are painful (Bentham, 1970: 1). This *hedonistic* position seems to have been accompanied by a *materialistic* one. Thus, whereas Bentham acknowledged that individuals often consciously act upon their own intentions, he went on to note that any given act may be neither intentional nor conscious. In fact, it can be "falsely conscious"; that is, the individual may think that he or she is acting for one reason when an opposite reason may actually be behind the act (Bentham, 1970: 71). Implicit in this argument is the materialistic assumption that the pleasurable or painful physical ("material") consequences of the act have more causal significance in explaining it than the intentions and states of consciousness which preceded it.

Bentham's *utilitarian* ethical stance was consistent with his hedonism and materialism. Specifically, if an act brings individuals pleasure it is in harmony with human nature, and should therefore be judged favorably. Similarly, since conscious intentions may neither cause the act nor mitigate its painful consequences for other individuals, they are a less satisfactory basis for moral judgment than the consequences themselves.

Given this view of human nature, all one really needs to predict, explain, and judge an individual's activities is a set of assumptions about the pleasures and pains that stimulate the individual to act or refrain from acting. One must first decide which among all the conceivable consequences of an individual's actions are pleasurable and which are painful, and preferably which among these are more or less pleasurable or painful. Here Bentham seems to have had little trouble in asserting the following list of pleasures (those with lower numbers are more important):

(1) The satisfaction of such physical appetites as hunger, thirst, and the desire for sex, intoxication, and novelty
(2) The acquisition and possession of wealth
(3) Skillful performance (e.g., playing a musical instrument)
(4) Self-recommendation and a good reputation with others
(5) Power over others
(6) Things like piety, benevolence, and malevolence

His list of pains for the most part contains opposites to these pleasures; for example, one's physical desires are not fulfilled because one lacks wealth, one is awkward, and so on.

It is then helpful to know which general properties of pleasures and pains make them more or less effective. Here Bentham suggested that they will be more effective the more certain they are to follow the act, the sooner they follow the act, the more intense they are, and the longer they last.

These ideas of Bentham still form the core of "Behaviorism" (more or less literally meaning a focus upon overt behavior rather than introspective accounts of intentions and consciousness), one of several major schools of thought in modern psychology. Much of the work of Behaviorists such as B. F. Skinner (1953) has essentially been an attempt to extend and verify empirically Bentham's propositions — that the anticipation of "rewards" or "punishments" is the major source of an individual's actions, that the effectiveness of rewards or punishments will vary with such properties as the likelihood that they will actually follow these actions, and that thinking or cognitive processes within the individual are either less important than, or at least no different from, links between "stimuli" and overt behavioral "responses" which can be objectively observed and measured. In fact, Skinner (1971) and some other Behaviorists (e.g., McConnell, 1970) even expose utilitarian ethics.

It is not my purpose here to elaborate upon the work of the Behaviorist school.[2] However, it will become clear that one cannot fully understand the nature of more sociological theorizing in social psychology without a rudimentary knowledge of Bentham and Behaviorist theory. Thus on one hand a major school of sociological thought takes much of Benthamism as its starting point, and on the other another major school has to a large degree been provoked into existence as a reaction against this same body of thought.

In this regard we might note that Bentham's theorizing is not even particularly social, let alone sociological. His pleasures or rewards may be social, but in his scheme they are secondary to physical ones. The focus is upon single individuals rather than social *inter-action*, and there is little if any attention to social structure. In fact, one might ask, if everyone is in fact pursuing his or her own interests, how is cooperation or any other form of structured collective activity even possible in the first place?

Three answers to this embarrassing question can be gleaned from Bentham:

(1) Rather than simply what is good for single individuals, utility refers to what is good for the greatest possible number of individuals (essentially the majority). Similarly, since happiness varies within as well as between individuals, the happiness I have need not keep you from being happy, and there are therefore few serious conflicts of interest.

(2) Because being benevolent and receiving others' approval are pleasurable, cooperation as well as self-interest are built into human nature.

(3) Selfish activity is regulated by institutions representing society as a whole, either officially in the case of governmental and legal institutions, or unofficially in the case of public opinion and religious organizations.

Note that none of these explanations is particularly helpful. The first simply defines the problem out of existence. Furthermore, unless one were to assume that such pleasures as private property are limitless rather than scarce, one would have to consider this explanation contradictory to the original theory. The second explanation presents a similar problem; that is, since physical pleasure and private property are more important than benevolence, one would not expect cooperation to win out over self-interest. Finally, Bentham's theory provides us with no means for explaining the emergence of institutions or society as a whole. That he seems to have taken their existence and legitimacy for granted suggests that he presumed that those who administer such institutions would act in the interests of the majority. Why self-interested individuals would establish and obey an authority outside of themselves is never explained.

Similar problems accompany the theorizing of *Adam Smith* (1723–1790), the Scottish academic whose work is central to "classical economics." Specifically, if we are above all else motivated to "better our condition" and if this amelioration mainly entails working for ourselves and accumulating wealth (Smith, 1937), why do so many of us work for others in factories?

As with Bentham, one of Smith's answers was that "it's only human nature"; that is, humans, being rational, have a natural "propensity to truck, barter, and exchange" (Smith, 1937:13). The use of reason and speech permits us to act upon the realization that while each of us has a limited number of productive abilities, we can get whatever we want by exchanging what we can produce ourselves for something else. The productivity specialization permits then encourages us (for the most part unconsciously in the case of factory workers, whose rational capabilities are stunted) to specialize further.

Yet beside this psychological answer one also finds a more sociological treatment of the problem. Thus, Smith argued, one cannot satisfactorily explain the emergence of factories by assuming that workers were forced to exchange their labor for a wage because of their inferior abilities. Rather, their inferior abilities are much more an *effect* than a cause of their social position (Smith, 1937:15):

> The understandings of the greater part of men are necessarily formed by their employments. The man whose whole life is spent in performing a few simple operations, of which the effects too are, perhaps, always the same, or very nearly the same, has no occasion to exert his understanding. . . . He naturally loses, therefore, the habit of such exertion and generally becomes as stupid and ignorant as it is possible for a human creature to become. The Torpor of his mind renders him, not only incapable of relishing or bearing a part in any rational conversation, but of conceiving any generous, noble or tender sentiment and consequently of forming any just judgment concerning many even of the ordinary duties of private life . . . [Smith, 1937:734–735].

But if this characterization is true, why did people enter factories in the first place?

Here Smith seems to have more or less realized that for whatever reason, everyone does not have access to the resources which working for oneself requires. At one point, for example, he notes that beginning farmers must wait until harvest time before they can even acquire the means for their own subsistence let alone equipment for the next planting, just as weavers must wait until their cloth is sold. Under these circumstances independent workers may have to give up part of their product in exchange for the capital to tide them over. Alternatively, if through hard work and thrift independent workers have a particularly good harvest or large product, they may then be able to hire others to work for them (Smith, 1937:259).

Nor was Smith oblivious to the fact that once established, such capitalist-worker relationships involve conflicts of interest:

> The workmen desire to get as much, the masters to give as little as possible. The former are disposed to combine in order to raise, the latter in order to lower, the wages of labour.

and that force might therefore be necessary to maintain them:

It is not, however, difficult to foresee which of the two parties must, upon all ordinary occasions, have the advantage in the dispute, and force the other into a compliance with their terms. The masters, being fewer in number, can combine much more easily; and the law, besides, authorizes, or at least does not prohibit their combinations, while it prohibits those of the workmen. . . .

The workmen, accordingly, very seldom derive any advantage from the violence of [their] tumultous combinations, which, partly from the interposition of the civil magistrate, partly from the superior steadiness of the masters, partly from the necessity which the greater part of the workmen are under of submitting for the sake of present subsistence, generally end in nothing but the punishment or ruin of the ringleaders (Smith, 1937:66–67).

These observations notwithstanding, Smith is of course regarded not as competitive capitalism's leading critic, but as its foremost theoretician and apologist. While many of his modern counterparts have rather conveniently swept his reservations under the carpet, they have nevertheless correctly identified which side of the fence he was on, for apologize he did.

Thus, he argued, while the capitalist-worker relationship may not be completely voluntary, the behavior of capitalists as well as workers is usually heavily controlled by a built-in network of checks and balances. For example, it is not in the interest of the capitalist to pay workers below a subsistence level, because the latter cannot work if they are unhealthy, and will not work if there is little incentive to do so. If the wage is below its market value, as in the high external-alternative condition in the Thibaut and Faucheux experiment, the worker will simply go elsewhere. Although competition for jobs among workers occasionally drives wages down, this being the reason why English workers are usually paid less than American workers, most European workers are paid above subsistence level and are not greatly unhappy with their lot (Smith, 1937:68–74).

The presumed devastating effects of the division of labor upon workers' psychological condition caused Smith more discomfort. Yet this effect was seen as a price we must pay for competitive capitalism's increased productivity. To intervene directly in the capitalist-worker relationship would be to oppose human nature by removing the capitalist's incentive for high productivity. All one could hope to do was ameliorate the effects of the division of labor by having the state educate workers.

DETOCQUEVILLE'S JOY OF
JOINING IN THE MARKETPLACE
OF IDEAS

Alexis deTocqueville's (1805–1859) importance as a social theorist has been often overlooked, perhaps in part because his major theorizing is contained in a book of observations about the United States rather than a self-proclaimed theoretical treatise. However, this French nobleman in effect (although perhaps unknowingly) extended Smith's model of competitive capitalism to include political activity. His extension is still the most favored model of political activity among Western social scientists.

DeTocqueville basically accepted Smith's model of economic activity, arguing that Americans' prosperity was attributable to their "equality of conditions," or what is now referred to as "equality of opportunity." In contrast to the more aristocratic European nations, in the United States talented individuals from many different social backgrounds were encouraged to engage in business activity. Moreover, since the outcome was not fixed by aristocratic inheritance, entrepreneurs were also more likely to be stimulated by the excitement and risk of competition itself. There was indeed a danger of repetitive work stunting workers' decision-making abilities, but then again the United States was primarily a land of small rather than large industry. Similarly, there was a potential for an "aristocracy of manufacturers," but then business people were so preoccupied with competing among themselves that they did not form an organized class and therefore could not actually wield undue influence (deTocqueville, 1961, *II*: 184–189, 190–194).

As an aristocrat with an understandable distrust of political democracy (the French revolutionaries had not been particularly kind to France's aristocracy), deTocqueville was amazed that the same conditions which appeared to have stimulated so much business activity had not also led to anarchy and revolution, as he thought the advent of democracy in Europe had done. He went on to suggest two related explanations for this supposed paradox. We have already alluded to one; that is, with most individuals competing among themselves there has been no development of large-scale social classes such that conflict between them could tear American society apart at the seams. The other is that this competition does promote political organization, but in a form which integrates rather than disintegrates society because it involves most individuals in it.

In the first place, this competition among equals actually makes individual Americans feel powerless, but this same feeling of individual powerlessness goads them into forming a myriad of interest groups around particular interests, these interest groups being thought of as essentially political lobbying groups and parties. DeTocqueville was the first to refer to America as a society of joiners (deTocqueville, 1961, II:123–133). Second, membership in these interest groups has a moderating effect upon individuals' political outlooks.

For one thing, deTocqueville in effect seems to have argued that since political activity in a democracy such as the United States essentially amounts to free competition among interest groups, those with useful programs for governing society, like manufacturers selling goods in high demand, have a very good chance of having their interests represented in the outcome. This process then undoes individuals' initial sense of powerlessness, giving them a sense of personal involvement and purpose, and removing any desire for revolutionary social change. Furthermore, the objectively high chance of winning as well as the fact that the political game is played fairly (i.e., democratically) by all parties keeps individuals moderate until their turn comes around (deTocqueville, 1961, II: 138–149).

For another, because these interest groups are many and overlapping, individuals have numerous ties to other individuals. They are neither isolated from other people in general nor in wholesale conflict with any one other, large-scale class of individuals (deTocqueville, 1961, II:302–303).

Finally, the equal opportunity to participate and the multitude of groups to which the individual actually belongs give him or her a great deal of practice and skill in political matters. Chief among these are speaking abilities and deliberative powers, which in turn help individuals to develop capacities for compromise and consensus (deTocqueville, 1961, II:148–149).

DeTocqueville's assessment of the United States was not quite as rosy as the above summary might imply. For example, he did note that blacks had much less power than whites. (He later made an analogous observation regarding French Canadians.) Moreover, he complained, the stability of the free political market existed at the expense of serious theoretical controversy; that is, Americans never seemed to disagree on principles, only on trivial, pragmatic details. This orientation, in turn, often meant that public opinion demanded conformity and discouraged dissent. Paradoxically, however, equality and homogeneity actually frustrated Americans' natural desires to outdo others, such that they were prone to emphasize minute differences in status and jealously guard their privacy (deTocqueville, 1961, I:304–318; II:257).

For deTocqueville such conditions raised the specter of a *"mass society"*; that is, a society of homogeneous but isolated individuals who could be manipulated by a few well-organized elites. Yet he clearly preferred his *"pluralist"* model of the United States, "pluralist" meaning that power resides in a plurality of roughly equal interest groups rather than in a single dominant class, and this model is still the most popular one among Western business people, politicians, and social scientists (e.g., see Connolly, 1969).

"MODERN" EXCHANGE THEORY

Just as Behaviorists have followed in Bentham's footsteps, so "Exchange Theorists" have continued the Smith-deTocqueville theoretical tradition. This is particularly true for the latters' view of human nature, which, as can be gleaned from the above account, retains the hedonism of the Utilitarians but substitutes a more active, thinking individual for Bentham's near robot. Modern Exchange Theorists have also followed the Smith-deTocqueville account of the relationship between the individual and society, which is, in a nutshell, that the societies they were analyzing were the best possible reflection of individual members' interests and intentions.

Unfortunately, Exchange Theorists seldom explicitly commit themselves on this issue. Instead, while at the same time professing to develop a general model which explains most specific social actions and relationships, in their own empirical work they have tended to concentrate upon small-scale, informal interaction among those of similar social class, with only an occasional reference to structured political-economic relationships. However, since the general model they choose to apply to informal relationships is that of the market, of competitive capitalism, their debt to the classical political economists and their liberal, bourgeois political outlook should be obvious.

The extension of the classical economic model to informal social relationships has necessitated (1) translating such alleged rewards as social approval into economic terms, and (2) attempting to identify the set of rules or calculus that individuals with knowledge of these rewards use in deciding the most rational course of action. I shall briefly take up the latter problem first.

Homans' Distributive Justice and Thibaut and Kelley's Comparison Level of Alternatives

According to George Homans (1974), most if not all behavior can be explained with the following equation:

$$\text{behavior} = f\ (\text{profit}) = \text{rewards} - \text{costs}$$

Before acting the individual decides, "What do I get for doing it, and what do I lose?" John Thibaut and Harold Kelley (1959) have further suggested that the rewards to be gained are not only judged in absolute terms (how large they are), but also in relative terms (how much is it relative to what I could get elsewhere). Thus, for example, when the low-power subject in the Thibaut and Faucheux experiment is assured of a high outcome outside the game, he has what Thibaut and Kelley refer to as a high "comparison level of alternatives". Similarly, Homans has suggested that the costs of acting have an analogous component in "rewards foregone"; that is, acting means giving up the rewarding consequences of other actions. (The other component of costs is the absolute amount of effort or other resources one has invested in an action or social relationship.)

When the returns to participants in an exchange are as great or greater than their investments in the relationship, there is what Homans calls "distributive justice." When investments and returns are not commensurate, participants become dissatisfied, and perhaps hostile toward other participants.

Relationships are sought out and maintained for their return on investment, and one's involvement in them varies on the same basis. Furthermore, rewards and costs are subject to the laws of supply and demand. Although such social commodities as others' approval are more difficult to measure than material commodities, they are subject to much the same laws. Here it is useful to consider Peter Blau's application of these ideas to interpersonal attraction and love (Blau, 1964:76–85).

Blau's Excursus on Love

Looking first at why people are initially attracted to each other, Blau suggests that attractiveness is a function of market value. He says, for example that "how valuable a woman is as a love object to a man depends to a considerable extent on her apparent popularity with other men." Similarly, men prefer a woman "who cannot be easily won and who simultaneously indicates sufficient interest to make ultimate conquest not completely beyond reach."

In the early stages of a courtship each person actively attempts to manipulate his or her own scarcity so as to become more attractive to the other. Thus women withhold intercourse, realizing that the favors of a woman "readily engaging in sexual affairs" entail "less commitment to and ego support for a man than those of a woman who very rarely bestows them." The ability to withhold sexual favors will vary with one's market value or comparison level of alternatives. Thus, "A woman whose love is in great demand among men is not likely to make firm commitments quickly, because she has so many attractive alternatives to weigh before she does. The one who is not popular is more dependent on a man who takes her out and has more reason to become committed to him."

In general, the establishment of commitments and dependencies is a long, slow process, since becoming involved is costly — both absolutely in terms of effort expenditure and loss to one's ego if the other suddenly terminates the relationship (and particularly if he or she terminates it *first*), and relatively in rewards foregone; that is, in alternative relationships one has given up for the one in question. For this reason each person invests little in the relationship until it is clear that one will get an adequate return on one's investment.

Flirting and lovers' quarrels provide means for testing the other's commitment, but they do not permit the potential lovers to avoid what Blau considers a basic dilemma; that is, each has to indicate enough affection to keep the other interested, but only just enough, for to appear too interested would be to decrease one's market value in the other's eyes. The decision for women of whether or not to engage in sexual intercourse is said to be particularly problematic:

> A woman promotes a man's love by granting him sexual and other favors, as demonstrations of her affection and as a means for making associating with her outstandingly rewarding for him, yet if she dispenses such favors readily—to many men or to a given man too soon—she depreciates their value and thus their power to arouse an enduring attachment.

Blau implies that women usually choose a strategy of resistance in response to this dilemma. Thus,

> By prolonging the challenge of the chase until a boy has become intrinsically attracted to her, a girl exploits the significance of conquest to promote a more fundamental attachment that makes this incentive for dating her superfluous.

But what happens after a love relationship *has* become established? Blau implies that at that point love becomes an end in itself, yet he then immediately qualifies this implication by saying that "selfless devotion generally rests on an interest in maintaining the other's love." After failing to discover strong tendencies toward selflessness among actual couples in love, Zick Rubin (1973:87) has made much the same qualification.

Note that in the above account Blau has retained much more than a few trappings of Smith's theory. Thus individuals are not only rational and subject to the laws of supply and demand, but above all self-interested and competitive. Moreover, at least in his claims regarding men (and we shall have much more to say about this later), these individuals are presumed to value rewards more, the rewards in this case being love and commitment, when they are privately or exclusively owned.

The Approval-Conformity Nexus

The other area besides "interpersonal attraction" that seems to have received a great deal of attention from Exchange Theorists is that of social influence and conformity. Their thinking on these topics has been conveniently pulled together by Walter Nord (1969).

Having others conform to our own attitudes and actions is said to be rewarding for much the same reasons that approval is; that is, agreement from others reduces feelings of uncertainty and/or raises or maintains our self-esteem. Conversely, as with approval from others, conformity to others can be costly, particularly since independence from others is valued. As with other social commodities such as approval, the value of conformity is subject to the market processes of supply and demand. On the reward side, for example, others' conformity to one's own views will be more valuable, the more scarce it is. Similarly on the cost side, it is more costly to give out conformity indiscriminately or too soon, for then it will decrease in value for others.

Since approval and conformity have the same status as commodities, such that they both have abstract market values which can be compared, they can enter the same equation in individuals' "cost accounting" and be exchanged for each other. Put crudely, I can decide to conform to your wishes if I feel that I will gain your approval in return, and/or I can decide to approve of you if you will exchange conformity to me. According to this approach, therefore, conformity can be a sound investment practice. This equation is how the Exchange Theorist would explain ingratiation studies such as those described in Chapter 1; that is, a common way to gain others' approval later is presumably to invest conformity to their wishes now.

The Emergence and Maintenance of Social Structure: The Natural Order

The Exchange Theory account of social organization includes Blau's suggestions regarding the conditions under which informal interpersonal relationships are likely to become stratified by status and power. They are, briefly, that when some members initially invest superior contributions in the group, other group members must then exchange esteem and conformity for these superior contributions. Note that the above explanation is completely analogous to that of Adam Smith's for the emergence of the capitalist-worker relationship; that is, just as the capitalist was said to receive part of the worker's product in exchange for providing the worker with wages until the product actually gets produced, so the high-status or power member in the informal group is said to receive his or her status or power by providing other group members with the knowledge or other resources required for the group task.

Moreover, Homans (1974) at least takes such processes in the latter setting as the basic ones behind most stratified relationships. At one point, for example, he suggests that what individuals get out of society in income and status is usually equivalent to the amount of their investment in it (Homans, 1974:198–199). This argument has been officially known as the "Functional Theory of Stratification" (Davis and Moore, 1945: see Chapter 4), but it is equally amenable to Exchange Theory. Thus, so the argument goes, since the work of business people and doctors is more important for the functioning of society and requires greater risks, training, or commitment than does that of farmers or skilled workers, business people and doctors must be more highly rewarded with income, status, and power. As we shall see in Chapter 8, Blau is by no means so avid a fan of this position as is Homans, yet by choosing Exchange Theory as his most preferred model for social activity in general he has in many ways "voted with his feet."

On the question of why structured relationships are maintained, although again Blau will later be seen to differ considerably from other Exchange Theorists, we also find the Smith-deTocqueville position, which is, of course, that participants must derive some benefit from them. For example, their superior contributions to the group in the past may give leaders "idiosyncratic credit," which then permits them to deviate from group norms more than other group members (Hollander, 1960), but in the long run they must nevertheless continue to "deliver the goods" if they are to stay in power. This is, after all, the only answer which is completely in keeping with the voluntaristic assumptions underlying Exchange Theory.

On the other hand, *in spite of* the major thrust of their own theory, both Homans and Blau have attempted to develop a model of the processes by which relationships become institutionalized which includes some coercive and unintended elements. For example, group norms are presumed to arise contractually (i.e., intentionally), usually because they provide a more efficient means for group members to influence each other than a plethora of one-to-one influence attempts. However, once these norms are established, new members and even old ones may then be bound to them by group pressure, even when the norms in question no longer completely reflect their interests or intentions.

RETROSPECTUS AND PROSPECTUS

Several important features of the approaches to social psychology discussed in this chapter should be noted and kept in mind. In the first place, reflecting on Chapter 1, it is obvious that "Exchange Theory," modern sociology's version of classical political economy, epitomizes the voluntaristic/contractual approach which has dominated mainstream social psychology. People do what they want to do, what is in their own best interests, which means that the organizations and institutions they construct must also reflect their best interests.

Second, because Exchange Theory has taken this position, it is beset with the same problems as mainstream social psychology in general. Let us recall the lessons of Chapter 1 to see exactly why this is the case.

Thus Exchange Theory proper cannot adequately explain the fact that individuals in our society often act in violation of their attitudes and intentions. In defense of their theory they might have recourse to a cost accounting argument, claiming, for example, that the bystanders of Latané *et al.* or Milgram's subjects simply decided that the personal satisfaction of being a Good Samaritan was not worth risking others' disapproval. However, note that there is no provision in the theory to explain whether the fact that subjects expected to receive disapproval if they did or did not intervene or the presumption that the approval of, say, two others or one authority figure is more important to individuals in our society than the personal satisfaction of having acted upon one's own values in the face of countervailing social pressures. Nor, for that matter, is being coerced by others — receiving approval only if one does not act as one wishes to — an act of exchange, since an exchange is by definition a *voluntary* intention. Homans has tried to squirm out of this dilemma by claiming that even coercive interchanges have voluntary elements. For example, even if you stick a gun in my face and say, "Your money or your life," Homans says (1974:87), I can still decide to give up my life. Needless to say, this explanation is little more than "hocus pocus." Were Homans more honest (or perhaps less cute) he would follow Peter Blau (1964:116) in admitting that Exchange Theory simply cannot explain coercive interaction.

Of course *once* someone has stuck a gun in our face, Exchange Theory's less voluntaristic sibling, Bentham-Behaviorism, has little difficulty explaining our compliance with the demand to hand over our purse or wallet. On the other hand, why, for example, the authority figures Milgram's subjects had encountered would have exercised coercion in the first place is by no means clear, particularly since Behaviorists themselves claim to have demonstrated that rewards are more effective and efficient influence techniques than punishments.

Obviously the problem here is that both Exchange Theory and Bentham-Behaviorism provide inadequate accounts of social organization. In the theory of Bentham and Skinner "society" is on the one hand an ill-defined blob and on the other the status quo at its own word. Smith and deTocqueville could recognize large-scale conflicts of interest, but if their market-exchange conception of society is correct such conflicts should not occur. According to Homans and other modern Exchange Theorists they do not in fact occur. This is of course an empirical question which cannot be answered by proclamation, and for this reason we shall avoid answering it until we look at the evidence in Part 3.

Notes

[1]See also Patricia Marchak's book in this series (1974:4–7). For a more detailed account see Laski (1958).
[2]See, for example, Deutsch and Krauss (1965:77–109).

3

THE HISTORICAL MATERIALISTS' REVOLT: MARXIST AND NEO-MARXIST SOCIAL PSYCHOLOGIES

In its own time classical political economy was a relatively progressive approach to social science. On one hand its conception of the remnants of the feudal aristocracy as economically parasitical and politically authoritarian was a rallying point for agitation against the old order; on the other its emphasis upon economic and political freedom provided the basis for the considerable increases in production and civil rights which characterized the new. Yet classical political economy had largely been formulated by, for, and about the bourgeoisie. In their agitation they had proclaimed their outlook to represent the interests of humanity in general, but by freedom most of them really meant freedom for themselves. There should be neither government interference in the economy, since this involvement would interfere with their own class interests, nor universal suffrage, which would place those without property in a position to introduce such interference.

As the bourgeoisie used its new freedom and influence to establish large-scale industry, members of other classes increasingly became industrial laborers.[1] They were not long in pointing out the contradiction between the proclamations of the bourgeois revolutions ("Man is born free; and everywhere he is in chains.") and the bourgeoisie's new-found conservatism. From the standpoint of workers the *bourgeoisie* were economically parasitical, in that they obtained their living from the labor of manual workers, and politically authoritarian, in that they used their political influence to protect their own interests. In workers' clubs, workers and the occasional guest speaker–intellectual revived the ideas of Rousseau and other Enlightenment thinkers and gradually fashioned a conception of a new order, "communism," where property would be owned communally, social relationships would return to true community, and all individuals would finally realize their human potential.[2]

MARX'S ALIENATION

By the time he reached Paris in 1843, *Karl Marx* (1818–1883), a young German intellectual who had turned to freelance journalism after being denied a university position, was already reasonably familiar with these French conceptions of socialism and communism. There he began a more systematic study of this French tradition and English political economy. This confrontation of traditions had a profound effect upon his own theorizing: on the one hand he was led to drastically alter his German idealist presumptions; on the other he developed a comprehensive critique of, and alternative for, classical political economy. Here we shall be most concerned with this latter aspect of Marx's work.[3]

Marx began his critique of the political economists by praising their analyses of competitive capitalism. They had, he said, not only accurately *described* much of what went on in bourgeois society, but in some cases provided correct if incomplete *explanations* for these same processes.

Adam Smith, for example, had correctly observed that people tend to regard their *labor* as a sacrifice, and on occasion he even attributed this phenomenon to the fact that workers, being without property, were not working for themselves (Marx, 1973:614). Similarly, spurred on by their desire to demonstrate the parasitical nature of the feudal aristocracy, Smith and Ricardo in particular had greatly advanced our knowledge of capitalism by discovering a number of crucial laws concerning the *products* of labor. Thus they recognized that on the one hand, the value of products is determined by the amount of labor time that has gone into them (they even recognized Capital itself to be "stored-up Labor"), and that, on the other, different products appear to relate to each other according to their own laws (Marx, 1975, 3:239; *Capital I*: 76–87). Relationships with *others*, furthermore, are in fact calculated exchanges (in this respect there is some validity to Bentham and Smith's having seen bourgeois society itself as a series of exchanges among merchants and shopkeepers), which in the case of capitalist-worker relationships often take the form of open conflict (Marx, 1975, 3:217; Bottomore and Rubel, 1964:3-4). Finally, Marx clearly agreed that the division of labor has devastating effects upon workers' *selves*, in that it "mortifies" their bodies and "ruins" their minds (Marx, 1975, 3:274).

In spite of these breakthroughs, Marx went on, because they were attempting to defend as well as analyze bourgeois society, the political economists were committed to presumptions which prevented them from adequately explaining their own laws. Why, for example, if the present division of labor is the most rational way of organizing industry, do people regard their work as a sacrifice, and why are capitalists and workers at each others' throats? Why do people evaluate their products in terms of the amount of labor time "sacrificed" to produce them rather than in terms of their ability to satisfy human needs, and why are relationships with others so similarly selfish and calculating?

Political economy had only one "wheel" or dynamic with which to answer these embarrassing questions; that is, people are naturally egoistic, competitive, and desirous of private property. Although their labor is a salable or "alienable" commodity, their possessiveness makes it a sacrifice to give it up. But if this is true, why would people divide and exchange their labor? Because they have a natural propensity to do so. But given their natural selfishness, why do they permit others to acquire more private property from the exchange? Because the capitalist contributes more. But if labor is the source of wealth, how can this be true? Because individuals have natural differences in ability. But had not Smith himself admitted that differences in ability were much more a consequence than a cause of the division of labor?

Marx took it upon himself to extricate the analysis from this endless circle of explanations which always seemed to lead back to the same "it's only human nature" position. The first line of attack was to propose a very different conception of human nature, which, he claimed, leads one to conclude that the observations of the political economists are specific to capitalism rather than true for all time. He then set out to provide an historical account of how these phenomena came about, and how, under different social circumstances, people would be led to change them. Let us take up each of these aspects of the argument in turn.

The Alternative Conception of Human Nature and the State of Alienation

Far from being a sacrifice of one's time, Marx began, truly human or "*productive activity*" is the mediating link between humanity and nature. It is through spontaneous, conscious, and creative labor that individuals express, realize, and develop their peculiarly human potentialities. The objectification of their feelings and ideas through labor produces material objects and social institutions which satisfy some needs, permitting a concern with others, many of which are themselves created by the emergence of these same products. This two-way or "dialectical" relationship between subject and object, whereby the "resolution of contradictions" between the two ingredients changes both, is in fact the basis for the historical development of society.[4]

The other central feature of Marx's conception of human nature is what Isvan Mézáros (1970:149) has labelled "*sociality*." Specifically, human productive activity is of necessity social: it is undertaken consciously and cooperatively with others, and is based on the products and technologies of those who have produced in the past. Therefore human nature itself lies as much in "the ensemble of social relations" as in specific, biological individuals. Truly human individuality is therefore impossible without sociality, just as truly human relationships among people presuppose individuality.

This conception of human nature then served as a yardstick with which to criticize and explain the state of activity and social relationships described by the political economists. Given this criterion, he continued, one can only conclude that "economic man" is a shrivelled version of humanity, an object "estranged" or *alienated* from his or her essence.

In subsequent writings Marx elaborated upon, and, to some extent, systematized, this conception of alienation. Since it will figure prominently in Part 3, a brief summary will prove helpful.

In most general terms, the individual alienated from his or her true nature is separated from each and all of four sets of objects. One is productive *activity*, of which labor in the economic realm is the most important. A second is the *products* of this activity, which include social organizations as well as material goods. Third is alienation from *others*, defined in general and in terms of such social categories as classes. Fourth and finally is alienation from *oneself*. The individual's relationship to each of these sets of objects is then usually concretized in terms of four characteristics.

In the first place, to be alienated from the object is *to be indifferent to it, not involved with it, or detached from it.* Thus, for example, "as soon as no physical or other compulsion exists, labor is shunned like the plague" (Marx, 1975, 3:274), and "if capital were willing to pay it [objectified "Labor"] *without* making it labor it would enter the bargain with pleasure" (Marx, 1973:462). A similar indifference to the immediate product of labor, Marx suggested, is indicated by the fact that we do not even regard our own products as being ours. While we are clearly interdependent with others in our various activities, we do not consciously and collectively control our activities with them; instead, we live an egoistic, sequestered existence. Finally, since we are too exhausted and stupefied by our labor to escape successfully through leisure activities, we also have a detached, unreflective orientation towards ourselves more generally.

Related to the detachment of the alienation "syndrome" is a tendency *to use only a few of the objects' characteristics to achieve only a few egoistic, narrowly utilitarian ends*. Work in particular is regarded in this way; that is, as simply a means to "make a living" rather than as something one enjoys and uses to develop oneself. The same is supposed to be the case with one's products, with even the capitalist who "owns" the product simply using it to accumulate capital rather than to satisfy his own needs. People also "use" each other for their own selfish ends. In the case of the capitalist and the worker, there is " 'no admittance except on business,' " with the capitalist regarding the worker as simply a source of labor and the worker regarding the capitalist as simply the source of a job (Marx, *Capital* I:172; 1973;:310). Finally, peoples' very selves get treated in this way, being sacrificed to wage labor as a precondition for physical subsistence.

The third orientation is the opposite of the conscious, rational planning and control which would otherwise distinguish humans from animals: *rather than being under his or her own purposes and conscious control, the object controls the individual.* Labor becomes routine, mechanical, and uncreative. One is haunted by consumer products. One does not influence others, while others control one's needs and abilities through labor and consumption. At the same time, presumably, one cannot exercise self-control through long-range personal goals. As a matter of fact, one's physical life may actually be shortened as others use one for dangerous tasks.

Fourth, and finally, to be alienated is to *have certain "feelings" toward the object* of orientation. Thus, for example, one feels that one's working time is sacrificed, that one is only real when one is not working. One feels powerless, that "hostile objects" run one's life; one generally has "a feeling of misery rather than well-being" (Marx, 1975, 3:274–275).

Since social scientists have had a propensity to measure alienation solely by conscious attitudes, it is important to note that in Marx's own conception alienation is far from simply a state of conscious-ness. In fact, to act automatically, without reflection, is itself an indication of alienation, since the opposite is what distinguishes humans from other animals. Marx has sometimes been interpreted as having assumed, therefore, that being oblivious to one's own objective alienation, a state to which later Marxists have applied Bentham's term "false consciousness," is actually the highest possible level of alienation [Israel, 1971:80–81]. However, some of his state-ments imply that being aware that one is alienated by no means indi-cates that one is less alienated than someone who is not aware: ". . . the real estrangement of the life of man remains, and remains all the more, the more one is conscious of it as such . . ." (Marx, 1975, 3:313). Here Marx presumably meant that merely to be aware that one is alienated without at the same time changing the material con-ditions which produce alienation will simply make one feel even more frustrated. While these various considerations indicate the ambiguous role of consciousness for the state of alienation, Marx himself seems to have placed more importance upon its material aspects.[5]

The Theory of Alienation and Its Transcendence

Marx's theory of alienation has proven to be an embarrassment for many Marxists as well as an object of derision for Marx's detractors. Clearly there is an unabashedly moralizing and polemical tone to his conceptions of human nature and alienation. Similarly, as Bertell Ollman (1971:232) has pointed out, the presumptions of Marx's con-ception of human nature are not immediately "testable," let alone ob-viously valid. Given these considerations, some Marxists as well as non-Marxists have tried to draw a sharp distinction between Marx the youthful idealist and Marx the mature scientist. For a number of reasons, however, the approach taken here is a very different one.[6]

In the first place, the structure of Marx's conception of human nature is not all that different from that of most others in social psychology. Therefore to relegate Marx's conception to the realm of pure philosophy would be to invoke a double standard unfairly. The Exchange Theory presumption that people are naturally competitive, for example, is no less "ideological" and no more provable than Marx's contention that they are naturally cooperative.

Second, although Marx differed from these other theorists in his having presumed that rather than being now in their natural state people must instead struggle to attain it, he seems to have used his conception of human nature in much the same way. Thus most social psychological theories have taken the same form as Marx's, which, on one level at least,[7] is: "Given a certain theory of human nature, certain sociological processes will create certain psychological states" (Israel, 1971:55).

In what follows I shall elaborate upon this latter aspect of his theory. Although Marx himself did not explicitly do so, it will later prove useful to distinguish between a general and a specific social psychological theory of alienation in Marx.

⌈ The general theory would run more or less as follows: people will only engage in truly human productive activity and sociality when the social circumstances under which they think and act permit them to do so. More concretely, their *activity* must be subject to their own purposes and conscious control ("free, conscious activity" defines the "species-being"), otherwise individuals lose their spontaneous, creative involvement in it and regard it as simply a means toward a narrow end and a sacrifice of their time (hence Marx's frequent references to alienated labor as "enforced" activity under the service of an "external" need). Alienation from the *product* arises independently when it too is not under the individual's conscious control, and as a "generalization of learning" from the activity to the product ("How could the worker come to face the product of his activity as a stranger, were it not that in the very act of production he was estranging himself from himself?"). The reverse also applies, in that the absence of conscious control over the product is also likely to decrease one's involvement in production itself.

Similar principles apply to alienation from *others* and the self. For example, to the extent that circumstances do not permit conscious, *collective* purposes and control, one avoids others, uses them where possible, but nevertheless does not feel good about it. On the other hand, precisely because one's activities and relationships with others are unnatural and unsatisfying, when new circumstances permit, one actively joins others in combating the original alienating circumstances. Thus, Marx claimed (1975, 5:48), alienation can only be abolished after it has become "an 'unendurable' power, i.e., a power against which men make a revolution."

Whether or not Marx himself actually had such a general theory of alienation in mind, he was clearly more interested in expounding upon the actual historical circumstances which have denied individuals purpose and control. These circumstances, he felt, are central to capitalism.

The Historical Account

Marx did not claim that there was ever a primordial stage of history free of alienation, yet he did argue that social relationships in most precapitalist societies are more cooperative and less competitive. Much of this cooperation results from necessity, in that when people live on the subsistence level there is little extra to fight over and a lot to be gained from cooperation. New structural tendencies come about after cooperative labor arrangements permit a surplus production over and above subsistence. One of the first things to happen is that once everyone no longer needs to be directly involved in production, some people begin to specialize in making tools and engaging in other craftwork. Being somewhat removed from direct production, they eventually have the opportunity to plan and control production itself. This change is facilitated by their peculiar relationship to production, requiring as it does the exchange of products, and often leading to the marketing of production by the craftworkers as well. These conditions also eventually permit products and wealth to be accumulated by these specialists, whereupon other people begin to work "for them." However, since traditional forms of social control are not geared toward protecting such material privileges, some form of centralized government is established by the newly arising classes to cement their control. Such systems of domination nevertheless become unstable as subordinate classes revolt against the ruling classes. In the case of Western Europe, such developments have led to periods of domination by slaveowners, feudalistic lords, and now the bourgeoisie.

In bourgeois society production is increasingly carried out under the "capitalist mode"; that is, in work organizations owned and controlled by a relatively small class of capitalists with a near monopoly on the society's wealth. Most of the rest of the population is forced to exchange its labor power for a wage. The powerlessness of the wage earners vis-à-vis the ruling class, the bourgeoisie, also entails several other conditions. Whether or not they work at all depends upon market processes of supply and demand, and they must compete with other workers for their livelihood. Only owners and their representatives plan and direct production, such that class distinctions increasingly center around mental versus physical labor. Also, and especially for manual laborers, tasks become ever more specialized, with automation eventually leading to people's being planned and controlled by machines.

In Marx's account, therefore, private property and class conflicts of interest first emerged as *unintended* consequences of technological advances, productive surpluses, the division of labor, and exchange, because people's more or less voluntary "alienation" of their own labor (i.e., in this case their having given up conscious control of it to others) first made private property possible (Marx, 1975, 3:279–280). Once in existence, private property then led to class *conflicts of interest* which led some classes of people to alienate others *coercively.*

Note that this account fundamentally differs from that of the classical political economists. According to them, egoism, competitiveness, and private property are universal features of human nature from which exchange and the division of labor are said to result. People voluntarily exchange their labor for a wage or salary and collectively divide their labor, but according to Marx this freedom is illusory. Instead, he argued, given the domination of the bourgeoisie, based on state control and property, workers can at best "choose" their alienators.

Given that this argument is true, to continue Marx's historical account, workers have revolted, and will continue to revolt, against capitalism. Yet for a number of reasons he viewed this struggle as a long and protracted one. In the first place, the bourgeoisie is at first able to conquer not simply because of its direct coercive power, but because workers are divided amongst themselves by competition, individually and along racial, ethnic, and sexual lines (e.g., the antagonism between English and Irish workers is "the *secret of the impotence of the English working class*" (Marx, 1971:294). Second, bourgeois "ideology"—the set of claims that capitalism is the natural order, that people voluntarily exchange and divide their labor, that there is political democracy, and so on, which justify the bourgeoisie's domination—pervades the society's culture in general and serves as a smokescreen against awareness of the sources of alienation. Third and finally, as capitalism develops, the sources of alienation themselves become increasingly more complicated and difficult to grasp. One one hand everyday life in general becomes more and more fragmented, in that leisure is abstracted from work and the private sphere is abstracted from the public; on the other capitalism itself undergoes a number of complicated changes. These latter "second order" sources of alienation and false consciousness are important enough in their own right to warrant a brief exposition at this point.

These processes can be subsumed under the generic term *"the fetishism of commodities,"* which refers to the fact that as capitalism develops, more and more characteristics of people as well as their products become abstracted from them and treated as commodities; that is, as objects produced and sold for a profit rather than the immediate use of the producers.

On one side there is "reification" (literally, being transformed into a thing): here people take on the qualities of nonhuman commodities. Thus, for example, in their "cost-benefit" analyses "Management"* (an abstract category of individuals lacking individuality) tends to treat individual laborers as the equally abstract category, "Labor," basing its calculations not upon people's human characteristics but upon the so-called "Labor Market," itself an abstraction. Marx claimed that almost everything concerning people becomes treated in terms of its utility for capitalistic profit-making, such that one eventually has, figuratively if not literally, "universal prostitution" (Marx, 1973:163).

The other side of commodity fetishism is "hypostatization"; that is, the human powers temporarily lost to people during dehumanization are taken on by nonhuman objects. Money, which as we say, "talks," is one such object. It should be stressed that Marx conceived commodity fetishism to be objectively as well as subjectively alienating (Geras, 1971). Thus, for example, whereas money obviously does not *literally* talk, it *has* literally dehumanized many Capitalists, in that acquiring more of it has become their main objective in life, and in making decisions which affect "their" workers they are more influenced by money than safety and other humane considerations. Nor do the objectively alienating features of commodity fetishism rest solely upon "self-fulfilling prophecy," upon the mere *belief* that money itself is valuable and powerful. Thus as long as most other Capitalists are acting as misers, the Capitalist who is a nonbeliever in money and decides to be more humane toward "his" or "her" workers will be driven out of business, just as the Worker who decides to stop believing in money will starve. In a very real sense, therefore, "what was the domination of person over person is now the general domination of the *thing* over the *person*, of the product over the producers" (Marx, 1975, 3:221).

On the other hand, the subjective side of these complicating processes is obviously important in its own right, in that it makes it more difficult to pierce Capitalism's shroud. Thus Capital is seen as providing Workers with jobs instead of vice versa (according to

---

*From here on I have capitalized "Capital," "Management," "Labor," and "Worker" to signify that the "individuals" who make up these categories are not in fact individuals, but reified "personifications" of their respective roles in the class structure of capitalism. Similarly, the capitalization of Capitalism refers to its status as a hypostatized system.

Marx, in the capitalist mode of production, labor is the sole source of a product's value), just as the Stock Market lays them off. The source of stultifying work is not the capitalist but Factories and Machines. Equally important, moreover, Workers are hindered from recognizing that they, collectively, are the producers and that Capitalists, collectively, are parasites. Yet in Marx's account workers themselves are to dismantle this "fantastic form." How is this phenomenon to come about?

At the same time that alienated labor is "producing" commodity fetishism, Marx went on (1968:42–96), other contradictory tendencies are "at work." Thus if individuals in bourgeois society have become isolated from each other, the growth of Capitalism has nevertheless brought workers together physically, in large factories and segregated residential communities, where they are able to communicate. Though they are forced to compete with each other, they nevertheless encounter forces which provide them with common interests about which to communicate. Specifically, economic crises and consequent monopolization of the market force more and more members of the "petite bourgeoisie" (particularly owners of small farms and businesses) to become wage laborers. Furthermore, with the concentration of industry comes automation, which, through reducing skill and wage distinctions in general, and racial, ethnic, sexual, and national differences in particular, further reduces workers to a similar commodity status. Finally, as crises eat into Capitalists' profits and the number of unemployed workers competing for employed workers' jobs swells, Capitalists further decrease wages.

Given these motives and means, workers organize themselves on an increasingly wider scale. Instead of simply sporadic, localized acts of *sabotage* (literally, throwing a wooden shoe in the gears), one now finds trade *unions*. Given the above-mentioned homogenization, the increasing frequency and severity of crises, and modern means of communication, these trade unions also become superseded by *class* organization on a national level, which includes the formation of a political *party* to promote workers' interests in the official political arena. Finally, just as developed Capitalism does not "respect" national boundaries, so the Working Class eventually organizes on an *international* level.

Organization at each of these levels is supposed to be a collective learning experience for workers. Widening struggles against their employers reinforce their consciousness of having a common class interest opposed to that of the Bourgeoisie. They occasionally win these struggles, but even when they do not, they feel increasingly confident in their collective strength. In the process of struggle, moreover, bourgeois ideology is exposed for what it is. As the state intervenes on the side of the Bourgeoisie, for example, knowledge of the latter's political domination is added to the obvious fact that the economy is also monopolistic rather than one of "free enterprise." The class-dominance basis for commodity fetishism becomes self-evident.

Increasingly frustrated in their attempts to have their class interest represented within bourgeois society, workers eventually revolt and do away with it. "Doing away with It" means that industrial and other institutions are collectively owned and operated by people in general. While there is a period of Working Class domination of the State to provide time to construct a socialist society and eradicate the last vestiges of bourgeois society, once the class conflicts of interest upon which it is based have been eliminated, people let the State "wither away."

THE VICISSITUDES OF HISTORY AND NEO-MARXISM

Needless to say, history has yet to bear out most of Marx's expectations. Revolutions led by the working classes of Europe were to take much longer than Marxists had expected. Similarly, the Russian Revolution did not spread to the rest of Europe, as Marxists at the time expected, and presumably this is one of the major reasons why it was to turn sour. However, even after Russian workers had effectively lost control over their society, a buoyant optimism persisted among most Communist Party members in the rest of Europe. In fact, it appears, the longer capitalism persisted and the more authoritarian Russian society became, the more dogmatic became their use of Marxist theory. The materialism of many official Marxists became mechanistic in its economic determinism (i.e., all political and cultural phenomena are class based). Whereas according to Marx himself economic crises were to build workers' consciousness rather than to be major revolutionary events in and of themselves, now the success of the revolution became equated with the occurrence of such crises, almost regardless of the policies of workers' parties.

Most importantly for the present discussion, narrow economic determinism and an understandable embarrassment over developments in Russia appear to have led Marxists to shove a concern with alienation and humanism into the background. In fact, now that the discovery of Marx's early writing on alienation has sparked a renewed interest in such issues among Western Marxists, official Marxists usually argue that the concept of alienation itself is part of the individualistic ideology of bourgeois society and/or that alienation was by definition ended in the East with the abolishment of legal private property![8]

This trend toward "automatic Marxism" (Jacoby, 1971) led to attempts to reintroduce the two-way or "dialectical" relationships between the subject and object of Hegelian philosophy and between a society's culture or "superstructure" and its class-economic or material "substructure." Perhaps most interesting from a social psychological standpoint was the attempt by *Wilhelm Reich* (1897–1957), and later, various members of the "Frankfurt School" of sociology, to reintroduce the active subject through combining Marxian theory with Freudian psychology.[9]

THE FREUDO-MARXISTS: IS THERE A CAPITALIST CHARACTER STRUCTURE?

The rationale for doing so was cogently argued by Reich (1972:294): the rational thing for workers to do is collectively combat capitalism. That they have not done so concertedly must therefore mean that they are governed by an irrationalist rather than a rationalist psychology, as Marx as well as the political economists would have it. This is where Freud comes in:

> The moral inhibition of the child's natural sexuality, the last stage of which is the severe impairment of the child's *genital* sexuality, makes the child afraid, shy, fearful of authority, obedient, "good," and "docile" in the authoritarian sense of the words. It has a crippling effect on man's rebellious forces because every vital life impulse is now burdened with severe fear; and since sex is a forbidden subject, thought in general and man's critical faculty also become inhibited [Reich, 1970:30].*

Given that this is the case, it is pointless to simply exhort workers to revolution. Indeed, he claimed (1972:284), while the German Com-

---

*Excerpted with the permission of Farrar, Strauss & Giroux, Inc. from *The Mass Psychology of Fascism*, by Wilhelm Reich, newly translated from the German by Vincent R. Carfagno, copyright © 1970 by Mary Boyd Higgins as Trustee of the Wilhelm Reich Infant Trust Fund.

munist Party of the late 1920s and early 1930s "presented the masses with superb historical analyses and economic treatises on the contradictions of imperialism, Hitler stirred the deepest roots of their emotional being." The solution, therefore, is for communists to also get to the latter, largely through "consciousness raising" groups and reforms which will liberate peoples' sexuality.

If Reich's approach was heretical to the official Marxists of his day (he was expelled from the Party), it was equally so to his fellow psychoanalysts. Whereas Freud maintained that sexual repression is a necessary, if sometimes lamentable, feature of all societies, Reich (1972:237) equally dogmatically insisted that "it is only the private enterprise form of society which has an interest in sexual repression, and which requires it for the maintenance of two of its basic institutions, the permanent monogamous marriage and the patriarchal family." This in turn contributed to his expulsion from the psychoanalytic association, dominated at the time by Freud himself.

One of the contributions of *Herbert Marcuse* (1895–   ) of the Frankfurt School is an attempt to reconcile these opposing positions. Marcuse (1962: 31–34) suggests that whereas all social organization does indeed require some minimum amount of repression of individuals' needs (he refers to this as "basic" repression), because of its need to make more than subsistence work available for exploitation as well as to maintain the political domination of the ruling class, capitalism also requires an excess, "surplus" repression. With Reich, although through a somewhat different route, Marcuse sees this excess repression as producing fear of rebellion and destructiveness.

In his earlier work the dialectical potential for rebellion is nevertheless said to exist in an element of true sexuality protected from manipulation and repression through being active in our fantasy life. However, in his later writings Marcuse (1964) is pessimistic to the point of claiming that technology and consumerism have now invaded our fantasy life and private views of the world and closed off even this basis for revolutionary change. Understandably, therefore, he attributes more revolutionary potential to people on the fringes of society, to those not caught up in the closed system of relative affluence and "one-dimensionality." The irreverent, affluence-renouncing New Leftists of the SDS variety are seen as one such category, but obviously people in the underdeveloped countries, the "Third World," are even more likely prospects from Marcuse's point of view.

That Marcuse and other members of the Frankfurt School should have taken this turn toward regarding Western workers as "bought off" and un-self-reflective is particularly interesting because it parallels the concern of Marxists with imperialism on the structural level. This is also the direction which *Frantz Fanon* (1925–1961), a black psychiatrist and eventual revolutionary living first in the French West Indies and then in Algeria, took. His theorizing is also interesting for another reason; that is, just as many Freudians in general moved toward "ego psychology"—toward emphasizing the "self-concept" and other processes associated with the "ego" rather than sexuality and other instinctual drives[10]—so Fanon made "reality testing" (an ego function) and Adler's "inferiority complex" the centrepieces of his own theory of the psychological aspects of imperialism.

Colonialists' subjugation of Third World, and particularly black, peoples, Fanon suggested, is accomplished not simply by enforced economic dependence and coercion, although these are extremely important (Fanon, 1967:17, 31–34; 1966:41), but by a systematic derogation of native culture. This leads natives to derogate themselves, which promotes repression, and this in turn has a very important consequence: they direct their frustration-derived aggression against each other (or themselves) rather than the colonialist (Fanon, 1966:41–42, 204; 1967:25, 101–107). According to Fanon (1966:31), however, this "displacement" of aggression gradually ends because the social structure of imperialism, especially of whites over blacks, is so blatantly coercive and uncomplicated compared to the class struggles of developed capitalist countries (the enemy, for example, is both a foreigner and of another color). Moreover, the process of collectively combating the colonialist "frees the native from his inferiority complex and from his despair and inaction; it makes him fearless and restores his self-respect" (Fanon, 1966:62).

As Erich Fromm (1971:44–47, 146) himself a neo-Freudian neo-Marxist, has suggested, the attempt to wed Freud to Marx is in some respects strange. If on the one hand Freud's exposure of the "materialistic" roots of Victorian morality is somewhat analogous to Marx's deciphering of commodity fetishism, on the other his model of human nature—of isolated individuals naturally competing with and using each other for their own instinctual gratification—is much like that of the political economists against whom Marx constructed his theory of alienation! Although *Fromm* (1900–   ) himself has come under heavy attack from Marcuse and other members of the Frankfurt School for his ego-psychological leanings, his own theorizing, while sloppy, is actually closer to Marx's than is that of his detractors. This arises from the importance he attributes to competition and his conception of human nature which is more like Marx's than is that of orthodox Freudians.

According to members of the Frankfurt School, Marx's critique of political economy is now largely inapplicable because the growth of monopoly capitalism has eliminated the separation of private from public life and hence also competition (see Jay, 1973:104–105; and Connerton, 1976). Fromm (1955:65), however, claims that competition plays a major role in the formation of a capitalist character structure. Basically, he argues, competition frustrates a need for secure relationships with others and thereby leaves us "fixated" at this level, such that we are not free to proceed to a higher-level concern with creativity and other means of "self-realization." Instead, we spend our time attempting to overcome the attendant sense of insecurity by striving for individual wealth, power, and fame; by cluttering up our time with compulsive work; by marketing our personalities to others; and/or by slavishly submitting to them.

However reasonable an extension of Marx's theory of alienation this proposition may be, Fromm's theorizing suffers from a characteristic it shares with that of Marcuse, his most vigorous opponent. Specifically, whereas the original intention of appropriating Freud was to reintroduce the active subject to Marxist theory, Fromm follows Marcuse in making the subject largely an object. Whether this and the other innovations of the Freudo-Marxists—the transfer of concern from labor and production to private life and consumption, and, in the case of the Frankfurt School, from competition to monopoly—are warranted, of course, should be decided not on the basis of what is or is not most consistent with Marx's own theory of alienation, but on how well these various claims fit empirical reality. We shall consider such questions in Part 3.

RETROSPECTUS AND PROSPECTUS

By now it should be obvious that Marxian theory was constructed to overcome the limitations of Exchange Theory. Thus the bystander emergency effect makes more sense if we assume that the structure of our own society entails competition with and lack of support from others; Milgram's results make sense within the context of the structure of our society, where authority figures have typically had coercive power over us since the time we were born. That foremen and shop stewards should have very different outlooks makes a great deal of sense if we assume that our society is built upon a basic conflict of interest between Capital and Labor.

Note that Marxian theory is a sociologically oriented alternative to Exchange Theory; that is, whereas in the latter the explanation of last resort lies in human nature, in the former it lies in the structure of society. Yet private property and the class structure are said to have arisen in good part from the relatively unreflective psychological state of individuals in the past, from the unintended consequences of their actions. The unreflective apathy which capitalism is supposed to induce in those who participate in it is also seen as a major prerequisite for its continuance and development. In fact, Marx's major criticism of bourgeois society was precisely that its mode of production, and hence also most of the rest of its structure, is beyond the control of rationally acting, social individuals, such that it denies rather than develops their human potential (Marx, 1973:541; *Capital I*:85). Finally, it is their recognition of these facts, their class consciousness, which is supposed to lead workers to revolt against capitalism and consciously construct a new system.

These social-psychological features distinguish Marxian theory, although not necessarily official Marxism, from that of the school of thought we are about to take up. Although the two schools on occasion cross paths in their critiques of Exchange Theory, they differ more than they agree. In fact, of course, Marxian theory itself became a new position in the debate from which the members of other schools have taken great pains to distinguish themselves.

Notes

[1]For histories of these developments see Kuczynski (1967) and Rinehart (1975).
[2]See George Lichtheim (1970) for a capsule summary.
[3]For Marx's critique of Hegel see Marx (1975, 3:326-346) and Mézáros (1970). Mézáros is also a good source on Marx's critique of the political economists.
[4]For the Hegelian roots of these ideas see Note 3.
[5]The context of the statement quoted immediately above is an attack upon Hegel's idealism. For discussions of the ambiguous role of consciousness in Marx see Avineri (1968).
[6]For a summary and critique of these debates see Archibald (1976b).
[7]As well as being a social-psychological theory in the mainstream sense, Marx's theory of alienation clearly has Hegelian-philosophical and structural-descriptive aspects (see Archibald, 1976b).
[8]See, for example, Kon (1969). Interestingly enough, official Marxism's psychology is also the mechanistic, Pavlovian brand of Behaviorism.
[9]I had originally hoped to provide an account of the "Freudo-Marxists" much more detailed than the one which follows; however, space limitations inter-

vened. For more detailed reviews of the origins and other adherents of these approaches see Jay (1973) and Connerton (1976). Bruce Brown (1973) provides an ambitious attempt at synthesis.

[10]Floyd Matson's (1964:Chapter VI) summary account of the emergence of ego psychology in general is a nice one.

4

THE CONSERVATIVE IDEALISTS' BACKLASH: STRUCTURAL FUNCTIONALISM

Marxism has by no means been the only major tradition of reaction to the events accompanying the growth of capitalism, including classical political economy and related bodies of social theory. Here we shall look at another whose adherents were associated with neither the bourgeoisie nor the emerging proletariat but with what was left of the nobility. The French revolutionaries in particular had not been very kind to the latter class, and some of the earliest members of the present school (e.g., Louis de Bonald) were in fact exiles. Nor was the postrevolutionary political climate in France one that inspired confidence in anyone concerned with "law and order."

The theorizing of this school reflects these class, and, more generally, "law and order" roots. There is an aristocratic disdain both for power which derives from mere wealth rather than good breeding and/or intellect, and for the failure to fulfill one's paternalistic duties toward the "lower" classes (Comte, 1974b:536). There is also a distrust of the motives and abilities of the majority of the population, and hence often of political-economic democracy as well (Comte, 1974b:435–436). Understandably, these features are accompanied by two others: (1) a pessimistic, Hobbesian-Benthamist view of human nature, and (2) a conception of society as reified, as a living organism (fortunately, in their view) beyond the effective control of the majority of the population.[1]

COMTE'S POSITIVISM AND RESIGNATION

As did Marx, *Auguste Comte* (1798–1857) distinguished bourgeois society from the feudal society of the Middle Ages. However, in keeping with his own conceptual scheme we would be more accurate to refer to it as the "Protestant-democratic" as opposed to the "Catholic-feudal" period (Comte, 1974a:81). The "functional signifi-cance" of the ideas that guided the democratic revolutions in general, and especially the Protestant Reformation, he suggested, was that they had helped do away with the previous, antiquated regime. Comte attributed most of this change to the fact that by emphasizing freedom of religious interpretation and enterprise, the new ideas had loosened the Church's and feudal aristocracy's hold over science and industry (Comte, 1974a:96–107; 216–217).

As "a final essential part of the system of critical philosophy," political economy in particular had some of the same virtues, in that, for example, it had "proved, as to certain matters, far from being the most important, the spontaneous and permanent tendency of human societies towards a certain necessary order . . ." (Comte, 1974a:240; see also 1974b:461). Nevertheless, it is significant that Comte himself referred to the wider system of thought to which political economy belonged not as "Protestant-democratic," but as "Metaphysical," "Abstract," "Critical," or "Negative." The first two terms referred to his contention that the bourgeois theorists had a thoroughly "unscientific" view of human nature and society. The second two refer to his claim that, through these erroneous ideas, they had engendered among the general population an incessantly suspicious, dissatisfied orientation toward governmental regulation in particular and moral regulation more generally, without at the same time pro-viding an adequate substitute order for the feudal regime.

Metaphysics: The Transfer of Reason to Society

Comte first set out to refute the claims of such Enlightenment thinkers as Rousseau that humans are distinguished from other animals by the predominance of reason and enlightened self-interest. Instead, Comte argued (1974a:95; 1974b:380–398), most humans are so stupid and animalistic that they would hardly have labored enough to support themselves if the military-feudal regime had not forced them to. For this reason there is no question of social organi-zation having arisen from human nature, for this could only have led to the Hobbesian state of war of all against all. Rather, society evolves according to its own "natural," "necessary" laws which are for the most part beyond our control. Scientific knowledge does permit us to adapt ourselves better to the progress of civilization, and even to make minor modifications of it. Yet society's evolution is necessarily progressive, and were we to engage in the "ambitious chimera" of seeking to govern society's laws we would only wreak havoc (Comte, 1974a:147–148; 1974b:469–470). In effect, therefore, Comte transferred reason from individuals to society in an attempt to reify it and thereby justify opposition to radical social change.[2]

Negativism: The Ill-Fated Power of the People

Obviously, however, Comte then had to explain the blatantly "dysfunctional" features of societal evolution. Although he drew upon some of the same observations by the classical political economists that Marx was drawing upon at the time, observations which included the disruptive effects of private property and the division of labor,[3] as an idealist (Comte, 1974b:36) he emphasized the effects of nonadaptive beliefs and values, and among these he regarded the revolutionary philosophies as particularly dangerous.[4]

Chief among these "negative" beliefs and values is the doctrine of "Liberty of Conscience" or "free enquiry" that first guided the Protestant Reformation. After having served the function of emancipating art and industry, he said, it now encourages the intellectually inferior to try to control society, but for that matter, "social order must ever be incompatible with a perpetual discussion of the foundations of society" (Comte, 1974b:410). The "Dogma of Equality" has a similar effect; in fact, as scientific knowledge increases, natural inequalities among individuals also increase such that to preach equality is to preach anarchy. Finally, "Sovereignty of the People" condemns the intellectually superior to arbitrary dependence upon the inferior, which cannot help but impede the rational reorganization of society (Comte, 1974b:408–412).

Comte then added moral anarchy to the effects of the revolutionary doctrines. If for Marcuse, the neo-Marxist, imagination is a retreat from an alien social world, for Comte (1974b:673), "Vanity is pampered by the sovereignty given to every man by the right of private judgment," and "Pride and envy are gratified by the proclamation of equality." As a consequence, there has been a serious decline in public *morale*. Private morality was for a time insulated from degeneration, but especially with the "attacks on the hereditary principle and marriage." the latter of which include divorce and the emancipation of women, it too has become anarchistic. The predominance of egoism in public and private life, in turn, necessitates political corruption.

As an essential part of negative philosophy, political economy is subject to the same criticisms. For example, it is *its* stress upon the naturalness of self-interest and laissez-faire which has led industrialists to introduce labor-saving machinery without due regard for the welfare of the workers who become unemployed in the process (Comte, 1974b:448–449).

Positivism: The Transfer of Power to the Sociologists

Given that Comte believed people had simply not found the right philosophy of life, he benevolently offered his own — "Positivism." They should accept his organic model of society, complete with its claim that things are evolving progressively, and that even if they were not, people could not do much about it anyway. Positivism thus initially meant uncritical optimism as well as scientism (i.e., "stick with the facts").[5]

However, having already presumed most people to be too stupid to grasp the truth, Comte was faced with a very grave theoretical problem. Indeed, how *could* he have resolved the dilemma?[6] Given his emphasis upon idealism and "spontaneous order," it made him rather hypocritical, yet he in fact went on to propose an elaborate system of *material* institutions to enforce adherence to his ideas. His basic model was that of Plato's guardians or Hobbes's monarch. The main problem of the industrial order is that "the social affections, gradually concentrated among individuals of the same profession, become more and more alienated from all other classes," creating "a miserable indifference about the general course of human affairs" (Comte, 1974b:511–512). Therefore competent moral or "spiritual" authorities must step in to fill the gap.

Tellingly, however, Comte surpassed Plato's conservatism by suggesting that Capital retain its material or "temporal" power over Labor. One suspects that this move was initially as much a consequence of Comte's adherence to, and fear of disturbing, the status quo as it was theoretically based. The two bases merged in his apparent presumption that the existing superior power of capitalists had already demonstrated their mental superiority (Comte, 1974a: 104, 227), which meant, of course, that they would be readier to accept the new philosophy (Comte, 1974a:150).[7] Be that as it may, Comte left nothing to chance and went on to construct a theory of stratification tailor-made for legitimizing his proposed structure. This theory includes two of the three central elements of what is now known as the "Functional Theory of Stratification" (Davis and Moore, 1945).

In the first place, people are to be stratified much less by wealth per se than their "functional importance" for society as a whole (Comte, 1974a:104). "Contribution" or "functional importance" is determined by one's place in the hierarchy of the Positive Polity; that is, the more different occupations for which one is responsible, the greater is one's contribution. This means, of course, that sociologists such as Comte himself are most important, bankers come next, then merchants, industrialists, supervisors, manual workers, and so on (Comte, 1974a:128–134; 1974b:776–781).

Second, among the rewards for superior contributions to Society "social honor" will figure more prominently than wealth. Bankers, for example, will continue to make more money than sociologists. It is their recognition of this noble feature of the structure, as well as the criterion of functional importance and their having been spared the need to think, which will eventually lead workers to accept it. In fact, they will eventually learn what the rich are to learn from the Spiritual Authority; that is, that the rich really only hold their wealth "in escrow" for the use of the rest of Society (Comte, 1974b:777–780).

With an important exception we are coming to shortly, this was the basic structure for the Positive Polity. How, then, were these institutions to function? "Spontaneously," Comte answered, but this answer was again equivocal.

Looking first at the dynamics of *moral authority*, people are to become joyously involved in their work and work relations. *However*, in direct contrast to Marx's proposal, this involvement is to be accomplished by "the voluntary renunciation, on the part of most of them, of their sovereign right of free inquiry" (Comte, 1974b:422)! Nor are they to be allowed to "voluntarily" renounce this right, for they are to be conditioned for submission from birth (Comte, 1974a: 227–228).

This approach to education means repairing and sanctifying the third major institution of the Positive Polity — the patriarchal, monogamous family — for the subordination of Woman to Man is natural: Woman is too inferior for continuous and intense mental labor, "either from the intrinsic weakness of her reason or from her more lively moral and physical sensibility, which are hostile to scientific abstraction and concentration." Instead, given her natural aptitude for sympathy and morality, her role "must therefore be to modify by the excitement of the social instinct the general direction necessarily originated by the cold and rough reason which is distinctive of Man" (Comte, 1974b:502–506). Unfortunately, the fact that Comte stressed the family because of its superiority as a repressive institution is all too often overlooked.

How often, and to what degree, then, are capitalists expected to exercise their directly *coercive power?* Not very often or very much, Comte replied. If people have been properly socialized as children, most of the groundwork for their submission will already have been laid. They will have been conditioned to emphasize duties over rights and to be benevolent toward others "without any other certain recompense than internal satisfactions" (Comte, 1974b:779–781). Similarly, workers will already have been suitably propagandized by Moral Authorities. Specifically, operating on the principle that "the essential aim of all practical politics is, properly speaking, to avoid the violent revolutions, which spring from obstacles opposed to the progress of civilization," these authorities will have done so by "presenting a vivid picture of the ameliorations which the new system should bring about. . ." (Comte, 1974a:149, 156). *Some* coercion of workers would of course be necessary, but "their new leaders exercise no authority over them save what is strictly necessary for maintaining good order in their work, and this amounts to very little."

THE EVOLUTION OF ORGANICISM

As has Marxism, organicism has undergone a variety of changes, depending upon the societal culture from which its adherents have written and these adherents' own dissatisfaction with this or that aspect of the Comtean position.

As an Englishman from a laissez-faire tradition, for example, *Herbert Spencer* (1810–1903) was particularly concerned with Comte's having transferred reason to society. Instead, Spencer noted (1884, *I*:479), social organisms clearly differ from the human organism in not having a single "sensorium" or state of consciousness. This led him to conceive of society in more ecological terms — as the adaptations individuals, acting collectively, make to certain environmental problems (social as well as physical) they share in common. For example, when people are geared toward war they must necessarily suppress each others' individual liberties.

Later, *Emile Durkheim* (1855-1917) was to deal with this problem in Comte in a less individualistic, less voluntaristic manner. On the one hand, he suggested, the "function" of an institution should be conceived as its effects upon other institutions rather than as a purpose of "Society" (a reification) itself. On the other hand, society is neither as independent of individuals as Comte would have it nor as dependent upon them as Spencer would have it. Rather, institutions are partially "in" individuals because they are based upon consensus of values and because individuals therefore identify with them, and partially independent of individuals because they have peculiarly social properties which emerge only when individuals come together, as in a crowd, and because they persist beyond the lifespan of particular individual members (Durkheim, 1964b:19–20; 1973:66–73, 98). Still later, *Robert Merton* (1910–) was to make his well-known distinction between the "manifest" (intended) and "latent" (unintended) functions of institutions.

Spencer's own predilections led him in some curious and contradictory directions. First, his individualistic, laissez-faire leanings led him to incorporate the very "negative" philosophy, classical political economy, against which Comte had constructed his own theoretical system! Primarily, this took the form of postulating an ultimate evolution *toward* rather than away from individual liberty (his distinction was between "military" and "industrial" societies), and adding the third and final element — the *scarcity* of the goods, abilities, and capital which capitalists are presumed to bring to the labor-exchange relationship — to the "Functional Theory of Stratification." Second, however, he then negated much of this new-found voluntarism by introducing the theory of "social Darwinism." Here class, racial, and sexual inequalities are attributed not to individual differences in ability and effort, but to natural, biological, social-category-based inequalities. Hence, for Spencer (1884, *I*:740–742) defence of the status quo became equated with the very biological survival of society.

Spencer also greatly inspired Durkheim, who, in addition to extending his methodological position along the aforementioned lines, clearly in good part fashioned the distinction between "mechanical" and "organic" societies after Spencer's military-industrial dichotomy (see below). Nevertheless, Spencer was as much a negative as a positive influence upon Durkheim, for the former's allegiance to political economy was nothing less than heretical for the more orthodox Durkheim.

In terms of the particular debate we have been following here, Durkheim can be seen to have (1) reiterated and sharpened Comte's attack upon the political economists and social contract theorists more generally, and (2) developed certain aspects of Comte's theorizing along lines which provide (largely intentionally) a social-psychological alternative to both Exchange Theory and Marx's theory of alienation. Given limitations of space, we shall examine only the latter in detail here.[8]

DURKHEIM AND MERTON'S ANOMIE

As did Marx, Durkheim distinguished between a natural and un-natural state of society and human nature. However, his conception of and explanation for these states is markedly different.[9]

Restraint is Needed but Optimism is Justified

Altruism and morality, Durkheim argued, and indeed, society itself, presuppose constraint and restraint. It is true that the highest level of morality entails explicit, reasoned understanding of the need for, and hence also consent to, group norms or rules. However, the existence of such norms itself presupposes regularity in individuals' conduct, a sense of duty or obligation to an authority outside themselves, and a spirit of discipline which leads to self-restraint. These are prerequisites for morality because consent to the *content* of moral values can only be obtained through interaction with others. This learning through interaction is why children are more con-strained than others; that is, they must first be taught discipline and attachment to the group. Through the latter comes identification with the group, which fosters altruism and cooperation. Habitual coopera-tion then teaches the child specific norms and permits consensus and spontaneity (Durkheim, 1973:Part I).

In an obvious attempt to distinguish himself from Comte, Durkheim hastened to add (1973:49, 99) that he was speaking of the development of "enlightened allegiance" and not of "insidiously calculating a spirit of resignation in the child." Yet, we might well ask, *whose* interests are discipline and self-control supposed to serve? Who will educate the educators?

On one level, Durkheim answered, discipline and self-control serve the general interest. Following Spencer, he claimed that a society's response to its environment necessitates internal order, and, it would appear, that inevitable scarcities also require individuals' restraint (Durkheim, 1973:37–59).

On another level, constraint and restraint can be justified as benefiting particular individuals. Someone who does not exercise self-restraint, who is a slave of his or her irrational passions, for example, is in fact "alienated" — in an unnatural state which is so psychologically uncomfortable that he or she is likely to commit suicide. Having thus linked "alienation" with the *absence* of restraint, in opposition to Marx, Durkheim went on to speak of Society as liberating instead of alienating individuals (Durkheim, 1973:46–49, 68–71, 124; 1964a:254).

These essentially Positivist arguments were accompanied by a third; that is, society has been changing for the better, such that the amounts of constraint and restraint required have actually been decreasing. Here is the evolution of society from "mechanical" to "organic solidarity." The former exists mainly in primitive societies where labor is not divided and everyone therefore does much the same work. Under these conditions individuals are bound together not by economic interdependence, but by their common allegiance to traditional (primarily religious) beliefs and values. Because everyone thinks alike and because this *"conscience collective"* is the only basis for social order, the community cannot and does not tolerate individuality, but instead demands strict conformity to group norms. These norms, moreover, are highly specific, leaving little room for individual interpretation and initiative, and the punishments for violating them tend to be coercive in the extreme, in that they exact revenge to deter others rather than permit individuals to make good their damage to others. The term "mechanical," then, refers to the fact that individuals are "mass-produced" replicas from the same narrow mold, and are bound together, not through voluntary allegiance to cooperative relationships with each other, but by coercive conformity to the norms of society in general (Durkheim, 1964a:70–110).

"Organic" solidarity is analogous to order in biological organisms; that is, social order is based upon voluntary cooperation in individualized social units and allegiance to highly general norms that permit individual initiative. This initiative is said to be a necessary concomitant of the division of labor; specifically, when work is highly varied, individuals must be permitted a great deal of individual discretion. The move to the more general norms demanded by this change is made possible by the emergence of functional interdependence; that is, no longer having to rely simply upon conformity to traditional beliefs for social order, people can develop new beliefs to complement the change in material institutions. These new beliefs are still broadly religious, but they sanctify individuality rather than supernatural beings symbolizing Society (Durkheim, 1964a; also in Giddens, 1972:146–150).

"Individuality" was defined here essentially as humanity, as the realization of humans' distinctive characteristics, among which one of the most important is, as noted earlier, rational restraint. Allegiance to the norms of individuality eventually comes from having rationally considered alternative viewpoints, and therefore constitutes voluntary rather than blind allegiance to Society. The cult of the individual is therefore "a religion of which man is, at the same time, both believer and god" (Durkheim, in Giddens, 1972: 147–150).

Pathological States of the Social Organism

How therefore did Durkheim explain egoism and coercion? In most general terms, Durkheim argued, such "social problems" as egoism and coercion arise from the fact that organic solidarity has not fully emerged in all areas of society (Giddens, 1972:10). Central to Durkheim's theory of organic solidarity are the assumptions that the division of labor puts individuals into continuous contact with each other, such that new groups and new norms of individuality can arise, and that these norms will then restrain these same individuals. However, on occasion special circumstances remove individuals from group influence and/or otherwise prevent the development of clear new norms, or the disappearance of old norms which contradict the new. These latter two conditions define the state of *"anomie"* or "normlessness."

Although Durkheim never provided a systematic account of the special circumstances which produce anomie, he particularly stressed geographical and social mobility, and simply the rapidity of a variety of social changes, including the development of complexity of the division of labor. Among the social problems he attempted to explain with his theory of anomie are suicide and class conflict.

For example, although at first it might seem strange that suicides increase during economic booms as well as depressions, individuals are socially mobile in both cases, and mobility removes them from group ties and places them in unfamiliar situations where norms governing their aspirations and behavior may be unclear (Durkheim,

1966:246–254). The divorced or widowed, who are more likely than married persons to commit suicide, have also been removed from group influence (Durkheim, 1966:201–202). The same is true of religious differences: that the rate of suicide increases from Jews, to Catholics, to Protestants can be explained by the increasing stress upon individual freedom from the group and a decreasing degree of group solidarity that characterizes this ordering (Durkheim, 1966: 158–160).

Class conflict is said to have been largely caused by these same conditions. Thus whereas the medieval guild system united master and journeyman, just as the small factory still assures that employer and employee interact and realize their dependence upon each other and their respective social purposes, conditions in the large factory often make this contact difficult. The two parties infrequently meet at work, and they may no longer even live in the same community (Durkheim, 1964a:370). What interaction there is between them may be uncoordinated, such that, for example, some do more work than others, and the common social experiences which produce norms and identification with the organization are therefore limited (Durkheim, 1964a:390–392). Finally, the normal external constraints upon each party may be weak. Thus whereas traditional occupational, familial, and religious associations typically limited individuals' selfishness, geographical and social mobility in particular have now loosened all three types of associations, and work, family, and religious life have become divided (Durkheim, 1964a:361, 400). Similarly, legal regulation of employer-employee relationships has not been able to keep up with the rapid and far-reaching changes in such relationships (Durkheim, 1964a:367, 408).

Merton's later contributions to this theory of anomie appear to be twofold. First, whereas Durkheim himself took actual interaction in actual groups as a necessary preventative for anomie, Merton (1957) has argued that most individuals more or less automatically refer their own aspirations to group standards and adjust the former accordingly, with or without actual interaction. Moreover, in order to be effective the "reference groups" which serve as the sources of restraint need not be those to which the individuals in question actually belong. The socially mobile, for example, may socialize themselves simply through internalizing the standards of the groups to which they expect to belong. However, reference group theory also has implications that would not have pleased Durkheim; that is, these same individuals could also choose reference groups which raise instead of limit their aspirations. In one study Merton cites, for example, soldiers who spent World War II on American college campuses actually felt relatively more deprived than those on the battle lines in Europe, although their objective situation was obviously much more comfortable. That they should have felt more deprived, it is argued, arises from their having chosen as a reference group, not soldiers in Europe, but other college students, whose freedom was considerably greater.

Second, whereas Durkheim himself emphasized the absence of norms as a major source of lack of restraint in individuals, Merton (1938) has stressed the contradictions-between-norms aspect of anomie. As Durkheim had with suicide, Merton begins by disputing the popular assumption that poverty per se is the major cause of crime. What is interesting in this regard, he suggests, is that whereas the two are indeed highly correlated in the United States, this is not the case in many European countries. What one finds in the former, he continues, is a strong emphasis and value upon individual success in spite of the persistence of class-based inequalities of opportunity. As a consequence of this social structural contradiction, working-class individuals in particular are motivated to dispense with their allegiance to either or both of the goal of success or the legitimate means of attaining it. Hence, for example, the attempts to succeed through organized crime, or to renounce both success and the legitimate world of work through drug use.[10]

PARSONS AND BEYOND: PROGRESSION OR REGRESSION?

Durkheim's theory of anomie has had a large impact upon mainstream social psychology. Thus, within sociology there has been an abundance of empirical research loosely derived from the theory (see, for example, Clinard, 1971), and even the most popular conception of "alienation" among mainstreamists (Seeman, 1959; 1972) is a (very) loose hybrid of Marx's theory of alienation and Durkheim's theory of anomie. Although less research by psychologists has been explicitly based upon the theory, much of the theory and research of the "Human Relations in Industry" school (see Chapters 8 and 11) has Durkheimian roots, as is indicated by such concepts as "morale" and the concern that supervisors' expectations for employees be clear and noncontradictory (Kahn et al., 1964). Unfortunately, however, in my opinion, Durkheim's influence has been difficult to trace, and some of his more positive contributions lost, through the predilections and influence of *Talcott Parsons* (1902–   ).

Although Parsons (1964a:204) has warned against overly reified conceptions of society more vehemently than did Durkheim, much of his own theorizing is rightly known for its excessively abstract nature. According to Parsons (1964a:168), for example, we do not live in a society whose distinguishing feature is its capitalist political economy, but in one whose "occupational system directly institutionalizes the dominant patterns of value-orientation of the culture. . . ." If Durkheim and Merton were moved to criticize the class and sex structure for its not being meritocratic, Parsons has been much more inclined to push the Comtean-Spencerian position that all is right with these aspects of society. For example, Parsons (1964b:59–60) is notorious for having proclaimed the role structure of Bales's informal groups (see Chapter 1) to be a natural, universal one, and the one upon which our patriarchal family structure is based.

This overly conservative, overly idealistic position has led Parsons to a social psychology which emphasizes socialization and social control over the freedom of individuals to develop their positive human capacities, and "deviance" from societal norms over the inappropriateness of the norms themselves. This regression from Durkheim to Comte can be seen in Parsons' own appropriation of Freud. Although Parsons (1964a:222; 1964b:100) occasionally concedes to Freud that sexual repression can be costly, his own emphasis is unquestionably upon how beneficial the socialization process is for the child as well as society as a whole. From what can be gleaned from Guy Swanson's translation (1967:38–39), the benefits are allegedly these (there is no mention here of costs): in the "oral" stage of psychosexual development the child learns to be dependent upon others: in the "anal" stage s/he learns to be responsible; in the "phallic" stage the child is forced (given the Oedipal crisis) to generalize his or her dependencies and responsibilities from his or her parents to peers and others outside the immediate family; in a final stage s/he somehow also achieves "independence, or, more suggestively, . . . competent performance."

The evolution of organicism (by Parsons' time, "structural functionalism"), has by no means ended with Parsons. Rather, (presumably) in part positively stimulated by the "adaptation" and "goal attainment" needs he attributes to "social systems," and in part negatively stimulated by Parsons' own tendency to assume that the state of equilibrium to which the social organism returns is simply the status quo, many Functionalist sociologists have moved toward "open systems theory." Here, as with dialectical processes in Marxian theory, in the process of attempting to adapt to its environment the social system is usually assumed to change both its environment and itself, such that the new state of equilibrium is often quite different from the former. This particular liberalization of Functionalism appears to have won over a number of humanistic psychologists to Functionalism (see especially Katz and Kahn, 1966), but it does not appear to have added very much in the way of substantive theory to Functionalist social psychology.

RETROSPECTUS AND PROSPECTUS

As did Marxists, Functionalists first developed their theorizing in opposition to what is now known as Exchange Theory. Yet whereas his own purposes led Comte to recognize and attempt to explain egoistic competition and corruption, they also led him to explain them as temporary, *pathological,* instead of *inherent* features of bourgeois society. If for Marx individuals are *coerced* into these actions through capitalists' monopolization of wealth and power in bourgeois society, for Comte there is no such *fundamental conflict of interest.* Instead, egoism and corruption have arisen from the *absence of adequate moral regulation,* what Durkheim was to label "anomie." If for Marx unintended features of societal structure exist for the most part because capitalists have usurped the power of the majority, for Comte Society is, and should be, an integrated, *self-regulating system* beyond all individuals' control (except, perhaps, Comte's).

Therefore, the failure of bystanders to intervene in emergencies would presumably be attributed to the absence of clear norms for such situations, although we might well ask why "Society" has taken so long to develop them, or why existing norms do not become more salient as the number of bystanders increases. Milgram's subjects might perhaps be thought of as caught between prescriptions to obey authorities and prescriptions not to hurt others, although here too we have little means for determining which prescription should have the greater effect, why the experimenter's being absent from the room should make a difference, and so on. In this regard Functionalists have generally had little to say about the problems of power and support, except, as we shall see again in Chapter 8, that Organizations inevitably "require" power over, and support from, their members.

Our Functionalists would presumably explain the outlooks of

the fickle foremen by appealing to the concept of reference groups. As a *description* this explanation is quite adequate, since the foremen were indeed presumably choosing and evaluating their own outlooks in terms of the standards of their membership group. Yet we are left with two problems which have traditionally plagued reference group analyses: (1) what determines the very different outlooks of the different categories of individuals in the first place, and (2) why, since one's reference group need not be one's membership group, do individuals in fact choose their occupational group as their reference group? In this regard, note that unlike Marxian theory, Functionalist theory presumes away the conflicts of interest which presumably determine the opposing outlooks in question and force individuals to "choose" one or the other.

Were we to remove the emphasis from explicitly contractual aspects of the accounts of the emergence and persistence of social structure in Chapter 1 as, for example, Bales himself does in his account of role differentiation, Functionalists would be in their element. Whether we should lean toward their account or the Marxian is an empirical question we shall frequently ask in Part 3. *Do* our major social organizations constitute self-regulating systems? *Is* there consensus among all members about collective purposes, or are only some parties actually in control?

Notes

[1] The organicist model has undergone a number of transformations, some of which are touched upon later in this chapter. The newer terms include "structural functionalism," "systems theory," "general systems theory," "open systems," and a number of others. However, the concept of a self-regulating system is common to all of them.

[2] This approach is suggested by his very division of the sciences; that is, biology was to have exclusive dominion over the passions and innate intellectual capacities, sociology was to share the study of intellectual and moral development with it, and psychology was to be thrown out!

[3] See, for example, Comte (1974a:232, 238–239; 1974b:428, 449, 511–512).

[4] See, for example, the following quote:

> It is not only as an impediment to progress that the preponderance of material conceptions is to be deplored. It is also dangerous to order. When all political evils are imputed to institutions instead of to ideas and social manners, which are now the real seat of mischief, the remedy is vainly sought in changes, each more serious than the last, in institutions and existing powers. . . . An illustration of the case is presented by the discussions and attacks which have so often menaced the institution of Property [Comte, 1974b:428].

[5] In recent years the term has sometimes been used synonymously with "empiricism" or "the scientific method."

[6] Particularly in some of his earlier writings, he had suggested that civilization

was civilizing individuals, that property ownership or even simply having to subordinate oneself habitually to industrial leaders was gradually preparing people for the good society (Comte, 1974a:102–104). In his later writings he relied more upon the assumption that people have a natural instinct to submit to authority, an instinct which people will act on when competent authorities appear (Comte, 1974b:513–514).

[7]Some ten years later, after capitalists had for some strange reason *still* not accepted Positivism, Comte, ever the opportunist, then turned to workers. Why? In good part because their stupidity was supposed to have kept them from being warped by outmoded ideas (Comte, in Lenzer, 1975:348–371)!

[8]See Durkheim (1964a:250, 386, 415; 1964b:24, 94, 122).

[9]One should note, however, that Durkheim's ideological stance has been given fairly disparate interpretations. Contrast, for example, Giddens' (1972) with Zeitlin's (1968). While those who would make Durkheim out to be highly progressive often point to his having included the "forced" division of labor, which indeed reiterates certain aspects of Marx's analysis of alienation, they should remember that he was very much more concerned with the anomic conditions described below. Similarly, in his study of suicide, coercion as a possible cause of the phenomenon receives only a footnote. This is in direct contrast to the explanations for suicide which Marx himself preferred (Marx, 1975, 4:597–612).

[10]Merton has been justifiably criticized for having been vague on the question of when one will get one rather than another reaction to the contradiction (e.g., Deutsch and Krauss, 1965:202). The long line of attempts to solve the problem has been compiled and reviewed by Clinard (1971).

5

THE MODERATE
IDEALISTS' REVISION, I:
THE WEBERIANS

By the turn of the century Germany had still not achieved anywhere near the degree of political democracy that England or France had, the major cause being the blatant catering of the Prussian bureaucracy to the eastern landowning class, the Junkers. Without the active participation of a class of entrepreneurs, furthermore, the national policies growing out of Bismarck's unification of the country had not been particularly favorable to industrial capitalism, and as a consequence Germany lagged behind Britain and France in the imperialist rivalries of the day.

On the other hand, the same heavy-handedness which made for a politically timid bourgeoisie also greatly accelerated the growth of a social democratic labor party demanding political rights for workers, a party which understandably accepted Marxism as its official program. Also worthy of note is the fact that by this time many Marxists had already developed into the dogmatically materialist, "automatic" variety against which the neo-Marxists of Chapter 3 were later to rebel.

These two sets of conditions clearly had a very great effect upon such liberal German academics as Werner Sombart, Georg Simmel, Max Weber, and Karl Mannheim. Although these were by no means the *only* sources of intellectual stimulation for these thinkers, it is nevertheless true that they took as an important concern the development of bodies of theory which would justify *both* the liberalization of German society *and* the rejection of orthodox Marxism. Since the major counterposition to classical liberalism with which they grappled was that of Marx rather than Comte, it is hardly surprising that the products of these endeavors have more in common with Marxian theory than the Functionalism of, for example, Durkheim. Of these intellectuals Max Weber has unquestionably been the most influential, and it is to his work that we now turn.[1]

66

WEBER'S RATIONALITY AND IRRATIONALITY

Unlike Marx and Comte, Max Weber (1864–1920) did not explicitly state his agreements and disagreements with the classical political economists. One of the reasons for this lack may have been that as a liberal, his own position was closer to theirs than were those of Marx or Comte.

Certainly he appears to have been more concerned with the motives of individuals than have most Marxists and Functionalists. Nor did he seem to have been particularly concerned about egoistic competition, the cause célèbre of these previous reactions to the emergence of bourgeois society. For example, if for Marx the existence of the unstable market mechanism as the sole mediator between individuals' needs and production made capitalism an extremely irrational system, for Weber the profit-seeking motive is the reason for capitalism's unprecedented efficiency in production (Gerth and Mills, 1958:49). If for Comte competition promotes class conflict, for Weber, like deTocqueville before him, this same competition eventually breaks down classes, promotes political democracy, and decreases the likelihood of large-scale social cleavages. But for that matter, on occasion Weber even maintained that egoistic competition, far from reaching its highest level in a modern capitalist economy, had actually been greater in earlier economies (Weber, 1958a:58).

That Weber's theorizing is a "double-edged sword" in our debate is suggested by both his abstract theorizing and his analyses of concrete historical phenomena. For example, if for the political economists the rationality of individuals was simply taken as given, for Weber such rationality, which he labeled "purposeful," represented only one of several motivational bases for action. Thus an individual's actions may be oriented not towards choosing the most effective and efficient means for achieving a given goal, but towards rigidly following the dictates of such ideals as duty, honor, or devotion ("value rationality") or the "force of habit" ("traditional action"). Nor need there be any ulterior motive behind a given act, since one may simply do it because one is emotionally involved in it ("affective action") (Weber, 1964:115–118).

Weber can therefore be seen to have disputed the political economists' narrow account of individual motivation. But what was presumably his critique of the latters' position goes much deeper than this point. In the first place, Weber was obviously attempting to counter the crude materialism which characterized the Utilitarian position by stressing the importance of the meaning of the action for the actor.[2] Moreover, it is undoubtedly significant that the above-mentioned account of motivation was explicitly made with reference to *social* action, to action "oriented to the past, present, or expected behavior of others." Weber's point, in other words, was not simply that one must take into account the many different meanings which may guide an individual's actions, but that *these meanings are them-selves socially derived* rather than innately or psychologically given (Weber, 1964: 88–118).

The same moderate idealist position was behind much of Weber's critique of orthodox Marxism, although here the problem was not so much to emphasize the social and structural nature of such meanings, since Marxian theory was heavily social and structural at the outset. The problem was rather to emphasize the independent importance of social meanings vis-à-vis such material social conditions as class and power.

For example, if in orthodox Marxian theory class interests are often the only socially derived conditions around which individuals in bourgeois society are said to organize, according to Weber "Man does not strive for power only in order to enrich himself economically." Rather, "Very frequently the striving for power is conditioned by the 'social honor' it entails. . . . Nor," he continues, "is power the only basis for social honor. Indeed, social honor, or prestige, may even be the basis of political or economic power, and very frequently has been" (Weber, 1958b:180). Similarly, whereas Marx can sometimes be construed to have implied that individuals need not be aware of their class interests for significant degrees of class organization to occur, Weber countered that whether such organization does in fact occur is a function of a host of "cultural" factors, among which is the "*transparency* of the connections between the causes and the consequences of the 'class situation' " (Weber, 1958b:184–185).

But Weber is best known for what many (especially Parsons) have presumed to be his heavily idealistic attack upon the Marxist approach to religion. In fact, Weber did *not* disagree with the Marxian position that religious organizations are likely to be strongly conditioned by the class composition of their members.[3] He also did not wish simply to counter the thesis of Friedrich Engels, Marx's collaborator, that the Protestant Reformation reflected the bourgeoisie's rise to power, with the equally rigid thesis (of, for example, Comte) that the Reformation was even the major basis for modern capitalism (Weber, 1958a:91, 183, 277). He *did* in fact vehemently deny the orthodox Marxist contention that religious values are only a reflection of political-economic interests (Weber, 1958b:269–270), but what he wanted to substitute for this position was the more moderate one that "ideas become effective forces in history" (Weber, 1958a:90).

Weber's study of the relationship between Protestantism and capitalism is a logical place to begin an examination of the relationship between his substantive theorizing and that of Marx and the political economists. After examining this particular question we shall see how his account of the subsequent development of capitalism also differs from those of these two sets of theorists.

The Genesis of Modern Capitalism

The appearance of modern capitalism, Weber suggested, cannot be attributed simply to the breakup of feudalism and freeing of competition, which was Adam Smith's explanation, since previous societies were often even *more* competitive. Similarly, what characterizes the "spirit" of modern capitalism is *not* narrow hedonism, but

> . . . a unique combination of devotion to the earning of wealth through legitimate economic activity, together with the avoidance of the use of this income for personal enjoyment. This income is then turned back into the business. This is rooted in a value of efficient performance in a chosen vocation as a duty and a virtue [Giddens, 1971:126].

On the other hand, "the more naive historical materialism" is equally incapable of explaining the appearance of this spirit, since "in the country of Benjamin Franklin's birth (Massachusetts), the spirit of capitalism . . . was present *before* the capitalistic order" (Weber, 1958a:55; my emphasis; see also pp. 75,90).

Instead, Weber went on, this spirit had its strongest roots in the beliefs of such Puritan Protestant sects as Calvinism. Similarly, far from being purposively rational activity, for these early Protestants capitalistic activity was highly irrational, or at best value rational. Specifically, it derived in part from a sense of religious duty and in part from what amounted to a "chronic case" of anxiety induced by these same beliefs.

Thus in this belief system human activity "only has meaning in relation to God's purposes," *yet* these purposes cannot be comprehended by humans without His having revealed them, *and He may choose not to do so!* God chooses only a few people for eternal grace, and the choice has already been made, such that one cannot affect it, nor is there even any way of discovering whether one is in fact among the chosen (Giddens, 1971:128)!

Needless to say these beliefs put the member of the Protestant sect in a most unenviable position, for if "the Catholic confession of sins was . . . by comparison a means of *relieving* the person from the tremendous internal pressure under which the sect member in his conduct was constantly held," for the latter "like the bliss in the beyond, his whole existence in the here and now depended upon his 'proving' himself." Proving himself or herself, in turn, meant having to do so before God, "before men in the sense of socially holding one's own within the Puritan sects," *and* "to himself as well" (Weber, 1958b: 320–321, 291).

The consequence of this "extremely inhuman" doctrine was

> . . . *a feeling of unprecedented inner loneliness* of the single individual . . . .He was forced to follow his path alone to meet a destiny which had been decreed for him from eternity. No one could help him [Weber, 1958a:104; my emphasis].

Two related responses developed to this psychological state:

> Firstly, that the individual should consider it as obligatory to deem himself one of the chosen: any doubts as to the certainty of election are evidence of imperfect faith and therefore lack of grace. Secondly, that "intense worldly activity" is the most appropriate means to develop and maintain this necessary self-confidence. Thus the performance of "good works" became regarded as a "sign" of election—not in any way a method of *attaining* salvation, but rather of eliminating doubts of salvation [Giddens, 1971:128–129].

Subsequent Developments

Weber (1958a:181) agreed with Marx that once modern capitalism is well under way, most individuals are *forced* to take on a specialized task within the capitalist division of labor. On the other hand, this is by no means the *only* meaning which submission to authorities is likely to have for the members of capitalist society. Similarly, whereas economic self-interest is one of these other motives, it is by no means the only one. In fact, Weber suggested, in opposition to Marx, it is actually in the interest of capitalists to increase workers' wages. Rather than limit itself to "the appeal to material or affectual or ideal motives as the basis for guaranteeing its continuance," he suggested, every system of domination "attempts to establish and cultivate the belief in its 'legitimacy' " (Weber, 1964:324–325).

Weber's emphasis upon the importance of *beliefs* in the *legitimacy* of a social order, which could be "traditional," "charismatic" ("devotion to the specific and exceptional sanctity, heroism or exemplary character of an individual person, and of the normative patterns or order revealed by him"), or "rational-legal," was clearly another instance of his moderate idealist revision of the Marxist and Exchange Theory positions. Yet it should again be noted that Weber's claims in this regard were much more moderate than those of the Functionalists. For example, at one point he noted that people may submit not out of a belief in legitimacy but "from individual weakness and helplessness because there is no acceptable alternative." Similarly, he went on, when a system of domination is "so completely assured of dominance . . . *as often occurs in practice* . . . it can afford to drop even the pretence of a claim to legitimacy" (Weber, 1964:326–327; my emphasis).

Nevertheless, Weber was most interested in the fact that "the distinction between an order derived from voluntary agreement and one which is imposed is only relative" (Weber, 1964:131–132), and in the following account of his theorizing about concrete historical phenomena the often subtle relationship between objective conditions and subjective meanings, of "transparency" in general and legitimacy in particular, figures prominently.

Growth of Bureaucracies Versus Class Conflict

Marx's central criticism of classical political economy was that it regarded alienated individuals and capitalism as natural states. What is particularly noteworthy about Weber is that he in effect applied Marx's method to Marx himself, arguing that *property-class conflict and the alienation of individuals it engenders are only a moment in a much more general trend.* Specifically, whereas Marx had been correct that capitalists divide workers' labor in order to control them better and to increase the capitalists' profits directly through technical efficiencies, *he was wrong to have presumed that bureaucratic organizations are unique to capitalism.*

Thus, the formation of bureaucracies had first occurred not in a capitalist economy, but in feudal society. The monarch had learned that the only means by which his or her vassals could be prevented from usurping the monarch's wealth and power was to restrict each vassal's tasks and make someone immediately above him or her in the authority hierarchy responsible for the vassal's actions (Weber, 1958b:205–206). Similarly, given its superior efficiency and reliance upon technical expertise, bureaucracy is here to stay. Even if workers were to revolt, they could neither do away with the bureaucratic organizations which, for example, run transportation and communication facilities, nor run these facilities themselves (Weber, 1958b: 228–229; 1964:339). *In fact,* Weber argued, by breaking down the political-economic monopoly of the capitalist class, a socialist revolution would only hasten the development of bureaucracy in industry and government.[4] According to Weber, bureaucracies have already transformed the nature of modern capitalism, but in two highly contradictory ways.

The Generalization of Alienation

In the first place, what began as the expropriation of the wage worker's labor and product has now extended to the vast majority of the labor force. This is true not only for "clerical personnel and technically trained persons," but, given the dispersion of ownership through stockholding, managers, and, given the importance of finance capital, single owners as well (Weber, 1964:247, 259).

This phenomenon is as true of publicly owned as of privately owned work organizations. The result is that individuals have increasingly less influence upon governmental as well as industrial organizations. In fact, the same is even true of political parties, and here Weber especially singled out the German Social Democratic Party, which was officially a Marxist labor party, and the two major American parties, which, in spite of the rhetoric of democracy, were extreme cases of "machine politics" (Weber, 1958b:38, 211).

Weber made relatively little of the psychological consequences of the general lack of power, and made at least equally as much of the gains in technical efficiency from bureaucracy. This fact has led some of his left-wing interpreters (e.g., Israel, 1971) to conclude that alienation was of little concern to him. Yet two important considerations should be kept in mind here. In the first place, Weber labored under the illusion that his analyses were "value-free," and he in fact broke off some of his few accounts of psychological alienation with precisely this claim.[5] Second, since he attributed such alienation to bureaucracy in general rather than capitalism in particular, and since he regarded bureaucracy as inevitable, he may well have regarded it as fruitless to dwell upon conditions which could not be changed.

The Narrowing of Class Conflict

Weber did not claim that class conflict had disappeared during his own time, but he *did* claim that there had been fundamental changes in the nature of class conflict by the turn of the century. In the first place, he argued, economic ("class") struggles in the marketplace increasingly center around the price of labor instead of control over the means of production. Second, because of this change it is mainly during economic crises and major technological changes that "class" conflict comes to the fore. Otherwise status conflicts, often centering around occupational, educational, and/or income differences, are favored (Weber, 1958b:180–194).

As with the generalization of alienation, these changes are supposed to have arisen from the increase in bureaucracy. Specifically, the high degree of effectiveness and efficiency which characterizes bureaucratic administration requires technical expertise, such that managers, officials, and eventually production workers as well tend to be chosen for their education and other technical qualifications rather than the class position of their family of origin. Two major consequences follow from this trend: (1) as mentioned previously, the management of the large corporation becomes separated from its ownership, and (2) there is a general proliferation of occupational, educational, and income interests in the labor market and a proliferation of life-styles or status interests in the sphere of consumption. If for Marx and Engels property and *class* are the major determinants of an individual's "personal development" (see Chapter 8), for Weber it is increasingly one's *occupation* and, to a lesser extent, one's *status*, which determines one's "life chances."

These changes are also behind the transformation of class conflict, in that it is the general lack of property ownership and increasing importance of one's occupation's bargaining power in the labor market which tend to reduce "class" conflict to the issue of the price of labor. In addition, those without property are divided against each other by competing occupational and status groupings, and with these complications in the objective nature of the class structure it also becomes less transparent. "The ill will of the worker," for example, is directed not toward "the rentier, the shareholder, and the banker," but managers (Weber, 1958b:186). Similarly, the class structure is even *more* reified and opaque for the bureaucratic official, whose loyalty is not "to a *person*, like the vassal's or disciples' faith in feudal or in patrimonial relations of authority," but "to impersonal and functional purposes." These therefore "provide an ideological halo for the master" (Weber, 1958b:199). Finally, given the divided and opaque nature of the class structure, specifically political organizations are likely to lose much of their class character. These conditions, for example, have already "made possible the varieties of patriarchal socialism and the frequent attempts—formerly, at least—of threatened status groups to form alliances with the proletariat against the 'bourgeoisie'" (Weber, 1958b:186).

Related to the forming of bureaucracies in general and the democratization of the class structure which bureaucracies tend to promote is another major social change: the increasing legitimation of the social order through "rational-legal" means. Although this legitimation reflects and promotes a genuine increase in political democracy, remember that Weber also maintained that it hastens the further development of bureaucracy, which in turn *decreases* individuals' influence. "Bureaucracy," Weber said (1958b:234), "naturally welcomes a poorly informed and hence a powerless parliament—at least in so far as ignorance somehow agrees with the bureaucracy's interests." The belief that the social order is legitimate because it has been "voted in" by the majority can therefore legitimate individuals' powerlessness (Weber, 1964:131–132).

What Can We Set Against This Mechanization

Since bureaucracy is here to stay, counteracting it is not a question of doing away with the industrial and state bureaucracies, which was Marx's solution, but of *counterbalancing* them with other social organizations. Nor are these other organizations to be "workers' councils" within a city or region, which has been the more typical Marxian solution. Indeed, Weber felt, the internal "disruptions" caused by a revolution could only weaken Germany's position in the imperialist struggles of the time. In a disturbingly Machiavellian elitist manner, Weber then suggested that we turn to charismatic leaders such as the John F. Kennedy of 1960, the Pierre Elliott

Trudeau of 1968, or, perhaps (but perhaps not), the Nicolai Lenin of 1923 or the Mao Tse-Tung of 1957.

THE WEBERIAN LEGACY, LEFT, RIGHT, AND CENTRE

Given his attempts to separate politics from his sociology and the "if, and, but" nature of so many of his theoretical statements, Weber's theorizing has been used to buttress just about any other ideological-theoretical position that one can imagine.

For a "welfare" liberal such as John Kenneth Galbraith (1972), for example, or, to a lesser extent, John Porter (1965), Weber's arguments are said to justify regarding "big" Labor as as much of a threat to democracy as "big" Capital, the latter of which, in Galbraith's case, has little to do with property ownership and everything to do with the increasing power of the "technostructure." Similarly, more egalitarian education and the reform of existing parliamentary parties seems to be the preferred solution of such analysts. For modern deTocquevilleans such as Ralf Dahrendorf (1959), Weber is said to have provided a perfect rationale for rejecting both Marx and Parsons. Specifically, whereas "conflict" (for our present society read "competition") is "ubiquitous," in opposition to Parsons' "consensus," since the last century it has been completely transformed from large-scale–property-class conflict to small-scale–interest-group competition within an equally small-scale consensus that the "game" should be "played fairly" or democratically.

Although this usurption of Weber by liberals more mainstream than Weber himself has involved some distortion of his position, it has nevertheless produced some interesting and useful accounts of the social-psychological consequences of bureaucratization. Particularly important are Robert Merton's (1957) portrayal of the psychological condition of the bureaucrat, whose narrow sphere of responsibility and heavy dependence upon the whims of those higher than himself or herself in the authority hierarchy seems to make him/her particularly defensive in interactions with the bureacracy's clients, and William H. Whyte's (1957) The Organization Man, a study of how the change from the individualistic entrepreneur, at least secure within his own business, to the executive within the group-oriented corporation, who continually fears for his job, is supposed to have produced a slavishly conformist, neurotic human being.

For Parsons and his followers (Parsons, 1964c; 1968), on the other hand, Weber's stress upon the inevitability of bureaucracy, his presumed stress upon status as opposed to class, and religious values as opposed to material substructure, have been regarded as a total rejection of Marxism and reinstitution of the idealism behind such concepts as "value-orientation" and "normative action." Although many have now taken Parsons to task for these distortions (e.g., Giddens, 1972b), his interpretation has already become almost orthodoxy in North American sociology, where a concern with "socio-economic status" and pluralism has unfortunately replaced that of "class, status, and party."

In contrast to these liberal and conservative interpretations of Weber is a long and venerable tradition of left-wing Weberianism, beginning, in North America at least, with *C. Wright Mills* (1916–1962) and continuing through the work of such writers as *Norman Birnbaum, Irving Zeitlin,* and *Anthony Giddens* (1972b).

C. WRIGHT MILLS: MASS SOCIETY REVISITED

In his own analysis of motives, Mills (1940:904, 907) takes the radical position that they may largely be socially derived rationalizations which may not only be imputed to oneself and others *after* the act, but which serve as *causes* of the act, in that "often anticipations of acceptable justification will control conduct ('If I did this, what could I say? What would they say?')." As a consequence, "individuals are skeptical of Rockefeller's avowed religious motives for his business conduct because such motives are not *now* terms of the vocabulary conventionally and prominently accompanying situations of business enterprise" (Mills, 1940:910). In the same manner, Mills (1956:225) later accused Marx of having used the Renaissance's model of craftmanship as a baseline for alienation when it is in some respects no longer applicable.

The point here was not that Marx was incorrect in his analyses of the *objective* state of workers, in that craftsmanship does indeed no longer characterize most work. In fact, Mills himself proceeded to document the proletarianization of "white-collar" workers. Their work, he said, has been routinized and even automated. Operating as they do upon people more than things, and having to manipulate them in order to sell them something, white-collar workers must market their personalities in order to perform the job adequately. As a consequence, interaction between employee and employee and employee and customer becomes more shallow and insincere and the worker's very personality becomes the property of the enterprise. The narrowing of differences in income and working conditions between the white- and blue-collar worker, the increasing impersonality of the bureaucratic enterprise, and the enlarging of the white-collar labor force through mass education have also made it increasingly difficult for the salaried worker to borrow prestige, let alone make the traditional climb up the white-collar ladder.

Rather, Mills's point was that because craftsmanship is no longer available to most people as a model with which they can personally identify (that is, it is no longer in their vocabulary of motives), proletarianization is unlikely to have many of the subjective effects Marx postulated. "The historical destruction of craftsmanship and the old office does not enter the consciousness of the modern wage worker or white-collar employee; much less is their absence felt by him as a crisis, as it might have been if, in the course of the last generation, his father or mother had been in the craft condition" (Mills, 1956:227–228). This also means that capitalization, while a source of objective alienation, "has not been widely experienced as 'agony' or reacted to by proletarianization, in any psychological sense that may be given these terms" (Mills, 1956:297). Rather than experiencing alienation subjectively, Mills suggested, many white-collar workers are governed by a "status panic" which leads them to simply try and catch up, through unionization, to blue-collar workers and their rising incomes. But for that matter, even awareness of alienation "often seems more likely to be accompanied by political apathy than by insurgency of either the left or right" (Mills, 1962:112–113).[6]

If historical changes in work and the class structure have fostered the development of a "mass" of individuals characterized by political apathy, the latter has also been reinforced and promoted in the spheres of politics and culture. Specifically, the bureaucratization of politics has more directly produced political alienation by fostering reliance upon the technical expert and professional politician, centralizing decision making about the more important decisions generally (e.g., control of the economy and foreign affairs becomes the sole prerogative of the federal government, and often even municipal government becomes "regionalized"), and requiring that elite decision makers then sell these decisions by manipulating the opinions of the majority of the citizens through such vehicles as the mass media. These two mass-producing factors, furthermore, feed upon each other; that is, just as individuals who lack the support of relevant interest groups and for whom political issues are therefore meaningless are more susceptible to manipulation, so more susceptible individuals increase the likelihood that political decision making will become still more centralized and manipulated. Finally, as Mills claimed is now the case in the United States, there is only formal democracy (Mills, 1959:317). This fact of course raises the important question of *who* is doing the manipulating for *what* purpose.

By referring to elite decision makers as the "power elite" instead of "ruling class," Mills followed Weber in avoiding the presumption of Smith and Marx (and deTocqueville, in the case of the "aristocracy of manufacturers" in his mass society model) that political power is more or less synonymous with economic power (Mills, 1959:277). Specifically, the power elite consists not simply of large-scale capitalists or upper-level executives, their direct representatives, but also (since the New Deal) of professional politicians and (since the Cold War and its "permanent war economy") high-ranking military officers. Nor is the protection and enhancement of private property their sole goal; rather, these various elites share wealth and power with and borrow prestige from each other in the process of exercising power in their respective spheres of influence. Finally, whereas "there is . . . little doubt that the American power elite . . . has also planned and has plotted," it is by no means simply a conspiracy. Indeed, "Often the outcome of their liaison has had consequences which none of them foresaw, much less shaped, and which only later in the course of development came under explicit control." Similarly, "No matter how great their actual power, they tend to be less acutely aware of it than of the resistance of others to its use" (Mills, 1959:292–293, 4–5).

These Weberian qualifications notwithstanding, according to Mills (1956: 101), "Power has not been split from property; rather the power of property is more concentrated than its ownership." Whereas Mills agreed that "the powers of decision are now firmly vested within the state," he added that "there is no countervailing power against the coalition of big businessmen . . . and the ascendant military men" because the former, "as political outsiders, now occupy the command posts" (Mills, 1959:267). While denying that the power elite is an aristocracy (i.e., replenished through inheritance), Mills clearly considered it to be a class in the Marxian sense of the term, and it is precisely these features, in contrast to the nonclass (disorganized) features of the working "class," which have assured its ascendancy. Thus the various members of the power elite come from similar class backgrounds and have had similar educational experiences. Moreover, they actually interact with each other, not only in the "key organizations," the boards of directors of the major corporations, but also socially. As a consequence, although their consciousness of class can take several different forms, "nowhere in America is there as great a 'class consciousness' as among the elite; nowhere is it organized as effectively as among the power elite" (Mills, 1959:281–283).

Old Left, New Left

According to Mills, the "historical agency" of social change for socialists, the working class, is now as inappropriate a choice as voluntary associations, the traditional agency of liberals. Mills bases this position not only upon the aforementioned trends, but upon the bureaucratization of working-class organizations themselves. Given the mass psychology of their individual members and the bureaucratization of politics, he claimed, trade union officials, far from providing leadership for the fight against capitalism, have increasingly begun to vie for personal power, status, and income with the national power elite. When combined with their peculiar backgrounds as members of the labor elite, this tendency has promoted its own peculiar status psychology (Mills, 1967:100–101). In fact, he claimed, most of the intellectuals of the "Old Left" (the 1930s) have themselves succumbed to the increasing bureaucracy of the labor movement and the culture they analyze, which has meant a de facto capitulation to the status quo.

To Mills (1967:257), therefore, the new historic agency of change seemed to be the younger intelligentsia, the "New Left" which had already emerged by the time of his death in 1962. They were already taking on, he said, the two major tasks which had arisen with the new societal developments: (1) the fight against the influence of bureaucracy on culture, which they were fighting within the very milieus where culture is produced (for example, the universities), and (2) (through the "peace" movement), the fight against imperialism and militarism, which have helped transform labor (i.e., by providing a bigger pie) as well as the ruling class (Mills, 1967: 233–235).

Notes

[1]The social context within which Weber worked is more fully described by Gerth and Mills (1958) and Giddens (1971; 1972b).

[2]Which is not to say that all human behavior is therefore meaningful (Weber, 1964:93).

[3]Marx had suggested that religious beliefs in general reflect humans' alienation on earth; that is, believers' submission to God is in many respects a projection of their submission to authorities in the here and now. Similarly, what Marx took to be a naive emphasis upon community in the face of fundamental class conflicts of interest and "pie-in-the-sky-when-you-die" instead of equality on earth, led him to characterize religion as the "opiate of the masses," an ideological weapon for the bourgeoisie.

[4]In this regard he avidly followed the first Russian revolution of 1905 and predicted that should Russia lose a major war and the proletariat come to power, Russia would experience a degree of bureaucracy hitherto unknown.

[5]Weber (1958a:182; 1958b:216–217).

[6]That Marxists have argued otherwise, Mills suggested (1956:324–327), stems from their having retained the Utilitarians' rationalism.

6

THE MODERATE IDEALISTS' REVISION, II: THE SYMBOLIC INTERACTIONISTS

Since our debate began with the classical political economists' use of the Enlightenment ideal of human rationality, it is interesting to trace the subsequent fate of that ideal. Comte, having found the ideal too threatening, denied its empirical validity and instead entrusted progress to Society. Marx retained the ideal, but argued that the rationality of the craftsperson had in fact been transferred to the capitalist and the machine. Weber then went on to argue that rationalization had also expropriated the rationality of the bureaucratic official and the public.

Given this consensus on the current rarity of rationality, it is interesting to note that, during Weber's time, many psychologists were turning away from the more active strain of Utilitarianism (Exchange Theory) and towards Bentham's relatively passive version. The results included Pavlov's and Thorndike's famous experiments on conditioning and Watson's attempts to develop a more general psychology of Behaviorism. This approach entailed both a suspicion of internal states of awareness and an attempt to explain thinking itself as simply the repetition of learned associations between environmental "stimuli" and one's own "responses." Social phenomena were in turn treated as simple cases of conditioning, or of "imitation," where the human or other organism simply mimics others. So popular was this type of approach, in fact, that it produced entire sociologies and social psychologies, whose proponents, such as Gabriel Tarde, Gustav LeBon, and Edward Ross, often intimated that modern democracies may be ruled less by rational publics than the "mob mind" of the crowd.

Needless to say this move toward involuntary psychological processes flew in the face of traditional bourgeois ideology, and especially, one might note, the frontier and free enterprise ethos of the fledgling United States. The result was a series of counter-

psychologies stressing the continuing rationality of humans as compared with other animals. Within psychology these took the various
forms of what is now referred to as "cognitive psychology";[1] within
sociology, a somewhat parallel tradition emerged in "Symbolic Interactionism." Were one to restrict one's comparisons to the metatheoretical level, the Symbolic Interactionists' heavy stress upon the
socially derived meanings of individuals' behavior would lead one
to classify them with the Weberians. However, in their search for a
substantive theory of social structure it was to the Darwinist branch
of Functionalism rather than to Marxism that the Interactionists
turned — Marxism (and the more systemic forms of Functionalism)
having been "un-American." As a consequence there is a world of
difference between the original theoretical contributions of the two
schools of thought.

COOLEY'S SOCIALLY MINDED
SELF AND SELF-MINDED SOCIETY

Charles Horton Cooley (1864–1929) met the Behaviorists halfway by
conceding that much of human behavior is broadly instinctive, and
that much of human social behavior is "suggestion," or mechanical
reflex activity, and "imitation." However, he continued, humans are
distinguished from other animals by a much larger degree of reason
or choice, "a principle of higher organization, controlling and trans-
forming instinctive energies." It is this facility, involving "reflective
awareness" rather than material instincts, which determines the
specific actions a person takes. In fact, he went on, his own observations of children suggest that "a novel imitation is not at all mechanical, but a strenuous voluntary activity, accompanied by effort and
followed by pleasure in success" (Cooley, 1964:26–33, 51–61).

Yet it was not Cooley's intention simply to reiterate the rational-
istic hedonism of the Exchange Theorists. Instead, he continued,
any conception of an unchanging content to human nature is unten-
able. Human nature is not, for example, characterized by either
"pecuniary selfishness or generosity. . . . It may be selfish, inefficient,
quarrelsome, conservative now, and a few years hence or in another
situation generous, peaceful, efficient, and progressive; all turns upon
how it is evoked and organized" (Cooley, 1964:33). Equally unten-
able is the approach of most Exchange Theorists that "each person
is held to be a separate agent, and all social phenomena are thought
of as originating in the action of such agents"; or the approach of

Hobbes and Bentham that "there is the same premise of the individual as a separate, unrelated agent; but over against him is set a vaguely conceived general or collective interest and force" (Cooley, 1964:43–44).

The alternative Cooley went on to offer was the "interactionist" perspective of an organic relationship between the individual and society, with each evolving with the other.

This criticism was directed against the Functionalists as well as the Exchange Theorists. Functionalists ignore the "continuously evolutionary" process arising from the influence specific individuals have upon the course of social interaction, in favor of a conception of society as "tending toward an ideal condition of moving equilibrium" (Cooley, 1920:141; 1964:49–50, 337–339). In order to argue his position Cooley began at the level of face-to-face interaction and then proceeded to try to demonstrate the links between such interaction and social organization.

"Sympathy," Self, and Social Relationships

Cooley began with the rather radical idea that rationality itself is "an organization of comparatively complex social relations." Part of what he had in mind here was the Comtean idea that "precisely as the conditions about us and the ideas suggested by those conditions become intricate, are we forced to think, to choose, to define the useful and the right, and, in general, to work out the higher intellectual life." But he went still further to suggest that rather than simply providing stimuli for thought, social relationships are actually internalized, such that thinking itself is in fact "team-work in the mind" (Cooley, 1964:53, 30).

Cooley meant that there is little direct connection between our own and others' instinctive impulses and our awareness of these impulses. Rather, our awareness is informed by our imagination of how others would act toward our own and/or their own actions. This capacity for "sympathy," or what we more typically refer to as *empathy*, is an evolutionary development in humans that permits them to achieve the reflective awareness which characterizes rationality, and this awareness in turn permits them to adapt to each others' actions in much more complex ways than other animals can. For example, it is through internalizing parents' reactions to his or her own behavior ("Johnny is a good boy for using the toilet instead of his pants.") that the child develops self-awareness, self-evaluation ("I'm a good boy."), and self-control ("I should not use my pants."). For this reason one's self is really a *social* or "looking-glass" self.

According to Cooley (1964:155), as an adaptive mechanism, empathy is something we are most likely to engage in when there is a problem to be solved, when, as Mead later put it, there is resistance in the environment to our attempts to manipulate it.

If this assessment is true, any social conditions which make the environment resistant to our influence should facilitate empathizing. For example, we should be more likely to empathize with those upon whom we are dependent (for example, other members of the immediate family) and/or who have most power over us (Cooley, 1962:270 referred to professionals who are dependent upon the rich for their livelihood). Similarly, those who are more typically dependent upon others, such as females as compared to males (Cooley, 1964:202–203), and, presumably, working-class as compared to middle-class people, should generally be more empathic.

Another matter about which a theory of empathy should enlighten us is what happens after we have in fact empathized with another. Now, if empathy is indeed an adaptive mechanism, after having empathized with others we should be much better able to adjust our own actions to theirs, to overcome or circumvent their resistance, than before. "Sympathy, therefore, is a requisite for social power" (Cooley, 1964:327–331, 140). Yet note the serious contradiction this proposition introduces to the theory; that is, if dependence upon and powerlessness in the face of others facilitates empathy, and if empathy makes one more powerful, then the weak should be more powerful! Women and workers, in other words, should surely have taken over the world by now.

The contradiction vis-à-vis women seems to have been simply avoided, whereas that regarding workers led to some rather tortuous squirming indeed. Hence, we find him saying on one hand that the strong are also the sensitive (Cooley, 1964:140–141). Yet elsewhere he seems to have realized that such a social Darwinist position *also* contradicts the democratic adage that all people are basically equal, or at least that it is not nice to speak as if they are not. *There* we find him suggesting that for a number of ad hoc reasons (those in power are overloaded with problems to solve, workers are less encumbered by the superficial "prop" of property and hence are closer to the more essential, "earthy" social experiences, or *American* workers are so much more intelligent than *European* workers) the weak may in fact be as sensitive as, or perhaps even more sensitive than the strong after all (Cooley, 1964:146–153; 1962:135–136, 289).

There is another fundamental problem with Cooley's theory of empathy which also surfaces when one compares the theory to the democratic ideal (upon which his theory is clearly based), particularly where, as in the relationship between classes, there are power inequalities. Specifically, whereas the democratic ideal very clearly specifies that the strong should be particularly sympathetic toward the weak, the theory itself predicts that the strong should receive more sympathy from the weak than vice versa!

The more general problem here is that the theory does not in fact predict that anyone will be more *sympathetic* to another after having empathized with him or her. Rather, as Cooley himself admits (1964:137), "I may imagine how a suffering man feels — sympathize with him in that sense — and be moved not to pity but to disgust, contempt, or perhaps admiration." Presumably, whether one reacts to another's suffering with sympathy or antipathy depends upon whether one's relationship with the other is based upon cooperation or a conflict of interest, a fact of which Cooley himself (1964:192, 392) again appears to have been well aware.

Perhaps for this reason as well as his tendency toward Positivism, he more typically argued that "the commonest and most obvious form of selfishness . . . results from the apathy of the imaginative impulses" (Cooley, 1964:214). As a consequence, his analyses of class relationships usually appear more than a little strained (Cooley, 1964:72–73; 1962:251). Similarly, after making the highly progressive suggestion (in spite of his occasional social Darwinisms) that the rich are more to blame for poverty than are the poor, he proceeded to suggest that "the chief hope of improvement is in arousing the consciences of those who are able to do away with such surroundings and so check the evil at its source" (Cooley, 1962:297; 1964:420). Nevertheless, he provided a sensitive and reasonable account of the effects of these and related relationships upon the selves of the powerless, and it is only fair to summarize this account before moving on.

In order to develop and maintain a "healthy" self, Cooley suggested, one must be able to feel that one can exert a reasonable degree of control over the immediate environment, which includes other people. The self-respect which in part arises from this control is supported by the evaluations of one by other people. However, he continued, "No one can study sympathetically the actual state of men and women in our social order without being convinced that large numbers of them are denied some or all of these fundamentals of human living." Moreover, "An unhealthy self is at the heart of nearly all social discontent" (Cooley, 1964:245–260).

Unemployment, Cooley wrote (1964:290), produces "a terror like that of a child in the dark; just as impulsive, perhaps just as purposeless and paralyzing. . . . It is well known," he continued, "that such fears play a conspicuous part in hysteria, insanity, and other weak and morbid conditions." Similarly, of the nature of the work itself he suggested that "very commonly their work itself does not admit of that exercise of the will and growth in skill and power which keeps the sense of self alive and interested" (Cooley, 1964:261). Of what Marx would have regarded as being treated in terms of one's exchange value as a commodity, he claimed (1962:304), "At present the common man is impoverished not merely by an absolute want of money but by a current way of thinking which makes pecuniary success the standard of merit, and so makes him feel that failure to get money is failure of life." Finally, "It may well be that resentment and occasional rebellion are the only way to preserve his self-respect" (Cooley, 1964:261).

Cooley then went on to suggest that these same ideas could be extended to racial, ethnic, and sexual conflict. Although here too one can see a similarity to Marx, the difference is that Cooley preferred to see the source of such callousness on the part of the powerful as lying mainly in unfortunate misunderstandings rather than in the structure of unequal power relationships themselves. Such an approach, I shall now argue, was inherent in Cooley's own theory of the social organization of the wider society.[2]

The Social Organization of the "Larger Mind"

The existing conception which obviously pleased him the most, and obviously because it is the most consistent with his theory of empathy, is the Durkheimian position that solidarity arises through functional dependence and communication, and that egoistic competition arises through rapid social changes and the slowness of the emergence of norms regulating class and other relationships.[3] However, since as a liberal Cooley also found the reified aspects of Functionalism distasteful, he went on to offer a theory of social organization still more consistent with his presumption that the world runs on sympathy.

It is through empathy that individuals are able to discover the nature of others and then adjust themselves to these others. The predictability which arises from this process of adjustment provides one of the necessary means for the emergence of more organized forms of social activity. The second basis also arises through empathizing. Specifically, through entertaining others' points of view one is supposed to acquire a sense of justice, as, for example, in the Golden Rule, and of morality more generally (Cooley, 1964:388).

Such experiences are then said to provide the basis for agreed-upon moral principles, although Cooley implied (1964:147, 296–297) that group norms as such do not appear until there is an increase in group size and complexity to the point where "universal sympathy" becomes "impractical"; that is, where it becomes too effortful to empathize with each-and-every other group member, such that the adjustment necessary for group activity is left to conformity to group norms. Even with the emergence of this more efficient form of social influence, however, empathy plays a crucial role, in that the anticipation of disapproval from the rest of the group provides the major motivation for conformity to the norm (Cooley, 1964:276–280, 293–294).

Now this conception of the social-psychological basis for social organization by no means made Cooley blind to all coercion of individuals by institutions. We have already noted his claims regarding the effects of certain institutions upon selves, and he conceded more generally that "the effect of formalism [his term for bureaucracy, or at least "red tape"] upon personality is to starve its higher life and leave it the prey of apathy, self-complacency, sensuality and the lower nature in general" (Cooley, 1962:343). Yet for all his having noted that institutionalized activity tends to recede from our consciousness, the very point of Cooley's account is that it for the most part emerges and continues through the conscious actions of sympathetic individuals. In fact, Cooley (1964:134, 121) went so far as to maintain that "society is simply the collective aspect of personal thought. . . . The imaginations which people have of one another are the *solid facts* of society, and that to observe and interpret these must be the chief aim of sociology."

One implication of such a view is that any failure to attain such ideals must be attributed neither to bad intentions nor coercion but "in part to moral weakness of a personal character, to the fact that our higher nature has but an imperfect and transient mastery of our lower," and in part to "the difficulty of organization" (Cooley, 1962:52–53). Another is that those incidences where institutions appear to coerce individuals are likely to take the form of a majority democratically resisting the will of a minority (Cooley, 1964:41). Finally, according to Cooley most social problems arise from misunderstandings in communications. However, both communicative skills and democratic ideals are preserved in "primary groups" (intimate, face-to-face groups such as the family or neighborhood). Therefore there is still hope, both for industrial organizations, "for the most part unfree," and for a more developed "public will" which will plan the United States's economic, political, and religious development more effectively (Cooley, 1964:427; 1962:419).

MEAD'S SYMBOLIC INTERACTION AND SOCIAL BEHAVIOR

George Herbert Mead (1864–1931) suggested that Cooley had succeeded in establishing "the self and the others upon the same plane of reality in experience" and had undertaken an "impressive study of society as the outgrowth of the association and cooperation of the primary group in its face-to-face organization." However, by continually referring to the "imaginations" the individual has of others without ever explaining where these imaginations come from, he *too*, if unwittingly, had placed the psychological before the social! Similarly, by focusing upon such imaginations *within individuals* as the "solid facts" of *society*, an objective organization of overt behavior as well as states of consciousness, much of society was in fact closed to him. For example, in studying society through introspection "the actual effect was to take the mental organization of society as it lay in his own liberal and wholesome view as the standard by which primitive impulses must be tested" (Mead, 1964: xxxvii, xxxiii; see also Mead, 1962:224).

To Mead, what is required is a more objective or *behavioristic* explanation for consciousness and the self, although one which retains Cooley's attempt to stress the self's *social* nature. Also needed is a more objective account of the social organization within which social behavior takes place.

Symbolic Interaction, Others, and Self

From where, therefore, *does* one get one's imaginations of others and their views of oneself? The secret, Mead suggested, lies in the peculiarly human ability to make vocal gestures.

As opposed to the case of other animals, when humans use a vocal gesture to refer someone else to something in the immediate environment, they can *hear* what they say (Mead, 1962:69). The gesture therefore "affects the individual who makes it just as much as it affects the individual to whom it is directed." It is a "significant symbol," in that it has the same *meaning* for the speaker as it has for the other. For example, when giving someone directions, "we are ready to do the thing and perhaps become irritated by the awkwardness of the other and insist on doing it ourselves" (Mead, 1936:379).

Mead referred to the process of assuming the "attitude" (disposition to act) of the other as *taking the "role" or standpoint of the other*. He made this choice of words in order to emphasize that it may be simply a "rational" or cognitive rather than emotional process, as implied by Cooley's concept of "sympathy" or empathy (Mead, 1936:375).[4] Certainly Mead's own conception of these processes has done much to clarify what often appears in Cooley's writings as a "transplant" of minds. For example, in doing so he was able to extend Cooley's reinterpretation of the Behaviorists' "imitation" as a more voluntary and social process. " 'Imitation,' " Mead suggested (1962:65–66), "depends upon the individual influencing himself as others influence him, so that he is under the influence not only of the other but also of himself in so far as he uses the same vocal gesture."

In this reworking of the process of empathy "thinking" is therefore really a conversation with others "in the mind" (Mead, 1962:47, 141). The phrase "in the mind" is actually misleading because the meaningful reactions of others to one's own attitudes, and the language which makes the whole process of internally rehearsing such conversations possible in the first place, have arisen in and are really only a phase of objective, on-going processes of *symbolic interaction* with actual others. Moreover, the self is "so evidently a social individual that it can exist only in a group of social individuals" (Mead, 1936:382). Mead then elaborated upon the nature and development of the social self.

Here it is instructive to return to Cooley's rather strained attempt to account for the development of a unified sense of self. "Imagination," Cooley suggested (1964:280), "presents us with all sorts of conflicting views, which reason, whose essence is organization, tries to arrange and control in accordance with some unifying principle. . . ." In keeping with the general thrust of his own theorizing, Mead attempted to provide a less mentalistic and more social account.

"The unity and structure of the complete self," he suggested (1962:144), "reflects the unity and structure of the social process as a whole." It is because our relationships with others are socially organized that we can relate to different others with our different selves but still maintain a relatively unified sense of self. Similarly, this relatively unified sense of self is greatly facilitated by the fact that the conceptions of others which we "carry around inside us" have evolved into a "generalized other." Again, this evolution has occurred as a consequence of the organization of the on-going social process rather than as an effect of Reason as such (Mead, 1962: 154–155).

When a child plays alone, for example, he or she will often have conversations with an imaginary playmate, yet these conversations tend to involve only one-to-one relationships: "He plays that he is, for instance, offering himself something, and he buys it; he gives a letter to himself and takes it away; he addresses himself as a policeman." Moreover, in this form of play "there is no basic organization gained. In that early stage he passes from one role to another just as a whim takes him." However, when the child participates in an organized *game* with several others, such as baseball, "he must have the responses of each position involved in his own position. He must know what everyone else is going to do in order to carry out his own play" (Mead, 1962:151). It is through experiences such as this latter one that the individual is said to develop a sense of the generalized other, and it is the taking of the role of the *generalized* other which characterizes the morality and self-control of the mature individual.[5]

Mead's Society: Mind or Organism

Although Mead himself (1962:7) insisted that "we attempt . . . to explain the conduct of the individual in terms of the organized conduct of the social group, rather than to account for the organized conduct of the social group in terms of the conduct of the separate individuals belonging to it," he appears to have alternated between Cooley's "buildup from role taking" model and that of the Functionalists.

A moderate allegiance to the "buildup" model seems clear in Mead's stance on the determinist-voluntarist issue discussed above. The model also surfaces in numerous favorable references to social progress as "evolutionary" in the sense of a trial-and-error adaptation of individuals to collective problems, but not in the sense of Its having Its own, fixed goal (e.g., Mead, 1936:368–372). *In fact, we* even find Cooley's claim that there are certain universal features of face-to-face interaction which "work their way up" into larger-scale organizations. One of these is the "neighborliness" of the primary group, which finds its way into organized religion; the other is a more socialized form of Adam Smith's exchange process (Smith was wrong to have seen it as essentially egoistic), which is of course reflected in our economic and political institutions (Mead, 1962: 281,286).

Now Mead was well aware that the interaction in the above account *"has to occur in a cooperative process"* (Mead, 1962:300; my emphasis), and that by undertaking such an account he was therefore committing himself to the position that the social processes of our own society are basically cooperative. This commitment did not mean that he was blind to conflicts of interest, as in the case of capital versus labor, or buyers versus sellers, yet it did mean that he was predisposed to deemphasize their importance (see, for example, Mead, 1962:323).

It seems clear that Mead had the Functionalist model in mind here, and he in fact expressed his greater admiration for Comte and Spencer than for Marx in several different places (see Mead, 1936). What this emphasis meant in concrete terms was that when he worked his way "down" to face-to-face interaction between people of different classes and other groups in conflict, any problems he discovered there were accounted for in terms of Comte's, Durkheim's and Cooley's systems.[6] Similarly, it is the Functionalist model of integration rather than the Marxian model of alienation which is said to best forecast our immediate future as individuals (Mead, 1962:318).

THE NEO-INTERACTIONISMS, CENTER, RIGHT, AND RADICAL CHIC

As I have attempted to show in the above account, Cooley's theory of empathy, while intriguing, is fraught with ambiguities and contradictions. Moreover, as Mead pointed out, his "sympathetic introspection" or "understanding" has serious limitations as a method for validating and developing the theory. Mead (1964:xxxvi) took Cooley to task for this latter limitation, but his own interests were primarily philosophical, so that he himself did little to practice what he preached in this regard. Furthermore, although Mead did a great deal to clarify the nature of role taking, his belief that the individual's adjustments to others after role taking are, in his own words, "uncertain," and his "armchair" approach to empirical data seem to have limited his own attempt to clarify and develop the theory of role taking itself. One suspects that when coupled with the greater prestige psychological Behaviorists have derived from their precise, if often mundane, experimentation, these problems with the classic formulations of Symbolic Interactionism account for its subsequent fragmentation into a variety of only very loosely related subschools.[7]

Strangely enough, the neo-Interactionists who have claimed orthodoxy, the so-called "Chicago School" (see Petras and Meltzer, 1973), have contributed little to the theory of role taking, the substantive tour de force of Symbolic Interactionism.[8] Instead, many of them have contented themselves with ritualistically reiterating the old metatheoretical platitudes. Similarly, Mead notwithstanding, many of these particular sectarians (see especially *Herbert Blumer*) have insisted that the only legitimate method for a Symbolic Interactionist is Cooley's sympathetic understanding!

In direct opposition to the claims of the Chicago School that human interaction is often unpredictable and must be studied with methods peculiar to Symbolic Interactionism is the approach of the "Iowa School" and of "Role Theorists" more generally. Here empirical researchers have tended to focus upon a few of the traditionally Interactionist hypotheses and "test" them with more mainstream methods. *Manfred Kuhn* (1960), for example, has demonstrated that the older one gets, the more social roles one includes in one's self-concept. Similarly, researchers in this tradition have repeatedly demonstrated that we do tend to evaluate ourselves as others evaluate us, at least when the others in question are those with whom we interact in small face-to-face groups (see Archibald, 1972). Many of the basic tenets of Role Theory more generally can indeed be found in the writings of Cooley and Mead (see especially Cooley, 1964:276–277). However, rather than epitomizing the more general process of role *taking*, the role *playing* of "Role Theory" with its Hobbesian or "empty organism" view of human nature and its involuntary conformity (Wrong, 1963) actually reverts to the very Watsonian Behaviorism which Cooley and Mead took such pains to criticize!

Members of the remaining strains of Symbolic Interactionism have not been all that much more concerned with role taking than the so-called Role Theorists. Indeed, by reintroducing a somewhat more active individual mainly as one who "works" rather than freely and cooperatively constructs the role system, these theorists can be (and often have been) legitimately considered the Spencers of Symbolic Interactionism.

GOFFMAN'S DRAMATURGY AND GARFINKEL'S ETHNOMETHODOLOGY

Erving Goffman's (1922–) arguments for this reintroduction are twofold. First, the roles we typically play are much more situation-specific than the Role Theory account implies, such that the moral legitimacy and consensus surrounding them are more problematic and less coercive. Second, such actors are *required* to actively work hard if their roles are to be "realized" and the entire show is to "come off" (Goffman, 1961:88–93).

Although this stance moves Goffman back toward Cooley and Mead, his conception of interaction is more "collusive" than cooperative, since in addition to maintaining "focus" (pursuing the official task of the encounter), individual participants are seen as attempting to achieve and maintain "face" (a favorable image of themselves). Indeed, Goffman appears to regard most of the norms or rules which emerge in face-to-face interaction as quasi-consensual attempts to deal with the dilemma of maintaining focus when participants are usually more interested in "face-work," and the problem of preventing each others' faces from being "lost" during focus or attacks from others.

For example, rules of commitment and considerateness require that once a participant has staked out a claim to a particular face, s/he must play through the role to avoid having the interaction break down and others lose face (Goffman, 1967:5). However, the image which s/he first projects may be one not freely chosen by himself or herself, but one imputed to him or her by others on the basis of his or her dress, deportment, or whatever. Hence, both the need to prevent one's low outside status from entering the encounter and the need to make good an image which one may not in fact deserve are likely to discourage open communication and encourage duplicity. Goffman (1959:17–76) suggests that the latter is in fact so common in our everyday lives that it is seldom subjectively felt to be a problem.

Technically, the "rules of irrelevance" should prevent others from imputing images to participants on the basis of their outside characteristics; however, the latter often figure into the "transformation rules" (those specifying who is to get what portion of the winnings). For example, it would be unfair of my students to make fun of my basketball playing on the grounds that my high status as professor requires me to excel at everything. On the other hand, the more likely outcome, as with the emperor's new clothes, is discrimination in my favor; that is, my students will be more likely to avoid noticing my faults than they will those of lesser-status others. This means that in general the feelings of low-status persons are much more likely to be disregarded than are those of high-status persons (Goffman, 1967:26; 1961:57, 130).

Goffman's interest in such dilemmas (and we have only scratched Goffman's surface, so to speak) has led to widespread speculation as to his preferred theoretical and ideological allegiances.

His concern with inequality might remind us of Marx, but Goffman himself (1967:59–61; 1961:80) is adamant that face-to-face interaction follows a pluralistic and not a class model. "The race-group status of one participant in a focused gathering," he says, "can have something of the same effect as the harelip of another; the route through which socioeconomic factors enter an encounter is one that is equally open to a strange and undignified set of vehicles." Not only are there "deference obligations that superordinates owe subordinates," but also:

> Two individuals are likely to be related to one another through more than one pair of capacities, and these additional relationships are likely to receive ceremonial expression too. Hence the same act of deference may show different kinds of regard, as when a doctor by a paternal gesture shows authority over a nurse in her capacity as a subordinate technician but affection for her as a young female who is dependent on him in his capacity as a superior older male [Goffman, 1967:61].

The various dilemmas, arising as they do from contradictions between norms, in effect indicate anomie, and at some points Goffman (1959:245) specifically relates them to the conditions of mass society. Unlike Durkheim, however, Goffman does not see any way out. Indeed, whereas some interpret him as lamenting "the decline of civility" (Manning, 1976), Goffman himself usually attempts to convey value neutrality to the point where others simply describe him as an avid participant in, as well as chronicler of, the everyday lives of the new middle classes as they ingratiate themselves with the capricious and defensive bureaucrats upon whom their livelihood and status depends (Gouldner, 1971; Petras and Meltzer, 1973).

Be that as it may, Goffman's claim (1959:251) that individuals are less concerned with actually meeting moral standards than "with maintaining the *impression* that they are living up to the many standards by which they and their products are judged," that "as performers we are merchants of morality," fairly well describes the subject matter of *Harold Garfinkel*'s approach.

Calling it "Ethnomethodology" (a nearly literal translation would be the study of the "methods of the folk"), Garfinkel (1967) and his followers (e.g., see Turner, 1974) make it their business to study the hidden procedural rules (roughly, "cultural truisms") underlying the norms or explicit rules, which, while taken for granted and largely invisible, are necessary for interaction to take place. For example, in one notorious series of studies Ethnomethodologists "excavated" these assumptions by deliberately violating them; students, for instance, acted as if they were only boarders in their parents' homes and then reported upon how the (very confused and angry) other members of their families dealt with these actions (and particularly how they justified them or explained them away).

Although when viewed only in these terms Ethnomethodology could be easily integrated with other, more conventional paradigms, Garfinkel himself (1967:30) appears rather to be extending Goffman's merchandizing of morality argument to the point of arguing that the underlying assumptions the Ethnomethodologist studies are much less part of an objective social structure existing "out there" than flimsy rationalizations interactants use to try and *convince* themselves that what they do is orderly and meaningful! Keeping the "folkways" invisible, therefore, is said to be functional for, and perhaps even motivated toward, making any interaction at all possible.

As William Maryl (1973) has so convincingly argued, the problem with this latter, stronger interpretation and use of Ethnomethodology is that it is a "sociology without society." If "Role Theory" can be said to have brought Symbolic Interactionism back to Behaviorism (perhaps legitimately, if Marxian claims about alienation are correct), Ethnomethodology would seem to have undone Mead's critique of Cooley by again making society dependent simply upon the specific "definitions of the situation" of the individuals who (voluntarily) do the structuring. As we shall now see in Part 3, this is an "advance" we do not need.

Notes

[1]See Matson (1964).

[2]In fact, however, Cooley entertained many. For complimentary references to deTocqueville's pluralistic model and uncomplimentary references to the mass, "unruly mob" model of Tarde and LeBon see Cooley (1964:307–309; 1962:92–99, 116–119, 155–160, 199–201, 235–242, 309), and to social Darwinism, Cooley (1964:151, 299–304, 327, 337–339, 404; 1962:35). For (highly qualified, essentially social democratic) praise of the "economic interpretation of history" see Cooley (1964:192, 423; 1962:140, 252–261, 268–269, 274–287). Also, for a Weber-like concern with bureaucracy see Cooley (1962:231–232, 239, 343).

[3]See Cooley (1964:149, 258, 288, 310–311, 422–428; 1962:89, 128–129, 158–159, 177, 288–296, 330, 383).

[4]Elsewhere, however, Mead (1962:147–149) suggests that we may be less likely to empathize than take a role on a cognitive level. Here he appears to argue that being in a state of emotional arousal is likely to distract us from taking another's point of view. While this has led Coutu (1951) and others to insist that role taking is a cognitive *rather than* emotional process, one should note, in addition to the passage cited in the text, another where Mead (1962:299) appears to argue that cognitive role taking is simply the *first step* in the processes of empathy and sympathy.

[5]That individuals are therefore heavily determined Mead denied. Even if one accepted this, he said (1962:201–202; 1964:xxxvii), each person will have encountered a unique set of others, and access to others outside any given relationship provides the stimulus and support to be critical of it. However, individuals selectively attend and respond to their environment (Mead, 1962:25, 176), and their reactions to others in turn modify the course of interaction (Mead, 1962:179).

[6]See Mead (1962:256, 288–289, 293–294, 326). Role taking is seen as "fleshing out" the Functionalist position by explaining how cooperative activity is possible.

[7]For an ambitious and impressive attempt to integrate most of the various Interactionisms (by a true believer, which I clearly am not) see the recent text by John Hewitt (1976).

[8]There have been important exceptions among those who would probably identify themselves as Chicago types, but a much greater amount of such work has been undertaken by Piaget and his students and other psychologists (see Archibald, 1972).

3

A POLITICAL ECONOMIC APPROACH TO SOME PRESSING SOCIAL PSYCHOLOGICAL PROBLEMS

7
EXCHANGE, COOPERATION, AND COMPETITION

Since our debate among sociological social psychologists began with the Exchange Theorists' conception of human nature and their claim that society reflects that nature, it seems reasonable to begin our empirical investigation of the various perspectives by examining the phenomena of exchange, cooperation, and competition. Are people naturally egoistic or self-interested, eager to compete with each other and to cooperate only on a contractual basis, or is the *opposite* perhaps the case? *Do* such propensities themselves perhaps vary considerably with variations in social conditions, and if so, *do* such conditions characterize alienation, anomie, or faulty communication? These are the questions we shall try to answer here.

FUN IN GAMES AND COALITIONS

Of the situations social psychologists have used to study cooperation and competition, by far the most popular are those associated with experimental games. For this purpose, the most popular game studied, the "Prisoner's Dilemma," is in some respects ideal, for built into the game are fairly equal incentives to be cooperative and competitive, such that if one finds a preference for one or the other it should presumably tell us something about the players' normal predilections in everyday life. Luce and Raiffa (1957:95) describe the thinking behind the Prisoner's Dilemma in this way:

> Two suspects are taken into custody and separated. The District Attorney is certain that they are guilty of a specific crime, but he does not have adequate evidence to convict them at a trial. He points out to each prisoner that he has two alternatives: to confess to the crime the police are sure they have done, or not to confess. If they both do not confess, then the District Attorney states he will book them on some very minor trumped-up charge such as petty larceny and illegal possession of a weapon, and they would both receive minor punishments; if they both confess they will be prosecuted, but he will recom-

mend less than the most severe sentence; but if one confesses and the other does not, then the confessor will receive lenient treatment for turning state's evidence, whereas the latter will get "the book" slapped at him.

In actual experimental situations subjects are usually presented with a "matrix" of choices and outcomes which simplifies the information they must consider in making their choice. Thus, for example, Edward Jones and Harold Gerard (1967:563) quantify the prisoner's situation in approximately this way:

	Prisoner B	
	Not confess	Confess
Prisoner A — Not confess	One year each	Ten years for A Three months for B
Prisoner A — Confess	Three months for A Ten years for B	Eight years each

More typically, however, subjects play for points or money on the basis of a matrix such as this one:

	Player B	
	Choice X	Choice Y
Player A — Choice X	4¢, 4¢	—8¢, +8¢
Player A — Choice Y	+8¢, —8¢	—12¢, —12¢

Note that if you were a subject, this latter situation would present you with a dilemma somewhat analogous to that of the actual prisoner: that is, it is in your self-interest to be uncooperative by choosing Choice Y if you are Player A and can safely assume that Player B will be nice and choose X (your outcome is on the left), but if Player B acts the same way you will both lose much more than if you had cooperated.

How do Canadian and American college students typically act in such a situation? While the percentage of X or cooperative choices may range anywhere from 10 to 90, depending upon a number of different conditions, the average tends to be about 45 percent (Scheff and Chewning, 1968: cited in Secord and Backman, 1974:270; Vinacke, 1969). In other words, subjects are more likely to be competitive than cooperative in these situations, *in spite of* the fact that they lose out by being so! Surprisingly, this outcome often persists even after subjects have had a chance to see previous outcomes (e.g., Kelley and Grzelak, 1972). In fact, knowing that one's opponent has been completely cooperative, what Lave (1965) calls the "Ghandi" pattern of nonviolent behaviour, does not increase the likelihood that one will also be cooperative. Rather, one tends to exploit him or her by taking advantage of the other's cooperation (Bixenstine, Potash, and Wilsen, 1963; Lave, 1965).

Now, on the one hand such findings can and have been interpreted as supporting Exchange Theory. However, a moment's reflection reveals that they hardly flatter it. Specifically, whereas in this theory competitiveness is supposed to be the result of, and basis for, rationality, in that it is said to be an effective means for individuals to satisfy their best self-interests and for a society to satisfy the interests of the majority of its members, in such situations as the Prisoner's Dilemma the competitiveness we find appears anything but rational. Nor, one should also note, do such findings support the Positivism of Exchange Theory's Functionalist and Symbolic Interactionist critics.

The defense of our rationality and/or basic cooperativeness has usually taken either or both of two forms. Experimental games, so one argument goes, are after all games where the stakes are so low that it is not in fact very irrational to lose by competing. The second argument is that since they are "only games," subjects are expected to be, and expect their opponents to be, competitive. Hence when there is no communication between players it is actually rational to presume that one's opponent will not cooperate and therefore to act in kind. Similarly, when subjects do not actually communicate they will understandably suspect the motives of an unconditionally cooperative opponent; however, when they can communicate and dispel this distrust, cooperation will ensue.

These arguments have indeed received considerable support in subsequent research. Thus increasing the size of the stakes does seem to increase cooperation in the Prisoner's Dilemma (see Vinacke's review, 1969), as does permitting subjects to communicate (e.g., Swingle and Santi, 1972). Hence on this round, at least, Exchange Theorists can breathe a sigh of relief. Yet note that even these additional findings do little for those who would apologize for our own society by concluding that we are basically cooperative.

In the first place, the Prisoner's' Dilemma clearly has a built-in incentive to cooperate; that is, if the players do so, they will receive lighter sentences. Similarly, that they in fact initially distrust each other and have to communicate for some time before becoming "cooperative" (in this case, not destroying each other) probably tells us something in and of itself about the propensities of people in our society, or at least, of our college students. Finally, there is reason to believe that when subjects do communicate in such experiments they are at least as likely to threaten retaliation if the opponent does not cooperate as to appeal to latent propensities to cooperate (Deutsch and Krauss, 1960).

Secondly, while Jones and Gerard (1967:577) among others appear to have concluded from the stakes-and-communication results that people will therefore be more cooperative in real life than in experimental games, the validity of such a conclusion is by no means obvious. In the "Great" Depression of the 1930s, for example, the stakes were extremely high and there was a great deal of communicating, yet people sometimes even stole their own friends' jobs by offering to work for less pay (Broadfoot, 1975). Similarly, when I give my students a particularly difficult examination question I often encourage the class to discuss the answer collectively, yet many students actually refuse to participate on the grounds that they will give away their own, presumably good, ideas.

The thrust of these two examples is, of course, no deep mystery, for both entail a fundamental conflict of interest which appears to have overridden any cooperative effects which high stakes and accurate communication might otherwise have had. Nor need such a conclusion rest upon such selective examples, since it is already implied in the very experimental research we have been considering. Morton Deutsch (1960), for example, found that communication did indeed increase cooperation after subjects had been instructed to simply concentrate upon winning without worrying about how much their "opponent" won, but not after other subjects had been instructed to win over/against their opponent.

Given such findings as these, whether the our-society-is-okay interpretation of studies reporting increased cooperation after communication is valid depends a great deal upon the particular juxtaposition of interests built into the experimental social structure. Certainly a considerable amount of other experimental research with high stakes and communication indicates high levels of competition.

For example, subjects with the choice of entering several different coalitions with differing degrees of inequality of outcomes for the two partners were much more likely to choose the coalition which brought themselves the highest individual outcome than the coalition which would have made the outcomes more equal and *still* permitted the coalition to be a winning one (Gamson, 1961). Similarly, following a suggestion by Simmel, Theodore Mills (1960) found that in a group discussion where members were supposed to agree upon a story about a picture, the dominant tendency was for two of his male subjects to participate more than a third and express more liking and support for each other than for the third member of the group. Interestingly, given Blau's excursus on love, when the groups are of mixed sex the two members in the majority sex appear to compete for the third, minority member of the opposite sex. This is suggested by Reginald Robson's findings at the University of British Columbia (1971:15), which indicate that the most frequent coalition is one "between the minority-sex member and one of the two members of the other sex."

Clearly what is needed to resolve the issue of whether the competition and cooperation which occur in the laboratory are representative of the wider society is a more systematic attempt to compare different interaction settings.

One interesting attempt to do so is an experiment by William Dorris (1972), who had college students interact with rare-coin shop owners in the Los Angeles area. Each student described his situation to the coin dealer in one of two ways: in a *"Neutral"* condition he simply said that he was getting rid of his coins because he had decided to give up coin collecting, while in a *"Moral Appeal"* condition he said that he was selling his coins because he needed the money for school books and other things connected with going to college. Furthermore, in this latter condition the student added that he was worried about being exploited, and that he had been told by another coin collector who knew the dealer that the dealer could be trusted. The results clearly indicate that students were offered more for a particular coin in the Moral Appeal than in the Neutral condition (i.e., an average of $13.63 as compared with $8.72). Furthermore, additional information suggests that the dealers were more concerned with the personal welfare of the student in the Moral Appeal condition, in that there was more eye contact with the student, the dealer stood closer to the student, took longer to make his offer, gave more information about the coin, and was more likely to suggest a more profitable alternative to accepting his own offer.

Dorris suggests that aside from offering higher stakes and greater opportunities for communication than most laboratory game situations, his experiment gives the potentially exploitative player a reason for his opponent's unconditionally cooperative behavior. That is, since the student says he wants to sell his coins because he is no longer interested in collecting or needs the money, and knows very little about their real worth, he reduces the likelihood that his opponent will mistrust his motives in being unconditionally cooperative. Furthermore, whereas opponents are often anonymous in laboratory games, in the present experiment they are face-to-face and can identify each other.

Dorris' arguments make sense, particularly in explaining the differences in results between the Moral Appeal and Neutral conditions. The importance for the student of getting a good price for the coin is indeed more obvious in the Moral Appeal condition and, as we shall see later, exploitation generally seems to be more difficult if one is face-to-face with one's exchange partner. However, whether these findings of higher levels of cooperation than is usually the case in laboratory games warrant the degree of relief Dorris expresses is questionable.

First, remember that in the Moral Appeal condition the dealer is supposed to have been recommended to the student by another collector who attests to his trustworthiness. For one thing, this may put the dealer in the position of having to live up to a reputation that, while he may not in fact deserve it, is nevertheless flattering and hence worth living up to on this occasion. For another, however, and this is considerably less flattering, this knowledge places the self-interest of the dealer in the Moral Appeal condition much more clearly in line with that of the student; that is, because he has been recommended to the student by another coin dealer, the dealer in the Moral Appeal condition may be likely to feel that he will lose business if he violates his reputation and exploits the student.

Second, it is important to look at the absolute levels of the prices offered to the student. Specifically, while Dorris suggests (1972:394) that "discussions with informants indicated that offers of \$12 and greater should be considered fair and that a dealer might legitimately offer considerably less if he had no particular need for the coins or honestly felt they were overgraded," we should note that the average of \$8.75 for the Neutral condition is obviously unfair. Also, it is important to ask whether most buying and selling situations in our society are characterised by neutral or morally appealing conditions. The answer is not easy to come by, but one suspects that the personal testimonies of Dorris' Moral Appeal condition are in fact less frequent than the impersonality of his Neutral condition. Although this may be changing for the better of late, one suspects that most of us would still be embarrassed to give strangers such "sob stories." The very ease with which we evoke the latter term, and others such as "What's his line?" or, "Yeh, I've heard that one before," suggests that impersonality, not personality, is the rule rather than the exception in our business dealings. Supporting this reasoning is Edward Hall's observation (1959:208) that we maintain a greater physical as well as social distance from others while doing business than other things with them.

From the evidence we have considered thus far, one can only conclude that while Exchange Theory has not come through untainted, it has fared a great deal better than its Functionalist and Symbolic Interactionist critics. Specifically, however "rational" their competitiveness may appear, *the North American people studied hardly strike one as beacons of cooperation.* Similarly, *whereas in these studies communication sometimes increases cooperation,* as Durkheim and Cooley would have had us believe, *it is doubtful that it does so where there are substantial conflicts of interest.*

Should we therefore become Exchange Theorists? Two other considerations arising from the findings of experimental research by social psychologists suggest that this would be premature at this point.

In the first place, by no means all of the experimental subjects in these studies have evidenced the competitiveness we have been describing. This has been particularly true of women. While sex differences in competitiveness in Prisoner's Dilemma-related games have never been great, and, by the present time, appear to have disappeared altogether,[1] in coalition formation experiments women have been much less egoistic. In the Gamson-type experiment with "material" stakes, for example, females have been much more likely to form three-way (really *non*coalitions) than two-against-one coalitions and divide the outcome equally instead of unequally on the basis of initial input-advantages (see Gamson, 1964). Similarly, when approval is the "good" in question, as in Robson's research, women again tend to avoid establishing coalitions which exclude third parties.

Secondly, there is considerable evidence against the claim that, when it does occur, competition has more beneficial effects than cooperation. The classic experiment here is again one by Morton Deutsch (1949). In this study, students in an introductory psychology course were given the option of participating in an experiment instead of attending the normal three one-hour classes a week. Those who volunteered were divided into groups of five, each of which worked on several tasks. Some of these tasks were logical puzzles; others were "human relations" problems, such as having to decide whether and how to discipline children in a summer camp. However, the conditions under which these groups worked on these tasks varied; that is, half of the groups were competitively and half were cooperatively oriented. The characteristics of the *Competitive* groups were similar to those of classes in the schools and universities of our society. Thus, whereas subjects were told that they were working "as a group," they were also told that their grade for the course would be determined by ranking their *individual* contributions to the solution of the "group" problems. *Cooperative* groups, on the other hand, were told that entire groups rather than individuals would be ranked, with individual group members' grades for the course being identical to the ranking of their entire group.

The results of this classic experiment hardly support the argument that competition is superior to cooperation. Looking first at the productivity of the two types of groups, one finds that Cooperative groups not only produced more and better recommendations as solutions for the problems, but produced them in less time as well. Moving on to other consequences of the two types of conditions, one finds considerable difference in the nature of the interaction among members of the two types of groups. Thus subjects in Cooperative groups were friendlier toward each other, communicated more, and communicated with fewer difficulties than did subjects in Competitive groups. It was probably this greater friendliness and communication which permitted the Cooperative groups to work together and coordinate their efforts better than the Competitive groups did, and the latter in turn probably accounts for the differences in productivity.

Deutsch's results are matched to a remarkable extent by those of a field study by Peter Blau (1955), conducted long before Blau became such a fervent exponent of Exchange Theory. Thus in examining two different sections of a public employment agency, Blau found that while the supervisor of section "A" "relied heavily on individual performance records in evaluating interviewers," the supervisor of section "B" did not, and was also more lenient in his evaluations. As was the case with the Deutsch study, the nature of the interaction of the interviewers within each section was also different; that is, those in section A were not only much more likely to avoid each other, but also to hoard the files of job applicants so as to get better individual performance records. This worked for some individuals, in that the more competitive an individual in section A was, the more productive he or she was. However, the overall productivity of section A, the Competitive section, was actually *lower* than that of section B, the Cooperative section. Interestingly, being competitive was not advantageous to individuals in section B, because whereas cooperative members of this section tended to tell each other about interesting job vacancies, competitive members tended to be excluded from this individually advantageous sharing process.

At the very least, these two new sets of considerations suggest a serious qualification to our previous conclusion. Specifically, *experimental research on cooperation and competition only appears to support Exchange Theory so well to the extent that one rather con-*

veniently excludes sex differences (and others we shall get to shortly) *and fails to compare the effects of cooperation with that of competition.*

Put otherwise, Exchange Theorists in our own time appear to have had a propensity to do what they did in Marx's; that is, to use *within*-system evidence to justify the *system* itself. If this is the case, then to better test the validity of Exchange Theory we should compare the potentially biased research findings we first considered with those obtained by studying people in societies whose political-economic institutions are very different from our own.

"PRIMITIVE" PEOPLES: ARE THEY "JUST LIKE US"?

Although this seems to be an eminently reasonable procedure, the amount of cross-cultural research on cooperation and competition by social psychologists is dismally small. To date, the major contri-

Figure 7.1

Conditions in the Kagen and Madsen (1972) Experiment*

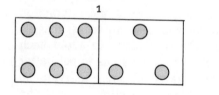
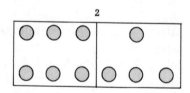
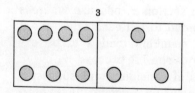
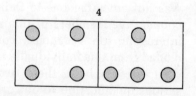

bution of social psychologists seems to be a single but impressive research program undertaken by Spencer Kagen, Millard Madsen and their associates, comparing particularly urban American and rural Mexican children.

In one of their experiments (Kagen and Madsen, 1972), children played a game analogous to the Prisoner's Dilemma, but simplified through the use of marbles and a pictorially presented set of matrices. These are presented in Figure 7.1.

The shaded circles represent marbles, which the children could trade in for toys after the experiment. The child faces the matrix from the bottom. Thus in Case 1 he is told that if he chooses the right-hand choice he will get two marbles and his opponent will get one, while if he chooses the left-hand choice he will get three and his opponent will get three. The reader can use this example to figure out the outcomes for each of the other three cases. The important thing to notice here is that two different motives are being tempted. Thus in Case 1 the child can choose to be rivalrous or outdistance his opponent by choosing the right-hand choice, but if he does so he actually gets less than if he chooses the left-hand choice, which would equalize his and his opponent's outcomes. In Case 2 the absolute gain is constant and the choice is simply between rivalry and cooperation. In Case 3 one can win over one's opponent or let him win but still get more, and in Case 4 one can easily both win and get the maximum possible amount for oneself, the alternative being to take less and share more.

The results of this experiment could hardly be clearer. In the first place, the American children were more likely to choose the right-hand, more rivalrous move, in all four cases, that is, even when they got less for doing so. Second, if we look at the behavior of specific individuals from each of the two societies across the different cases, we find that more Americans were always rivalrous while more Mexicans were never rivalrous. Third, if we make the reasonable assumption that egoism and competitiveness are things children learn as they grow up in a particular society, we should not be surprised to learn that the behavior differences between the two sets of children increased with age. Fourth, there is little question that children who were rivalrous intended to be so, as Kagan and Madsen themselves clearly state (1972:218)*:

Spontaneous comments of the children corresponded to their rivalrous behaviour. Some rivalrous Anglo-American children jeered at their
peers, saying, for example, "I only gave you one. Ha! Ha!". In discussions after the experiment, rivalrous children quite readily explained
their behaviour. When asked why they chose the side with less absolute
gain in Condition 1, they replied, "Cause I wanted to give Jerry only
one," "I wanted her to have less," or "Proque gano (because I win)."
Even some 5-year-old children were able to verbalize their rivalrous
intents. As one 5-year-old Anglo-American girl made her choice, she
spontaneously exclaimed, "I'm going to give the most ones to me."
After the experiment, another 5-year-old Anglo-American girl told the
experimenter, "I wanted to have more than her."

Now, although Nelson and Kagen (1972) cite comparable findings
from a study comparing Anglo-Albertans and Blackfoot Indians by
Anthony G. Miller and Ron Thomas (1972), one can hardly throw out
Exchange Theory after so few comparisons. Instead, we must ask
whether the results obtained for rural Mexicans would be typical of
those for people in "less developed" societies more generally.

Whereas Marx and Engels had drawn upon the work of such 19th
century anthropologists as Lewis Morgan to formulate and support
their claim that most precapitalist (and noncapitalist) peoples could
be characterized as predominantly cooperative ("primitively com-
munistic"), classical political economists at the time were still insisting that human nature is everywhere the same (except, perhaps, that
primitive people are less intelligent). This insistence has persisted
into the present among so-called "Economic Anthropologists," who
claim to see markets and egoistic competition in such ritualistic
practices as the exchange of gifts between a bride and groom's
kinship groups (e.g., see Leclair and Schneider, 1968). In a different
"Culture and Personality" approach, Ruth Benedict (1960) and
Margaret Mead (1937) in particular appear to have attempted to
neutralize any criticism of our own society by assuming a random
distribution of competition across societies.

Probably a majority of contemporary anthropologists would agree
that *none* of these three extreme positions adequately describes *all*
of the facts. Nevertheless, an interesting assortment also appear to
agree that it is the first claim, imputing *primarily* cooperation, rather
than the other two which *best* describes them.

This is not to say that most of these anthropologists would agree
with the Marxian explanation for this difference, as we shall see
shortly. Some are Marxists (Godelier, 1972; Mandel, 1970), but
others are such well-known Functionalists as Mauss (Durkheim's
nephew and student)(1970) and Redfield (1962). Still others (Polyani,
1957; Sahlins, 1972), whose skepticism of the primary importance of

either evolution or capitalism gives them some affinity with Weber, have labelled themselves "substantivists" because of their attempt to develop a culture- (and ideology-) free set of concepts for the cross-cultural comparison of political-economic systems.

In spite of their diverse starting points, these various critics seem to agree to a remarkable extent on the reasons for the discrepancy between their own observations of primitive peoples and those of Exchange Theory and Culture and Personality adherents in anthropology.

In the first place, they claim, the latter observers' use of our political-economic categories for *primitive* societies is misleading, for whereas in our own society "economic" activity tends to be separated from family, religious, and other activities, such is not the case in these primitive societies. Nor, for that matter, are individuals in these societies likely to function as separate individuals, egoistically or otherwise. As a consequence, behavior which appears to be egoistically competitive to the outsider (e.g., haggling over a "bride price") may not actually have this function within the *context* of the society in question (e.g., Mauss claimed that the function of the bride price is to establish and cement broader social relationships among entire kinship groups). Similarly, even when such behavior *does* have this function, within the context of the society as a whole it may play a tangential rather than a dominant role.

Second, particularly when one abstracts particular behavior patterns from their context in this manner, one can easily misconstrue the *meaning* which they have for the primitive peoples themselves.

Third, whereas there may have been a time when it made sense to think of these various societies as relatively autonomous units, their discovery and contact with (and often colonial subjugation under) the "civilized" world often invalidates such an assumption. Hence many of the competitive practices attributed to primitive people (for example, the charging of "interest rates") may well have been introduced from the outside and may not have been an integral part of their original culture.

In order to illustrate these problems, probably no example is more fitting than the *"potlatch"* of the Indians on the coast of what is now British Columbia, for according to our two sets of apologists, these people were *more* competitive than we are, so much so that their culture is said to have been a *parody* of our own (Benedict, 1960: 195). Here is a typical account of the potlatch*:

---

*From *Habitat, Economy and Society* by Daryll C. Forde. Published in the United States by E. P. Dutton & Co., and reprinted with their permission.

The noble families within a single village and those of neighboring settlements were in continual rivalry each to establish its greater prestige. . . . And it is for this reason that the famous ceremonial feasts or *potlatches* of the Northwest Coast Indians had such compelling importance . . . .

Every important social event demanded a lavish ceremony: the birth of a child; the ceremony when a girl reached puberty; the burial of a relative; the assumption of a predecessor's rank and titles; the building of a new house. . . . For them large stores of food and gifts were accumulated in advance. New carvings were made to represent the crests of the feastgiver, who generally assumed a new name and in a dramatic performance, for which elaborate masks and costumes were worn, enacted mythological events connected with his titles.

. . . The giver of the feast made presents of sea otter skins, blankets, coppers and even canoes. While some of these were for services, the greater part were gifts made to the guests according to rank. Although the glory of munificence was everywhere paramount, the obligations of repayment played a prominent part, especially among the Kwakiutl. The acceptance of gifts at a feast there involved an obligation to repay them with considerable interest when the guest in turn gave a feast. A Kwakiutl would sometimes borrow material beforehand, again at high interest, in order to increase the lavishness of his gifts at the feast. Careful record was kept by official tally keepers of all these gifts which were practically forced loans, and the extent of all obligations was publicly known. Farther north, however, the repayment obligations and the idea of interest were unknown.

Property was also destroyed. Canoes and coppers were often deliberately broken, slaves were sometimes killed and valuable olachen oil would be squandered by pouring it on the fire until the leaping flames set the roof timbers on fire. By some or all these means the feast giver challenged his guests to greater orgies of destructiveness.

Renown depended on the frequency and lavishness of these celebrations [Forde, 1963:88–90].

While many of the facts cited in the above description are correct, others are not, and still others are cited so out of context that they greatly distort the true nature of the original potlatch. Thus, while one can hardly dispute that Kwakiutl chiefs were exchanging material goods for individual prestige and status and that there was considerable rivalry involved — something that is clear when one reads accounts of actual potlatches (e.g., Boas, 1969:15, 85–87) — one must hasten to add that the process was nowhere near as self-seeking as Forde implies.

In the first place, rather than viewing the potlatch primarily as a competition between individuals, the Kwakiutl viewed it as a collective effort, with everyone in the chief's kinship group contributing food and other goods to be given away at the potlatch. Nor, as Forde would have us believe (1963:88), was there in any way a "free-market" competition among individuals, such that a commoner could acquire noble status by giving a potlatch. The few instances of this happening occurred only after the white man had arrived and disrupted traditional Indian customs (Piddocke, 1968:291).

Second, while the chiefs' rivalrous rhetoric was indeed rampant, the actual competition was very much more sedate. For example, all four Kwakiutl tribes were usually invited to a potlatch, and after it was over they did not go off into a corner and "plot" how best to outdo the most recent performance. Rather, all four sat down together, and in their own word, "discussed" when the next potlatch would occur and what the level of gift giving would be. In this process "a Kwakiutl would subject himself to ridicule by demanding interest when he received a gift in requittal of one of like amount made by him" (Curtis, 1915:143–144). Furthermore, the actual ruining of a rival appears to have been unknown. Here our Exchange Theorists would do well to pay more attention to the meaning the Kwakiutl gave to their own behavior. For example, references to cooperation and sharing are rife in the Kwakiutl songs and dreams recited by George Hunt and recorded by Boas, and considerable embarrassment about acquisitiveness seems to be evident, as when one chief says, "Am I not going to become excited and am I not going to cause to disappear the one who has the great name the Great-Cause-of-Fear, the great property, the great one that causes people to lose their senses, the one that makes people unmerciful . . ." (Boas, 1969:169).

Third and most important, in their haste to assure us that the Kwakiutl prove the generality of their theory of human nature, Exchange Theorists have ignored or conveniently forgotten the major significance of the potlatch. Specifically, whereas hedonistic man is an acquisitive one, Kwakiutl man was concerned to *give away* wealth![2] As Curtis says (1915:143–144),

> A man can never receive through the potlatch as much as he disburses, for the simple reason that many to whom he gives will die before they have a potlatch, and others are too poor to return what he gives them. . . . When a recipient holds a potlatch he may return an equal amount or a slightly larger amount, or a smaller amount with perhaps the promise to give more at a future time.
>
> *The feeling at the bottom of the potlatch is one of pride rather than greed.* Occasionally men have tried to accumulate wealth by means of the potlatch and of lending at interest, but . . . a man can never draw out all his credits and keep the property thus acquired. Before his debtors will pay, he must first call the people together and inaugurate a potlatch, thus ensuring an immediate redistribution. [My emphasis].

Note that whereas the Kwakiutl redistributed most of their wealth (contrary to the claims of Exchange Theorists), "philanthropy" in our society is a rather isolated and puny enterprise. For example, Canada's most generous "good corporate citizen" in 1971, Labatt's Breweries, gave a grand total of 1 percent of its profits to charity. The average for corporations in Canada in general was .67 percent (Misgivings, 1972).

Now needless to say, the case against Exchange Theory cannot rest upon a few examples, nor has it been my intention to have it do so. At the same time, however, space does not permit a detailed examination of the vast amount of evidence on this matter. For present purposes, therefore, let me simply use the summaries of anthropologists who have reviewed this evidence.

Thus Marcel Mauss, the Durkheimian, after examining gift giving and other exchanges in a fairly wide range of societies (including the Northwest Coast Indians), concluded (in 1925) that:

> It is something other than utility which makes goods circulate in these multifarious and fairly enlightened societies. Clans, age groups, and sexes, in view of the many relationships ensuing from contacts between them, are in a perpetual economic effervescence which has little about it that is materialistic; it is much less prosaic than our sale and purchase, hire of services and speculations [Mauss, 1970:70].
>
> There, if one hoards, it is only to spend later on, to put people under obligations and to win followers. Exchanges are made as well, but only of luxury objects like clothing and ornaments, or feast and other things that are consumed at once. Return is made with interest [sic], but that is done in order to humiliate the original donor or exchange partner and not merely to recompense him for the loss that the lapse of time causes him. . . .
>
> It is only our Western societies that quite recently turned man into an economic animal [Mauss, 1970:73–74; my emphases].

Later, Karl Polanyi (1944:43) was to repeat much the same conclusion:

> In spite of the chorus of academic incantations so persistent in the nineteenth century, gain and profit made on exchange never before played an important part in human economy. Though the institution of the market was fairly common since the later Stone Age, its role was no more than incidental to economic life.

Similarly, still later his student, Marshall Sahlins (1965), elaborated upon the specifics after a seemingly exhaustive examination of exchange practices in primitive societies.

Sahlins classifies such relations into three pure types. What he refers to as "generalized reciprocity" entails giving something to another with no expectation that a particular amount of another good will be returned at a particular time, or, perhaps, even that there will be any return at all. Pure gift giving would be the best example of this form of exchange. A second type is what Sahlins calls "balanced reciprocity." Here the exchange contains expectations "which stipulate returns of commensurate worth or utility within a finite and narrow period." "Barter," where goods are exchanged for goods, usually "on the spot," would be an example of this type. Third and finally, there is what Sahlins calls "negative reciprocity," where the goal is not really to exchange things equivalent in value, but to "maximize utility at the other's expense." The word negative refers to the fact that while one gives the other person something, the object is to get more in return than one has given. What we call "dealing in commodities" in our society, for example, buying 500 pigs one day and selling them at a profit the next, would be a pure form of this type of exchange. Sahlins' classification of exchange relations thus runs from considerable altruism/cooperation on one end to self-interested or egoistic competition on the other.

His major conclusions of relevance to the present discussion can be summarized as follows:

(1) "The societal profile of reciprocity . . . most often inclines towards *generalized* modes" (Sahlins, 1965:179; my emphasis).

(2) "Exchange in primitive communities has not the same role as in the economic flow in modern industrial communities. . . . Typically, it is *less* involved than modern exchanges in the *acquisition* of means of production, *more* involved in the *redistribution* of finished goods through the community" (Sahlins, 1965:140; my emphasis).

(3) In primitive communities as compared with our own, when balanced and/or negative reciprocity *do* occur, they are more likely to be *restricted to particular roles* (e.g., the trader) *and for particular others* (e.g., those, such as strangers from another tribe, with whom no lasting social bond exists; Sahlins, 1965: 149–150). In this regard, differences in status rank do *not* entail the absence of a social bond, *and*, in fact, "differences in fortune between them compels a more altruistic (generalized) transaction than is otherwise appropriate" (Sahlins, 1965:165). Nor, for that matter, is negative reciprocity necessarily the typical relationship with strangers (Sahlins, 1965:172).

(4) In primitive communities as compared with our own, when balanced and/or negative reciprocity *do* occur, they are more likely to involve *highly restricted categories of "goods"* which cannot be exchanged for goods (including "monies", if they exist) in other categories. In this regard, "One does not exchange

things for food. . . . Staples are insulated against pecuniary trans-actions and food shared perhaps but rarely sold" (Sahlins, 1965: 170–172). Similarly, even where generalized exchanges are usually restricted to those with whom one has a lasting social bond, generalized exchanges in food will often not be so restricted (Sahlins, 1965:172).

In summarizing the theoretical implications of his own research Sahlins reiterates Mauss's conclusion, which now should surely be our own:

> Here has been given a discourse on economics in which "economiz-ing" appears mainly as an exogenous factor! The organizing principles of economy have been sought elsewhere. To the extent they have been found outside man's presumed hedonistic propensity, a strategy for the study of primitive economics is suggested that is *something the reverse of economic orthodoxy* [i.e., Exchange Theory; Sahlins, 1965:186; my emphasis].

EXCURSUS ON THE CORRELATES OF TRUCKING, BARTERING, AND EXCHANGING

According to Marxian theory, it is revolutions in the *technology* and social relations of production (more specifically, the *division of labour* and *ownership* of the means of production) which provide the major impetus for changes in the nature of exchange relation-ships. In this causal chain, increases in a community's *surplus,* in the amount of production over and above that required for the physical subsistence of its members, play a crucial role, for it is only when there are "extra" goods which might be hoarded that one can have egoistic exchanges. Similarly, it is only after control over the means of production and the products themselves have passed into the hands of a class of nonproducers, and that control has been cemented with political control over the society as a whole, that pro-ducers can be forced to work for others and production itself can be directed wholly toward exchange rather than the immediate use of the producers.

In this account other factors also play an important role. Of *population size and distribution,* for example, Marx suggested that the concentration of people in towns, leading to a large demand for agricultural goods, provided one of the major impetuses for com-modity production. Similarly, the *breakdown of norms traditionally governing social relationships* which accompanies the division of the population into town and country, and dominant and subordinant classes, in turn facilitates the pursuit of naked self-interest. However, note that in this case these factors are filtered through the (allegedly) more central factors of technology and the class structure, and this clearly distinguishes it from Durkheim's version of Functionalism.

In the latter, population size and density are the *major* bases for the division of labour, and even when the latter involves the division into classes, it is not the division of labour and private property per se which leads to anomie and hence egoistic competition. Rather, it is rapid increases in population size and density and geographical and social mobility which produce it, particularly through breaking up traditional groups and thereby creating problems in coordinating the activities of different individuals and limiting their aspirations.

Probably inspired by the recent concern with "overpopulation," a number of anthropologists (e.g., Barth, 1965; Harner, 1970) have recently revived yet another version of the population size/density argument. This is the theory of Thomas Malthus, an offshoot of classical political economy later elaborated by Spencer, that dramatic increases in population size and density will outstrip a society's ability to provide subsistence for all of its members, producing a serious *scarcity* of goods and thereby also a fierce *competition* for them. Eventually, so this social Darwinist argument continues, it is the fittest individuals and adaptive institutions, including kinship, class, and political as well as more narrowly economic structures, which survive. For example, after studying a tribe of sheep- and goat-herding nomads in South Persia, Fredrik Barth (1965:124) has suggested that their institution of private ownership of herds by household is a necessary adaptation to population pressures. Specifically, since grazing land is scarce, private ownership of herds limits the number of economic units which must live off it and shifts responsibility for the effects of droughts and the like from the community as a whole, which might well perish if it had to ensure that all individuals survive, to individual families whose members can exchange shepherd labour for subsistence or settle in permanent villages as craftspeople and merchants if they cannot compete successfully.

To successfully apply general models such as those summarized above to specific societies and the host of unique conditions which are likely to characterize them is a very difficult process indeed, particularly if one attempts to abstract certain of these characteristics from their societal context in order to make cross-cultural comparisons. Nevertheless, if we are to choose among them, such a procedure is necessary.

Let us begin with the pattern suggested by Marxian theory. Here we might begin with a study of 415 preindustrial societies conducted as early as 1915 by Hobhouse, Wheeler and Ginsberg (1965).

Their major classification of these societies is by their productive technology, which many evolutionists also take as a rough index of surplus (it is presumed that the more sophisticated the technology, the more productive labour is and hence also the higher is the level of surplus), although the degree to which labour is divided into crafts is also treated as part of this classification. Their term "Lower Hunters" (abbreviated as "LH") refers to hunting and food gathering societies such as the Bushmen of Africa and the Aborigines of Australia, who use no metals and only poorly maneuverable canoes in their hunting and food gathering. Similarly, they have no pottery and do no spinning of yarn or weaving of cloth. The "Higher Hunters" (HH), who include the Eskimo and Micmac of Canada as well as such Northwest Coast Indians as the Kwakiutl, have a more advanced productive and craft technology with regard to the previously mentioned practices.

As is still accepted among those who take an evolutionary view of technological development, Hobhouse et al. see two lines of development beyond hunting and foodgathering. One, the "Pastoral" line, entails shepherding and animal husbandry. "Pastoral 1" (P1) societies have little or no agriculture, little use of metal, and few handicrafts whereas "Pastoral 2" (P2) societies, which would include Barth's nomads, have much more of all three of these things. The second line of development is Agricultural. In the case of such Indian tribes as the Algonquin, Iroquois, or Ojibway, "Agriculture 1" (A1), one finds people living mainly from hunting and foodgathering, but also practicing a rudimentary agriculture. Whereas there is no metal use, there is a rudimentary use of pottery and textiles. "Agriculture 2" (A2) societies, such as the Pawnee and Seminole in the Southwestern and Southeastern United States, use agriculture as their main means of subsistence, and engage in pottery making, spinning, and weaving. "Agriculture 3" (A3) societies, which include the Hopi and Zuni Indians of the Southwestern United States, rely almost wholly upon agriculture, use irrigation, manuring and some rotation of crops as well as the plough, and have woodwork, metal, and textile activity as specialized industries.

The two lines of development can be pictured as follows:

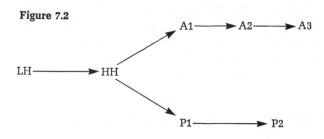

Figure 7.2

The reader should remember here that as separate lines of development, the Pastoral and Agricultural are not really comparable, and
should be compared more with hunting and food gathering societies
than with each other.

Although Hobhouse et al. do not provide us with actual figures,
their first result of interest is that the incidence of trade, obviously
a form of exchange which, being most likely to involve strangers,
would also be most likely to permit balanced and negative as
opposed to generalized reciprocity, also tends to increase as one
proceeds up the evolutionary scale. In this regard, in a recent quantitative analysis of a representative sample of 100 societies, Dean
Shiels (1969; 1972) found that the incidence of marketplaces, exchanges with those within one's own community, and exchanges of
goods involving various degrees of calculativeness (i.e., barter,
money for only a limited number of goods, money as a generalized
medium of exchange) all increase with the level of agricultural technology and the division of labour. Similarly, Ernest Mandel (1970)
makes a good case, not only for Marx's claim that trade tends to be
first irregular with outsiders, then regular with outsiders, irregular
with insiders, and finally regular with insiders, but that these
changes, at least through the early stages of technological development, tend to occur with the appearance of surpluses.

Returning to Hobhouse et al., two further sets of results, reported
here in the accompanying table, are particularly interesting.

In the first place, should the Exchange Theorist still insist that we
regard the exchange of a bride for a bride price as well as the
exchange of nonhuman goods for nonhuman goods as a calculated,
egoistic exchange, then s/he will find that as with the leasing of land,
these exchanges *also* tend to increase with level of development!
(We shall have more to say about the reasons for this in Chapter 9.)

Second, as the technology and division of labour become more complex, so the incidence of communal ownership of land and tools decreases and that of private property increases. Similarly, ownership by chiefs and nobles, including the ownership of slaves, also tends to increase. To this should be added Michael Harner's (1970) and Stanley Udy's (1970) more recent findings that the existence of a centralized government as well as a class structure tends to be highly correlated with the level of technology.

TABLE 7.1
PERCENTAGE OF SOCIETIES AT VARIOUS STAGES OF TECHNOLOGICAL DEVELOPMENT WITH CERTAIN EXCHANGE AND PROPERTY-CLASS CHARACTERISTICS
(HOBHOUSE ET AL., 1965)

A. PRODUCTIVE TECHNOLOGY

	LH	HH	[P1	P2]	A1	A2	A3
B. EXCHANGE							
a. Leasing land	0%	2%	[0%	0%]	1%	4%	7%
b. Bride purchase	10	42	[61	83]	31	53	69
C. PROPERTY AND CLASS							
a. Communal property	69	80	[57	62]	64	54	29
b. Owned by chiefs and nobles	0	8	[9	33]	0	12	37
c. Slave-owning	2	32	[37	71]	33	46	78

Third, the fact that private property classes tend to accompany egoistic exchange disputes the Exchange Theory position that such exchanges remain "free" or voluntary. To the contrary, it suggests the contradictory development which Marx noted; that is, whereas surpluses and the division of labour may free the individual from traditional obligations and permit him/her to engage in individualized exchange relations, the accumulation of private property and class formation subsequently limit this same freedom. This contradiction is even more apparent in a study by Stanley Udy (1970), whose results concerning the exchange and more directly coercive expropriation of labour can be seen in the accompanying table.[3]

Note first the striking findings in row a; that is, *individual choice decreases* rather than increases with societal development. Furthermore, in line with the hypothesis of contradictory development, the incidence of *forced labour increases*. Finally, contractual work, as a relatively free form of work relations, is actually more frequent in less-developed societies than is forced labour.

Nevertheless, there is little reason to believe that the relative absence of egoistic competition among primitive peoples is not in good part a function of norms prescribing cooperation and prohibiting competition, and that the breakdown of such norms during periods of social upheaval (such as, for example, those which usually result from the invasion of Euro-American culture) does not play an equally important part in changing this dominant pattern. Indeed, there is every reason to believe that this is the case.

TABLE 7.2
RECRUITMENT TO WORK ORGANIZATIONS BY SOCIETAL COMPLEXITY IN UDY'S STUDY (1970)

METHOD OF RECRUITMENT TO WORK ORGANIZATIONS	COMPLEXITY OF SOCIETAL STRUCTURE			
	I and II	III	IV	V
a. Up to individual	46%	28%	22%	0%
b. Balanced reciprocity between families	5	26	22	13
c. Contractual	7	31	21	27
d. By force (slavery or feudalism)	1	14	33	35

We have already encountered some of the specific norms which have this function (the restriction of potlatch giving to chiefs among the Kwakiutl is one example), and it is not difficult to find others. Moreover, there it was also noted that the invasion of Euro-American culture appears to have weakened the effects of these same norms. Here it is also interesting to go back to the cross-cultural game research of Kagen and Madsen, for there we find one experimental variation whereby one child was given the toy and only the second child could make the moves which would determine whether or not the first child could keep the toy. Under these circumstances the rivalry of the Mexican children was not significantly less than that of the American children. Presumably, this was a result of some combination of the decrease in interaction and, perhaps, therefore also the heightened suggestion to the Mexican children in particular that rivalry was what the experimenter really wanted.[4]

Up to this point, therefore, we should conclude that while the Marxian explanation for differences in egoistic competition appears to have considerable validity, this does not preclude the operation of processes, such as those postulated by Durkheim, which are not central to the Marxian argument. However, several crucial issues remain.

One is obviously whether the operation and dissolution of norms regulating exchange relations depend upon technology, the division of labour, the level of surplus, and private property, as postulated by Marxian theory, or upon population size and density and other social disruptions peripheral to the development of capitalism *as such*, as postulated by Durkheimian and neo-Malthusian theory. Another, even more important than the first, is whether the phenomena of exchange purportedly explained here by Marxian theory, with or without the intervening normative processes, might not be better explained by such factors as population pressure *as such*.

These are issues which existing information does not permit us to conclusively resolve at this point, least of all in the present format, but I shall leave the reader with several matters for his/her further consideration.

In the first place, such analysts as Evans-Pritchard and Sahlins appear to be of the opinion that among primitive peoples "it is scarcity and not sufficiency that makes people generous, since everybody is thereby ensured against hunger" (Evans-Pritchard, quoted in Sahlins, 1965:165). While this runs counter to the neo-Malthusian argument, there may well be a threshold of scarcity, caused by such conditions as unusual population pressures, below which the relationship reverses, as Sahlins himself (1965:168–169) suggests may be the case.

Second, in the previously mentioned study by Shiels, population size was found to be as highly correlated with the various exchange variables as was technology and the division of labour.[5]

Third, there is certainly reason to believe that the social regulation of individual propensities, including those toward being egoistic in exchange relations, becomes more difficult with increasing population size. In fact (although the validity of such results may be restricted to college students in our own society), there is even some experimental evidence for this. Thus, in a study by Gerald Marwell and David Schmitt (1972), subjects in a Prisoner's Dilemma game began by cooperating 38 percent of the time in two-person but only 25 percent of the time in three-person groups. In Durkheimian fashion, Marwell and Schmitt suggest that as more players are added it becomes more difficult to coordinate each others' behavior and establish relations of trust.

Where, therefore, do we go from here?

Perhaps the first thing to keep in mind is that the technology/surplus and population size/density factors are not independent of each other. Specifically, on the one hand a community will not be able to feed more members in a more concentrated area unless it has a more productive technology, and the latter in turn is likely to require a more complex division of labour and settled living pattern; on the other, increases in population size and density will increase the demand for higher levels of production and a more productive technology, and supply the larger numbers of people in a settled area to make the technological change possible. Hence one might well expect *both* sets of factors to increase the incidence of egoistic exchange, not because, or at least only because, they initiate separate and competing processes, but because they are both part of the *same* processes.

In an attempt to examine the validity of this argument John Gartrell and myself reanalyzed Shiels' data and compared the relative effects of both technology and "population pressure" (size and density) upon the various exchange characteristics. As expected, technology and population pressure are highly correlated with each other. Furthermore, when one statistically removes the effects of the other, each of technology and population pressure is independently and significantly related to the incidence of exchange. However, the relationship between technology and exchange is closer than that between population pressure and exchange.[6]

The second consideration is that any such abstract comparisons of necessity ignore the unique configurations of structural features which characterize particular societies. To paraphrase Marx, for this reason there is no way to avoid coming to terms with these unique configurations when one analyzes specific societies. Hence, for example, to the extent that the behavior of individuals in a particular preindustrial society is egoistic as well as highly public, we should presumably look for the causes of egoistic competition in such things as conflicts of interest deriving from property ownership rather than population processes as they are treated in Durkheimian theory.

In the next few chapters we shall attempt to do precisely this for our own type of society. Egoistic exchange will continue as an underlying theme, but now the focus shifts considerably. Specifically, whereas in the present chapter we have tended to lump the specific relationships among very different types of people together, as if there were no differences among them, in these next chapters we take a closer look at such differences. Whether "egoistic exchange" is in fact a good or complete characterization of these various relationships is one of the many questions we shall try to answer.

Notes

[1]However, Wiley (1973) reports that females are still less competitive when playing against males. The implications of such a finding are taken up in Chapter 9.

[2]It should be noted that while many anthropologists would agree that the competitiveness of the potlatch has been greatly exaggerated by Exchange Theorists, not all of them would agree that its main function was to redistribute wealth.

[3]Udy's random sample of all known societies was subdivided as follows. Type V societies, the most developed, have all of the following: agriculture in settled villages, exclusive proprietorship with regard to land, a complex stratification system aside from kinship considerations of at least three levels, and a centralized government exercising control over several geographically distinct communities. Type IV societies have these less the complex stratification system, Type III also lack a centralized government, and Type II societies differ from Type I in having exclusive proprietorship.

[4]Kagen and Madsen themselves say only that their results demonstrate that the rural Mexican children do not therefore lack competitiveness.

[5]Harner (1970) even uses agricultural societies' dependence upon hunting and foodgathering as a measure of the absence of scarcity rather than the absence of a surplus. Since there is relatively good information on these societies' population size and density (Harner uses the same data as does Shiels), this seems inexcusable. Also, a very large number of Harner's societies are dependent upon others in the sample (even in a sample of only 100 societies, Shiels found fully 37 to be dependent upon others; Harner uses the entire population of 1170 societies), and he makes no attempt to compare the validity of competing models. On this latter question, see the discussion which follows.

[6]Shiels's 100 societies are drawn from the well-known *Ethnology* listing. To measure technological level we combined the variables "agricultural system" (gathering; digging stick; hoe; plow; commercial) and "agricultural tool materials" (none; wood; stone; bone; iron; steel); population pressure "population size" and "density"; and exchange Shiels' three variables mentioned earlier. The actual "beta coefficients" for technology—exchange and population pressure—exchange are .46 and .40, respectively (the closer these coefficients are to 1.00, the closer is the relationship between the two factors).

8
CLASS, STATUS, AND POWER

As we saw in the previous chapter, the monopolization of wealth and power associated with social class is associated with and presumably arises from cooperation, competition, and exchange. On the other hand, right from its inception, competition is not completely free, with those groups favorably situated in the division of labor having better access to wealth and power, and others being eventually forced to rely upon one major form of exchange in order to subsist — the exchange of their "labor power" for a wage or salary. In the Marxian conception, cooperation therefore becomes increasingly characteristic of relationships among people *within the same class* as they try to maintain or enhance their collective competitive position, while competition and (eventually) open conflict over political power becomes increasingly characteristic of the relationship *between classes*.

Since relationships between individuals characterized by class-based egoism and conflict fall under the rubric of alienation, then should the former be shown to play a central part in our social relationships alienation would provide a logical means for integrating the two topics. In this chapter we shall examine the effects of class, status, and power, more or less as defined by Marx and Weber, not only upon our relationships with others, but upon our relationship with work, its products and ourselves. However, two things should be kept in mind with regard to this way of dividing up everyday life. One is that these aspects are highly interdependent rather than empirically separate, and this will necessitate some skipping back and forth among them. The other is that the very ease with which we are able to segment different aspects of our everyday lives may itself be an indication of alienation, since it has been shown that "work" and "leisure" were not so clearly demarcated for preindustrial people (Sahlins, 1972; Thompson, 1967).

Work

Are most people in our society highly involved in their work, or would they be better characterized as psychologically alienated in the Marxian sense of the term? The answers mainstreamists have typically given to this question have been heavily informed by the data from two research traditions: (1) studies of the "job satisfaction" of members of the population in general, and (2) studies of the effects of specific working conditions upon such attitudes. The results of the first type of study are very straightforward; that is, a clear majority of the Canadian population — 85 percent, in fact[1] — say they are satisfied with their jobs. The results of the second type of study have not been as clear or as consistent, but they too are persuasive.

Robert Blauner (1964), for example, claims to have shown that the assembly-line technology to which autoworkers are subjected is much more alienating than the craft technology of printing or the "continuous process" (fully automated) technology of the oil and chemical industries. His results are not quite as clear as this claim implies, in that textile workers, whose specific working conditions are very similar to those of autoworkers, were not as consistently dissatisfied with their work as were the latter, and chemical workers were not consistently satisfied.

Nevertheless, not only have Fullan (1970) and Shepard (1971) replicated Blauner's findings using between-industry comparisons, but Kern and Schumann (1970) have also done so by classifying workers according to the technologies with which they actually work rather than simply by industry, an important step considering that not all automobile workers work on the assembly line and not all oil or chemical workers work with continuous processes. Similar findings have been obtained in smaller-scale studies distinguishing among automobile (Kornhauser, 1965) and chemical (Fürstenburg, 1969) workers themselves according to the technology with which they actually work. Finally, in two separate studies Shepard (1971) and Kirsch and Lengermann (1972) have fairly successfully applied Blauner's hypothesis to white-collar workers by comparing bank and insurance clerks (presumed to be analogous to craft workers), computer "key punch" and "sorter" and addressograph machine operators (mass production), and computer console operators, programmers, and analysts (continuous process).

What is less clear is what inferences about the extent of actual alienation one can legitimately make from such studies. The intent of those who have conducted them is clear; that is, according to them such studies indicate that most people in our society are *not* alienated from their work. In Blauner's case this is said to follow from the fact that although autoworkers are highly alienated, workers who work on assembly lines are a minority among even blue-collar workers, let alone the general population. Furthermore, that chemical workers appear to be so satisfied indicates that contrary to popular belief (and Marxian theory), automation may liberate workers from, rather than enslave them to, alienating work. However, such inferences are not so straightforward as they might seem.

Consider first whether job dissatisfaction itself is an adequate measure of alienation. In fact, whereas only 15 percent of the Canadian work force say they are dissatisfied, well over twice as many (39.4 percent) agree that they wouldn't mind being unemployed for a while, and twice as many say they work more because they have to than because they like to! Furthermore, whereas approximately 75 percent of blue-collar workers say they are satisfied with their jobs, little more than half this many say they would choose them again if they had the choice to do so, or recommend them to a friend. These inconsistencies among attitudes themselves are matched by inconsistencies between attitudes and behavior, in that job satisfaction is at best a poor-to-moderate predictor of a person's productivity, absenteeism, or tendency to change jobs ("turnover"). Various other pieces of evidence suggest that job dissatisfaction grossly underestimates alienation from work.

A moment's' reflection reveals why this might be the case; that is, very few people in our society actually get to choose interesting and otherwise involving jobs, such that their expressions of satisfaction with them are likely to reflect less their true underlying orientations toward them than their attempts to "come to terms" with them, to "make the best of a bad situation'" (Kornhauser, 1965). As various workers themselves have put it, "If I didn't enjoy it I would be miserable" (Zweig, 1961:77); "A true worker *brings aspirations to level of job*. That's why a new man is not so good. The first six months are the toughest. I was at the verge of quitting. *After a while, you get used to it*" (Blum, 1953:85; my emphases). People also don't like to think of themselves as deserving only dissatisfying work, and this too probably biases job satisfaction upward.[2]

That such a coming-to-terms process is widespread is suggested by the fact that young workers in our national survey (see also the Upjohn Institute, 1973), whose aspirations for interesting work and options for obtaining it are more open (they actually do more job-switching), express much more dissatisfaction than older workers with the very same work, and the fact that blue-collar workers in particular tend to rate the nonwork aspects of their lives (their family, garden, or stamp collection) as being much more important to them than their work (see Faunce, 1968, and below).

These considerations suggest that *alienation from work is much more extensive than most survey researchers would have us believe.* However, in and of themselves they do not refute the claims of Blauner and others that alienation from work, rather than being uniformly high throughout most of the work force, varies considerably according to specific working conditions. Indeed, turnover rates as well as job dissatisfaction tend to follow the pattern Blauner has suggested (Fullan, 1970).

Blauner attributes his differences in alienation by industry to the relative amounts of control over work which different technologies permit workers. Specifically, printers, like artisans, do an entire sequence of tasks from start to finish. They not only have control over the quantity and quality of production, but its speed as well. However, work on the textile or automobile assembly line involves the complete antithesis of these conditions. Although fuller automation does not provide chemical workers with very much more control over the quantity and quality of production, it makes them less tied down to and paced by the line (they mainly "check dials," "push buttons," and do a great deal of socializing with fellow workers). Furthermore, if the high demand for their skills gives printers much more job security than autoworkers, the low ratio of investment in labor to investment in machinery leads the management of chemical industries to be willing and able to provide workers with more job security and other fringe benefits.

There is reason to believe that some of Blauner's differences in alienation can be attributed simply to differences in pay, in that printers and chemical workers are paid considerably more than autoworkers. Some of their satisfaction with their work may therefore indicate not a *lack* of alienation, but simply a different type; that is, they may still be only "instrumentally" attached to their work (the means-ends dimension mentioned in Chapter 3).[3] However, the results of a more recent survey study suggest that while pay is indeed a source of job satisfaction, job security, and especially control over the work itself, are more important sources (Sheppard and Herrick, 1972). Experimental studies using behavioral as well as attitudinal indicators of alienation also attest to the importance of the amount of control over work which specific working conditions permit.

Thus, increasing the variety of tasks people perform through "job enlargement" or "enrichment," seems to decrease the amount of alienation people express (see Shepard, 1970), as does increasing employees' decision-making power. For example, when workers in a pajama factory "resisted" the introduction of increased automation, Coch and French (1960) divided them into three different experimental groups. One group, "No Participation," was simply told in the usual manner that the changes would take place, whereas another group, "Participation through Representation," was given more detailed information and permitted to elect those among them who would be the first to learn how to use the new machinery and teach the others. Those in a third group, "Total Participation," were permitted to meet in small groups and make suggestions about how the new jobs might be redesigned. Especially since even the "Total" Participation group's input was token (i.e., they could not decide to forego the machinery or even choose among several types), the results were indeed dramatic, with the productivity rate greatly increasing and the turnover rate greatly decreasing for the "Total" as compared to the other groups. After reviewing such studies as these, Paul Blumberg (1968:123) concludes: "There is hardly a study in the literature which fails to demonstrate that satisfaction in work is enhanced or that generally acknowledged beneficial consequences accrue from a genuine increase in workers' decision-making power."

At least one of Blauner's claims, therefore, is undoubtedly true; that is, *alienation from work varies considerably by specific working conditions.* However, let us examine his other inferences more closely.

One concerns the distribution of such conditions, not only by industry, but over *time.* Specifically, one assumes from his optimism about the future of alienation that Blauner must assume that all people who will ever work on an assembly line are already doing so, such that any further automation is toward continuous process production and an alienation-free existence. Whether or not Blauner believes this to be the case, the facts completely contradict such an assumption, in that *most people are somewhere between the craft and mass production stages, and therefore in store for a great deal of alienation* (Faunce, 1968:53–54). But for that matter, even the move from mass to continuous process production is far from as rosy as Blauner would have us believe. Specifically, after studying actual changes which took place after plants become fully automated, Kern and Schumann (1970) discovered that a substantial portion of the employees are left with no job security; that is, they are fired, and that a quarter to a third get to work, not with the new continuous process machinery, but with various semiautomated machines which do not increase their freedom at work. In fact, Kern and Schumann found a *decrease* in job satisfaction for these latter workers.

Another such inference concerns the distribution of working conditions by *class*. In this regard, by having demonstrated large differences in alienation *within* the category of blue-collar workers, what some take to represent the "working class," Blauner (1964:3) considers himself to have also refuted Marx's claim that property and class, capitalism as such, are the ultimate sources of alienation. Later, after reviewing some recent studies which purport to have demonstrated few differences in alienation between white- and blue-collar workers, the Upjohn Institute (1973:31–32) concluded with an analogous defence of capitalism.

Right from the start, there are two problems with drawing such inferences from these data. First, as Joachim Israel (1971:223) has also noted, one cannot infer the absence of differences *between* classes simply by examining differences within them. Rather, there could be large differences between as well as within at the same time. Second, Harry Braverman (1974) has forcefully argued that the proletarianization of white-collar work of which Mills spoke has proceeded at such a pace that the white-versus-blue-collar distinction is next to useless as a categorization of the distribution of actual working conditions. I believe that Braverman states the case too strongly, in that there are still substantial blue-white differences in job security and variety in and control over work (Bain, 1970:67–71; Kohn, 1969; Coburn, 1973). Nevertheless, there is probably little point in making much of the differences in working conditions between, say, secretaries or bank clerks and most blue-collar workers, and there are in fact few differences in psychological alienation from work between them (Shepard, 1971; plus see below). Either way, the blue-white distinction as such is not the most relevant class distinction for evaluating Marx's theory.

Clearly, the distinction between those self-employed and those employed by others, resting as it usually does upon differences in ownership of the means of production, is much more relevant. However, when one examines studies which have made the comparison one finds that the results are mixed. Thus, while Eden (1973) and Kohn (1976) report significantly lower alienation among the self-employed, Rushing (1970) and Wilkening and Rodefeld (1972) found no differences between farm owners and, respectively, farm workers or farm managers. In fact, Bonjean (1966) reports that whereas production workers were more alienated than self-employed businessmen, the latter were in turn more alienated than business managers, and this difference was still stronger in a later study by Nelson (1968).

Although the results of these particular studies do not permit us to affirm Marx's theory, it would also be unwise to simply dismiss it. For one thing, the indicators of alienation in almost all these studies were attitudinal. In the one study containing a behavioral measure (how often interviewees reported being absent from work), Eden did find much more alienation among the other-employed. For another, whereas few of the above researchers paid much attention to the size of the firm or personal income of those they studied, vulnerability to the market and the whims of large-corporation buyers and sellers make the "job security" of small businesspeople and farmers tenuous indeed (Johnson, 1972). It should not be surprising, therefore, that after analyzing further results of the survey employed by Eden, John Gartrell, Owen Adams and myself discovered that while the self-employed were much more likely to say that they would choose the same job again if given the choice (70.3 percent as opposed to 46 percent), they were *less* likely to say they would recommend it to a friend (48.5 percent as opposed to 65.4 percent)! Such considerations don't warrant dispensing with the self-versus-other employment comparison, but they do point to the need to distinguish among the self-employed as well as the other-employed.

When we do so with our national Canadian sample, and also distinguish between direct attitudinal and more indirect (quasi-behavioral) measures of alienation, we obtain the results in Table 8.1. The reader will note, there is little difference between the

TABLE 8.1

ALIENATION FROM WORK BY EMPLOYMENT STATUS AND OCCUPATION IN THE NATIONAL CANADIAN SAMPLE

	JOB ENJOYABLE	COM-MITTED	CHOICE OF IN-TRINSIC	WORK OVERTIME WITHOUT PAY
Self-employed	88.3%	88.9%	57.9%	82.9%
Other-employed	81.5	68.7	39.7	45.1
Executives, managers, proprietors	90.2%	87.0%	46.2%	81.8%
Professionals	91.6	79.1	57.4	74.3
Sales	92.5	75.0	29.8	70.1
Clerical	86.1	68.0	49.1	43.3
Skilled laborers	79.6	67.7	33.8	31.8
Unskilled laborers	62.4	57.1	28.5	25.0

self- and other-employed in the percentage saying the job is enjoyable, but there is a large (and statistically significant) difference in favor of the self-employed in those claiming to feel a strong sense of commitment to it. Furthermore, when asked which factors would be most important in choosing another job, the self-employed were more likely than the other-employed to choose such intrinsic factors as "more interesting work," while the other-employed were more likely to choose such means-ends factors as "higher pay." The former were also much more likely to "work overtime without extra pay," and to "come in on own to catch up" (not shown in the table).

When we compare occupational categories rather than employment status, as in the lower section of Table 8.1, we see that the differences between the "top" and "bottom" categories are usually large indeed. Note that those occupations where people have the most likelihood of being able to plan production (i.e., "Executives, managers, proprietors" and "Professionals") usually have much lower rates of alienation than do those where the likelihood is least (i.e., "Skilled" and "Unskilled laborers"). Interestingly, however, the lack of clear and consistent differences on intrinsic orientation toward work indicates considerable (means-ends) alienation among high-status–white-collar as well as low-status–blue-collar "workers."

When combined with other, well-established findings about differences in alienation between broad categories of the work force,[4] these results require a conclusion contrary to that of Blauner and others. Specifically, *substantial class differences in alienation are not only not precluded by substantial differences within "classes," but in existence.* However, the question of the precise importance of *capitalism* in particular, as opposed to simply bureaucracy in general, remains.

If we are to believe mainstream textbook writers,[5] the answer is already clear. That is, as with the Functionalist and Weberian positions, a highly specialized division of labor, and therefore some minimum alienation from work, is said to be inevitable for *any* industrial society. (The same is said to be true for class *inequalities* in alienation.) However, much of the alienation now in existence is said to be a product of neither capitalism *nor* industrialism in general, but management policies based upon Taylorism ("time and motion studies") and other allegedly outmoded conceptions of work and workers. When workers are treated with "sympathetic understanding" and given even token participation in the work process, these Cooleyan and Human Relationist writers claim, alienation is much lower.

THE TRUTH . . .

One should first concede the truth in these claims.

{ In the first place, the very existence of commodity production — of having to produce for others through some such impersonal mechanism as the market — probably promotes alienation by imposing purposes other than their own upon producers' work. Nelson Graburn (cited in Martyn, 1964:558) discovered this after Eskimo carvers began producing sculptures for the tourist market rather than simply their own amusement or to provide tools or toys for their children. Similarly, in a most intriguing series of experiments, Edward Deci (1972) discovered that college students deeply involved in solving intrinsically interesting puzzles would subsequently become alienated from the task if they were paid to do it! (Presumably, this led them to question whether they were doing it for themselves or "simply for the money."[6])

Second, this seemingly inherent alienation must surely be heightened under "economies of scale," particularly because it undoubtedly requires considerable coordination, and workers considerable supervision. This is suggested by the fact that some workers appear to be uncomfortable when their supervisors do not emphasize rules and supervise them closely (Kahn et al., 1964:161). (More of this later.) It could also be inferred from the classic study of boys' clubs by Kurt Lewin and his students (White and Lippitt, 1960). Here groups of subjects producing soap sculptures under a laissez-faire leadership not only produced less than did groups under an authoritarian leadership (here every conceivable detail of work and relationships with others was spelled out by the adult leader), but were less interested in their work, more discouraged and exasperated, and more aggressive with each other.

Third and finally, the argument for the ameliorating effects of sympathetic management receives some support in the correlation between perceptions of sympathy from supervisors and job satisfaction, and, although to a lesser extent, productivity (Kahn and Katz, 1960; Likert, 1961). Furthermore, organizations where workers perceive themselves to have more influence upon management and production are not only more satisfying, but more productive (Likert, 1961; Tannenbaum, 1968). Finally, a democratic leadership style in the Lewin et al. experiment produced higher quality sculptures and more intrinsic involvement in work (e.g., the boys were more likely to keep producing after the leader had left the room).

This said, we must surely ask a number of searching questions.

How many of whose other purposes are required by "production in general"? Are the "outside" purposes simply those of consumers? How much scale and how much supervision is required by all "modern" work organizations? How much of what we have is actually in the "general interest"? What is the actual frequency and distribution of sympathetic management? How dependent upon the latter is control over work?

BUT NOT THE WHOLE TRUTH

Note that all of the above arguments are based on a common assumption; that is, that workers and owners or managers share a common interest in high productivity which overrides any competing interests they might have. Indeed, some Human Relationists claim to have established this empirically. For example, that work organizations where rank and file members perceive themselves to have more decision-making power are also likely to be those where *management* perceives itself to have more power has been taken by Arnold Tannenbaum and his associates (1968; see also Likert, 1961) to indicate the absence of any serious conflict of interest.

In fact, of course, these analysts have rather conveniently left out the pursuit-of-profit purpose which defines our "private enterprise" system. The hardly inconsiderable stamp this has made upon work in our society should be obvious, but one searches in vain for a trace of it in mainstream texts. At best, we are fed pablum about the new, "soulful" corporation which is no longer interested in profit maximization (see the devastating critique by Baran and Sweezy, 1966).

First, one might note that the initial emergence of other-employment was far from a case of workers waking from their beds in the middle of the night and exclaiming, "I'm going to produce collectively for society!" Rather, as Stephen Marglin (1971) among others has noted, workers usually began producing for others through a "cottage" system where they produced in their own homes and marketed the goods through a middleman buyer-and-seller. Their movement from home to factory was a long and painful process of coercion and cajolement whereby the middlemen, mainly to exercise enough control over the cottagers to extract the maximum amount of profit, were able to largely force them into factories through the use of "search-and-seizure," anticompetition, and antiloafing laws. Other workers were obtained through the "enclosure" system in Britain and preventing immigrants from obtaining land and "loafing" in

Canada and the United States (Teeple, 1972). By far the largest proportion of Canada's first laborers were Irishmen who had been forced off the land in their home country and had presumably become resigned to working for others. The upshot of all this is that most people work for others (still) because the option of self-employment is not a serious option. (In 1973 63.4 percent of Canadians still say they would rather work for themselves.) Any imputation of a consensual basis for our work organizations is therefore highly questionable.

Second, to return to an earlier period again, the introduction of machinery and the division of labor to the factory, far from serving an alleged general interest, served the interests of profit-making. Specifically, fragmentation of tasks and close supervision were designed less for higher productivity *as such* than to lower costs by controlling workers. Hence, as Taylor and other "scientific management" types argued (Braverman, 1974; Rinehart, 1975; Heron and Palmer, 1976), workers waste too much time when they are permitted to make decisions and socialize. Hence all planning of work must be transferred to the capitalist and workers must be closely supervised, preferably by someone who himself has not planned production and who is therefore less likely to be compromised when workers complain about the pace of work and the rate of pay. From that point on automation serves a double function. It increases the number of products for sale, to be sure, although this too is not geared directly to consumers' needs, but it also controls the worker's work more effectively and cheaply than continuous human supervision. Indeed, automation (past the mass production stage, at least) is designed to rid capitalists of the "inefficient" worker altogether.

This structuring of work for profit (usually someone else's[7]) has a myriad of effects upon work and alienation in our own time. In most general terms, it means that when there is a conflict between the "needs" of profit-making and the needs of individual producers, which is often, the former usually take precedence. As a result, workers receive the "commodity treatment."

This heavily determines not only how little or how much control workers have over work itself — how fast the line moves, how closely they are supervised, and so on — but how secure their job is and how much pay they receive. Nor is the commodity treatment restricted to industrial workers:

> I don't think they'd ever hire a male receptionist. They'd have to pay him more, for one thing. You can't pay someone who does what I do very much. It isn't economically feasible. (Laughs) You're there just to filter people and filter telephone calls. You're there just to handle

the equipment. You're treated like a piece of equipment, like the tele-pone [Terkel, 1972:29].

In fact, William Whyte (1957:184) occasionally uncovered somewhat similar treatment of relatively high-level executives, one of whom, after having been transferred with no explanation, told Whyte, "What is the purpose? What is the end? . . . I hope the company isn't playing checkers with me."

However, there is a very real difference between the objective situations of most workers and most managers. Specifically, the latter are much closer to and hence much more likely to personally identify with profit-making purposes. (High-level managers not only have a large degree of decision-making power, but personally own a substantial number of stocks in the companies they "work for" (Zeitlin, 1974).) This probably explains why, in the words of Marx (1975, 4:36) and the accompanying cartoon, the capitalist class (managers in this case) "feels at ease and strengthened in this self-estrangement, it recognizes estrangement as *its own power*. . . ."[8] The working class, on the other hand, is said to feel "annihilated in estrangement; it sees in it its own powerlessness and the reality of an inhuman existence."

Figure 8.1

Courtesy of Chicago Tribune-New York News Syndicate, Inc.

Given Marx's other writings on alienation, it is safe to conclude that he meant the latter statement literally as well as figuratively, and it bears remembering that it is unfortunately still true today:

> Five painful years ago, [Malcolm Nicholson] slid and fell on a ramp in the cigarette factory he worked for, Rothmans of Pall Mall Canada, on Dufflaw Rd. Today after nine gruelling operations on his back, he's still in a brace and still not back to work. And Nicholson isn't the kind of guy who doesn't take safety precautions. In fact, as a member of his company's safety committee, he had written several reports sharply critical of that same dust-covered incline. The day after Nicholson's accident, the company covered the ramp with a graphite slip-proof material. "It seems like it always takes an accident to make a company move, doesn't it. They're not interested in safety—it costs too much money," he says bitterly [Roseman, 1974:1].*

> One night a guy hit his head on a welding gun. He went to his knees. He was bleeding like a pig, blood was oozing out. So I stopped the line for a second and ran over to help him. The foreman turned the line on again, he almost stepped on the guy. That's the first thing they always do. They didn't even call an ambulance. . . . You're nothing to any of them. That's why I hate this place ["Jim Grayson," auto worker (Ford) interviewed by Terkel, 1972:167].

Nor, it should be made perfectly clear, are these a few isolated cases dredged up for their shock value:

> One out of every 10 Canadians killed accidentally is killed on the job. One out of every five Ontario workers has been injured on the job this year. Almost three times as many man days are lost to on-the-job injuries as on strikes and lockouts [Roseman, 1974:1].*

And, to these statistics on industrial accidents should be added those on such diseases as asbestosis, silicosis, and lung cancer.

Where, then, do these considerations leave us? We must conclude, I submit, that *however much "basic" alienation is inherent in industrialism or bureaucracy in general, capitalism per se imposes its own share of "surplus" alienation from work upon us, and this share is considerable.* If sympathetic management and token participation in the planning of work can sometimes lessen the pain, the exigencies of profit-making make them infrequent and puny (see Chapter 11). According to one owner-manager, sympathetic management "never existed in corporations," and family-owned corporations with paternalistic orientations toward their employees have simply been forced out of business (Terkel, 1972:410–411). Nor, for that matter, would individual managers' sympathy necessarily be of much use to

---

*Reprinted with permission — the Toronto Star.

workers. For example, in the previously described case of an auto-worker lying bleeding on the floor while Ford's holy assembly line kept rolling, we find for a manager, *not* an ogre, but a personable sort who told Terkel that he has good personal relations with all his workers.

This is *not* to say that "capitalism" as we know it is the only modern industrial system which produces surplus alienation. Certainly the social structure of the Eastern, so-called "Communist" countries also appears to have produced it (see Blumberg, 1968; Zdravomyslov et al., 1970). The point here is not to deny that these other systems are alienating, for they certainly appear to be, but to note that whether or not it is a *necessary* cause of surplus alienation, capitalism is indeed a *sufficient* cause. Certainly the argument that surplus alienation, like inflation or cancer, is currently "world-wide" is of little use to alienated Western workers. ⟶

Products

If it is true that capitalism is the source of a great deal of surplus alienation from work in our society, why don't people fight capitalism? They in fact *do,* as we shall now see, yet the very fact that capitalism persists is proof that they have not done so very effectively.

In this section we shall consider how and why this two-pronged situation exists through examining people's relationships to the products of their work, both physical and social structural, but mainly the latter. We begin at the workplace, the immediate point of production, and then proceed through wider organizations such as classes to more explicitly political processes.

PRODUCTIVITY AND SABOTAGE, COMPANY AND UNION

In one way or another workers have been struggling against the conditions they face at work since the inception of capitalism. More than a few prominent social scientists began their careers by helping management break this resistance. Not surprisingly given their choice of sides in these disputes, the first such researchers (Roethlisberger and Dixon, 1964) tended to view such things as the "restriction of output" by work groups as irrational behavior. High productivity, they argued, benefits everyone, worker and capitalist alike; workers will dispense with their resistance to such things as the introduction of new machines if they are educated as to their nature and the defensive conformity pressures of the work group are diffused. Later the argument took a more sophisticated turn in the hands of the Human Relationists. Here the presumption of irrationality on the part of discontented workers is watered down, in that they are said to be reacting less from ignorance than their (albeit largely unarticulated and perhaps unconscious) desires to have some small measure of control over their work and be sympathetically respected as human beings. Instead, it then became old-fashioned and inflexible *managers* who are said to need education so that the energies of workers and the work group can be harnessed toward, instead of provoked against, higher productivity.

In fact, however, studies of "restriction of output" and other patterns of "counterproductive behavior" indicate anything but irrationality among workers. For example, when management pays workers on a "piece-work" basis (i.e., so much for every unit they produce), they usually have a maximum day's pay in mind, such that they have actually been known to reduce (or eliminate) the piece rate if workers' productivity levels put them over the maximum day rate. Understandably, under these conditions workers often restrict their output to a level which will earn them the equivalent of the underlying day rate (see Roy, 1969, and Eldridge, 1973). Similarly, Stanley Mathewson (1969:86) has noted that "the wage-earner . . . restricts his output as a means of postponing layoffs, steadying his employment, and stabilizing his earnings." Many wildcat strikes are (often successful) attempts to have fired workers reinstated or hazardous working conditions rectified. In the previously mentioned case of an autoworker lying bleeding on the floor, for example, it was a sit-down strike by his fellow workers which got the line shut down and the worker to safety. Also relevant here is the infamous "time-study" man. As one of the autoworkers Terkel (1972:120) interviewed complained, it is often simply not worth learning shortcuts in one's work, since "when you learn these shortcuts, all of a sudden time standards: he's gonna come around and he's gonna time your job." Given these conditions,

> The more settled a fellow gets, he quiets down. He'll set a pace. See, I set a pace. You just work so fast and you do just so much work. Because the more you do, the more they'll want you to do. If you start running, they'd expect you to do a little bit more. . . .

More collective responses to such conditions are the wildcat strikes which frequently occur when the speed of the assembly line is increased.

This is not to suggest that all forms of worker resistance are equally rational (Taylor and Walton, 1971). Many individualized acts of sabotage, for example, appear to be little more than "blind lashings out". Yet even these may halt production and provide much-needed relief, particularly for assembly-line workers, who in fact spend much of their working day hoping and praying that the line will break down. The same could be said of the intense conformity pressures which are often behind collective acts of resistance (e.g., see Rothlisberger and Dixon, 1964; Fried, 1973:173). Specifically, whereas newcomers are indeed likely to be coerced into the "deviant" ways of the work group (and there are usually no holds barred when it comes to "scabbing" during a strike), the old-timers usually have little choice but to enforce these norms, as newcomers themselves will often later admit (e.g., Terkel, 1972:522).

Note, however, that in the cases we have been examining "resistance" is a most appropriate term, for while some of the acts in question have temporarily modified managements' control, few of them have explicitly challenged it, fundamentally changed it, or even acknowledged it, and especially its basis in capitalism as a system. Even where restriction of output or wildcat strikes can be attributed to workers' explicit concern with wages relative to profits (e.g., Roy, 1969:xxv; Israel, 1971:225–226), the villain may still be assumed to be a particular company or supervisor rather than capitalism more generally.

Since trade unions usually organize workers well beyond particular workplaces, one might expect them to have carried the fight much further than these acts of subtle resistance or sporadic "guerilla warfare" and promoted levels of consciousness other than those of individualist rebellion and "factory" consciousness, as Huw Beynon (1973:98) has called it.

In the early stages of their development they often did just that. Nevertheless, in the present period the vast bulk of trans-plant activity has taken the form of waves of wildcat strikes which have occurred in spite of, rather than because of, the stance of trade union officials.

Some portion of this new-found timidity on the part of trade union officials can undoubtedly be attributed to the Millsian proposition that unions are bureaucratic organizations whose officials are as interested in their own power, wealth, and status as in fundamentally improving the lot of the rank and file.[9] However, rank-and-filers

themselves are notoriously poor meeting attenders, which is interpreted by many union officials as meaning that they regard their
unions as simply "service organizations" for higher wages and minimum job security, and, at least on the surface, much survey research
appears to support such a conclusion. In fact, some studies do seem
to indicate that union officials are more liberal than their rank and
file, and some suggest that many of the latter even share the "general
public's" distrust of trade unionism itself![10]

These two processes are probably dynamically related; that is, the
more "bent" union officials become, the less possibility of and interest in controlling their unions workers have. However, the more
apathetic rank-and-filers are, and the more they tend to reduce their
attachment to their unions to a "bread-and-butter," means-ends level,
the more bent officials can control them. Alternatively, officials who
really do want to mobilize the rank and file to fight more fundamental issues find it very difficult to do so. However, it is important
to try and sort out where each of these processes has come from
rather than attribute them simply to a Weberian-Michelsian "iron
law of oligarchy" (Michels, 1962).

Any such attempt will certainly have to incorporate the historical
fact that just as workers have been forced to "come to terms" with
their work individually, unions as organizations have had to (well,
understandably *felt* they have had to) come to terms with capitalism
as a system. The chief vehicle through which unions become institutionalized — that is, recognized as more or less legitimate and eventually "protected" by law — was and is the collective bargaining
agreement, into which employers would, and will, only enter when
the union concedes "the right of management to manage." The
"pruning down" of union demands to "bread-and-butter" and other
issues which do not directly challenge management's control has
therefore been more or less assured from the very beginning, and the
"Wobblies" and other contrasystem movements have been systematically and brutally smashed. Indeed, one suspects that for every
unorganized worker who disapproves of unions there are two who
are simply too intimidated to join one.[11]

By the same token, once this collective coming to terms has taken
place, alienating working conditions help assure the apathetic and
instrumental orientations of workers to their unions. Specifically,
management is left free to select workers (for example, married men
with children) who will be most likely to be compliant (Beynon,
1973; Serrin, 1973); workers with the most instrumental orientation
toward work preselect themselves for the most alienating jobs
(Goldthorpe et al., 1969; Beynon, 1973); and the hours, pace, and

routine of so many jobs is so physically and emotionally exhausting (and/or the pay so inadequate that workers must work overtime or moonlight anyway), that participation in unions and other "voluntary" associations, or even reading their literature, is often very difficult for rank-and-filers (Michels, 1962; Meissner, 1970; Serrin, 1973:227).[12]

Given these conditions, it is not difficult to see how, as Mills suggested, aspirations for nonalienating work have been lowered over the years. Indeed, there may even be workers who are not aware that their work is objectively alienating (Mills, 1970; Kern and Schumann, 1970), and even where they are aware of it, their low aspirations often limit the degree to which they are frustrated by its absence (Blum, 1953; Lane, 1962; Runciman, 1966). On the other hand, whereas this paints a rather grim picture, there have already been changes which may swing unions toward fighting alienation from work more seriously.

In the first place, with the recessions and spiralling inflation of recent years unions have not been able to "deliver the goods" on those demands which they *have* raised. Increases in the number of unofficial strikes have presumably resulted from these changes, and in the scramble of officials to catch up with their rank and file (perhaps through changes in leadership) many unions may become democratized and revitalized in general, and more concerned with alienating work in particular.

Second, long term changes in the work force have been taking place, and these changes may in turn affect the nature of worker-union relationships. In particular, there has been an increase in the proportion of young and more highly educated workers in the labor force, and their higher aspirations for fulfilling work are presumably behind their greater readiness to make other than bread-and-butter demands (Sheppard and Herrick, 1972; Aronowitz, 1973). At the same time, younger workers, having escaped (until very recently, at least) the security-seeking experiences of the Depression of the 30s (Broadfoot, 1975) and the leftist-phobic experiences of the McCarthy era, may well be more receptive to calls for democratic control of work.

CLASS AND CLASS CONSCIOUSNESS

With so many of workers' collective attempts to combat alienation "nipped in the bud," it is hardly surprising to find little organization on the class level. Instead, with various sectors of the class at best fighting for their own "slice of the pie" we find a myriad of specialized and sometimes conflicting interests within even blue-collar workers, most notably between the skilled and semi or unskilled, even within the same industry (e.g., Form, 1973), but also between industries, sectors of the economy, and geographical regions (Johnson, 1972; O'Connor, 1973). There is far from complete residential segregation or endogamous marriage by class (see the section entitled "Others"), nor are there always blatant differences in life-styles or values in line with class interests. Finally, peoples' subjective awareness of their class position is by no means synonymous with their objective class interest (Jackman and Jackman, 1973), and most are obviously not engaged in explicit, class-wide battles with the capitalist class.

This is the element of truth to the "classlessness" claim of mainstreamists (e.g., Brown, 1965:135). However, what they conveniently fail to mention is that the same is *not* true of the ruling class. As Mills noted, the ruling classes of North America and Western Europe consist of very small proportions of these populations, who not only own highly disproportionate shares of the means of production (Johnson, 1972; Zeitlin, 1974), but who in many ways can be legitimately referred to as interest "groups." That is, they frequently interact with each other in a variety of settings, often on a national basis, to the exclusion of most people from most other social categories, and their life-styles, values, and awareness of themselves as a group are similar and well developed (Porter, 1965; Domdoff, 1971). Given the existence of this elite class, we would be irresponsible to react to the evidence concerning the apparent absence of a developed working class (a class "for itself") by throwing out "the economic baby with the psychological bath." Rather, "if psychological feelings and political outlooks do not correspond to economic class, we must try to find out why . . ." (Mills, 1956:294).

Perhaps the first thing we should note is that even typical (attitudinal) measures of class consciousness, as inherently poor as they are, indicate that class consciousness is by no means as low as mainstreamists claim. For example, after surveying the residents of London, Ontario, by all accounts a very *status*-conscious city, James Rinehart and Ishmael Okraku (1974) discovered that fully 75 percent of blue-collar workers identified themselves as "working class." The percentage of people in this study *identifying* themselves as working class is roughly the same as one finds in national surveys of Canadians and Americans (Pineo and Goyder, 1973), nor has this percentage changed since World War II (Schreiber and Nygreen,

1970). Finally, at least some consciousness of *opposition* is evident in the sense of "them and us" which one finds among most North American (Gans, 1962; Leggett, 1968) as well as British workers (Hoggart, 1958). The problem, therefore, is less that of explaining the total *absence* of working class consciousness than why class identification and a crude sense of opposition have so seldomly been accompanied by a sense that the class structure affects one's *total* life and that the problem can only be solved by an *alternative* form of society (Mann, 1973:13).

Marcuse (1964) and other members of the Frankfurt School, the reader will recall from Chapter 3, essentially answered the question "Why doesn't a hungry man steal?" by arguing that (1) with the growth of capitalism he is in fact no longer hungry, and (2) with the new-found complications and stabilization of the system he can't see what needs stealing anyway. However, the shattering of "the myth of the happy worker" (Swados, 1962) and documentation of the high frequency of class identification require us to reject this particular answer. All one can say in its defence is that class consciousness is indeed higher (1) in those countries (France and Italy) which, it could be argued, are developed enough to have developed working classes but not so developed that capitalism has been able to deliver many of the economic and political goods workers aspire to (Mann, 1973), and (2) (sometimes) among those who are in a sense on the fringe of the system — that is, those who have recently come from rural living situations — who have presumably had considerable control over their working conditions, and those who are currently unemployed, whose secondary, means-ends attachments to the system have presumably been cut off (Hamilton, 1967; Leggett, 1968; Rinehart and Okraku, 1974).

On the other hand, whereas several studies seem to indicate that more highly paid workers are less class conscious (Leggett, 1968; Rinehart and Okraku, 1974), this is not always the case (Hamilton, 1967; 1972), and historically the relationship has often been the reverse, with skilled workers raising more demands which challenge capitalism (Mann, 1973:60). Furthermore, there is another problem with this particular explanation. Specifically, as Westergaard (1970), Israel (1971) and others have pointed out, the presence of a means-ends or instrumental orientation toward work and union does not necessarily assure low levels of militancy and class consciousness. Rather, when one's psychological links to work and society are so few, one's commitment to capitalism may be an extremely brittle one. Thus, the increased militancy of the past few years has presumably occurred precisely because the worsening state of the economy has prevented capitalism from "delivering the goods" so easily.

These considerations suggest that the Frankfurt School's position is at best seriously incomplete, and that we would do well to develop alternative explanations, to it, and perhaps to Marx's as well.

Marx's position, remember, was essentially that (1) workers will inevitably fight alienation collectively, and (2) their experiences during the fight will inevitably heighten their class consciousness. However, we have already seen that while workers do indeed fight, they often do not do so collectively, and those collective actions which occur are often circumvented by their unions as well as employers and the state. One suspects, therefore, that while the collective experiences of many workers do indeed make the oppressive nature of the system transparent, as Marx claimed, they may be as likely to promote a sense of fatalism as optimism in their collective strength. Certainly my own observations and discussions with workers are in line with such an explanation ("Yes, but there's nothing we can do about it," is the most common comment). However, it requires more systematic documentation.

One thing which can be said in its defence is that whereas traditionally British workers have been more class conscious than their North American counterparts, they have also been less militant (Edelman, 1969). Other evidence that participation in collective combat against capitalism need not greatly increase workers' consciousness is suggested by the results of a West German study by Michael Schumann and his associates (1971). These researchers compared coal, steel, and chemical workers who had participated in a wave of wildcat strikes in September of 1969 with those in the same industries who had not. Most of the relevant results are presented in Table 8.2.

If we can presume that the two sets of workers had roughly equal levels of class consciousness before the strike wave, we conclude that having participated in it has made them more class conscious. Thus those who had participated were more positive about their relations with their workmates and somewhat more likely to view their society in class terms. Furthermore, they were more impatient with their unions, somewhat less likely to restrict themselves to bread-and-butter issues, and in spite of (or perhaps because of) expecting class inequality to get worse in the future, they were more likely to say that they would participate in the next strike wave, even if their own union were against it. On the other hand, if these survey results have actually measured the effects of these different

TABLE 8.2
THE CLASS CONSCIOUSNESS OF STRIKING AND
NONSTRIKING GERMAN WORKERS (SCHUMANN ET AL., 1971)

INTERVIEW ITEMS	WORKERS IN STRUCK FIRMS	WORKERS IN FIRMS NOT STRUCK
1. Most important task of union is to achieve higher wages	56.5%	65.3%
2. Safety from unemployment is among top four tasks	34.5	19.0
3. Unions could obtain much more for workers	61.5	40.0
4. Society made up of "over" and "under" rather than equal groupings	62.5	54.5
5. Rich will get richer without everyone else's position getting better	27.5	11.0
6. Relations with workmates "very positive"	46.0	30.7
7. September strikes have given workers courage and made them conscious of wider goals	68.5	54.0
8. Would participate if happened again	81.0	46.5
9. Would do so even if their union were against it	75.6	54.5

experiences at all adequately, many of these effects are far from large.

Although we have no way of knowing for this particular case, whether even dramatic experiences such as those provided by militant wildcat strikes are particularly consciousness-raising probably depends upon, (1) the purposes behind such collective action, (2) the way in which workers' experiences in them are interpreted (Parkin, 1972; Mann, 1973), and (3) their degree of success. In this West German case the apparent sources of the strike wave were classic ones; that is, there was a downturn in that sector of the economy after a long period of "rising expectations," whereas the dip was not as marked for other industries, and compared with the wage increases of these latter workers, those in the struck industries had been low. These limited purposes may therefore also have limited the conclusions which workers drew from their success. Similarly, union officials finally caught up with their workers and helped end the strikes, and the interpretations they presumably provided workers of their activity as well as the limited success of the latter may also have limited the level of consciousness attained by the strikes.

POLITICS AND POLITICAL IDEOLOGY

One cannot say that there is no class basis whatsoever for Canadian politics, in that the majority of those who do vote for the New Democratic party are blue-collar workers, and especially those who identify themselves as working class, and the bulk of its support has come from the largest unions. Nevertheless, one also cannot say that open class conflict has often surfaced in official politics in recent years. If NDP governments have been voted in in several regions of the country, they look little different from other party governments, especially in their treatment of labor. A majority of blue-collar workers have never voted for the party on the national level; in fact, the proportion of Canadian workers who vote NDP is smaller than the proportion of U.S. workers who vote for the Democratic party (Alford, 1963).[13] Why, then, does class figure so relatively little?

Those who still espouse the deTocquevillean pluralist model take these facts to herald the demise of class conflict, which is happily said to have gone out with the Second World War, if not the century. Such a model, however, falls in ruins in the face of two well-established facts: (1) *blue-collar workers hardly participate at all in official politics* (voting, after all, does not indicate very much involvement, and workers do less of it anyway); and (2) *their sense of "political efficacy,"* of having any influence within the official political process, *is much lower than that of middle-to-high-status white-collar workers* (Milbraith, 1965; Pateman, 1970; VanLoon, 1970; Verba and Nie, 1972).

Those mainstreamists who have been brave and responsible enough to admit the existence of these facts, especially the first, have understandably been forced to revise the classical model. Low participation, they suggest (see Pateman's review, 1970), is inevitable, if not by human nature, as Michels would have it, then at least by the increasing scale and technical complexity of government. Given that this is the case, the interests of the "little people" are now said to be pushed by elite representatives. The low participation of their constituents, therefore, arises from the latters' interests having been so successfully represented by elite others. Indeed, some have gone so far as to refer to ours as a "politics of happiness."

The fly in this ointment, of course, is the *other* fact; that is, the low sense of political efficacy. If one is going to argue that the little people have a great deal of influence, then one must explain why they believe otherwise. In this regard, those who have stooped to do so have found the task painful indeed. What comes out is a political version of the aforementioned "irrational worker" conception. Rick VanLoon (1970:394), for example, suggests that because they lack the educational and other resources to actively participate in politics and therefore do not in fact do so, workers indeed have less effect upon government policies. Hence their feelings of political powerlessness are in part a consequence of their initial ignorance and in part a consequence of their failure to participate.

There is, of course, another explanation which is at least as plausible, and certainly less elitist. First, assume, as is indeed the case, that most of the population *want* to have "economic-class" issues of equality and the like processed through the political system, but that most of our wonderful elites, being themselves upper-middle class, do not, and do not provide viable parties and platforms for doing so (Hamilton, 1972; Ogmundson, 1976). Second, assume, again with rather clear evidence for doing so (e.g., Deaton, 1968; Miliband, 1973; Domdoff, 1971; Lewis, 1972), that the actual outcomes of political decision making in our society are oriented more toward the interest of capital than labor.[14] As in labor-management relations, therefore, it might seem pointless to workers to participate politically, and such feelings might well be *reinforced* rather than reduced if they *did* actually participate. Although the evidence for these latter steps is not airtight, it is persuasive.

Note first that *rather than being more ignorant of the actual outcomes of official political processes, workers are actually less so than their middle- and upper-class counterparts* (Form and Rytina, 1969; Mann, 1970). In the Rinehart and Okraku study, for example, the people interviewed were asked to choose which of two models, a pluralist or a Marxist, they thought best represented the reality of Canadian politics:

1. No one group really runs the government in this country. Instead, important decisions about national policy are made by a lot of different groups such as labor, religious, and educational groups, and so on. These groups influence all political parties, but no single group can dictate to the others, and each group is strong enough to protect its own interests.

2. Big businessmen really run the government in this country. The heads of the large corporations dominate the political parties. This means that things in Ottawa go pretty much the way the big businessmen want them to.

As can be seen in Table 8.3, blue-collar workers were much more likely than others to choose the Marxian model. They were also more likely to agree that government leaders "hardly care what people like myself think or want."

TABLE 8.3

	MODEL OF POLITICS	
OCCUPATIONAL GROUPING	PLURALIST	MARXIST
White collar	62.0%	38.0%
Blue collar	36.8	63.2

Source: Rinehart and Okraku (1974), "A Study of Class Consciousness." Reprinted from the Canadian Review of Sociology and Anthropology, Volume number 11.3, by permission of the author(s) and the publisher.

This suggests, therefore, that it is much less ignorance than a sense of *fatalism* which leads to the low participation by workers in interest groups and the official political process. In this regard, it is noteworthy that feelings of powerlessness have been shown to limit information seeking, political participation (Seeman, 1972a), and within-system protest activity (Gore and Rotter, 1963).

Second, note the considerable support for the second implication — that to participate is to become even more alienated (see also Cutler, 1973). Nelson (1968), for example, found that participation in associations like the chamber of commerce *increased* rather than decreased the likelihood that small businessmen would view their environment in general as threatening. Similarly, Rushing (1970:175) suggests that the farm owners he studied may have expressed more powerlessness than farm laborers because their greater organization and political involvement increased the likelihood of their "feeling the constraints of a bureaucratized society." Finally, Gilmour and Lamb (1975:63–65) report that the political alienation expressed by American youth was actually lower in the mid-sixties than that expressed by the rest of the population. This, of course, was the time when their participation in campaigns such as Eugene McCarthy's was at its highest. After 1968, however, presumably after the events surrounding the Democratic party's convention had indicated the futility of participation, this age group showed the steepest increase in political alienation. Also, while a large proportion (39 percent) of those members of the general U.S. population who are generally apathetic and did not participate in the 1972 election expressed extreme political alienation, a much larger proportion (66 percent) of those generally *interested* in politics, but who did not then participate, expressed such extreme alienation.

To be avoided, however, is any implication that knowledge of political outcomes and fatalism are equivalent to a fully developed class consciousness. Rather, a great deal of evidence points to extensive ideological inconsistencies within and between workers. For example, many are even ambivalent about the legitimacy of unionization and union support for nominally working-class parties (Parkin, 1972; Westergaard, 1970). Whereas blue-collar workers have been consistently more progressive on social welfare and other issues having to do with governmental redistribution of wealth and power than have white-collar people (Form and Rytina, 1969; Mann, 1970; Hamilton, 1972; Ogmundson, 1976), they have also been more conservative on civil liberties issues such as freedom of speech for Communists and other political dissenters (McClosky, 1964; Ransford, 1972; Davis, 1976).[15] The voting behavior of workers more generally tends to be more inconsistent across different but ideologically related issues and the same issue over time than is that of the rest of the population (Converse, 1963; McClosky, 1964).

The task of explaining such inconsistencies is an important one to which we shall return throughout the rest of the chapter. For the present, a number of reasonable suggestions can be noted. One, of course, is the general ideological hegemony of the capitalist class (Mann, 1970). Another is the highly fragmented life most workers lead, what with their workplace activities depoliticized and their political activities, where they exist, "declassified" (so to speak). This (and, perhaps, their relative lack of education) may explain the curious way in which workers often give lip service to the system's homilies but take a clear and unwavering class position when it comes to their concrete, everyday activities (Parkin, 1972; Westergaard, 1970). A third is the fact that more generally, workers have less opportunity to formulate and act upon general class-political issues, and that this is true collectively as well as individually may explain the lesser consensus among blue- than white-collar workers (Mann, 1970).

Aside from such inconsistencies, another matter concerning workers' ideology of cynicism and fatalism should be kept in mind. This is that such a stance, as Mills stressed, may limit class and revolutionary action as well as within-system participation. For example, Melvin Seeman (1972b) reports that those most likely to subsequently take an active part in the (nearly revolutionary?) events in France in 1968 were not those who felt *most* powerless, but those who felt *moderately* powerless!

Finally, however, what has been true until recently need not remain so. Thus, a good case can be made that the same downturn in the economy which has increased the frequency of wildcat strikes and other industrial protest may well have wide-ranging political consequences. This has been true to some extent in Quebec of late, and in the recent struggles against "wage-and-price" controls.

Others

In this section we shall see that people's everyday relationships with each other under capitalism go a long way toward explaining their relatively low level of class organization, consciousness, and ideology. We begin with the ways in which class conflicts of interest affect "interpersonal" relationships between people of *different* classes and then proceed to a discussion of relationships between people within the *same* class. As we shall see, one cannot understand either relationship adequately without the other.

CLASS-TO-CLASS, "FACE-TO-FACE"

In the section on "Work" we had occasion to examine the "commodity treatment" — management's use of workers as beasts of burden to be controlled, and, if their existence interferes with profit-making, to be dispensed with in the process. There are many other things about this means-ends orientation which should be noted. For one thing, this tendency for those of one class to *use* those of another is reciprocal; that is, if management uses workers simply for their labor power, workers use owner-managers simply for jobs (Marx, Capital *I*: 195). For another, it represents one of few "pull" factors in a relationship which is otherwise characterized by a great deal of *avoidance*, what was referred to in Chapter 3 as the "detachment" orientation.

The latter is evident in the very physical organization of the workplace. Managers and other salaried employees often have separate parking lots, entrances, elevators, and cafeterias, and offices physically separate from the shopfloor. They are also "protected" from workers by foremen, supervisors, and other "go-betweens" (Goffman, 1967:110). But it is also very evident in the fact that once beyond the workplace, where the classes are clearly dependent upon each other and must therefore interact to some minimum extent, they avoid each other even more: they are residentially segregated and their spouses and friends are heavily drawn from the same class (see Archibald, 1976c). When they do get together it is also likely to have instrumental overtones:

> You look up from your menu in an exclusive restaurant to see an unlikely couple enter. The woman is a strikingly attractive blonde in

> her late twenties. . . . She is smiling down at her escort, who is a short, balding man some fifteen years her elder, with small, beady eyes and protruding ears. . . . If you entertain the possibility that he is extremely rich . . ., the chances are good that you would be right. Both the beautiful woman and the wealthy man have something of value to offer one another. She can please him aesthetically, and, perhaps more importantly, she can enhance his esteem in the eyes of others. . . . He, in turn, can provide her with a standard of living that she would not otherwise be able to attain [Rubin, 1973:67–68].

This avoiding-using dialectic suggests that the class conflict of interest between them makes them *threatened* by each other — that they deliberately (although not necessarily consciously) keep the interaction between them to the minimum necessary to get the job of producing-exploiting-existing done.

This seems obvious in the case of workers, since their "superiors" have a great deal of control over their fortunes. Indeed, there is evidence to suggest that the threat is sufficient to affect workers' behavior well beyond the workplace. Hurwitz, Zander, and Hymovitch (1960) for example, found that low-status professionals in the mental health field (social workers and high school guidance counselors) were not more likely to like high-status professionals after discussing mental health in an experimental setting. However, they did tend to overestimate the extent to which "Highs" liked "Lows," which the authors themselves explain as a defensive "need, realistic in these discussion groups, to feel that relations with Highs are satisfactory and pleasant. . . ." In a second study (Gross and Doob, 1968), motorists behind a car whose driver deliberately failed to drive on after the traffic light turned green were much more likely to honk their horns if the car was a beat-up Ford than a flashy Chrysler (85 as opposed to 50 percent). In fact, two of the former even *hit* the Ford! Threat also seems evident in the *hostility* which workers do express when conditions are more favorable: in the lunch room and other "backstage" regions at work; when discussing those few members of the neighborhood who are of higher status (Young and Wilmott, 1960; Dobriner, 1963; Lorimer and Phillips, 1971).

But threat is also likely to be experienced by owner-managers and other privileged people, for whereas their privileges depend upon maintaining control over workers, such control is far from always assured. Indeed, as Goffman (Goffman, 1967:83) has noted, the privileged must be extremely careful not to provide the underprivileged with any information which might bring the legitimacy of the status quo into question. That Highs are indeed threatened by Lows can be seen in the results of several series of studies.

For example, in a study of supervisors in five different light manufacturing companies, David Kipnis and his associates (Kipnis and Cosentino, 1969:465; Goodstadt and Kipnis, 1970) found that as the number of workers they had to supervise increased, supervisors decreased the amount of time they had to spend with "problem" workers by simply giving them official warnings. However, in a subsequent simulation with college students these researchers also found that the larger the work group, the less likely "supervisors" were to correct nonproblem "workers." Presumably, when there are more workers present the threat of rebellion and the severity of its consequences are greater, such that supervisors exercise more caution so as not to provoke it.

In a second series certain features of the class structure were simulated experimentally by giving one team of working-class boys the exclusive right to do such things as jump on members of the other (Thibaut, 1950), or distinguishing between the work of teams of college students in terms very similar to the manual/nonmanual distinction (Kelley, 1960). The researchers attributed the fact that Lows communicated more to Highs, and especially more criticism of their own team's work, than Highs communicated to Lows to the insecurity of Highs. That is, they were embarrassed at having been arbitrarily assigned higher status than those of similar status outside the laboratory, and fearful of losing their tenuous position. Conversely, in another study Zander et al. (1959) found that the more power a psychiatrist perceived himself to have over psychologists and social workers, the more contact he reported having and desiring to have with them.

Finally, the hostility of workers toward owners-managers is reciprocated by the latter, and this hostility appears to vary according to the distance workers maintain from them. In their study of an English middle-class suburb into which working-class families were moving, for example, Wilmott and Young (1960:5-6) found that the large numbers of middle-class people leaving the district tended to imply threats to their status (e.g., "The better class of people," as one man put it, "are moving further afield.") as well as the property value of their homes as reasons for leaving.

That "individuals" of different classes are so threatened by each other may partially explain a curious fact mentioned in the "Work" section; that is, that many workers appear to want the very rules which so often work against them. A reasonable explanation is that these workers "want" these rules not out of a love of rules as such (for more on such a claim see the "Self" section), but because such rules make the interaction with threatening others more predictable, and hence less threatening. Indeed, as Goffman (1961:128) has noted, strict conformity to the rules can provide both certain secondary benefits and a more secure position from which to express class hostility. Specifically, the more closely one follows the rules, the more justified one feels in claiming to oneself and others that "That really wasn't me; my true feelings weren't expressed by my actions." If one replies to a distasteful directive with "Yes, *sir!*" the boss might answer with something of the order of "Don't get lippy," but he would do so only at the risk of more open rebellion.

The latter fact points to the other side of the coin: that those of high class, being threatened as well, are also very concerned with predictability in spite of their greater power to withstand chaos. This is suggested by the results of a study by Harold Gerard (1957), where even subjects who thought of themselves as "the boss" gave fewer directions to other subjects when they had not been closely coached by the experimenter. It is also suggested by management rule books, which clearly state that it is more effective to manage by reward than punishment, since the latter is more likely to provoke rebellion and hence remove the interaction from management's control.

That threat and a concern with predictability are mutual probably goes a long way toward explaining the emergence and persistence of the intricate rituals of class protocol. Some of these are both blatant and blatantly under management's control. I speak here of the well-established fact that communication and influence patterns, beyond as well as within the workplace, are heavily "top down" (see Berger et al., 1972; Archibald, 1976c), and that the same is true for expressions of familiarity:

> In the research hospital, doctors tended to call nurses by their first names, while nurses responded with "polite" or "formal" address. Similarly, in American business organizations the boss may thoughtfully ask the elevator man how his children are, but this entrance into another's life may be blocked to the elevator man, who can appreciate the concern but not return it [Goffman, 1967:64].

Another way of putting it would be to say that *the typical patterns of control-purposiveness are asymmetrical.* Other patterns, however, are much more subtle.

For example, in attempting to explain why one sometimes finds more bottom-up than top-down communication, Brewer (1971) discovered that insurance underwriters, being more highly educated and knowledgeable about their jobs than their immediate supervisors, are permitted to communicate upwards because supervisors have little to communicate down, and because any such communication would probably be strongly resented. Goffman has documented numerous other patterns of "repressive tolerance," to borrow a term from Marcuse. Management, he suggests, on occasion feigns informality as a social control mechanism (Goffman, 1967:65; 1959:199), with this tactic sometimes even verging on surrogate rebellion. "The 'good guy' informality of the surgeon," he suggests (1961:131), "can give his subordinates a feeling that they are not the sort to tolerate strict subordination, that in fact the surgeon must see this and has adjusted himself accordingly, yet this is, of course, a vicarious rebelliousness carried out principally by the very agency against which one would ordinarily rebel."

If the preceding account of interclass relations is thoroughly out of whack with most treatments, it is because the latter use, not an alienation model, but one or another version of the Exchange-Functionalist theory of stratification. There it is usually presumed that workers agree that high-status persons deserve their status, and therefore conform or otherwise defer voluntarily (see Archibald, 1976c).

I certainly do not mean to imply here that this never occurs, even with class relations in the workplace. Indeed, there is reason to believe that many workers will subscribe to the mainstream model.[16] The ruling class, after all, aided by workers' own adherence to social distance rules, often does a masterful job of controlling information about itself, such that, for example, it would not be surprising if owners-managers come to be regarded as such because they are leaders, rather than leaders because they happen to be owners or managers (Marx, Capital *I*:314–315). In this regard, the results of some experiments (Reicken, 1958) suggest that those who talk the most tend to be attributed the best ideas, even when these ideas are objectively identical to those of other group members!

However, it is very important to remember that the conditions of equality and freedom which usually obtain in small informal groups (from which most of the data supporting mainstream claims are drawn) simply are not met when *classes* meet. Rather, as Blau (1964:210), himself an Exchange Theorist, notes,

> Although managerial authority in organizations contains important leadership elements, *its distinctive characteristic*, which differentiates it from informal leadership, is that it is rooted in the *formal powers and sanctions* the organization bestows upon managers. Their official position and sanctioning power provide managers with tools that make it easy, *even for those with only moderate leadership qualities*, to broaden the scope of the limited authority initially invested in them through the employment contract . . . [my emphases].

The dangers of generalizing from the former to the latter conditions are strikingly evident in mainstream texts. For example, consider Homans' claim (1974:81), later reiterated by Secord and Backman (1974:295), that the direction of communication flow in a status structure is bottom up rather than top down. The evidence invoked for this claim is usually Blau's study of work groups in a government bureaucracy (Blau, 1955), where low-status members tended to ask high-status members for advice rather than vice versa, and the Thibaut (1950) and Kelley (1960) experiments where low-status members communicated more to Highs than the latter did to Lows. Yet in the Blau case Highs have presumably received their status in the first place from their superior advice, and from this alone. Under such circumstances Homans is probably correct that they avoid Lows because any symbolic indications of dependence upon Lows might lower their status, whereas Lows clearly have both an interest in approaching Highs and not much to lose by doing so. But as we have seen, neither the same conditions *nor the same direction of communication flow* holds in the case of class and formal status structures. Similarly, whereas Secord and Backman take Thibaut and Kelley's experimental situations to be typical of stratified structures in general, we noted earlier that the similar class backgrounds between Highs and Lows and the swift "rags to riches" assent of Highs could not have helped but make Highs particularly timid and Lows particularly bold.

CLASS WITHIN CLASS: PERSON-TO-PERSON OR WINDOW-TO-WINDOW?

If it seems obvious that people in different classes are alienated from each other, it is much less clear that this is true of their relationships with others in the *same* class. Nor is it clear that Marx's theory predicts that they necessarily will be. Thus he did claim that each person in a capitalist society tends to "view the other in accordance with the standard and the relationship in which he finds himself as a worker" (Marx, 1975, 3:278). This presumably means that because one is in competition with others for subsistence, one tends to treat them as commodities; that is, in a means-ends manner (see especially Ollman, 1971:209–211). Yet remember that Marx also claimed that working-class people would overcome much of their alienation from each other in the process of fighting capitalism.

We do know that there are certain senses in which one might consider (blue-collar) working-class people to be more alienated from each other than middle-class people are from each other. Thus, on the average, blue-collar workers are less likely to interact with other workers at work than are middle- and upper-status–white-collar workers. Since blue-collar workers are more likely to work with physical technologies which limit interaction and social technologies which preclude officially sanctioned consultation and collective decision making, this fact is hardly surprising. Yet the reader may be surprised to learn that blue-collar workers are also less likely to interact with their workmates after work (Blum, 1964; Goldthorpe et al., 1969; Fried, 1973). Furthermore, in addition to belonging to fewer voluntary associations, which provide one important arena in which socializing can take place, blue-collar workers report somewhat less interaction with friends. Indeed, they even report having fewer friends! (See Blum, 1964; Bradburn and Caplovitz, 1965; Tomeh, 1967; Phillips, 1969.) Finally, on the average, blue-collar husbands and wives also interact less with each other than do white-collar spouses (Komarovsky, 1967; Fried, 1973).

If these facts imply greater detachment among blue-collar workers, others could be construed to imply class differences in the quality of interaction. Goldthorpe et al. (1969:103), for example, claim that the workers they studied tended not to interact with their workmates after work because they oriented toward them in a means-ends manner; that is, that through union organization, workmates were mainly means towards protecting and enhancing economic interests. Similarly, the fact that blue-collar workers tend to pursue relationships with relatives and neighbours more than workmates, whereas white-collar workers do the reverse, is sometimes interpreted to mean that the former's relationships are chosen more for the mutual aid in job finding and support during unemployment, childcare, and sickness that they provide than for the common interests and intrinsic attraction that one usually associates with friendship.

Others stress the greater conformity pressures that presumably characterize the "close-knit", typically working class, "network" of relationships (where most of the people with whom one socializes know each other), in effect arguing that because of such pressures individuals in such networks have less control-purposiveness over their own activity. (The similarity to Durkheim's "mechanical solidarity" is often explicitly noted.) Bott (1971) characterizes the gossip in such networks as oppressive, and Blum (1964) suggests that fear of violating the highly agreed upon norms in such networks keeps working-class people from cultivating a greater number and variety of friends. Similarly, Gans (1962) and Bernstein (1973) have claimed that because individuals in the network are so similar in occupation and kinship, they develop less role-taking skills and individuality, which in turn hinders the effective communication of abstract ideas and personal feelings. Any claim that communication *in general* is less effective among working-class than middle-class people appears to have been decisively refuted (see especially Labov, 1972), but there is evidence that working-class people have more difficulty communicating abstract ideas (Bernstein, 1973; Strauss, 1968; Tallman and Miller, 1974).

Finally, one is more likely to find overt *hostility* and violence towards others in one's own class among workers than among middle-class people. The greater frequency of "crimes of violence" is one indication, but one tends to find a greater stress upon physical toughness among working-class people more generally (Cohen and Hodges, 1963). One is reminded, for example, of the incredibly brutal fights in Toronto's Cabbagetown of which Juan Butler (1970) has written.

Yet, for all these indications of greater alienation from others among working-class people, any such conclusion must be highly qualified, in that *some class differences represent more qualitatively different interaction patterns than simply quantitative differences on a single dimension of interaction.*

Perhaps the first thing to consider here is that the quantity and quality of interaction need not be related in a one-to-one manner. Form (1973), for example, reports only a weak relationship between the two for autoworkers. Indeed, Fried (1973:96) follows Hoggart in claiming that the lower number and range of people with whom working-class people typically interact actually increases solidarity and intimacy:

> If we want to capture something of the essence of working-class life in . . . a phrase, we must say that it is "dense and concrete," a life whose main stress is on the intimate, the sensory, the detailed and the personal . . . [Hoggart, 1958:105].

Similarly, Bott (1971) has suggested that while blue-collar husbands and wives are more likely to move within separate networks and hence see relatively little of each other, this is often regarded as natural, with each spouse deriving adequate satisfaction from his or her respective network.

Another working-class interaction pattern which can be easily misconstrued is the relative absence of having nonkin friends or neighbours "in for dinner." While this trend is marked, it must be considered in light of the fact that working-class men often meet in a local pub or corner store instead of individuals' homes, and that their wives socialize on the street or while shopping. Similarly, after studying a long-standing, working-class community Herbert Gans (1962:39, 75) claims that working-class relations with kin and neighbours are at least as inter*personal* as middle-class relations with nonlocal, nonkin friends, in that

> The rules of selection—which are informal and unstated—are based less on closeness of kinship ties than on compatibility. . . . Neighbours also may be included in the group if they are friends, but they are not eligible merely because they live next door.

Finally, many question that the greater conformity pressures in close-knit, working-class networks actually represent, on balance, greater alienation of individual members. Hoggart (1958:85, 90–91), for example, suggests that the "extensive and sometimes harsh pressure to conform" mainly concerns class solidarity itself. That is, there is great intolerance of snobbishness or, for that matter, any individual behavior disruptive of group solidarity. Yet there may actually be greater tolerance for such activities as prostitution or suicide that working-class people sometimes engage in to adapt to their disadvantaged situation. In this regard it is interesting that in the quasi-experiment from which Fried (1973:197) concludes that working-class people are more conformist, people were asked to predict what they would do if they disagreed with the decision of fellow workers to strike. Quite aside from the fact that such a situation would be completely hypothetical and indeed, perhaps even contradictory to their own class interests for many of the middle-class people who were asked this question, it may simply be one where working-class conformity is, understandably, exceptionally high.

Gans (1962:40–41, 80–89) approaches this issue from a somewhat different direction. He argues in the first place that whereas middle-class people have jobs and a general class position which permit greater individuality, working-class people can only derive and express their individual identity through interaction in close-knit peer groups. In this sense, therefore, the solidarity underlying the conformity pressures of such groups is liberating rather than confining. Second, he suggests that whereas "West Enders also regulate their conduct by involuntary conformity of the type expressed in the phrase 'what will the neighbours think,' . . . as so much of life is based on routine, there is little incentive for nonconforming behavior. Thus most conformity is quite voluntary." On these grounds

Gans labels the view of peer group life "as a prison for its member," a "caricature."

A second general qualification in assessing the relative alienation of working-class people is that *general differences are often small, and rather than clear-cut general differences, one often finds a great deal of variation within the working class, particularly by skill level, industry, and the nature of the community in which workers reside.*

Thus skilled workers, although often less than professional white-collar workers, tend to have more solidary relationships with work-mates on and off the job than do semi and unskilled workers (Meissner, 1970; Form, 1973). Conversely, unskilled workers may be more threatened by people in general, as suggested by Cohen and Hodges' (1963:316) finding that they were more likely to agree with such statements as "I am not the sort of person who enjoys starting a conversation with strangers on a bus or train." Similarly, other studies besides Blauner's indicate that the nature of the technology with which workers work can markedly affect their relationships with workmates (Meissner, 1970; Form, 1972; 1973). Finally, solidary interaction with workmates is likely to be less in small workplaces where the situation of the worker typically "brings him into direct association with his employer or other middle-class influentials and hinders him from forming strong attachments to workers in a similar market situation to his own" (Lockwood, 1968:103–104).

According to David Lockwood (1968), whether workers form solidary relationships with workmates and others more generally also varies considerably with the community in which they live. Thus in stable working-class communities, especially in single-industry cities, but also where peoples' workplaces are near their residences more generally, relations with workmates are more likely to carry over after work. However, Lockwood claims that working-class solidarity in this type of community, which may be rapidly declining in numbers, is in marked contrast to that in at least two others. Thus the "deferential" worker in a small factory with a paternalistic boss is also likely to live in a small, mixed-class rural community where everyone knows everyone else and more or less agrees upon each other's status. Thus his or her nonwork relations tend to reinforce rather than compensate for his/her alienated relationships with workmates at work. Similarly, the "privatized" worker is typically one who may work in a large factory, but who also resides in a transient urban area, far from those he or she works with and the close-knit networks of the traditional working-class community.

Michael Young and Peter Wilmott (1960:161–163) provide a vivid picture of the contrast between relationships in these two types of communities. Thus whereas in Bethnal Green, a traditional working-class district of London, England, male workers typically partake of the "conversation, warmth and merriment of the beer-shop, where they can take their ease among their 'mates' and are judged more in the round, as a person,"

> How different is Greenleigh. . . . Where nearly everyone is a stranger, there is no means of uncovering personality. People cannot be judged by their personal characteristics . . . Judgments must therefore rest on the trappings of the man rather than on the man himself. If people have nothing else to go by, they judge from his appearance, his house, or even his Minimotor. . . . People in Greenleigh want to get on in the light of these simple standards, and they are liable to be anxious about it just because they no longer belong to small local groups. *Their relationships are window to window, not face to face* [my emphases].

Such community differences may account for a number of apparently contradictory sets of findings that have been reported for within-class interaction differences (see also Shostak, 1969, and Bott, 1971). Thus, for example, the high degree of solidarity that Fried (1973) reports occurs in a traditional working-class community, whereas the privatization that Goldthorpe et al. (1969) report does not. Similarly, Litwak and Szelenyi (1969) find only a few, weak differences in help giving favouring blue-collar workers and Wellman et al. (1971) find few at all, but unlike Fried (1973:114), who reports high levels of help giving among blue-collar workers, both sets of researchers studied transient, mixed-class communities.

In summary, some of what might be construed to be greater alienation from others among blue-collar workers does *not* represent true alienation. Clearly, however, some of this seemingly greater alienation *is* bona fide alienation. How do we explain the latter? Marx's theory clearly seems to *describe* this greater alienation, but can it actually *explain* it? The facts indicate that it can, but that the social-psychological processes we usually associate with the theory tell only part of the story.

The obvious truth of the theory is this: the conditions of the capitalist labor market and division of labor often lead workers to compete with each other, and this conflict of interests produces the avoiding and using tendencies we have just examined. One worker, for example, has suggested that "It would be messy to get to be friends with guys you're supposed to be . . . you're supposed to perform against"; another, that "You're there to get what you can for yourself" (Sennett and Cobb, 1972:104–105). Experimental evidence also attests to the disruptive effects mobility aspirations have upon "workers' " relations with each other. In the Kelley (1960) experiment, for example, half of the Low groups were led to believe that they might later join the High group, and the cohesiveness of these groups was considerably less than that of the groups whose members did not expect to move up. However, it is not clear how frequently such competitive conditions actually occur and precisely how they are distributed across the class structure.

Typically, of course, given their presumedly higher status consciousness, we are more likely to attribute competitive conditions to white- than blue-collar work. However, while such a hierarchical, "one-rung-up-the-ladder" consciousness may indeed be more frequent among white-collar workers (e.g., see Whyte, 1957:177), blue-collar workers have at least been more likely to have to compete with each other for *any job at all*. This has been especially true during economic crises, where the ranks of the "reserve army of the unemployed" have been particularly large (the Depression of the 30s often set even friend against friend (Broadfoot, 1975:215)), but it bears remembering that at least until very recently, blue-collar workers have had much higher rates of unemployment. Certain sectors of the class — most notably, those, and especially those in the skilled trades, in the monopoly sector of the economy — have been less subjected to these conditions, but they represent a minority of the class as a whole. Furthermore, even where competition does not continuously exist, employers often manufacture it on those occasions where "divide-and-rule" tactics are especially useful; hence, the frequent use of strikebreakers ("scabs").

As well as producing alienation from others through competition, however, capitalism affects workers' relationships with each other through many other routes. Thus, as Marx noted, the fact that their individual contracts with their employers leads them to feel that they are related to each other only through Capital is likely to limit the solidarity among them. The structure of work itself has similar effects; that is, because workers do not collectively plan and oversee production, because they are physically and psychologically separated by the fragmentation and automation of work, they are denied the opportunity to develop solidarity on a truly collective basis (Aronowitz, 1973:417).

Both competition- and noncompetition-derived alienation from others, it should be noted, extend well beyond the workplace. We have already seen hints of this in the previous description of workers' alienation from each other; for example, in the competitive *consumption* relations in Greenleigh (Young and Wilmott, 1960). This alienation beyond the workplace occurs through a wide variety of processes. Most of them, however, in one way or another derive from the structure of capitalism, and especially its work structure. Indeed, as noted at the beginning of the chapter, the very separation of the nonwork from the work sphere is in good part unique to capitalism (Zaretsky, 1973). Specifically, this separation accompanied the transfer of production from entire communities and extended families to factories controlled by capitalists. The subsequent development and glorification of the nuclear family and personal or "private" life cannot be adequately understood without considering the interaction between this separation itself and the development of alienation at and from work.

The latter point provides a good place to begin a discussion of alienation beyond the workplace, because *much of the peculiar quality of working-class socializing appears to derive from workers' attempts to escape from and compensate for alienating relations with others at work.* Thus, its "close-knit" quality would seem to represent a "mutual insurance scheme" (Cohen and Hodges, 1963:307–9), not just "against" unemployment, industrial accidents, and the lack of time and money to care for children, but against one's alienating relationships with others. These others are especially those in other classes, in that most of those who have studied working-class communities note that fear and hostility toward "them" (Hoggart, 1958), the "external" (Bott, 1971) or "outside" world (Gans, 1962), seem to be behind the local peer group orientation of working-class people (Fried, 1973), but it is probably also true of those with whom one works and is often forced to compete. *However, one of the meanest tragedies of capitalism is that those who have been most driven to cultivate personalized relations outside of work also have the greatest obstacles to overcome in order to do so.*

In the first place, the unemployment to which workers are more subject has been found to disrupt their interpersonal relationships. In a classic study from the 1930s, for example, Wight Bakke (1969) found a marked drop in most types of socializing with unemployment. Many of the reasons for this were very straightforward. As Bakke himself (1969:17) put it, "The plain fact is that the decline in recreation results from a decline in income. . . ," and the people he interviewed indicated why this was the case: socializing is usually "greased" with food and drink, outings which provide interesting topics of conversation, and so on, but these all require money.

Unemployment insurance has probably eased these particular effects of unemployment, but others much less so. I refer here particularly to the stigma associated with unemployment, a stigma which affects socializing in a myriad of different ways. Not being able to provide what Goffman calls the "sign-equipment" for socializing is itself likely to be demeaning, but more than this, the presence of employed friends and family continuously provides a negative reference point for oneself. Sometimes employed friends simply break off the relationship, but perhaps more typically, they unwittingly force the unemployed person into a demeaning position by, for example, saying, "Well, I'm glad it's you and not me!" However, simply being dependent upon others for favours has these demeaning connotations in our society. One of the workers Bakke (1969:11) interviewed, for example, said that "Even though they don't say nothing you know they wonder what's wrong with you."

Threat to self-esteem as well as a decrease in income is therefore behind the fact that "friendships between those who hold jobs and those who do not tend to break up." Nor is the worker's "mutual insurance scheme," his or her close-knit network, likely to provide a completely satisfactory "premium," since relationships between spouses and other relatives are also strained by unemployment, so much so that one is most likely to find the "unstable family situation" that social work and legal authorities complain so much about in precisely those sectors of the working class most susceptible to unemployment. Nor is there a complete return to normal patterns of socializing after reemployment (Pope, 1964). Nevertheless, close-knit relationships and greater experience in coping with unemployment may actually help "traditional" blue-collar workers deal with unemployment more successfully than white-collar workers. For example, Stuart Crysdale (1971) found that the decline in socializing among those "let go" in the transfer of an electrical equipment factory from St. Catharines to Toronto was greater among white- than blue-collar workers, although, of course, many more blue-collar workers were let go.

Given these effects of unemployment one can readily extrapolate the effects upon socializing of having a low income more generally (Goffman, 1959:123, 221–222; Tomeh, 1969:65; Phillips, 1969:114). Another obvious source of class differences in socializing is shift work. Try organizing a meeting of blue-collar workers and you quickly realize the profound effects this must have upon their socializing:

> Regularized sex relationships are often disrupted; ordinary family activities are often curtailed because the breadwinner is sleeping during the day; . . . family meals and ceremonials, often important to the social cohesion of the family, are sporadic. . . .
> Informal relationships—the visiting of friends and neighbours—are only slightly less curtailed . . . The lack of a predictable shift means

that for long periods it is often impossible to spend an evening with close friends in the same occupations. A respondent reported an attempt to organize a date with another couple for an evening of bridge, and it was a month and a half until the two men were free during the same evening, so that the four could get together [Lucas, 1971:159–160].

Unfortunately, shift work is one of the many aspects of capitalists' control over work that workers and union officials seldom question. Rather, as Lucas (1971:164) follows Mott et al. (1965:13) in observing, "The majority consider that it is an integral part of the work situation and accept it with fatalism and resignation."

More subtle ways in which the division of labour alienates workers from each other are suggested by the research of Martin Meissner (1970). He found that workers who were most constrained by their work (tied to a fixed workplace, paced by a machine, etc.) and isolated from others at work were also somewhat less likely to socialize on workdays. On days off those most constrained at work tended to make up this difference by more frequently visiting others and talking and drinking beer, but those who were most isolated at work still remained more isolated *after* work.

The first difference can be fairly simply explained: that is, those who are most constrained on the job require longer to recuperate off it. Similarly, the further finding that the most constrained compensate for the lost socializing on their off days also suggests that the previous difference does not have a profound motivational basis; that is, these workers are probably not psychologically alienated from others in the sense that they purposely avoid them more. But the finding that those who are more isolated at work remain so after work is more problematic. Meissner himself claims that those who do not interact at work do not keep up the social skills that socializing requires.

This may well be true, particularly given the fact, as noted earlier, that unskilled workers, those most likely to be constrained and isolated are most likely to fear meeting strangers, least likely to participate in voluntary organizations, and most desirous of reliable, predictable friends. Yet there may also be other motivational bases for these findings. In the first place, their isolation may prevent them from developing the solidary relationships with workmates that characterize traditional "proletarian" workers. Second, this isolation may lead them to associate "work" mainly with the work itself; that is, the relative absence of solidary relationships with workmates may deny them one of the proletarian's only rewards at work. These two conditions may then interact to produce a motivated avoidance of workmates; that is, in the absence of some more enduring basis for the relationship, to associate with workmates after work simply on the basis of work that one wants to avoid would only prolong the misery.

In fact, because the absence of solidarity on the job prevents frustration from being collectively vented against the employer, this frustration may be "displaced" towards other workers, including those in one's own family, the result being the hostility mentioned earlier:

> I work so damn hard and want to come home and sit down and lay around. But I gotta get it out. I want to be able to turn around to somebody and say, "Hey, fuck you." You know? (Laughs) The guy sitting next to me on the bus too. *Cause all day I wanted to tell my foreman to go fuck himself, but I can't.*
>
> So I find a guy in a tavern. To tell him that. And he tells me too. I've been in brawls. He's punching me and I'm punching him, because *we actually want to punch somebody else.* The most that'll happen is the bartender will bar us from the tavern. *But at work, you lose your job* [Terkel, 1972:3; my emphases].

This worker's self-psychoanalysis may be rare, but still other accounts allow us to draw the same conclusion without the same prompting from the subject. For example, each time the hero of Juan Butler's *Cabbagetown Diary* beats the hell out of a fellow slum resident, or even contemplates it, he becomes deathly afraid that his employer will hear about it and fire him from his job, which, incidentally, pays all of $60 a week (Butler, 1970:9). In other words, whereas this worker seems obsessed with the *consequences* for his job of aggression against fellow workers, the close association between the two may belie the fact that his alienating job and class position more generally *cause* most of this aggression in the first place.

Alienation from Others and the "Why Doesn't a Hungry Person Steal" Problem

We have already seen several ways in which alienation from others probably affects alienation from work; that is, on the one hand alienated relationships with those in *other* classes give work itself its most important alienated qualities, and on the other, alienated relationships with those in the *same* class may prevent one from deriving substitute satisfactions from the work realm. Before leaving the discussion of alienation from others, I would also like to draw some of the connections between it and alienation from the products of work.

In the first place, given how threatened working people are by the great amount of control that employers have over them, it is hardly surprising that so many of them have not yet unionized; that is, many of them are simply too afraid to. Similarly, the fact that employers' interpersonal control over their employees extends far beyond the workplace cannot help but have far-reaching political implications. Specifically, if people appear to be so concerned about honking their horn at a high-status driver, how much more concerned they must be about expressing antisystem politics (Miliband, 1973: 163)!

Second, if and when working people are also alienated from each other, their powerlessness vis-à-vis capitalists is increased in a large variety of ways. It means, on one hand, that many of the alienating aspects of everyday life go unchallenged or underchallenged. Similarly, whereas the "proletarian" worker interacts with his workmates after work and is likely to view management as foreign to the community, giving him a sense of the totality of class, "deferential" and "privatized" workers are hindered by the apparent discontinuity between work and nonwork life. Finally, in the absence of means for collectively interpreting information in one's own class interest, capitalists' cultural "hegemony" more generally may go unchallenged.

With regard to the latter point something should be said of the mass media, one of the indirect ways in which capitalists attempt to exert influence upon workers. Hoggart's thesis (1958) is that through encouraging consumerism and the loss of distinctively working-class symbols (such as language) and values, the media have been a major cause of the breakdown of traditional working-class culture. Much of its alleged success is attributed to its successful manipulation of that very culture, as, for example, when advertisers play upon the greater person-orientation of workers by exhorting them not to be different from the group. Similarly, Marcuse (1964) assigns great importance to the media: on the one hand, it creates false needs for consumerism which rising affluence then satisfies, while on the other it directly manipulates people's ideology in a conservative direction.

While the issue is difficult to settle empirically, it would appear that the effectiveness of the media has been greatly exaggerated. Certainly available evidence, thoroughly reviewed by Judith Agassi (1970), does not support the claim that workers in general are more susceptible to media influence. Nor does it appear that "consumerism" per se has a conservatizing effect upon workers' ideology (Gans, 1962:183). Finally, Gans (1962:187) also disputes the claim that the media directly modify workers' values. Instead, he claims, "West Enders accept themes that mirror their own values, and reject others as illustrating the immorality and dishonesty of the outside world." However, there are two reasons for believing that Hoggart and Marcuse are not completely "out in left field," so to speak.

In the first place, in a classic study of the effects of the mass media Elihu Katz and Paul Lazarsfeld (1955) discovered that rather than directly affecting individuals, the messages of the media were filtered through local "opinion leaders" who passed them on to those in their peer group. It is precisely this filtering process to which Gans (1962:194) attributes the weakness of the media's effects: West Enders preferred to get their local news from each other, and watching TV was a collective, debunking event. *Yet this presumes that workers are not alienated from each other. To the extent that their everyday lives are actually "deferentialized," or "privatized," they are presumably more open to the media's influence* (Lockwood, 1968:113).

Second, the media may more subtly affect workers' ideology through reinforcing existing ideological presumptions which, rather than simply originating with the capitalist class, workers themselves extrapolate from their own everyday experiences. For example, just as they are likely to conclude from the latter that trying to do away with capitalism is a losing battle, so the news conveys how the system seems to return to "normal" after even the most militant strikes and protests. Similarly, the media's presentation of life in supposedly "communist" societies probably does reinforce the belief that there is no suitable alternative system for which to fight.

Yet ideological influences per se, whether they derive from everyday interpersonal experiences or culture-promoting instructions and technologies, are probably not the major reason for the relatively low levels of workers' consciousness. To the contrary, most workers are very much aware of class relations in general and class domination of politics in particular, as we saw in the "Products" section. Rather, one suspects that *the alienation from others that many workers experience greatly reinforces their feeling that they are unable to change the system.* The underlying process is probably as follows: to successfully "buck the system" one needs a great deal of support from others. However, if one is not sure that one will actually get that support from fellow workers, perhaps simply because isolation deprives one of experiences that would develop trust, then some form of "coming to terms" is more likely than revolt. The apparent fact that "no one (besides me) is willing to do anything" then further confirms both the feeling that others cannot be trusted and the belief that (perhaps because others cannot be trusted) the system is immovable.

One can find illustrations of this process among workers themselves, but the validity of this reasoning is probably one of the best established facts in mainstream social psychology. That even a single dissenting model greatly increases the likelihood that a person will resist undesirable influence and revolt against authority, for example, has been demonstrated in many experiments besides Milgram's.[17] Similarly, the crucial role of anticipating support from others has been shown in a series of experiments designed to simulate revolutionary situations. In these experiments by Andrew Michener and his associates (1972) college student subjects in a game situation typically face a powerful leader who violates initial understandings about the distribution of collective winnings by hoarding most of them for himself. When given an opportunity to coalesce with another "worker" against the leader, many subjects do. However, Edward Lawler (1975:176) has shown that "dissatisfaction is not sufficient to engender coalitional responses—subordinates must also anticipate that others share their sentiments and will respond favorably to overtures regarding joint action."

Self

Given what we know about the everyday lives of people in different classes (or, more accurately, occupational groupings), what, if any, differences in orientation towards *themselves* might we expect?

SELF-DIRECTION VERSUS CONFORMITY

Melvin Kohn (1969) has suggested that since white-collar persons are likely to be less closely supervised, to work on "active" people or data rather than "passive" material products, and to have particular tasks which are complex and require them to make judgmental decisions, they will be more "self-directed" than blue-collar workers. That is, they will be more concerned with their own attitudes, intentions, and other *internal* states, and upon acting upon them (i.e., with *autonomy*). Conversely, blue-collar workers, being more subject to the power of others and less able to exercise reflective self-control, will be more concerned with their overt behavior and its objective consequences for others (i.e., with *external* states), and with *conformity* to these others. In Kohn's own words (1969:87), "Self-direction, in short, is consonant with an orientational system premised on the possibilities of accomplishing what one sets out to do; conformity, with an orientational system premised on the dangers of stepping out of line."

Unfortunately, most of the direct support Kohn and others (e.g., Coburn, 1973) have marshalled for this claim concerns how individuals relate, not to themselves, but to their children. Furthermore, the indicator of self-versus-conformity direction has been the choice of adjectives such as "curious" versus "clean" or "self-controlled" versus "obedient" to describe the kind of person they would like their child to be like. However, there does seem to be a consistent, if often small, difference between occupational groupings, and the relationship between the actual nature of specific parents' work and their child-training orientations is stronger than that between the latter and occupational grouping. Moreover, other studies with more behavioral measures of orientation indicate parallel differences.

Robert Zajonc and David Wolfe (1963), for example, found that the belief structure of employees in a large business became both more differentiated and more organized, the higher the employee was in the authority hierarchy. Since an earlier study (Zajonc, 1960) clearly shows that more complex and organized inner states come from having to *act* upon them, it is reasonable to interpret the Zajonc and Wolfe results in Kohn's terms. Basil Bernstein (1973) and his associates (see Sigelman, 1972) have also discovered interesting language differences between occupational groupings which could be construed to indicate differing self-orientations. Specifically, working-class children often make less use of such internal, subjective pronouns as "I" and "we" and more of "he" or "she," "you," and "they." Similarly, their descriptions of people and events are often less taken up with intentions and more context bound, in the sense that they make more use of terms such as "you know." Bernstein argues that these features indicate that blue-collar workers are more likely to treat the listener as if s/he moves within the speaker's own inner circle, and hence less likely to role take (a complex internal process oriented toward others' internal states). Finally, after observing actual interaction between mothers of different strata and their 4-year-old children, Robert Hess (1970) and his associates found that middle-class mothers were more likely to use internal-dynamic and abstract-logical as opposed to conformity techniques in instructing their children in how to deal with such real-life problems as their first day at school and a number of experimental learning tasks.

One suspects that much of whatever truth there is to the highly uncomplimentary characterizations middle-class researchers draw of blue-collar workers derives from this apparent coming to terms with their everyday lives on the part of workers (especially "un-skilled" workers).

For example, claims regarding genetic class differences in *intelligence* are hopelessly bogged down in middle-class-biased instruments and research designs.[18] Similarly, many of the intelligence-related claims we have just examined cannot be legitimately attributed to class differences in native *ability*, genetic or otherwise. Thus, whereas at first Bernstein and his associates related language differences to abilities, their critics (Robinson, 1965; Lawton, 1968) have now demonstrated that working-class children clearly can, and will, when pressed, use the abstract language which middle-class children more typically use. Nevertheless, given that workers are not permitted to utilize their native intelligence in their working and political life, it should not be surprising if their minds, in Marx's term, sometimes appear "ruined" (see also Baran and Sweezy, 1966:317).

There may even be some truth to the (convenient) claim of main-streamists that such differences derive from class differences in child-training practices, in that, for example, in the Hess et al. studies differences in the latter were in turn correlated with the child's performance on both verbal IQ measures and the experimental concept-formation tasks, regardless of the mother's own IQ. How-ever, if one is to assign *blame* for such practices, as mainstreamists often implicitly do, one must consider the fact that, as Kohn notes (1969:201), blue-collar parents are simply (but, obviously, implicitly) preparing their children for a world which not only they, the parents themselves, know, but which the vast majority of these children, regardless of their native intelligence, will also be forced to know. Indeed, Kohn and Schooler (1973) have demonstrated that the job affects one's psychological functioning more generally much more than the latter affects what kind of job one will get.

Nor, of course, can all of children's present "intelligence" by any means be attributed simply to their *parents'* treatment of them (or the latters' genes). Thus, in one classic experiment Rosenthal and Jacobsen (1968) led teachers to believe that some of their pupils were particularly bright and would show a "spurt" in IQ over the next year, whereas others would not. Although the two groups were in fact matched on initial IQ, only the former pupils in fact evidenced the spurt. Later research by Meichenbaum et al. (1969) and others (see Rosenthal, 1974) suggests that teachers spend more time with and encourage more those students whom they already expect to do well, and working-class students are probably expected to do less well. The "tracking" system then institutionalizes the class-biased expectations of school authorities, and available research indicates that it too is a "self-fulfilling prophecy" (Rosenbaum, 1975).

In another favorite characterization, workers are said to have an "inability" to "*delay gratification,*" to control themselves enough to put off gratification until later, after one has allegedly accomplished other, better things and the rewards are more substantial. This claim and the research which purports to prove it is fraught with the same middle-class biases as the intelligence issue.[19] Nevertheless, working-class children *are* less likely to delay gratification, as indicated, for instance, by their greater tendency to choose a 10c chocolate bar now than a 25c bar next week (e.g., Cameron and Storm, 1965).

However, one cannot simply attribute the lesser delay of gratification to their parents' lack of self-control, since it is now *white* rather than blue-collar parents who are more permissive (Bronfenbrenner, 1958)! Similarly, the pursuit of immediate gratification does not reflect a native *ability*, but an adaptation to situational circumstances and one's own powerlessness over them. Both of these claims are supported by an experiment (Seagull, cited in Miller, Riessmann, and Seagull, 1968) where middle-class children learned that the 25c chocolate bar might not in fact be delivered next week. Under these circumstances the middle-class children miraculously lost their "ability" to delay gratification.

Related to claims concerning delay of gratification are those of "*achievement motivation.*" That working-class children, at least, "have" less of it is well established. Furthermore, in a manner reminiscent of their parents' work orientations, their achievement motivation is aroused more by "material" than "symbolic" rewards, while the reverse is the case for their middle-class counterparts.[20] Some of this class difference can again be attributed to parents' socialization techniques (see Brown, 1965; Smith, 1968; Hess et al., 1970). However, some of this may itself be attributable to parents' self-other orientations; that is, working-class parents who are themselves pessimistic about the possibilities of accomplishing tasks and concerned that their children "keep their noses clean" may make fewer adventurous demands and show more irritation when those demands which are made are not met, as is suggested by the Hess et al. studies.

Certainly the *outcome* of the socialization process is consistent with such an interpretation. Specifically, contrary to the early claims of Hyman (1953) and others, working-class adults and adolescents do not *value* education and occupational mobility any less than middle-class persons; rather, they simply do not *expect* to be able to achieve them, and hence appear to have (largely realistically) lowered their aspirations for themselves (Han, 1969; Clark et al., 1975). Finally, those who have claimed that our school system itself is highly alienating are legion (e.g., Reimer, 1972).

At least as popular a characterization as the foregoing is that of "working class *authoritarianism*." Here workers are said to be more likely to harbor resentment toward authority figures, mainly because of the restrictive and harsh treatment they are alleged to have received at the hands of their parents. This resentment, however, having been both dangerous to express and guilt provoking, is said to surface in reverse forms. On the one hand there is slavish conformity to authority figures in general, on the other rigid, envious resentment toward those, especially of low status, who do *not* conform. (The latter may simply be different, through being members of a minority racial group, etc.).

Certainly workers score higher on typical measures of "authoritarianism," and authoritarianism in general has been related to restrictive and harsh child-training practices.[21] However, all of the pieces of the puzzle simply do not fit. First, working-class parents do not appear to be more restrictive and prone to use physical punishment enough (Erlanger, 1974) to account for most of the class difference in authoritarianism, or in such correlates as bigotry (McCord et al., 1960:721). Second, the authoritarianism scores of blue-collar workers are less closely related to "authoritarian" responses on other questions than is the case among nonmanuals (Miller and Riessman, 1961; Lipsitz, 1965; Fried, 1973).

These gaps in the argument lead one away from the above, largely Freudian, interpretation of "authoritarianism." This is not to suggest that working-class authoritarianism has no frustration/displacement-of-aggression component whatsoever. Indeed, as we noted in the previous section, there is every reason to believe that many workers are highly frustrated and highly aggressive, but forced to displace the latter. In keeping with such an argument, Lewis Lipsitz (1964:951) reports high degrees of punitiveness as well as fatalism among autoworkers on the assembly line. However, it is not necessary to assume, as Reich and the Frankfurt School as well as mainstreamists would have it, that this frustration and the authoritarian's typical ways of dealing with it arise in childhood (usually over issues of sexuality) rather than adulthood. Rather, all one need do is reflect upon the demands our system typically makes of blue-collar *adults,* as Cohen and Hodges (1963:320) have lucidly done:

> (a) They are formulated in relatively concrete terms: *"Do this"*—rather than in terms of broad goals, to be implemented in ways that commend themselves to his discretion. He is not expected, to the same degree as members of other strata, to "exercise judgment," which means to weigh and balance alternatives, consider the circumstances, and reconcile conflicting principles. (b) The demands are less likely to be justified or rationalized to him in terms of more ultimate goals or principles. The authority of those who issue the demands is supposed to be enough to legitimize them. (c) The alternatives, when confronted with these demands, are few: compliance or defiance or, in some cases, withdrawal.

Hence, what was true of the assembly-line workers in the Lipsitz study was much less true of autoworkers elsewhere in the plant. Similarly, Kohn (1969) and Coburn (1973) report significant correlations between authoritarianism and the amount of complexity in and control over work more generally, and Ransford (1972) reports a high correlation between workers' own feelings of powerlessness and their resentment of student protestors.

At the same time, a substantial portion of working-class "authoritarianism" probably does not have deep psychodynamic roots of *any* kind. Rather, it probably derives from the fact that blue-collar workers are (1) more likely to have recently come from rural background and (2) likely to have less formal education. These demographic characteristics would in turn provide them with (1) the conservatism of rural life, and (2) greater isolation from the recent liberalization of official ideology with regard to race relations, sex education in the schools, and so on. Supporting such an interpretation are a number of well-established facts. First, by far the best predictor of "authoritarian" beliefs is *neither* collar color *nor* childhood experiences, but formal education (Hyman and Sheatsley, 1954:91–96; Lipsitz, 1965). Second, agreement with authoritarian beliefs is higher among farmers than blue-collar workers, and in the Southern United States, long known for its "red-necks," blue-collar workers are often less authoritarian than their middle-class counterparts (Hamilton, 1972:432–452).

By way of summary, we might reflect upon what, if anything, these considerations have to do with alienation. That any such connection is a distant one should not surprise us, since these concepts have not in the least been inspired by the theory of alienation. Indeed, if Marx used the latter to lambast capitalism as a system, mainstreamists use the former to foist most of the system's ills upon workers' personalities. A moment's reflection reveals that such concepts even serve to explain away the class structure itself, in that the very position of blue-collar workers is attributed to their low intelligence, lack of self-control and ambition, and/or rigid and dangerous resentments.

Let us first concede that such traits undoubtedly have *some* "feedback effect" upon individuals' position in the occupational hierarchy. A child with low achievement motivation, after all, may well acquire less formal education. However, recall the strong evidence against making a great deal of class differences in personality: (1) such differences are not as large as is often implied, and (2) for most of these traits the direction of the relationship is more from class to personality than vice versa. Furthermore, to these facts should be added another: (3) most such personality traits only explain about 10 percent of the variation in overt behavior to begin with (Mischel, 1968)! Here again we see mainstreamists' voluntaristic presumptions at work, *in spite of* the fact that, ironically, (4) the very logic of the class structure is that it is "*upper-middle-class*" persons who will be much more able to act upon their personal predispositions! We have already seen this to be the case for authoritarianism, and one suspects that the same would be found for delay of gratification and achievement motivation.

With these provisos in mind, note that workers *do* appear to "find their conditions of life predetermined, and have their position in life and hence their personal development assigned to them by their class, thus becoming subsumed under it" (Marx and Engels, 1976, 5:77). Similarly, to act with relatively less self-reflective intelligence, to be less concerned with the future consequences of one's actions or one's own and others' autonomy, and/or to be less likely to initiate action in the first place, is (in effect) to be psychologically alienated from oneself. Finally, a substantial portion of these orientations has been shown to derive from workers' greater personal powerlessness in our capitalist system.

In effect, therefore, it might be legitimate to reconstruct the conceptualization of such personal predispositions as the above in terms of detachment from oneself (e.g., a relative lack of self-reflective intelligence), treating oneself as a means toward narrow ends (immediate gratification, low ambition, and authoritarianism), and *under* controlling oneself for one's *own* ends (immediate gratification and low ambition) but *over* controlling oneself for *others'* ends (authoritarianism). Given this apparent applicability of the theory to various personality orientations, let us consider several others, which, to be sure, often build upon these three dimensions of alienation, but which are more explicitly related to the fourth, "feelings" dimension. These are the feelings of powerlessness and "misery rather than well-being" of which Marx himself wrote, and the phenomena of "low self-esteem" and "mental illness" which have been identified since his time.

ITS OWN POWER VERSUS ITS OWN ESTRANGEMENT, WELL-BEING VERSUS MISERY

That blue-collar workers are more likely to feel personally powerless over their lives in general is a well-established fact. It is already implicit in the results of the research on the above personality traits, in that alleged measures of immediate gratification, low ambition, and authoritarianism often include such questions as "Planning only makes a person unhappy since your plans hardly ever work out anyway," "People cannot be trusted," and so on, but it is also true when such feelings are the major focus (Battle and Rotter, 1963; Seeman, 1972; Tudor, 1972; Shepard and Panko, 1974).

The same is true for feelings of misery as opposed to well-being, in that blue-collar workers rate themselves as less "happy" than white-collar workers do (Bradburn and Caplowitz, 1965; Cantril, 1965). Such feelings (and those of powerlessness) have been shown to derive from the poorer physical condition of workers (on the average, they are more subject to illness and die eight years sooner than white-collar workers![22]; Fried, 1973), their lower income (Bakke, 1969), their lesser control over their work (Kornhauser, 1965), and their lower and less satisfying contact with others (Bradburn and Caplovitz, 1965; Phillips, 1969).

Feelings of self-depreciation, or "low self-esteem," are in some respects feelings of misery whose object is more defined and concrete. Their obverse, feelings of self-worth, presumably derive from the two sources suggested by Cooley (see Chapter 6): (1) a sense of competence from having been able to control one's environment (and, in terms of Marx's theory, having been able to create with it through intrinsically involving activity), and (2) others' positive evaluations of one's accomplishments and one's person. Since most blue-collar workers, given their working conditions and low social status, are deprived of both sources of high self-esteem, it is hardly surprising that they are more likely to evidence low self-esteem:

> I'm just a meter reader. . . . A lot look down on us, I suppose. . . . There's no reason they should look down on me for that. . . I needed a job with regular hours because I've got two kids with muscular dystrophy. . . . That's why I'm a meter reader. At least, that's what I tell myself. Maybe the real reason is that I'm no good for anything else but reading meters. I'll never know, will I [Alderman, 1974:12]?

More generally, researchers at the Upjohn Institute (1973:35) claim to have found "an almost overwhelming sense of inferiority: the worker cannot talk proudly to his children about his job, and many workers feel that they must apologize for their status," and Sennett and Cobb (1972:182) report considerable self-doubt — the "hidden injury of class" after which their book is titled — among the workers they studied.

One suspects, with Fromm, Robert Lane (1962), and Sennett and Cobb, that this self-doubt is an important pivot around which much of workers' everyday lives revolves. Specifically, in Sennett and Cobb's (1972:94) paraphrase of an aerospace worker's comments on his daydreaming at *work*, "The more a person is on the receiving end of orders, . . . the more the person's got to think he or she is really somewhere else in order to keep up self-respect." On the question of why he is threatened and deferential in his interactions with upper-middle-class *others*, a house painter told one of them that:

> It's not you, you're all right—but see—um—whenever I'm with educated people, you know, or people who aren't my own kind—um—I feel like I'm making a fool of myself if I just act natural, you know? See, it's not so much how people treat you, it's feeling like you don't know what to do [Sennett and Cobb, 1972:115].

According to Lane (1962) and Sennett and Cobb (1972:147,135), this same self-doubt sets workers against each other by provoking a "contest for dignity," as evidenced, for example, by the bricklayer's reference to people on welfare and his own ideology of sacrifice: "I *work* for my money." Ironically, therefore, the class structure, the source of their self-doubt, is also its *product*, not only because workers are too divided amongst themselves to combat it collectively, but also because "they are not rebellious in the ordinary sense of the word; they are both angry and ambivalent about their right to be angry" (Sennett and Cobb, 1972:79).[23]

Perhaps more surprising is that more workers are not overwhelmed by such feelings. In this regard, several processes have been found to moderate the status-esteem relationship. For one, the status structure is not always transparent. Howard Kaplan (1971), for example, discovered that low status was less likely to lead to self-derogation when people are geographically and/or socially mobile, but more likely when they live in mixed-class ("deferential") communities and/or have lived in any one community for more than five years. For another, workers use various "ego defenses" to protect themselves. After studying a (very) small sample of American workers in the late 1950s, Robert Lane (1962:62–64) suggested that they tended to compare themselves with other workers rather than middle-class people ("insulation"), deny the importance of status distinctions by telling themselves that there is nothing more they can do ("resignation"), and/or assure themselves that their status will in fact improve.

More recently, William Faunce (1968) and Sennett and Cobb have greatly elaborated upon workers' use of "insulation" defenses, arguing that they tend to lower their aspirations for fulfilling work and instead emphasize the importance of job security, pay, and such nonwork matters as family relationships. Similarly, withdrawing affect from work and the competitive struggle for status in general are said to be very prevalent, the argument being, in the words of "Carl Dorian's uncle," that:

> See, if you care about something, you gonna get hurt like as not. . . .
> I don't let myself hope, I gotta hold back a lot of times from getting
> involved in how well things are going, you know, the job, what my
> kids are doing with themselves. . . . I don't like it—but I tell you, I get
> scared if I care too much . . . [Sennett and Cobb, 1972:217].

However, Sennett and Cobb maintain that there was little resignation among the workers they studied in the 1970s. Instead, they claim, workers are now more likely to defend themselves by pointing to the great personal sacrifices they have made — especially in terms of working overtime and having two jobs so that their families can have the modern conveniences and perhaps send the children to college — as evidence for their own personal worth. Nevertheless, some considerable measure of self-doubt is likely to remain, and if the Lane-Sennett analyses are correct, even those workers who express less self-doubt than others may be highly defensive. These two conditions may then promote two others.

In the first place, someone who doubts him/herself, and/or has withdrawn affect from his/her everyday activities, may well exhibit an exterior of toughness for fear of exposing him/herself. Similarly, someone whose self-respect rests mainly upon his/her claim to self-sacrifice may be particularly concerned that (1) the spouse and children for whom s/he is sacrificing acknowledge it and exchange deference in return, and that, (2) those who appear to have been able to avoid such sacrifices (for example, "welfare bums," college students, and racial minorities helped by "positive" discrimination) be denigrated. Put otherwise, whether or not it is valid to label as "authoritarian" someone who agrees that "an insult to your honour should not be forgotten" or that "the most important thing to teach children is absolute obedience to their parents," the dynamics behind such an orientation may be very different from those suggested by the hypothesis of "working-class authoritarianism." Specifically, "authoritarianism" among workers may be much less of a childhood-derived demand that all authority figures be obeyed than a "back-to-the-wall," "last-ditch" demand that one be respected as an adult (Sennett and Cobb, 1972:121–150, 158–159, 217–218).

Second, since someone who is "mentally ill" is usually thought of as being especially self-derogatory and/or defensive, we might well inquire as to the relationships among class, alienation and mental illness. Here Sennett and Cobb (1972:191–219) vehemently deny that the workers they studied were "on the edge of nervous collapse," and instead take the interesting position that it is precisely their defensive alienation which shields workers from going insane: "The more a man's actions are split up in his own mind the less chance he has of being overwhelmed as a whole." I would agree that many more workers would be driven to insanity if their alienation did not help them defend their self-respect; however, I also suspect that there is a great deal more to the class-alienation-insanity relationship.

Perhaps the first thing which strikes one in examining accounts of mental illness is the close parallel between *descriptions* of these states and psychological alienation (Becker, 1964). Martin Seligman (1975:45), for example, quotes this description of "reactive depression":

> Loss of interest, decrease in energy, inability to accomplish tasks, difficulty in concentration, and the erosion of motivation and ambition all combine to impair efficient functioning. For many depressives the first signs of illness are in the area of their increasing inability to cope with their work and responsibility. . . .

Similarly, of "schizophrenia," another "psychosis," R. D. Laing (1965:42) has written that:

> The individual in the ordinary circumstances of living may feel more
> unreal than real; in a literal sense, more dead than alive; precariously
> differentiated from the rest of the world, so that his identity and
> autonomy are always in question. He may lack the experience of his
> own temporal continuity. He may not possess an overriding sense of
> personal consistency or cohesiveness. . . . He may feel more insubstan-
> tial than substantial, and unable to assume that the stuff he is made of
> is genuine, good, valuable. And he may feel his self as partially di-
> vorced from his body.

Yet the parallels are still more striking, for when one examines
some of the more popular *explanations* for such states, one also
discovers that they center around powerlessness.

Thus Seligman (1975) and his associates appear to have essentially
produced depressive passivity in the laboratory by making their
subjects helpless in the face of stress, first with dogs who were
unable to escape electric shock, and then with college students faced
with insoluble puzzles. In other experiments, furthermore, students
who were already depressed did not change their expectations for
success any more on tasks described as requiring skill than on those
requiring only chance, which suggests that "learned helplessness,"
as Seligman puts it, may in fact be at the root of depression in
real life.

Although schizophrenia is said to have much more of a genetic
component, here too learned helplessness has figured prominently
among the social causes suggested for the state. Of "James," for
example, Laing (1965:97) reports: "What happened was that he had
developed his subjectivity inwardly without daring to allow it objective expression." Similarly, Gregory Bateson (1972:214–217) describes
the "double bind" process so common in the backgrounds of schizophrenics as follows: "In a relationship, the most important of his life
and the model for all others, he is punished if he indicates love and
affection and punished if he does not; and his escape routes from the
situation, such as gaining support from others, are cut off." Under
these circumstances the severing of one's conception of others
and oneself from reality becomes understandable: "He would be
'punished' for learning to discriminate orders of messages accurately.
. . . To survive with her he must falsely discriminate his own internal
messages as well as falsely discriminate the messages of others."

By now the point of my apparent diversion into mental illness will
probably have become clear to the reader; that is, the learned helplessness of the "depressive" or "schizophrenic" is not unlike the
situation of the adult worker. More specifically, s/he is prevented
from being secure and freely expressing and controlling his/her
desires and abilities at work, in politics, with other people, and so

on, and then criticized as lazy, irresponsible, and unintelligent for his/her passivity and rigidity. S/he is usually prevented from withdrawing by, if nothing else, the scarcity of less alienating activities, but if s/he rebels against the circumstances which alienate, s/he is *also* severely punished! It is, in a nutshell, "enough to drive anyone crazy." *Does* it in fact drive workers crazy?

Here the data are very clear in at least one respect; that is, *the lower one's social status, the more likely one is to exhibit the symptoms of a variety of mental illnesses* — depression, and especially schizophrenia, being among them (Roman and Trice, 1967; Kohn, 1968; Dohrenwend and Dohrenwend, 1969). Since many of these "symptoms" are the alleged indications of the personality traits we have discussed previously in this section, one suspects that some portion of these class differences are simply the result of class-biased labelling procedures. Nevertheless, some of these symptoms clearly point to considerable psychological anguish, and others to the cessation of "normal" functioning, by working-class as well as middle-class standards of normality. Could one therefore legitimately regard some types of mental illness as "extreme cases" of psychological alienation, arising from, among other processes, those structural processes central to capitalism?

Two striking findings in the stress literature are the apparent lesser importance of childhood as compared to adulthood stresses, and the presence of marked class differences in stress in adulthood but not childhood (Langner and Michael, 1963:345; Kohn, 1968:167; Berkman, 1971). Some of the difference in favour of adulthood stresses may have arisen from the fact that the adults in question were asked to recall childhood stresses they may have encountered, yet in some of these studies the same persons' events and symptoms were measured at several different points in time (Dohrenwend and Dohrenwend, 1969:126–130; Myers et al., 1972), and the results of such studies confirm the importance of adulthood stresses in the occurrence of mental illness.

It is also interesting to note which adult stresses observed in these studies appear to be particularly important for one's mental health. Thus having "work worries," being dissatisfied with one's occupation, and being unemployed all figure prominently, as do having few friends and being in poor physical health. Furthermore, as suggested by the material reviewed previously in this chapter, blue-collar workers are more likely to have suffered from all of these different stresses (Langner and Michael, 1963).

Yet in most of these particular studies it is difficult to determine how important such factors are relative to other adulthood "stresses"

and whether, as many have claimed, "inadequate occupational performance" and unemployment might be better thought of as *effects*
rather than *causes* of mental illnesses. However, several more speci-
fically-focussed studies appear to have provided the answers.

Harvey Brenner (1973:ix), for example, has discovered that "insta-
bilities in the national economy have been the single most important
source of fluctuation in mental-hospital admissions or admission
rates." Using New York State hospitals' classification of their
patients as more or less capable of financially supporting themselves
rather than patients' occupations prior to admission as an indicator
of class status, he also found that it is the rates of admission for the
poorest persons which are most affected by increases in the level of
unemployment (Brenner, 1973:124–126). Individual-level data demon-
strating the importance of "the commodity treatment" have recently
been provided by Jay Turner (1973). Thus as can be seen in the left-
hand portion of Table 8.4, patients in public and private hospitals in

TABLE 8.4
SEVERITY OF SCHIZOPHRENIA BY EMPLOYMENT STATUS AND EMPLOYMENT STATUS BY SEVERITY OF SCHIZOPHRENIA (TURNER, 1973)

	MINIMAL-MILD	MODERATE-SEVERE		EM-PLOYED	UNEM-PLOYED
Employed	37.6%	62.4%	Minimal–mild	90.5%	9.5%
Unemployed	12.1	87.9	Moderate–severe	69.2	30.8

New York State who were unemployed during the six months
prior to being interviewed were much more likely to be rated as
moderately or severely schizophrenic. Furthermore, since prior
employment status predicts severity of illness much better than
severity of illness predicts employment status (for the latter results
see the right-hand portion of the table), employment status is presumably also much more of a cause than an effect of severity of
illness.

The consequences for one's mental health of a lack of control over
working conditions are more difficult to determine. Nevertheless,
here too the evidence is persuasive. Arthur Kornhauser (1965), for
example, constructed "mental health" scales for autoworkers in
Detroit. Since most of his subscales more or less measure subjective
alienation as we have conceived of it here, it is hardly surprising
that "mental health" was found to decrease with each descending
level of the skill hierarchy. Nevertheless, regardless of whether one

calls what these workers "had" alienation, mental illness, or both, one finding strikes one as particularly important; that is, this relationship was little affected by a host of childhood and other background characteristics, suggesting that these workers' "sickness" was contracted on more than brought to the job. One also notes that assembly-line workers doing repetitive work were much more likely than skilled workers to be rated as "frustrated, unhappy, maladjusted," and that, supporting the "social causation" as opposed to the "social selection" hypothesis, middle-aged workers were more likely than young workers to be so rated (Kornhauser, 1965:258). Still other research (Kohn, 1969:166–176; Kohn and Schooler, 1973; Coburn, 1973:52–56) suggests that being propertyless, closely supervised, time-pressured, and forced to work overtime are all likely to increase one's anxiety level and decrease one's psychological well-being more generally, even when the effects of one's background characteristics are held constant.

All told, therefore, even readily available evidence suggests that our society should have a package label attached to it: "Warning — social scientists have determined that capitalism is dangerous to your health." Yet one claim in particular in the standard literature — that blue-collar workers are more susceptible to mental illness, regardless of the level of stress they encounter — should be taken up before we leave the matter.

That this claim is true for many mental illnesses, and especially schizophrenia, is now beyond dispute (see Kohn, 1968; 1972). Similarly, there is good reason to suspect that some of the greater susceptibility to schizophrenia in particular is genetic (Kohn, op. cit.). Yet the latter can by no means totally explain even this latter difference. How, therefore, might one explain it?

At one point or another, most of the presumed class differences in personality discussed in this chapter have been invoked for this purpose. Of blue-collar workers, for example, Kohn (1968:166) has suggested that:

> Their occupational conditions and their limited education gear their thinking processes to the concrete and the habitual; their inexperience in dealing with the abstract may ill equip them to cope with ambiguity, uncertainty, and unpredictability; their mental processes are apt to be too gross and rigid when flexibility and subtlety are most required. Or, a related hypothesis, the lower- and working-class valuation of conformity to external authority, and disvaluation of self-direction, might cripple a man faced with the necessity of suddenly having to rely on himself in an uncertain situation where others cannot be relied on for guidance.

Langner and Michael (1963:438), on the other hand, give special prominence to workers' presumed lack of self-control and the suspiciousness of, and hostility toward, others which is supposed to result from it. Finally, Dohrenwend and Dohrenwend (1969:141–143), Ryan (1969:52–56), and others have suggested that feelings of powerlessness and low self-esteem make it more difficult for workers to combat stress.

Since blue-collar workers do not in fact lack self-control in general, as we have already seen, we can dispense with that particular explanation. Yet some of its weaker forms are more plausible. For instance, if class differences in "self-direction" include differences in introspectiveness, then blue-collar workers might have more difficulty rationalizing negative events which threaten their self-respect.[24] Alternatively, if we are correct that their low status has made many workers highly defensive (in effect, overly self-controlled), further stress might well prove to be "the last straw." Finally, Hollingshead and Redlich (1958) have suggested that blue-collar workers are more likely to "act out" their reactions to stress, while upper-middle-class persons are more likely to react internally by becoming anxious.

Each of these possibilities is consistent with the finding of the latter researchers and Langner and Michael that, while blue-collar workers are more susceptible to psychoses, middle-class types are more susceptible to neuroses, the "bottled-up" anxiety disorders. An additional finding of Langner and Michael (1963:412–413) is especially interesting in this context; that is, whereas the greater the level of stress, the more likely blue-collar as compared to middle-class persons are to exhibit psychotic symptoms, the reverse is the case for neurotic symptoms.

One way of summarizing these suggestions for explaining class differences in susceptibility to the more debilitating forms of mental illness would be that the structure of our society produces insanity by unequally distributing, not just stress, but also the "inner resources" for coping with it. At the same time, however, it is by no means clear that inequalities in inner resources are more important than those from other sources:

> Part of the explanation for lower-class people dealing less effectively with stress may be that the stress-producing situations they face are less alterable by individual action than are those encountered by people of higher social-class position. Many of their stresses arise from economic circumstances over which few individuals have much control, lower-class individuals least of all. Moreover, lower-class people have little money or power to employ in coping with the con-

sequences of stress. It also appears (cf. Dohrenwend and Dohrenwend, 1969:137–139) that fewer institutional resources are available to them, either for escaping stressful situations or for mitigating the consequences of stress [Kohn, 1972:299].

In addition to such class differences in powerlessness vis-à-vis the products of one's everyday activities, differences in interpersonal support from others may also be crucial. Specifically, to the extent that lower-status blue-collar workers do indeed have fewer friends, and to the extent that politically/economically-derived hardships have been more likely to disrupt their family relationships, they may receive less support from others in facing stressful situations. (See Kaplan, Cassell, and Gore, 1973, for the importance of social support in general.) Yet, as mentioned in the "Products" section, workers often combat alienation collectively, and, interestingly, many observers (e.g., Fanon, 1966; Ryan, 1969) report decreases in the incidence of psychiatric symptoms in communities where workers have collectively organized themselves.

Notes

[1]This study of 1067 Canadians in 1973, known as the "Work Ethic" study, was conducted for the Department of Manpower and Immigration by Burstein et al. (1975).

[2]For an excellent discussion of other sources of bias see the forthcoming paper by James Rinehart in the Canadian Review of Sociology and Anthropology.

[3]This tendency is no doubt reinforced by the very low degree of skill involved in fully automated work, as Braverman (1974:224) and Rinehart (1975:135) note.

[4]Thus, white-collar workers, even with "manual," clerical, and sales workers thrown in, have had lower rates of absenteeism and turnover (Judek, 1968) and been less likely to emphasize the importance of working conditions "extrinsic" to the work itself (Faunce, 1968:117; Goldthorpe et al., 1969).

[5]Using titles such as "social organization" or "industrial sociology," "organizational" or "industrial" psychology.

[6]That it is the implications of being paid for the meaning or purpose of the activity rather than some other feature is suggested by the fact that paying the subjects *after* the first session with the puzzle without their having expected to be paid does not alienate them from the task (Lepper et al., 1973).

[7]Although we commonly exempt "public" corporations and governments from this charge, remember that governments are required to obtain their revenues without seriously infringing upon either the wealth or the power of the large corporations and the class of individuals who own and run them (Miliband, 1973; O'Connor, 1974). As a consequence, corporate contributions to Canadian government revenues has decreased as a proportion of total revenues whereas individual contributions have increased. Furthermore, given such things as

hidden sales taxes (e.g., there are at least 150 such taxes included in the price of a loaf of bread), income taxes tend to be far less progressive than they appear on the surface (Deaton, 1968).

[8]Needless to say, this ambiguous statement has led to many contrasting interpretations. Although many take it to mean that the theory predicts no objective differences in alienation between classes, I prefer to see the problem as one of levels (see Archibald, 1976b). Specifically, whereas the capitalist is less psychologically alienated (that is, s/he is more involved in his/her work, etc.), in objective, structural terms s/he is not well-rounded, being instead something like a misanthropic miser, and, given his/her class interest, will not be among those to usher in the new society. Another way of stating the latter is that s/he too is ultimately determined by his/her class position, just as the worker is. See especially Marx's restatements of the issue (Marx and Engels, 1976, 5:77).

[9]This seems abundantly clear in a number of case studies (Beynon, 1973; Aronowitz, 1973; Mann, 1973:22; Serrin, 1973), although there have also been cases of the reverse reported (e.g., see Mann, 1973:37, and Note 10 below). Certainly it is shop stewards rather than full-timers who are most likely to be ahead of the rank and file on control-related political issues.

[10]See, for example, Form (1973b). This also true of Britain, whose trade union traditions are considerably longer than North America's (Mann, 1970; Parkin, 1972; Westergaard, 1970).

[11]As is clear from my own and others' attempts to interview workers (e.g., Terkel, 1972:243), it is not uncommon to have workers start out insisting that all is right with the world, only to open up later in the interview to complain about a host of working conditions and then say, *"We have no protection."* Just how extensive and serious the problem is became clear in London, Ontario recently when *legal* secretaries complained that their *lawyer*-bosses were intimidating them to keep them from unionizing!

[12]This may partially explain why skilled workers have higher levels of participation in their unions (Form, 1973), and why some of the most internally democratic unions have been composed of skilled workers. Note, however, that these are precisely the (blue-collar) workers who benefit most from the system anyway.

[13]For other analyses of class voting in Canada see Chi (1973) and Ogmundson (1976); for Britain, Runciman (1966) and Goldthorpe et al., (1969); and for the United States Hamilton (1972; 1975) and Verba and Nie (1972).

[14]For example, see Note 7 above.

[15]Contrary to the "hard-hat" image, however, this was not true of positions on the Vietnam war (Hamilton, 1975:194).

[16]Attempts to test the subjective validity of the Functionalist theory of stratification (Lewis and Lopreato, 1963; Lopreato and Lewis, 1963) have had only mixed success, and many have suggested that to the extent that the prestige of occupations is associated with the attribution of functional importance, it is the former which determines the latter rather than vice versa. However, recent interview studies, especially Sennett and Cobb's (1972), indicate that most workers are probably at least skeptical of the abilities and contributions of those in higher strata.

[17]Asch (1960), Allen and Levine (1968), Moscovici et al. (1969).

[18]For reviews, see Kamin (1974), and Gartner et al. (1974).

[19]See especially the critical review by Miller, Riessman, and Seagull (1968).

Such claims are also centerpieces of the "culture of poverty" position, which has been critiqued by Ryan (1971).

[20]For class differences in achievement motivation in general see Brown's review (1965); for the research on the differing effects of material and symbolic rewards (Cameron and Storm, 1965). As Smith (1968) notes, the standard, projective measure of achievement motivation is far from a pure measure of *intrinsic* motivation; rather, it measures individualistic competitiveness as well, and in this respect (and perhaps others) it is class biased.

[21]For the first finding, see Lipset (1963), Lipsitz (1965), Kohn (1969), and Coburn (1973); for the second, Brown (1965) and Byrne (1974:98–101). For critiques see Hyman and Sheatsley (1954), Miller and Riessman (1961), and Hamilton (1972).

[22]The eight-year figure is based on U.S. data (Antonovsky, 1967). Unfortunately, the secretiveness of Canadian governments has prevented my colleagues from obtaining comparable Canadian data. For a review of class differences in health with some Canadian data see Siemiatycki (1974).

[23]This then becomes the basis for their own interpretation of working class authoritarianism:

> The man who is displaced by Harvard or the people whose sons are dying in the war do not believe that whatever authority does is right. Rather, a sense of self-doubt intervenes to make them unsure *they have the right* to fight back. Is it any wonder that they often lash out . . . at those who receive the unfair rewards, feeling cowed as they do in the face of the rewarder [Sennett and Cobb, 1972:159]?

[24]On the other hand, under some circumstances feelings of powerlessness may actually protect one from harm. Specifically, if one believes that whatever happens to one is not one's own fault, one may have a ready-made rationalization for failure which dampens its effect upon one's mental health (Rotter, 1966). See Dohrenwend and Dohrenwend (1969:141–143) for a review of the evidence for and against these two possibilities and some suggestions as to conditions under which one might find one or the other.

9
RACE, ETHNICITY, AND SEX

Marx and Engels' explanation for the persistence of, and increase in, antagonism between the English and the Irish was that, (1) English capitalists had used the Irish as cheap labour both in Ireland itself and by importing them to England and that, (2) since their extreme poverty in Ireland made them readier to accept low wages, the Irish were understandably regarded as competitors by English workers. Much the same is implied for male-female relationships: "The bourgeoisie has made the most of the opportunity of employing and making profitable the labour of women and children afforded by machine work"; "The less the skill and exertion of strength implied in manual labour, in other words, the more modern industry becomes developed, the more is the labour of men superseded by that of women" (Marx and Engels, 1975, 4:377; 1968:42).

In addition to this combination of exploitation and competition in the labor market, several less direct sources of racial-ethnic and sexual antagonism are suggested.

One is the often deliberate exacerbation of existing racial-ethnic conflicts (through "the press, the pulpit, the comic papers, in short, by all the means at the disposal of the ruling classes") in order to keep the working class divided, such that, for example, the English or southern American worker is offered a feeling of superiority over the Irish or black worker in compensation for his own lowly status (Marx, 1971:293–294).

A similar, if less often intended, process occurs in the family where, "in the great majority of cases, the man has to be the earner, the breadwinner of the family, at least among the propertied classes, and this gives him a dominating position which requires no special legal privileges" (Engels, in Marx and Engels, 1968:510). The man's "dominating position" is presumably also buttressed by the fact that women (and children) derive a lesser status from their lower exchange value on the labor market. (Marx and Engels (1968:36) suggested that capitalism "has resolved personal worth into exchange value," and wage-labouring women earn less than men while housewives have no direct exchange value whatsoever.) That the domination and derogation of women and children might then partially compensate men was noted by Marx himself (Marx and Engels, 1975:4:605):

> The most cowardly, unresisting people become implacable as soon as they *can exercise their absolute parental authority. The abuse of this authority is, as it were, a crude compensation* for all the submissiveness and dependence to which they abase themselves willy-nilly in bourgeois society.

These various "investments" in racism and sexism notwithstanding, Marx and Engels claimed, racial-ethnic and sexual antagonisms would work themselves out in the common struggle against the bourgeoisie. Thus workers of different racial-ethnic groups and sexes will eventually recognize that they have more to gain by combining against the bourgeoisie than competing amongst themselves. Similarly, as capitalism expands and more and more women are drawn into the labour market, the dominance of the husband-father will necessarily be undermined (Marx and Engels, 1968:50–51, 579).

Certainly among social psychologists studying "prejudice and discrimination," the first and most enduring focus has been not upon the labor-market processes of exploitation and competition, but the *compensatory* functions of prejudice for individuals' personalities. "Frustration" "displaced" upon low-status scapegoats (because they are safegoats) became the byline, the most popular example being the antagonism of white workers in the southern U.S. toward blacks.[1] Later the class structure seems to have lost its position of prominence among the conditions regarded as frustrating, its place being taken by the childhood experiences of the "authoritarian personality" (Adorno et al., 1964; see Note 1). By the time Lipset published his thesis on "working class authoritarianism" (see the previous chapter), therefore, the way had already been cleared to attribute workers' racism much more to their childhood than their adulthood experiences. That workers became the sole, or at least major, perpetrators of racism was of course significant in itself.

Probably because it retains the compensation approach's focus upon workers as the source of racism, *competition* eventually became the preferred rational-interest argument (see for example, Williams, 1964, and Blalock, 1967). Indeed, the position of neoclassical economists such as Gary Becker (see the reviews by Arrow, 1972, and Blau and Jusenius, 1976) has been that *only* workers have an interest in racism and sexism, since employers would be better off to hire nonwhites and women. (By increasing the number of workers competing for jobs, so they argue, such a move would eventually decrease the average wage.) Should there be discriminatory employers, they must therefore have a nonrational "taste" for prejudice, as a carry-over from precapitalist times, or because they are pressured to discriminate by their self-serving employees.

The remaining element of the original Marxian analysis, *exploitation*, was in fact vigorously reiterated by Oliver Cox (1970) and Carey McWilliams (1948) in the 1940s, so much so that even mainstream textbook writers (e.g., Allport, 1954; Simpson and Yinger, 1965) have felt obliged to acknowledge its importance. Yet this recognition has often been only grudgingly given. Alternatively, in Cox's account in particular, exploitation has been almost as abstracted from competition as the latter has been from exploitation in mainstream accounts, and this unfortunate practice has carried over to more recent accounts by Marxists (e.g., Michael Reich, 1971).

Interestingly, on the other hand, competition as well as exploitation appears to have been overshadowed by yet another explanation, which claims, in effect, that much if not most prejudice and discrimination is not tied to *any* political-economic interest. This is the "*cultural*," "group norm," or "conformity" approach, whose central proposition is that racism and sexism are simply aspects of a society's or subgroup's culture which are passed on to children in the socialization process and maintained through adulthood by group pressures toward conformity (Allport, 1954:285–296). According to Simpson and Yinger (1965:109), this approach can best explain "why any particular group should be selected as the object of prejudice." "Why," for example, "will a stable and secure person exhibit prejudice against the brown skin when he has a very low amount of hostility, has never even known a Negro, and has no conceivable economic or political interest to be served?" Their answer, presumably, is that he has been conditioned to do so, if not directly by others, then through exposure to the media, or perhaps simply to a language where "dark" symbolizes sexuality and evil.

In what follows it should become clear that all of these various claims contribute something to our knowledge of race, ethnic, and sex relations. However, whereas mainstream authors tend to treat the various factors as independent of each other, such that their eclecticism often amounts to theoretical agnosticism, I shall argue here that these factors, the "cultural" included, are often intimately related in patterns highly suggestive of the original Marxian analysis within which most of them were originally integrated.

THE RECORD: WHO DISCRIMINATES, WHO BENEFITS?

Were one to simply accept at face value much of what appears to occur in our society at the present time, one might well endorse the cultural model. Thus, it might be argued, many of our number are racist and/or sexist without either exploiting or directly competing with native people, blacks, French Canadians or women in the labor market. According to Simpson and Yinger (1965:112–113), the logical implication to be drawn from this — that prejudice and discrimination are simply part of our general culture — is supported by the fact that if one asks individuals to indicate the degree of intimacy they would permit between themselves and a typical member of various racial and ethnic groups, one finds that the "social distance" rankings (see Banton, 1967) for such groups tend to be roughly comparable across various occupations (businessmen, school teachers, and college students), regions of the United States (west versus east), and several decades. Others note that even whites who have solidary relationships with blacks on the job tend to discriminate against them socially (see the review by Secord and Backman, 1974:188–194); that even large proportions of relatively unprejudiced college students would not agree to undertake various activities with a black person, particularly when the activity involved intimacy and/or would be made public (Warner and DeFleur, 1969), and that much of this discrimination without apparent prejudice can be attributed to conformity pressures from family, friends, and the general public (Linn, 1965:362). Finally, there is ample evidence that children acquire racial and sexual prejudices from parents, playmates, and presumably the media (Goodman, 1964; Vener and Synder, 1966).

There is therefore some truth to the model of racism and sexism as unintended features of our social structure. However, such an analysis is "post festum" and piecemeal; that is, it ignores both the historical processes through which our society arrived at its reified state and the underlying political-economic processes which currently buttress and perpetuate it.

One cannot claim, for example, that our orientation toward native people has mainly reflected general cultural beliefs. Rather, the wholesale slaughter and/or colonization of native people on reservations coincided with the demands of white settlers for their land (Blalock, 1967). Prejudice and discrimination against blacks and orientals has had much less to do with their simply being here and being different, but their having been deliberately brought here as cheap labor to be exploited, and their subsequent position as competitors of white workers (Bonavich, 1975; Roy, 1974). On the other hand, given these political-economic interests in prejudice, the latter was deliberately promoted, by, for example, slave owners and southern politicians in an attempt to foster antagonism between poor whites and blacks, and slaves and freedmen (Doyle, 1968), and later, Andrew Carnegie and other leading capitalists who funded the "Eugenics" movement (Blumer, 1958).

Although many would have us believe that such occurrences are a thing of the past, a closer look at our present society reveals that such is not the case. Thus, employers often pay native (LaRusic, cited in Frideres, 1974:30) and black workers (Schiller, 1976:121–122) less for the same work, and Michael Reich (1971; see also Szmanski, 1976) has demonstrated that the greater the disparity between the incomes of blacks and whites in a metropolitan area of the United States, the greater is also that between those of the uppermost stratum and white workers. On the other hand, other research indicates that the greater the proportion of blacks in a given occupational category, the lower is the income of white males, and the greater is the tendency for blacks to become segregated in the lower-paying jobs of the occupational category (Synder and Hudis, 1976). Nor are such processes of exploitation and competition restricted to the labor market, since servicing Indian reservations and black ghettos (or, having to maintain workers whose standards of living are low) is big business for some (Robertson, 1970; Blauner, 1969), and a serious drain on the personal incomes of others through taxation (e.g., Ransford, 1972:345).

The record of prejudice and discrimination in ethnic relations in our country looks much the same. Specifically, the need to deride French Canadians as a "race" did not occur until they were conquered militarily, and ungratefully rebellious in 1837–8. They too are now often paid less for the very same work, after having received the same education, as Anglo-Canadians (Milner and Milner, 1973; Beattie, 1975), and their higher rates of unemployment and lower standards of living attest to *their* status as a special category within the "reserve army of the unemployed."

French Canadians have in turn had to compete with various ethnic immigrant groups (Joy, 1972:24–25), and this may account for their greater prejudice against, for example, Jews (see Curtis and Lambert, 1975, below). Such immigrant groups as the Irish and Italians, it should be noted, have had to face considerable exploitation and competition (Winks, 1971:144; Richmond, 1967), and prejudice and discrimination against them, far from being a near-constant feature of our culture, have varied tremendously according to political-economic conditions (e.g., see Avery, 1975).

Although we tend to relegate sex, or better, "gender," relations to a different category (too close to home, so to speak?), they too have followed more or less similar patterns. Thus, if it is true that women have been subordinate to men in most known societies, it is not true, as Parsons would have it, that the sexual division of labor as we know it is universal. Rather, on the average (for all known societies), women contribute 44 percent of the food for subsistence (Aronoff and Crano, 1975), and political-economic developments have seen a more or less progressive deterioration of the power and status of women, first, with the move from hunting and food-gathering societies to settled agricultural societies with class structures based on private property (Gough, 1971; see also Chapter 7), and second, with the move to commodity production outside the home (Sullerot, 1971; Johnson, 1974).

The subsequent use of women as a convenient subsector of the reserve army and cheap source of labor more generally is well known. Driven out of the work force altogether or segregated in the least skilled, lowest paying jobs after large-scale commodity production had gotten underway, they were first impressed back into civilian service during the two world wars (the "Rosy-the-riveter" image began to flourish at these points), and then driven out or resegregated when the military troops returned (hence, the "feminine mystique" and "home-sweet-home" images) (Women's Press Collective, 1974; Boutlier, forthcoming; Ferber and Lowry, 1976; Royal Commission on the Status of Women, 1971; Marchak, 1973; Schiller, 1976; Synder and Hudis, 1976). That employers greatly benefit from the fact that the wives of male workers maintain and replace their husband's labor power at a cost far below what such services would be worth on the labor market (Middleton, 1974; Women's Studies Group, 1976) should be obvious.

If the record clearly discounts any claim that "cultural" processes are the only or even most important "wheels" upon which racism, ethnocentrism, or sexism turn, it does the same to claims which would seize upon only one of exploitation, competition, or compensation as the material or "substructural" forces underlying these phenomena. For example, if it is difficult to explain the rampages of unemployed soldiers through early Canadian black communities (Winks, 1971) as anything but compensatory "scapegoating," one also cannot find a greater incidence of frustration and/or authoritarian personalities among South African or southern American whites (Pettigrew, 1959). If discrimination and prejudice have often occurred among white male employers and other high-status persons (e.g., for sexism, see Kanter, 1975), as the exploitation account would have it, this has also been the case for white male workers (e.g., Geoffroy and Saint-Marie, 1971; Roby, 1975), as the competition account would have it. However, when one controls for such things as region of the country and the group against which respondents are prejudiced, one finds that even class differences in *attitudes* have been greatly exaggerated.

Richard Hamilton (1972; 1975), for example, has demonstrated that while American workers in the South are more prejudiced against blacks than are their middle-class counterparts, this is not true in the North. Other studies (see Allport, 1954:80; Williams, 1964:54, 199) indicate that whereas blue-collar workers in the United States, taken as a whole, are *more* prejudiced against *blacks,* they are often *less* prejudiced against Jews. As can be seen in Table 9.1, English Canadian workers appear to be more prejudiced against both blacks and Jews, but there is no difference by occupational grouping in prejudice against blacks among French Canadians. Similarly,

TABLE 9.1

REJECTION OF VARIOUS "OUTGROUPS" BY OCCUPATION, EDUCATION, AND RELIGIO-LANGUAGE GROUP (CURTIS AND LAMBERT, 1975)

	ENGLISH CANADIAN PROTESTANTS			ENGLISH CANADIAN CATHOLICS			FRENCH CANADIAN CATHOLICS		
	Blacks	Jews	French Cana-dians	Blacks	Jews	French Cana-dians	Blacks	Jews	French Cana-dians
OCCUPATION									
Nonmanual	4%	6%	14%	2%	10%	7%	9%	16%	5%
Manual	9	12	14	9	19	7	10	30	10
Farmer	13	14	20	13	21	21	8	30	10
EDUCATION									
Some university or more	2	4	9	0	7	3	4	10	10
Secondary school	5	8	15	3	11	6	8	21	9
Elementary	16	18	18	19	25	11	13	30	8

Source: Reprinted from the Canadian Review of Sociology and Anthropology, Volume number 12.2, by permission of the author(s) and the publisher.

English Canadian blue-collar workers are no more prejudiced against French Canadians than are English Canadian white-collar workers. (Note that in general, education tends to predict prejudice better than does occupation.)

However, there are still more serious problems in drawing conclusions about class differences from such studies. Specifically, it is not clear that such measures of prejudice tap class differences in underlying predispositions toward *actual discrimination*. Thus, when one examines responses with more of a predisposition-to-act as opposed to simply a belief component, blue-collar workers often appear *less* rather than more racist (Greenblum and Pearlin, 1953; Stember, 1961).[2] Similarly, after investigating the images of women in white- and blue-collar women's magazines, Cornelia Flora (1971) discovered that they were more passive in the *former* than the latter. *Nor is it clear that any such predispositions are the major sources of individuals' behavior.* In addition to the aforementioned research with relatively unprejudiced college students, one might note the cases Hamilton (1972) cites where upper-middle-class Americans expressed less prejudice against blacks than did blue-collar workers, but subsequently voted overwhelmingly for a racist candidate while workers voted for a solid liberal. Similarly, whereas American middle-class couples express a more egalitarian sex ideology, their actual behavior patterns usually fall far short of the ideal (Babchuk and Bates, 1963). Indeed, in some studies middle-class wives have been found to have *less* actual decision-making power in the family (Gillespie, 1971). In a British study, blue-collar husbands were more likely to follow the dictum "father knows best" by exercising disproportionate power in family decisions, but also more likely than white-collar husbands to help their wives with the housework (Gavron, 1966).[3]

RACISM AND SEXISM AS ALIENATION

If one reflects upon the nature of racism and sexism, one discovers not only that they are heavily affected by class-related conflicts of interest, as we have just seen, but that the behaviour and feelings we usually think of as indicative of racism and sexism on the "interpersonal" level are also indicative of alienation from others.

To exploit or compete with others solely on the basis of their race, ethnicity, or sex, as with their class, for example, is to use them for one's own narrow self-interest (the means-ends dimension). To maintain "social distance" is to avoid them (detachment). To exclude and/or segregate them is also to avoid them, and perhaps also to control them for one's own purposes (control-purposiveness). Finally, hostility (feelings) certainly comes to mind when one thinks of the defining features of racism and sexism.

Given that this is the case, it is interesting to consider just how far such an analogy might take us. Also, to the extent that such alienation exists, to what can one attribute it?

The class-related conflicts of interest discussed earlier clearly provide one possible explanation. However, it is more commonly assumed that racial-ethnic and sexual conflict are largely independent of and often more basic than class conflict. The relative importance of class versus racial-ethnic and sexual conflicts per se in explaining alienated relationships among people, therefore, is an important issue to attempt to resolve.

Let us begin by examining the fit between the model of alienation from others and race, ethnic, and gender relations.

Others

As we saw in Chapter 8, class relations are characterized by a most interesting dialectic: on the one hand, individuals of different classes attempt to avoid each other "like the plague," yet, being interdependent, they must nevertheless come together in order to "get the job done." The least-worst solution for both sides, therefore, is to limit the terms of the interaction to narrowly defined roles, in the hope that the less one reveals of one's true feelings, the more likely the interaction is to come off.

THE AVOIDING-USING DIALECTIC

Avoidance is in fact what "social distance" is presumably all about; that is, the more distant the minority group from oneself, the less willing one is to interact with them under such presumably intimate circumstances as friendship or marriage. On the other hand, circumstances requiring little intimacy are more easily tolerated.

Here the data are very clear with regard to *black-white* relations in the United States, in that whites tend to rank blacks much lower than the members of white minority groups. Furthermore, in experiments where white subjects have actually been given the opportunity to interact with blacks or other whites, whites tend to choose whites over blacks, and the more intimate the circumstances, the less likely they are to choose to interact with blacks.[4] Observations of *native-white* relations in northern Canada indicate the same pattern (see Hughes and Kallen's, 1974:133–134 summary of Dailey and Dailey's research). In southern city settings some Indian workers move within all-white friendship networks, but this occurs mainly when the Indian is light-skinned enough to pass as white (Denton, 1975:66), or on "skid row," where "whites do many 'jobs' with Indians: whites have Indian girl friends, with whom they cooperate for the purposes of hustling and petty theft; much drinking is done by whites and Indians jointly" (Brody, 1971:48). More typically, the Indian has moved in all-Indian circles, avoiding discussions of race relations and otherwise attempting to "formalize relations with whites whom he did not know well so that encounters were impersonal and brief" (Denton, 1975:66). This has also been true, incidentally, where both the whites and Indians in question have been middle class (Dosman, 1972:55).

Surprisingly, although *French Canadians* are a much more numerous group than native people, much less is known about "interpersonal" relations between them and English Canadians. Do the groups represent, as Hugh MacLennan (1945) has phrased it, "two solitudes"?

We do know that on occasion, English and French workers have gotten along well on the job, so much so that they have learned each other's language well (Taylor and Simard, 1972). At the same time, at least one early study of French-English relations on the job indicates exclusion of the French, particularly in the socializing activities so important among executives and other high-status white-collar employees (Hughes, 1943). Similarly, "Although the two language groups [in Montreal] may meet during their working hours, . . . each tends to retire to its own sections of town when evening falls" (Joy, 1972:107). Nor have the vast majority of English Canadians made an effort to learn French, even when the proximity of French Canadians would seem to warrant it. Although there are few differences in bilingualism among English-speaking males in different occupations in Montreal, those that exist make sense in means-ends terms; that is, salesmen and the self-employed, who presumably are the most likely to have commercial relations with the French, are also most likely to be bilingual (Lieberson, 1970:142).

What, therefore, of *male-female* relations? In effect, the avoiding-using dialectic is already implied in the segregation of industries and jobs by gender, but it also occurs where the genders have an opportunity to interact. As Jessie Bernard (1968:283) quotes an early commentor as saying, "men dread the prospect of having women around." Rosabeth Kanter (1975:63) has summarized the results of later studies by noting that "when men and women interact in organizations, they often do it across barriers like that of social class. . . ." Thus, lone women in all-male groups tend to be isolated and invisible, in part through rejection by male colleagues, and in part through a series of accommodative strategies such as "keeping a low profile" and not taking credit for their own accomplishments. Interestingly, furthermore, such women tend to take on one of a number of restricted roles in such groups: " 'mother'; 'sex object' or 'seductress'; 'pet' (group mascot); [or] 'iron maiden' (militant and unapproachable)" (Kanter, 1975:57).

But *surely*, the reader will continue, don't particular men and women meet after "work" and go home together? True, yet

> Even in our own democratic society where marriage is supposedly based on romantic love there may be little communication between the partners in marriage. . . . Women have been known to say that although they have been married for twenty years, their husband is still a stranger to them. . . . In light of these considerations, some doubt may be cast on the propriety of placing marriage on the positive extreme of the social distance scale . . . [Hacker, 1951:64].

The major complaint of wives, it appears (Bernard, 1968: 232–248; 314–325), is that their husbands do not talk to them enough and reveal enough of their inner feelings, choosing instead to limit most of their encounters with their wives to the physical act of love-making. If it needs saying, it therefore looks suspiciously as if many, and perhaps most, men tend to regard even (especially?) their own spouses in a means-ends manner — as, in short, sex objects and personal servants.

Although it could be construed from this discussion that white-anglo males do all the avoiding and using, many minority group members and women have made the best of the options open to them by "working" the system for various secondary benefits. If, for example, whites feel more comfortable interacting with blacks or native people when such interaction is stereotypical, then sometimes a black or native can derive some pleasure from being "the life of the party" (Denton, 1975:67). Similarly, if men insist upon treating women as sex objects, some women can and do market their sexuality in order to achieve jobs, promotions, or other favours which they might not otherwise obtain. Alternatively, the housewife who really fears that she is not capable enough may use her husband as an excuse for "vegetating." "If it weren't for you," she suggests, "insisting as you do that I be your personal servant, I would be rich and famous in my own right" (Berne, 1967:103).

The detachment/means-ends dialectic, therefore, appears to describe majority-minority group and gender relations rather well.

THE CONTROL-DEFERENCE AND OPPOSITION-HOSTILITY DIALECTICS

In the slave society of the American south, complete submission was required of the black slave, and close to complete predictability of the other's actions toward oneself as was possible was as necessary for the slave as the master. These conditions were principally effected through two means. One was the manner in which the black African was first delivered to the slave master: s/he was first subjected to the shock of capture, then a long and brutal march to the sea among other slaves who seldom spoke the same language, sale to European slavers, travel through "the dread Middle Passage" in the hold of a ship, and finally to sale again in the West Indies. The other was the "closed authority system" of the American (and, to a somewhat lesser extent, the Canadian) slave system itself (Elkins, 1963: Chapter III).

Remarkable for their intricacy were the patterns of control and deference — the "etiquette" — which characterized the latter. First were fixed forms of address, the master being referred to as "massa" or "sir," his wife as "miss," and the slave by his/her first name (which was usually all there was), or "boy" or "girl." The slave having thus signified that s/he knew his/her place, the conversation could begin. The initiation of each interchange, however, was usually left to the white individual present, and as a slave, one was expected to continue to "give off" signs of deference throughout the entire conversation. This one usually did by tugging at one's forelock, shuffling one's feet, maintaining a toothy grin, and agreeing with virtually everything the white(s) said.

As long as one remained strictly within the rules of etiquette, some small measure of rebellion might be permitted, as through various "song-and-dance" routines (e.g., see Doyle, 1968:79–80). Anything beyond this, however, was undertaken only on pain of physical abuse, and perhaps death:

> Does a slave look dissatisfied? It is said that he has the devil in him.
> . . . Does he speak loudly when spoken to by the master? Then he is
> getting high-minded, and should be taken down a buttonhole lower.
> Does he forget to pull off his hat at the approach of a white person?
> Then he is wanting in reverence. . . . Does he venture to vindicate his
> conduct, when censured for it? Then he is guilty of impudence, one of
> the greatest crimes a slave can commit [Frederick Douglass, a former
> slave, cited by Doyle, 1968:8].

Although this etiquette became modified in different settings and time periods, its essential ingredients remained. Indeed, according to Bertram Doyle (1968:15, 92), the etiquette was more rigid in the towns and cities, where whites and blacks would encounter others whom they did not know and whose behaviour they were therefore less able to predict; between whites and free blacks for the same reason; and, in some respects, more *after* than before the Civil War. Similarly, much the same etiquette was still in force at the time that Doyle wrote his book (1937).

A great deal has changed since that time, such that now, in northern cities, at least, one is as likely to see black youths jostle whites off the sidewalk as conform to the traditional etiquette, which was to yield the "right of way." However, as John Griffin (1961) discovered after he took drugs to darken his skin colour and travelled in the South, the etiquette has far from disappeared. Nor has it been entirely restricted to the South, since, for example, in experiments as late as the early 1960s, black workers and college students were still participating and initiating less than whites (Katz and Benjamin, 1960). Similarly, it is still not unheard of for blacks in academia as well as the (other) entertainment occupations to "slip into the old song-and-dance routine."

According to Heather Robertson (1970), similar patterns can often be found among native people and white Canadians, there being wide swings between slavish deference and outright rebellion (for example, urinating on the barroom floor; see also Denton, 1975). Unless I am mistaken, however, native-white interaction has now undergone many of the same changes as have black-white relations, with opposition and hostility now being at least as common as passivity and deference.[5]

To what degree English-French relations have followed these same patterns is more difficult to say. As to the very beginning, Michel Brunet (cited in Rioux, 1971:28) has written: "All the historians have emphasized the very cordial relations which were established between the French Canadians and their conquerors from the first months of the English occupation. The fact is undeniable. . . ."

Although there is little here that explicitly points to the "black Sambo" process, British predominance and French dependence are also undeniable. Brunet himself suggests a rather interesting explanation for this exaggerated deference from the French:

> Fearing the worst, the vanquished discovered to their astonishment that the conqueror treated them with benevolence. Their exaggerated fear explains, in good part, their almost spontaneous submission at the beginning of the English occupation.

To this Rioux adds that, as we saw in the case of black slavery, "One might also invoke the profound divisions afflicting the country at the end of the French era."

Much hostile opposition was to surface in the rebellion of 1837–38, but after it was crushed, "Even the most committed French Canadians are filled with despair." In the words of Etienne Parent, a former *Patriot*, "We French Canadians are so situated that our only alternative is to resign ourselves with the best possible grace" (Rioux, 1971:55).

As to the more recent past, we have little in the way of hard observation of the presence or absence of the control-deference pattern in "interpersonal" relations. However, we shall see shortly that several important concomitants of such a pattern have persisted into the present, and the hostility of French Canadians toward the English has been no closely guarded secret. It has surfaced, for example, in their resistance to conscription during the two world wars, and in the number of French Canadian politicians who have implicitly (and recently, explicitly) ridden to power on the nationalist sentiments of the Quebecois.

Although there is even more resistance to viewing male-female relations in these terms, there is actually more hard evidence here than in the case of either native-white or French-English relations.

Thus, in mixed gender work groups, simulated juries, social gatherings, and experimental games, women:
(1) Participate (talk and make suggestions) less than men
(2) Initiate less (but have their suggestions interrupted more), and
(3) Agree with others more, but have their own suggestions agreed with by others less, unless, of course, such suggestions happen to be surreptitiously taken up by a man (Bernard, 1968:137–149; Smith, 1975; Lockheed and Hall, 1976)

Nor can one attribute these patterns to "natural" sex differences in personality rather than the social *situation* in which women find themselves. Thus, whereas early studies did suggest that women in all-female groups follow a strategy of accommodating and supporting others (see Gamson, 1964; Kanter, 1975), of, if you will, "stroking" instead of "poking," more recently, women, at least in experimental games, have become as competitive as men (see Note 3, Chapter 7). Some studies, furthermore, indicate that "in a conflict-type situation, they tend to be *less* cooperative than men," in spite of the fact that when interacting with men they tend to be *more* cooperative (Bernard, 1968:301–302; see also Horner, 1972; Wiley, 1973)!

That "something extra" which women encounter in their inter- actions with men is not particularly elusive; that is, men appear to be threatened by women, and some even verbally express a desire that male-female encounters remain ritualized (Bass et al., 1971)! More typically, however, the coercive power of men over women becomes most evident when a woman fails to remain "in her place," for at that point she is criticized as a "shrew." Should she try to dispense knowledge to other women (heaven forbid), she is a "witch"; if she dares to take initiative away from men more generally, she is a "bitch," or, to use a term which exposes the threatening nature of such behavior even more, a "castrating" woman. As Jessie Bernard (1968:284–287) has shown, recognition of this fact and strategies for dealing with it have long been codified in the etiquette books for office "girls," who right through the present have been cautioned not to argue, but agree, with their boss; not to criticize his ideas, but find a way to get one's own accepted without him and other men in the vicinity knowing where they have come from.

Nor, by the way, is this protocol simply restricted to the public sphere, with, as many have claimed, women actually gaining the upper hand in private. Thus, family decisions, at least the most important ones, *including*, by the way, whether or not the wife works outside the home and in which community the family will live, tend to be made by the husband, in the professedly liberal middle-class as well as the blue-collar family (see Gillespie, 1971; Bianchi and Brodie, 1974). Indeed, this gender protocol pervades that (allegedly) most intimate of interchanges, sexual intercourse.

There, men not only take the initiative, deciding, for example, the positions to be taken (men more generally touch women more than women touch men (Henley, 1973)), but implicitly send cues which are often far less endearing than they may appear on the surface. Margaret Laurence (1975:245) has captured this beautifully in *The Diviners*, reprinted by permission of the Canadian publishers, McClelland and Stewart Ltd., Toronto:

> "Have you been a good girl, love?" Brooke asks.
> It has become his game, his jest, before going into her, and indeed

before permitting his arousal or hers. If she protests the sentence, he will withdraw all of himself except his unspoken anger. She has to play, or be prepared to face the coldness. Either way she feels afraid. Yet he cannot help it, and she knows this. There can be no talk of it, for it is, after all, only a joke.

She smiles, hoping this will be sufficient, without having to use words in this service. And it provides enough. Brooke, poised above her, lowers his long body upon hers. Then she is angry and wants to shove him away, wants no part of him. But her flesh responds to him, and she rises to him, rises to his bait, and then everything is all right.

And yet, afterwards, when Brooke is asleep beside her, she cannot sleep, the body's spasm no longer being enough to shut off the alarm-clock head more than momentarily.

In fact, the male prerogative is *so* pervasive that Kinsey and his fellow researchers discovered most men to be highly resentful of the Fair Maiden, the woman who has resisted men's advances by remaining chaste and aloof, presumably because, as Bernard (1968: 125) suggests, her abstinence gives her greater bargaining power! At the same time, of course, many men still insist that their wife be a virgin.

As Bernard (1968:243) notes, whereas women may now be freer to take initiative in sexual intercourse, they apparently are not in the realm of conversation. Thus, in a study of married couples by Feldman, "Initiation of discussion by the wife was found to be negatively related to the amount of time spent talking with one another daily." One likely possibility, Bernard suggests, is that: "The more she tried to get him to talk, the less likely he was to want to talk. Understandably, therefore, such wife-initiated discussion left a negative affect."

Small wonder, therefore, that contemporary women, like the black slaves before them, should smile when they are angry! (Men tend instead to "mask" fear more than anger (see Hochschild, 1975:294).)

The "Wheels" or Dynamics: Which Ones?

To recapitulate, we can now say not only that there are broadly political-economic conflicts of interest between the members of majority and minority groups and men and women, as there are between classes, but that race, ethnic and gender relations, like class relations, can be characterized as (considerably) alienated. Having done so, it is tempting to conclude that there must be a causal relationship between these two facts, that people of different races, ethnicities, and genders are alienated from each other *because* there are political-economic conflicts of interest between them.

That there must be *some* truth to this can already be gleaned from some of the material discussed earlier, in that (1) white anglo men themselves have sometimes expressed concern over such conflicts of interest, and that (2) those whom one would expect to be most threatened by minorities and women tend to be most prejudiced against them. However, there are clearly other conflicts of interest besides those discussed earlier which might just as easily produce alienation, and we should perhaps consider some of these competing explanations before proceeding further.

In the literature on race relations in particular, revulsion for the members of minority racial groups is most typically attributed to either or both of culturally derived prejudices, or to threats to compensatory status which serves important functions for the bruised egos of, for example, unskilled workers. These are also the most popular explanations for gender conflict, although a host of other ways in which women may threaten men have been suggested.

Bernard (1968:215), for example, claims that men may be threatened by the greater capacity of women for both orgasmic pleasure and abstinence. Specifically, were women permitted to initiate sexually, men would be forced to recognize that they are incapable of fully satisfying them; were women free to refuse sexual overtures, men would have to do without more often than they now do. According to de Beauvoir (1961:446), such fears in turn explain much of the verbal and emotional silence between men and women: "Does she really find pleasure in the marriage bed? Does she truly love her husband? Is she actually happy to obey him? He prefers not to ask; to him these questions even seem shocking."

Unfortunately, there is no way of determining at this point whether these alternative possibilities are as important as, or perhaps more important than, directly political-economic conflicts of interest. Certainly there is no denying the existence of unskilled workers who avoid blacks and native people so as not to lose what little status they have. This seems clear, for example, from the Sennett and Cobb study (1972) discussed in the previous chapter.

Similarly, there is no denying the existence of the male ego, that amazingly brittle object which women encounter almost every day of their lives; that, as de Beauvoir (1961:xxiv) so aptly puts it, "the most mediocre of males feels himself a demigod as compared with women. . . ." This is presumably the most immediate cause of male possessiveness. Ironically, it probably also de-eroticizes sexuality (deBeauvoir, 1961:418; Bernard, 1968:325; Greer, 1972:146) and forces women to rebel in ways that could not be more disastrous for this same male ego:

> She is thus fated for infidelity: it is the sole concrete form her liberty can assume. . . . Only through deceit and adultery can she prove that she is nobody's chattel and give the lie to the pretensions of the male [deBeauvoir, 1961:76; see also Laurence, 1975:262–279].

Yet it bears remembering that *the exploitative-competitive nature of our society probably produces much of the very insecurity and status anxiety which feeds the racist's and sexist's ego,* as Reich and Fromm have suggested (e.g., see Curtis and Lambert, 1975). *Nor is this the only proximate cause of "interpersonal" racial-ethnic and sexual conflict which is conditioned by our political economy.*

When I was a youth in Nova Scotia, for example, I was once surprised to hear a girl defend her refusal to date Nova Scotian blacks on the grounds that they were "lower class." She had, she assured me, dated a black man in college, but he was an African prince! That some portion of racial prejudice and discrimination is in fact *class* prejudice and discrimination is suggested by the results of a number of studies, many of which have been conveniently reviewed by James M. Jones (1972:25, 80–85).

Thus, class has been found to be a more important determinant of some stereotypes than is race, but blacks are of course usually presumed to be "lower class." College students will choose to interact with whites rather than blacks; however, at least providing that the activity is not extremely intimate, they will choose blacks who agree and share common interests with them over dissimilar whites. These findings have also been replicated for native people and French Canadians. Indeed, white high school students in Winnipeg were *less* likely to reject a Metis than a white "when they both expressed strong intensity beliefs dissimilar to those of the majority" (Koulak and Cumming, 1973:211–212). Similarly, Lay and Cumming (1973) discovered that "English Canadians rated French Canadians more favourably than their English counterparts when they exhibited similarities to the English Canadian on either attitudes or personality." Although subjects need not presume that someone of a different race or ethnicity is also of a different class, and therefore has beliefs different from their own, this has often been found to be the case (Stein, 1966).

Whereas no such class conflict of interest separates most men from most women, class-related and class-like conflicts of interest could nevertheless be said to enter gender relations as well. For example, as mentioned in the previous chapter, class differences between men and women may increase the likelihood of sexual and status exploitation. Thus, middle-class high school boys may be more likely to use working- than middle-class girls merely as sex objects, and middle-class men who marry down are likely to be exchanging their own wealth and status for the sexual and perhaps status gains which having a young and "beautiful" wife presumably brings. Alternatively, Greer (1972:161) notes that men often use women to get at other men rather than to use the women per se, and Brownmiller (1976) cites cases where rape has been more an aspect of class and/or race than sexual conflict per se. (The reverse, of course, also occurs.)

Probably much more important, however, is the lesser access of women in general to the labour market. Specifically, deBeauvoir (1961:444) claims that the fact that "after some months or years they have nothing left to say to one another" ("they" being a husband and wife) can be largely attributed to the fact that "each one is entrenched within a private universe," that, in other words, husbands and wives may often share too few interests in common to empathize or otherwise communicate. Nor does communication necessarily produce common interests, empathy, and marital satisfaction (see the reviews by Bernard, 1968:105, 153, 237–248, 314–325; 1972). Conversely, where spouses do not lead such role-segregated lives, this being more frequent in the middle class and/or where the wife works outside the home, they are likely to empathize and communicate more, have *more* equal (but seldom equal) decision-making power in the relationship, and express more marital satisfaction (Oakley, 1974; Gillespie, 1971).

THE STANDARDS WITH WHICH THEY FIND THEMSELVES REGARDED

Being severely restricted from coalescing with others in one's own situation, the slave often derogated other slaves and attempted to acquire some measure of status for him/herself by borrowing it from the master, who himself had more or less status in the local community. In fact, the slave owners were apparently successful in getting many of their slaves to look down not only upon each other (the "house nigger," for example, felt him/herself to be better than the "field nigger") but upon *free* blacks as well (Doyle, 1968:72, 99; Genovese, 1976)!

Later, the internal stratification criterion was to become the lightness of one's skin. Hence, for example, after asking black children in the United States (North and South) to choose which, from among brown and white dolls, they found "nice" and wished to play with, Clark and Clark found that about two-thirds chose a *white* doll. These findings were replicated at least until 1970, whereupon matters appear to have become much more complicated (see Jones, 1972: 90–95). However, at that very time Roland Crooks (1973) discovered that three-quarters of the black children he studied in Halifax, Nova Scotia were still choosing a white doll. Similarly, Frances Henry (1973) reports that the black adults in two Nova Scotian communities, one rural and one semiurban, tended to exaggerate the degree to which their encounters with whites were frequent and friendly, since most such encounters were observed to actually be highly stereotypical. Also, "one-third or more of the sample agreed with negative statements about Black people" (Henry 1973:144).

Presumably this tendency to derogate the members of one's own race has everything to do with blacks' dependence upon, and deferentialized relations with, whites. By the same token, the few examples we have of this tendency among native people also occur under deferentialized conditions, when, specifically, Indian migrants to the city are attempting to "manage impressions of ethnic stigma" (Denton, 1975:67).

We know that French Canadians have been more "other-oriented" than English Canadians (Taylor, 1964; Aellen and Lambert, 1972). What we do not know is whether this difference is simply an autonomous aspect of Quebecois culture, or whether it might also be an implicit response to oppression. Since the Quebecois have both been discriminated against and fearful for the integrity of their culture, the latter would not be unreasonable. Interestingly, in Taylor's classic interviews with French- and English-speaking entrepreneurs, the former explain their own other-orientation as a response to a fear that without it, one's business would go under, or perhaps even that one would die! As one put it, "Like most French Canadians, I like to feel I can quit while I'm still alive."

We do know that whereas the assumption of a simple cultural difference between French and English Canadians would presumably lead one to predict that French Canadians should not derogate each other for want of succeeding, such has often not been the case.

Here, we fortunately have an extensive research program undertaken by Wallace Lambert (1967) and his colleagues. In their standard experimental procedure, subjects listen to

. . . the taped recordings of a number of perfectly bilingual speakers

> reading a two-minute passage at one time in one of their languages
> (e.g., French) and later, a translation equivalent of the same passage
> in their second language (e.g., English). Groups of judges are asked to
> listen to this series of recordings and evaluate the personality
> characteristics of each speaker as well as possible, using voice cues
> only [Lambert, 1967:93–94].

To the (initial) surprise of the experimenters, *French* as well as
English Canadian college students have tended to rate French
Canadian speakers more unfavourably than English Canadian
speakers. That this has been more marked among French men than
women could be a function of the former's having had more frequent
deferentialized contact with English Canadians. Similarly, rather than
simply being there from the beginning, such evaluations of one's own
group appear only after age ten, and then more among upper-middle-
class teen-agers, "and especially those who have become bilingual
in English."

Precisely the same arguments can be, and have been, made for
women. Thus, their aforementioned "accommodative" strategy has
been considered a given, if not necessarily a biologically given,
gender difference. Rosabeth Kanter (1975:53–54) concedes the difference and also concludes that "peer relations affect a woman's
decision not to seek promotion into managerial ranks, where she
will no longer be part of a group of women." "But," she *also* suggests,
"such orientations could also be seen as *realistic responses* to
women's structural situation in organizations, of the kinds of
opportunities and their limits . . . ."

> Yet, when we observe *men* disadvantageously located in the opportu-
> nity structure, they tend to demonstrate the same characteristics.
> What one line of thought considers a "sex difference," I consider a
> structural phenomenon [Kanter, 1976:417].

At the same time, where paternalistic relations with men are still
more prevalent, and, remember, women differ from the members of
minority groups in that they "live dispersed among the males," competition with and derogation of other women have often been
reported.

This is not to suggest that oppression has necessarily led all
women's relationships to be less intimate than men's. To the contrary, Alan Booth (1972) discovered that while middle-aged men
had *more friends* than middle-aged women, the women's friendships
were *more intimate*, in that female friends tended to confide in each
other more. Nevertheless, given some of the previously mentioned
experimental support for the legendary "cattiness" of women, this
intimacy may be largely restricted to dyadic relations with single

friends. In this regard, we do know that many, particularly professional, women prefer to interact with men more than women, and
Bernard (1968:320) cites examples of women derogating "women's
talk."

Certainly other research findings appear to support the contention
that women have often evaluated each other with the standards of
the oppressor. They have, for example, borrowed prestige from
individual men and evaluated each other accordingly. They [women]
as well as men have also been more likely to accept the content of a
lecture (or article) delivered by a man than one delivered by a woman
(Bernard, 1968:146; Goldberg, 1968). Similarly, in a series of experiments reviewed by Elliott Aronson (1976:178), college women
tended to discount the performances of other women, albeit often
very subtly, by, for example, implying that a woman had to try
harder than a man in order to produce the very same piece of
knowledge. Finally, after summarizing Candice West's findings with
regard to actual interaction between men and women in mixed-sex
groups, Dorothy Smith (1975:365) concludes by suggesting: "The
grammar of these relations is understood by *both* sexes. It is not
simply imposed by men upon women."

Self

The material we have just discussed clearly points to the same
"self-" versus "other-" or "conformity-" direction dimension which
was seen to characterize class differences in personality. We might
therefore expect blacks, native people, French Canadians and women
to have less "achievement motivation" and/or be more passive, to
have less of a sense of well-being and lower self-esteem, and to have
higher rates of "mental illness," than "WASP" males.

BLACK AND NATIVE PEOPLE

The lesser "delay of gratification" and "achievement motivation"
of black and native people have, in fact, been well documented.[6]
Similarly, that explanations for these differences analogous to those
discussed with regard to class are also appropriate here is suggested,
for example, by the fact that black and native children become more
aroused by material rewards than do white, middle-class children,
and that the underlying occupational preferences of the former differ

little from those of the latter. But these studies also tell us much more. Specifically, *where* blue-collar workers or their children have been employed as a comparison group, blacks and natives, most of whom are, of course, "working class," prove to be little different from other workers (see Jones, 1972:52). As Sydiaha and Rempel (1972:278) conclude with regard to the aspirations of Metis-Indian adolescents in northern Saskatchewan, therefore, "It would appear that cultural factors are less important than social and geographical location."

The question of self-esteem, however, is considerably more complicated. Certainly everything we know from the last chapter about the demeaning effects of being excluded from the active work force, segregated in the most alienating occupations, and dominated and derogated by others would seem to point in that direction. Even more directly suggestive is the aforementioned tendency for many black and native people to derogate each other.

As it happens, the lower self-esteem of blacks, or at least black children, in the United States is well established (e.g., Deutsch, 1967), although the "Black Power" movements of late have probably modified these effects (see Jones, 1972:92–93). Interestingly, furthermore, black children's preferences for white dolls, which, as Michael Banton (1967:341) notes, "probably reflect the incidence of self-hatred," "are stronger among those attending Northern integrated schools than among those attending segregated Southern schools."[7] (However, where equality has been successfully promoted in integrated schools, as it apparently was in a Halifax preschool studied by Crooks (1973), the reverse may be the case.)

Recently, on the other hand, the presumption that native Canadians have lower self-esteem has been challenged by a number of writers. Edgar Dosman (1972:78–79), for example, claims that at least among Indian welfare recipients in the city, such activities as heavy drinking are much more vehicles for group solidarity, and perhaps even incipient forms of protest, than an indication of self-hatred or psychological alienation from themselves more generally. By the same token, Rodney Clifton (1975) maintains that Indians in an integrated junior high school had not a "negative self-concept," but only moderately less positive self-esteem than white students in the same school.

To my own way of thinking, however, the evidence presented by these writers is weak indeed. That Indians may use drinking as a form of protest, for instance, in no way precludes their also having doubts about themselves. Certainly if one turns to the extremely high suicide rate and "pathology" rates more generally, it is difficult to avoid the conclusion that native people are more likely to be filled with despair. As to Clifton's data, we need only remember the unsatisfactory nature of such paper-and-pencil measures of underlying psychological orientations. Alternatively, or in addition, his findings may simply indicate that "Red Pride" is now cushioning some of the effects of racial oppression.

FRENCH CANADIANS

We have already seen not only how French Canadian entrepreneurs appear to have much less ambition for themselves than their English counterparts, but also how discrimination and (far from totally unrealistic) feelings of powerlessness may be at the root of their "other-orientation." However, according to Richer and Laporte:

> French Canadians are competing with English Canadians in terms of standards and work styles incompatible with their own. . . . Because *he is not cognitively equipped for this kind of competition,* the French Canadian will feel stress, will fail, will be frustrated, and ultimately perceive the English as the cause of his failure. Although this is a true perception, *the motive of prejudice often imputed to the English Canadian is here argued not to be the dominant pattern* [1973:56; my emphases].

There is no difficulty finding evidence for many of the individual aspects of this description. French Canadian children and adolescents, for example, not only score lower on measures of achievement motivation but show such concomitants as extremely high and extremely low aspirations (Aellen and Lambert, 1972; Yackley and Lambert, 1972). They also have a much more jaundiced view of the opportunity structure (Johnstone, 1969; Grabb, 1977). However, this evidence does not tell us whether their jaundiced viewpoint is, as Richer and Laporte claim, a consequence of or rationalization for failure, or whether it is an accurate view of a jaundiced structure.

Without denying that because of past discrimination and separate lines of subcultural development some French Canadians may be ill-prepared to compete with some English Canadians and therefore defensive, it is surely important to recall that discrimination against French Canadians *does* exist. Certainly all of the known facts do not fit the former "culture of poverty" position. Thus, whereas some researchers (Rosen, 1969) report that French Canadian parents demand self-reliance from their children later than English Canadians do, others (Aellen and Lambert, 1972) report no differences in how much independence they demand, or in how punitive they are. Interestingly, in Rosen's study *class* was a much better predictor of age at which self-reliance is demanded than was ethnicity, and Grabb (1977) has discovered the same for feelings of powerlessness.

As to self-esteem, we would again expect it to be lower among French Canadians, given, for example, the tendency for many of them to derogate each other. However, that this has not always been the case (e.g., see Aellen and Lambert, 1972:182) is presumably a function of the setting in question and/or changing times. As to differential rates of mental illness, we have little information, although emotional disturbances in children appear to be highest in some of the French districts of Montreal (Siemiatycki, 1974). However, this is presumably as much a *class* as an ethnic effect.

WOMEN

After reviewing studies relevant to the claim that females are more dependent than males, Eleanor Maccoby and Carol Jacklin (1974) conclude that this is in fact seldom the case. Women may be more sensitive to their physical environment than men are, in that, for instance, if one seats subjects in other than an upright position, women are more likely to become disoriented. On the other hand, if one examines orientations toward the social environment—toward propensities to role take, to perceive, learn, and remember material with "social content," or to cling to others in stressful situations—there are few consistent gender differences. Nor do girls appear to be more conditionable or susceptible to imitation, and, while they *are* more likely to comply with the directives of adults, they are not to those of peers.

Where gender differences in activity-passivity have been found, boys have been more active, but such differences have not occurred consistently "for all ages and experimental conditions," such that "it is not accurate to describe [boys] as generally more active" (Maccoby and Jacklin, 1974:177). As to gender differences in "need for achievement," there appear to be none whatsoever. Indeed, at least through undergraduate school, females actually get better grades than males. Nor can one claim that boys are generally more intrinsically involved in achievement tasks, while girls perform more to please others (Maccoby and Jacklin, 1974:142–146).

Given this absence of consistent gender differences in personality, we must also seriously question many of the folk wisdoms about the differential childhood socialization of males and females, or at least the all-determining importance many writers have attributed to it. In this regard, Maccoby and Jacklin (1974:Chapter 9) found that some of the more striking findings that have on occasion been reported in the literature have often not been replicated. Thus, mothers have not been consistently found to engage in more verbal and nurturant interaction with daughters than sons. "The bulk of the evidence is that there is little or no difference in the socialization of boys and girls when it comes to independence granting"; and "there has been no clear demonstration that one sex received more reinforcement for dependency than the other." Nor have mothers been shown to directly encourage competitiveness or achievement in sons more than daughters, although particularly after nursery-school age, boys do apparently tend to receive more of the "push-pull," positive-negative feedback from adults which has been found to relate to achievement motivation (see Brown, 1965).

Some of the true gender differences in the literature may well help explain each other, in that, for example, if girls really do comply more with adult directives, one might expect them to do better in school; if boys are more peer-oriented, they may be more likely to become distracted from school work. However, that so few differences in either early personality traits or socialization practices have been established raises a number of interesting possibilities.

Thus, since the majority of the studies Maccoby and Jacklin cite are of children, and especially preadolescents, it is certainly conceivable that there are important gender differences in personality which appear only at later ages. DeBeauvoir (1961), for example, maintains that social pressures against taking initiative are not great until adolescence, when "being feminine" becomes especially important. According to Bardwick and Douvan (1972:234), the imposition of more rigid role pressures at this time creates considerable ambivalence in women, in that, as they put it, one may find "the simultaneous enjoyment of one's feminine identity, qualities, goals and achievements and the perception of them as less important, meaningful, or satisfying than those of men."

Matina Horner's (1972) research on the "motive to avoid success" would seem to support such a claim.

In Horner's initial studies, college students in Michigan were asked to complete a story about John (if the subjects were male) or Ann (if they were female) who just finished his or her first term at medical school at the top of his (her) class. That women may be more likely to feel threatened by success, at least when it involves competition with men, is suggested by the fact that over 65 percent went on to say that Ann will feel anxious or guilty and/or become less feminine and be rejected by others, while less than 10 percent of the men responded in an analogous manner to the John cue. Indeed, in other similar studies some of the responses were downright bizarre, as in this story about "Jane" by a grade eight girl in Vancouver:

> Jane was a very good teacher, and she loved doing it. All through the year she had been a success with both the children and the parents. Jane was so proud when she heard it, that she got quite a swelled head. She is now thinking about how marvellous she is. Because her head got so swelled, Jane thought she was too good to teach at mere public schools. She began to be mean to the children, and when parents came to her she was extremely rude. She was soon fired, and instead of going to be a better teacher, she got mad and planted a bomb in the school. The bomb was found in time and Jane was sent to jail. This ruined her life because of a hot temper [Kimball, 1977:81].

On the other hand, Horner's interpretation of her results as indicative of differences in *personality* has been thrown into doubt by subsequent research. Thus, were we to accept such an interpretation, the fact that males are often more negative toward the Ann cue than females themselves (a boy in the Monahan et al. (1974:64) study suggested that "She is so overwhelmed she celebrates by letting all the boys lay her as she goes on studying. The future holds for Ann that she will go from whore to prostitute.") would have to mean that it is males rather than females who have a higher "motive to avoid success." Similarly, possession of high "motivation to avoid success" has not always proven to be debilitating for women in terms of actual achievement (Hoffman, cited in Tresemer, 1974; Sorrentino and Short, 1974). Ironically, therefore, whereas Horner's intent in introducing the motive was to explain the well-established fact that "need for achievement" does not predict the actual behavior of women anywhere near as well as that of men (for example, women high in need for achievement are less likely than men high in the need to choose challenging tasks or go on to graduate school), her own personality trait does not in fact fill the bill.

Nevertheless, the "fear of success" imagery elicited in Horner's research is probably indicative of something important, and this something is presumably "beliefs . . . that women who succeed in a traditionally masculine field encounter a multitude of difficulties" (Monahan et al., 1974:63). It may also reflect the threat which male-female competition produces in men as well as women. Although we cannot be sure of this interpretation at this point, it is at least consistent with these additional facts:

(1) In several studies in both Canada and the United States, fear of success imagery has been more frequent among older than younger girls (Horner, 1972; Kimball, 1973). [Although this was not the case in the Monahan et al. study, older girls did give more "nonadaptive" responses; that is, they were more likely to deny that Ann had, in fact, succeeded or to prophesy bizarre consequences from it.]

(2) Girls in coeducational schools express more fear of success imagery than do those in all-girl schools (Winchel et al., 1974).

(3) College women with high fear of success scores are much more likely to have boyfriends who disapprove of women competing with men (Horner, 1972).

(4) College women do not react as negatively to a woman's success in a traditionally feminine field such as nursing (Katz, 1973).[8]

If the achievement striving of women is indeed heavily affected by how threatening it is to men and the latter's willingness to permit it, we might well expect to find in women the same feelings of powerlessness that we saw earlier to characterize male youths from blue-collar families. Here Maccoby and Jacklin (1974:154, 157, 150) report that:

(1) Clearly, college men are more likely than college women to expect to do well, and to judge their own performance favorably once they have finished their work.

(2) [College women are more likely than men to believe that] their achievements are often due to factors other than their own skills and hard work.

(3) Both [male and female adolescents and college students] have a certain awareness of the kinds of occupations they may realistically hope to enter.

Interestingly, one common response to the lesser competitiveness and success of women on male-dominated tasks has been not to lament them, but to argue they are *good* things to have occurred, since they have left women freer to cultivate their (allegedly) natural feminine skills of understanding and nurturing others. The kernel of truth to this position is that women probably *have* been more understanding and nurturant than men. Thus, for example, whereas neither wives nor husbands are especially good at empathizing with each other (see above), wives are clearly better at it than their husbands (Thomas et al., 1972). Similarly, there is no question but that we could all use more understanding and nurturing than we currently receive in our society. On the other hand, this position fails to tell us a number of other important facts.

In the first place, as Phyllis Chesler (1973:263) has noted, *women have probably developed these traits less through choice than necessity.* This is already implied by the above-mentioned fact that they are prevented from competing equally with men. As we saw in Chapter 6, it is also a logical consequence of Symbolic Interaction Theory, in that those, such as women, who are dominated by others should have a greater need for role taking—that is, in order to understand the oppressor. Supporting such an interpretation is not only the above-mentioned finding that wives are better role takers than husbands, but that (1) this was *not* the case when the wife was dominant in family decision making, and (2) children, female *and* male, were better role takers than their mothers (Thomas et al., 1972)! Second, Chesler (1973:263–264) notes that "female emotional 'talents' must be viewed in terms of the overall price exacted by sexism," and among the prices she includes freedom and dignity. Since we have already seen a great deal with regard to women's lesser freedom, let us examine their dignity.

A great deal of what we have seen previously already implies that women would have difficulty attaining and maintaining it. They are, after all, more likely to be excluded from, or segregated within, the labor market in a society where one's position in it determines one's status as well as one's life chances. They are discouraged from taking initiative in a society whose dominant ethos is one of individualism, and, according to Bernard (1968:63–64) (see also deBeauvoir, 1961:335), "Having to wait for male initiative gives women a profound inferiority feeling." It must also be demeaning not to have one's initiatives accepted, or accepted but credited to someone else.

The final straw, one suspects, is not only that women have been looked down upon by each other as well as by men, but that the very social skills women have developed to adapt to their situation help "do them in." Specifically, the problem is probably not simply that women are derogated by others but that *they have been conditioned to be more sensitive to the opinions of others!* The findings of a study of role taking by Sheldon Stryker (1957) support such an argument, in that parents who accurately took the role of their children were by no means the happiest, since accurately perceiving their children's points of view often meant recognizing how different their children were from themselves. Nor, interestingly, do most women list their social skills as the basis for their self-esteem, the implication instead being, sadly, that women are "socially adept [so as] not to be rejected" (Stoll, 1974:116).

In fact, self-derogation by adult women has been reported in several studies (Gurin et al., 1960; Rosenkrantz et al., 1968). However, Maccoby and Jacklin (1974:150–163) note that this is far from a consistent trend even through college age. One conclusion the latter authors draw from this literature is that women may not, in fact, value success as much as men, such that their lesser achievement by *male* standards does not necessarily lead to self-depreciation. Having accepted such standards, on the other hand, those men who have not been successful *would* derogate themselves, the net effect being little difference in self-evaluation between men and women.

While this may in part explain the absence of consistent differences in self-esteem, it also bears remembering that explicit measures of self-esteem are likely to create defensiveness. One might therefore expect more self-derogation by women on less direct measures. Thus, the aforementioned derogation of other women is presumably also an indirect form of *self*-derogation, and the tendency for women to discount their *own* performances (see above) is even more suggestive.

Another consideration here is that almost by definition "ambivalence" implies something other than consistent self-derogation. Indeed, there is reason to believe not only that women are less free to act on their attitudes or "leave the field" when their actions or inactions are demeaning, but that they are encouraged to believe that unhappiness itself must be their own fault. This, of course, seems less than a healthy situation to find oneself in.

Nowhere is this clearer than in the case of "mental illness."

Perhaps the first thing to note here is that *the very conception of a "normal" adult female often seems unhealthy.* Inge Broverman and her associates (1970:6–7), for example, ask what is healthy about "being more submissive, less independent, less adventurous, more easily influenced, less aggressive, less competitive, more excitable in minor crises, having their feelings more easily hurt, being more emotional, more conceited about their appearance, less objective." In this regard, after comparing ex-mental patients and "normal" housewives, Shirley Angrist (see Chesler, 1973:50–51) was surprised to discover "that so many of the controls [normal housewives] were reported to have evidenced similar behavior as the ex-mental patients. Thus, 46 percent were described as restless; 59 percent as worn out; 60 percent as tense and nervous; 57 percent as 'grouchy'."

Can one therefore say that, as with blue-collar workers in general, the alienation of women shades over into mental illness, that women experience an analogous double-bind situation, where to react to alienating conditions with alienation is to be labelled sick?

The statistics for rates of (officially diagnosed) mental illness are certainly clear; that is, *for most illnesses, more women than men* have been diagnosed as ill, and more have been in the various forms of treatment (Chesler, 1973:33–57; Gove and Tudor, 1973). However, if the statistics are clear, the definitive way to interpret them is not.

One of the problems is that the diagnosing and treatment of women as mentally ill frequently appear to be a strategy of men to socially control women. Thus, after interviewing psychiatrically institutionalized women, Chesler (1973:165) discovered that most commonly, "these women were committed wholly against their will, through brutal physical force, trickery, or in a state of coma, following unsuccessful suicide attempts (Unhappy women must be sick?)!" Rehospitalized women tend to be those who, upon having returned home the first time, refuse to play the housewife role (see Chesler, 1973:51). Indeed, most female "schizophrenics" have characteristics directly opposite to those of male "schizophrenics"; that is, whereas previously hospitalized male schizophrenics tend to be more passive and withdrawn than male normals, female schizophrenics tend to be more active and dominating than female normals (see Chesler, 1973: 52–55).

So impressed is Chesler (1973:164) with such facts as the latter, and the implicit rebelliousness of many of the women she interviewed more generally, that she concludes: "Most women who are psychiatrically hospitalized are not 'mad'." However, she also offers two other explanations for the higher rates of "mental illness" among women besides this "labelling," social-control hypothesis.

One is based upon the well-established fact that women, presumably because they have been conditioned to be other-oriented, are simply more likely to seek help from others when they experience problems. According to Phillips and Segal (1969:69), this occurs not because there are "real sex differences in frequency of disturbance," but because of "man's greater reluctance to admit certain unpleasurable feelings and sensations" because he regards it as unmasculine.

However, as Gove and Tudor (1973:830) note, the latter explanation cannot explain the fact that the initiation of women into mental hospitals is typically undertaken by someone besides the woman herself. It therefore seems reasonable to follow Chesler (1973:37) in concluding that some substantial portion of the greater "mental illness" of women is probably real and a consequence of their oppression by men.

Is this explanation supported by the evidence?

Understandably, the most popular accounts have relied not upon alienation but "role conflict" and/or "anomie." Thus, in reviewing the most popular explanations for the higher rates of (genuine) mental illness among women, Gove and Tudor (1973:815–816) include these: "The role of housewife is relatively unstructured and invisible," allowing her to "put things off," to "perform poorly," *and* "to brood over her troubles." Also, "The expectations confronting women are unclear and diffuse," such that "it is likely that many women find the uncertainty and lack of control over their future frustrating." Pauline Bart's (1972:168–169, 172) analysis of depression in middle-aged women appears to support these claims. Thus, women who had experienced "maternal role loss" — that is, whose child (children) had left home — were more likely to be depressed, and this relationship was stronger when the women in question were "only" housewives and/or overprotective or overinvolved in their relationships with their children.

On the other hand, two considerations strike one as particularly important here. One is that *women's overreliance upon the roles of wife and mother for their self-concept cannot simply be taken as given. Rather, for many, this is presumably a consequence of their having been powerless to do otherwise,* of their having reacted to discrimination and sex-role conditioning by focusing upon housewifery as a secondary source of meaning and sense of importance, and Bart herself (1972:185) notes this in no uncertain terms. Supporting the latter proposition are her findings that "housewives have a higher rate of depression than working women," and that more generally, "It is the women who assume the traditional feminine role — who are housewives, who stay married to their husbands, who are not overly aggressive, in short, who 'buy' the traditional norms — who respond with depression when their children leave" (Bart, 1972:177, 185).

The other consideration is that women by no means "require" the loss of the traditional feminine role in order to become depressed or otherwise mentally ill. Rather, a great deal of evidence suggests that being confined to the role itself produces insanity! Chesler (1973: 116–117), for example, notes that gender differences in general adjustment are greatest "at the younger intervals," and indeed, they are greatest at *precisely* the ages (25–34) when men and women are most likely to be married with children living at home. "White women who were never married," furthermore, "reported fewer symptoms than white married or separated women."

The latter finding points to a most interesting paradox which Jessie Bernard (1973:Chapter 3) has made the centrepiece of her book, *The Future of Marriage*. In particular, *single* women rate themselves as being *less* happy than do married women, yet the evidence for actual mental health completely reverses this difference, with *married* women being much more *poorly* adjusted! (Ironically, furthermore, married women *without* children are more happily married than those with children.) The data for males, on the other hand, is completely different again, with *single* men being much less well adjusted than married men!

Bernard herself follows Durkheim in drawing the same conclusion I would like to emphasize here; that is, if one looks at mental health in general, a Functionalist-anomie explanation applies much better to men than women. Thus, contrary to the popular assumption that men are more hindered by marriage than are women, men may well "need" to have their desires and aspirations limited if they are to be mentally healthy. Women, however, are *alienated* by marriage, even though, ironically, most of them may consciously believe otherwise.

What is it about marriage, therefore, that is more alienating for women than men? Presumably, what marriage in our own society does is consolidate, legitimate, and hence strengthen the power of men over women. From what can be gleaned from accounts such as Chesler's, the consequences may closely parallel those for unskilled blue-collar workers in general.

Thus, given the (relatively) unskilled nature of sexual activity and housework, married women are often treated as expendable or replaceable by their husbands. In this regard, "A feeling of impending breakdown is reported more frequently by divorced and separated females than by any other group of either sex." To this, one might also add that discrimination makes paid employment, one of the chief mitigating factors for the effects of marriage, and presumably its dissolution as well, more precarious for women than men.

Similarly, to this first factor, Chesler (1973:33, 121) adds another: "White and/or wealthy women in private hospitals, black and/or poor women in general psychiatric wards are reacting to being both *overworked* and, paradoxically, to the beginning signals of their sexual and maternal 'expendability'" (my emphasis). That "overwork" may indeed be a factor is suggested by the above-mentioned fact that recommitted female "schizophrenics" are likely to have refused to do "their" housework "duties." Certainly we know that most men do very little housework indeed, even when their wives work, and even when the number of children in the family increases (Meissner et al., 1975).

One can, I suppose, refer to these latter circumstances as "role conflict." However, the crucial aspect would seem to be not that there are conflicting demands per se, but that housewives are forced to fulfill all of them. As Chesler (1973:277) puts it, "Paradoxically, while women must not 'succeed,' when they *do* succeed at anything, they have failed if they're not successful at everything."

If this latter point suggests a double *standard* which may make life insane for the married woman, other information suggests a double *bind* which cannot help but exacerbate the problem. Specifically, women are not only overworked, and, in the process, paced by the needs (and whims) of other family members, but denied the opportunity to "leave the field," or even to complain. When combined with the long periods of time many housewives are isolated from other people, this entrapment probably does wonders in fostering delusions and the like. As to the latter, all too many men have habitually used their superior social power to deny the validity of women's experiences. They do it by conveniently claiming that the things about which women complain are "all in your imagination," that "it never happened that way," or worse, that they should feel guilty for "always bringing it up" (Laing, 1967:31–32).

Work and Its Products

"Cultural" arguments abound on the question of minority group members' and women's psychological orientations toward work, class conflict, and the political system. Native people and the Quebecois, for example, have often been said to have "present time" and "other" orientations which make them less involved than "WASPs" in their work. Similarly, women have been presumed to place much more importance upon romantic-familial relationships with individual men than either their work or the class struggle which arises from and through it.

However, after studying the people of one Ontario reserve, including their "apparently casual attitude toward work," Richard Dunning (1974:77) concluded that "much of the behavior of the Indians in the contact situation, though judged or prejudged by others to be Indian behavior, is, in fact, normal behavior of the class (in the national socioeconomic system) in which the actors are." Similarly, after reviewing other, more recent studies, Dosman (1972:81) concludes that:

> The provision of relief does not appear to affect employment *where there is work*. Only where the alternative to subsistence relief was subsistence and exhausting work such as trapping, did the extension of relief change work habits, and even then the evidence is mixed.

Presumably, these authors mean here that when the only work available to them is insecure and/or otherwise alienating, and remember the evidence that Indian workers are discriminated against, native people's reactions to work are alienated. Interestingly, furthermore, these authors' (and Robertson's, 1970) explanations for political apathy also suggest the appropriateness of the alienation concept: "The position of chief appeared to be given (by means of elections) to a person who would not oppose anything or anyone on the reserve" (Dunning, 1974:83).

That native people have been slow to organize themselves as a political force is hardly surprising, given such conditions and the fact that it is only very recently that "Indians" have begun to think of themselves as such (as opposed to being members of specific tribes) (Frideres, 1974). By the same token, having been excluded from participating in the central labor markets in any significant numbers, they have probably developed little in the way of *class* consciousness.

If this is indeed the case, it is in direct contrast to the experiences of American blacks, whose inferior position *within* the labor market has usually *facilitated* class consciousness. In his study of Detroit autoworkers, for example, John Leggett (1968:100–103) found black workers to be much more class conscious than whites, regardless of how much they earned and the degree to which they were organized into unions, and the results of later studies (Form and Rytina, 1969; Hurst, 1972) have born this out. Interestingly, furthermore, given the suggestion in the previous chapter that workers in general do not participate in the official political process because they regard it as class biased, Hurst (1972:663) reports that "occupational status is more important than race in accounting for interest in politics."[9]

Although we have little hard data on the subject, one suspects that the "superimposition" of ethnicity upon class (Dahrendorf, 1959) has had an analogous effect upon the work orientations and class consciousness of the Quebecois.

Specifically, having been discriminated against, they will presumably evidence more of a working-class orientation toward work. In Beattie's study of federal civil servants (1975:65), for example, 22 percent of the French Canadians as opposed to only 9 percent of the English Canadians said that they joined the civil service because it was the only job available, whereas 20 percent of the English Canadians as opposed to 9 percent of the French Canadians said they joined for the uniqueness of the work, and the relative stress upon "work" (intrinsic) versus "benefit" (extrinsic) factors more generally followed this pattern. The French Canadians were also much more likely to say that they "were determined to leave after a definite period." Not surprisingly, they just happened to have been more likely to be in routine as opposed to creative jobs as well as to have earned less income.

As to class consciousness, we have little in the way of comparative-quantitative data. The qualitative data from the last few years, however, could not be clearer; that is, especially the Confederation of National Trade Unions, CNTU (Confederation des Syndicats Nationaux, CSN), but also the Quebec Teacher's Corporation (Corporation des Enseignants du Quebec, CEQ) and the Quebec Federation of Labor to some extent, the French-speaking union federations in Quebec, have been by far the best organized, and most militant and class conscious in North America, surpassing DRUM (Dodge Revolutionary Union Movement), the black workers' caucus in Detroit, in numbers and staying power. Similarly, the nationalism of many Quebecois more generally has often been explicitly set within a Marxist framework.[10] This relatively high degree of class as well as ethnic organization notwithstanding, French Canadians participate less in (federal) elections, even when the effects of ethnic differences in class position are ruled out.[11]

If belonging to a minority racial or ethnic group appears to have facilitated class consciousness among American blacks and French Canadians, this has yet to occur on any sizeable scale among women. In this regard, there has been considerable truth to the presumption by male unionists and employers alike that women have made more docile workers, in that, for example, they have been slower than men to form unions. On the other hand, it is doubtful that this has occurred simply for the reasons which have been most typically advanced.

Thus, the presumption that, because of greater commitment to individual men and the housewife role, women have been less concerned about and therefore less psychologically affected by paid work is simply false. For example, after studying male and female workers in several manufacturing industries and a large hospital in Southwestern Ontario, Terry White (1973:219–222) found that far from supporting the conventional wisdom, *"autonomy is a much more important predictor of job satisfaction levels for women than for men,"* and that although "the patterns for autonomy's relationships with worker effectiveness levels were similar for men and women, . . . they were considerably stronger for women."

Findings such as these require us to take a hard look at the conclusions which have typically been drawn from those differences in reactions to work which have been shown to exist (or, perhaps, to *have* existed). If, for example, women have had somewhat higher rates of absenteeism and turnover than men, as has been the case,[12] this may indicate *not* that women in general are less committed to paid work, but that, through discrimination against them, they have been segregated in objectively more alienating work. That this has indeed been the case has recently been argued by Kanter (1976), as we saw earlier in discussing women's relationships with each other, and by Marianne Ferber and Helen Lowry (1976:230–231).

This suggests that any researcher who would claim that differing "cultural" orientations make women less "reliable" workers than men must first control for discrimination and the lower position of women in the occupational skill hierarchy. Although controlling for occupational category alone by no means adequately does this, it is at least better than the typical practice of lumping all men and all women together, regardless of their occupation. When Owen Adams and I broke down the results from the national Canadian sample by sex, we obtained the results presented in Table 9.2.

TABLE 9.2
DEPENDENCE UPON, AND INVOLVEMENT IN, WORK BY OCCUPATION AND GENDER IN THE NATIONAL CANADIAN SAMPLE

OCCUPATION		DEPEND ON WORK	ENJOY-ABLE	COM-MITTED	CHOICE OF IN-TRINSIC	WORK OVER-TIME
Executives, managers, proprietors	Male	50.0%	92.9%	93.2%	44.2%	87.0%
	Female†	30.0	77.8	60.0*	55.6	55.5*
Professional	Male	29.7	91.9	77.4	54.9	78.9
	Female	27.1	92.6	83.1	63.6	63.8*
Sales	Male	28.2	93.7	78.9	25.4	84.1
	Female	17.2	89.6	65.5	40.7	35.7*
Clerical	Male	18.8	82.6	71.0	43.9	50.0
	Female	26.0	88.6	66.0	52.6	38.5
Skilled laborers	Male	22.2	78.0	67.7	31.7	31.0
	Female	34.0	88.0	68.0	45.7	36.0
Unskilled laborers	Male	22.8	61.4	57.4	27.3	25.8
	Female	14.8	64.1	56.6	30.8	23.5

†Except for the Clerical category, there are many more males than females in the sample. The ratios are about 2:1 for all except Executives and Skilled, which are about 5:1.
*Only these male-female differences are statistically significant.

The first column contains the percentage of respondents who, when asked to choose which, from among "friends, family, work, church or union," they depend upon the most for personal satisfaction, chose *work*. Note first that one can hardly claim that women depend less upon work than men. Thus, the differences go every which way, and none of them is statistically significant. Although the largest percentage difference (among "Executives, proprietors and managers") suggests that women depend upon work less, the unequal numbers of men and women and small number of women in this occupational category make it statistically unreliable; alternatively, where a sex difference comes closest to being significant ("Skilled"), women are *more* likely to say that they depend upon work.

If we now turn to the indicators of alienation from work in the remaining four columns, we see that the conventional wisdom is not supported here either. Thus, there are no significant differences between men and women in how enjoyable they say their job is, and while there is a slight trend toward more blue-collar women than men regarding their work as enjoyable, the trend for nonprofessional, white-collar women is in the opposite direction. The same can be said for the percentages of respondents saying that they are "strongly committed" to their job, and when asked to choose which, from among such "intrinsic" factors as "interesting work" and "extrinsic" factors as "pay," would be the most important consideration in choosing another job, women were at least consistently *more* likely to choose intrinsic factors. Finally, the only clear and significant differences in psychological alienation from work appear on the reported behavior indicator — whether respondents agree that they "often work overtime without pay." However, while women appear more psychologically alienated from work on this measure, this is only true for *white-collar* women. Since the inequality gap between men and women tends to increase as one goes up the occupational hierarchy, this difference is still very much in line with the discrimination as opposed to the cultural position.

In addition to questioning the conventional wisdoms with regard to women and *paid* work, such considerations also throw into doubt those with regard to *housework*. In brief, these wisdoms are that "working-class women would rather be full-time housewives than hold outside employment," presumably because "paid work available to the ordinary nonprofessional woman is intrinsically unrewarding or actively alienating, while housework is, in some sense, relatively rewarding and nonalienating labor."

Myra Ferree (1976:431–432) has recently questioned these assumptions, arguing that being a housewife can, and often does, produce

(1) a sense of powerlessness, since the lack of a wage gives one less bargaining power in family decision making, (2) isolation from others, which deprives one of one of the major compensatory satisfactions of paid work, and (3) low status and self-esteem, since one is not viewed as "contributing something of value to society as a whole." Ferree's own findings support these arguments, in that "a full-time homemaker is less likely to be satisfied in general than [are] those who hold paid jobs." Furthermore, like blue-collar workers in general, housewives were more likely than those doing paid work "to want their daughters to be 'mostly different' from themselves." Finally, Ferree presents independent evidence for the importance of all three of the above-mentioned sources of dissatisfaction with being a housewife.

The conventional wisdom left untested by Ferree — that housework itself, and housewives' alleged control over it, is intrinsically less alienating than paid work — can be examined with the results of a British study by Ann Oakley (1974).

In the first place, Oakley (1974:60–65) reports, "by and large, the women interviewed did not enjoy their work" (my emphasis). There were no class differences here in underlying psychological orientations toward housework, but 8 of the 20 blue-collar housewives who initially said they were satisfied turned out not to be as the interview progressed, suggesting that, if anything, it is greater normative pressures which distinguish blue-collar from white-collar women. Also of interest here, given the earlier suggestion that being "feminine" in our society may be tantamount to being ill, is that many of those housewives who were proud of their work could be construed to be "obsessive compulsives" (Oakley, 1974:108–111)!

Second, while more complicated than those for paid work, the results with regard to the effects of general working conditions provide more support than disconfirmation for the hypotheses of Chapter 8. Thus, when asked to state "the best things about being a housewife," by far the most common response was "being your own boss," and other characteristics having to do with autonomy also ranked high on the list. On the other hand, and this is presumably why dissatisfaction with housework predominates in spite of this relative advantage over paid work, the number of tasks which need to be done and the fact that the failure to do them has serious consequences ("the wrath of husbands and the ill health of children" were often mentioned) makes this freedom "more theoretical than real." Hence, the housewife is "exempt from supervision but not wholly free to choose her own activities," such that, for example, "the taking of leisure" puts one behind and is therefore "self-defeating" (Oakley, 1974:42–44).

Third, housewives' perceptions of and reactions to their specific working conditions were very much like those of unskilled (paid) blue-collar workers. Thus, they emphasized the repetitive, unconstructive nature of housework, so much so that they described their working conditions as *more* objectively alienating than did male factory workers in general, or assembly-line workers in particular! Similarly, the housewives liked best those tasks which were least routine and most skilled (especially shopping and cooking), and liked least those most routine and least skilled (washing and ironing) (Oakley, 1974:46–49, 87).

In summary, one can make a strong case that differences in orientation to work between women and men (and there do not appear to be many to begin with) are much less a consequence of their inhabiting different *subcultures* than different positions in the occupational structure, and hence of their also having somewhat different working conditions. One can perhaps make a stronger case for the importance of sex-role ideology when it comes to explaining why women have been less likely than men to actively engage in the class struggle and politics more generally, but here too structural (material) conditions can be shown to be important.

Interpreting gender differences in participation, however, is by no means a straightforward enterprise. For example, "In the United States in particular, men typically have shown up more often at the polls, have engaged more often in political organizations and have manifested greater political awareness and concern . . ." (Orum et al., 1974:197, 204). On the other hand, women by no means participate less in voluntary associations *in general*, in that, among middle-aged people, at least:

(1) "While white collar men belong to more voluntary associations than women, women spend as much time monthly on associations . . .";

(2) Whereas men are more likely to belong to such "instrumental" associations as professional or trade associations, governing boards, and political parties or protest groups, women are more likely to belong to such "expressive" associations as home-and-school associations, health-and-welfare fund drives, and religious associations, *and* to be leaders of the latter; and

(3) While class and marital status affect a woman's participation in the same way as they do for a man — that is, she participates more when she is white-collar and married — "they do not affect

her ties with expressive voluntary groups" (Booth, 1972:187–189).

Some of these latter findings can certainly be construed to support Thelma McCormick's claim (1975:18, 25) that women's participation is less a matter of "underperforming" relative to men than of men and women inhabiting *different* political *cultures* altogether. (Indeed, she suggests, the class struggle is primarily a male enterprise.) Studies of political socialization, furthermore, appear to support such a claim. Even as early as elementary school, for example, boys have shown more interest in, and knowledge about, official politics, and expressed less uncritical acceptance of particular personalities, parties, and institutions than have girls (see Orum, et al., 1974).

On the other hand, do the different orientations of women represent an autonomous subculture, or, as with the "social skills" of women more generally, are they more "second best" adaptations to alienation? To the extent that it may have had a certain autonomous existence in the past, does such a feminine subculture even exist at present?

In this regard, McCormick (1975:25) herself appears to play both sides of the fence, arguing not only that women have a different political culture but that "they bring other criteria [than the class-expediency criteria of men] to bear on public issues and persons in public life" *because they have been "kept out of power"* (emphasis added); because "long before a woman reaches voting age or is even told that politics is 'a man's world,' she can see that government is a male preserve." Her argument that the fact that women vote at all under these circumstances must indicate "a stronger sense of political efficacy than men" therefore seems strange indeed. *In fact,* gender differences in feelings of political efficacy have been in precisely the opposite direction. When, however, women work in the labor market, they feel more efficacious and participate more (see the review by Morris Levitt, 1967).

That recent studies of Canadians and Americans indicate only small gender differences in participation (Curtis, 1971) may reflect the increasing proportion of women doing paid work as well as the women's movements having liberalized the sex-role ideology somewhat. (For evidence for such changes, see Mason et al., 1976.) This may also explain why the most recent U.S. study of the political socialization of children turned up little in the way of gender differences in interest, knowledge, or conservatism (Orum et al., 1974).

To say that men and women are becoming more alike in their participation in the status quo, however, is not to say that women are joining either the class or the feminist struggles in droves. Nor should one necessarily expect most women to do so in the near future. Thus, whereas a clear majority of French Canadians and American blacks are blue-collar workers, such that many find it natural to express their frustration against discrimination through one or another form of the labor movement, women are much more evenly distributed across the class structure.[13] Furthermore, they are likely to encounter male resistance to their full-fledged participation everywhere: in unions, political parties, and from their own lovers and husbands. When coupled with the fact that they themselves have generally been middle class and had difficulty relating to blue-collar women, feminists have understandably had difficulty organizing women as a single interest group.[14]

Notes

[1]The classic study here is John Dollard's (1957). For reviews and critiques, see Allport (1954), Banton (1967), and Simpson and Yinger (1972).

[2]Harold Alden found this material in the process of doing his MA thesis at the University of Western Ontario, and I thank him for it. Actually, in the case of the Curtis and Lambert results presented above, "prejudice" in this case was measured by having respondents indicate, on a "feeling thermometer" (a scale of 0 to 100) how much they liked or disliked various groups. As such, the measure is in some ways more like a "social distance" measure (see below).

[3]An important exception here is rape; that is, in this case men from blue-collar backgrounds are apparently more likely to "act out" their sex prejudices (Brownmiller, 1976).

[4]For a good review of these various studies, see Jones (1972:80-85).

[5]Living near a reservation for the past four years has given me many examples of this. Thus, in one case, a male of about 15 followed me around the local grocery store, asking me, "What can we do for you, *white boy?*"

[6]See, for example, Katz (1967) and Coleman et al. (1966).

[7]Nobles (1973) has sometimes been cited as having refuted this claim. However, from my reading of him (p. 22), it appears that his argument is more that blacks do not *now* use negative identification with their own race as a source of self-hatred than that this has not occurred frequently in the past.

[8]Although Sorrentino and Short (1974) found that women high in the "motive to avoid success" did *better* on a *male*-oriented task, the fact that the task involved only classroom-type competition (i.e., the results are not very visible and hence punishable) may not have produced enough threat to replicate the conditions of Horner's earlier experiment. Maccoby and Jacklin (1974: 141) appear to agree that women do not regard classroom situations as particularly competitive.

[9]On the other hand, blacks as a whole actually participate somewhat *more* than whites (Olsen, 1970). Why this should be the case is not clear.

[10]See Milner and Milner (1973). This has also been the case for French Canadian academics, as Jim Curtis has reminded me.

[11]Curtis and Lambert (1976). However, it is possible that French Canadians participate more in Quebec provincial politics.

[12]The U.S. data are reviewed by Ferber and Lowry (1976). Although Marchak (1973) is undoubtedly correct that too much has been made of male-female differences in absenteeism and turnover, I don't think they are quite as negligible as she implies they are.

[13]Actually, the question of assigning a class position to married women in particular is a thorny one which has been hotly debated. See Oakley (1974) and Eichler (1973) for various positions on the issue.

[14]For studies of male barriers to female participation in unions and professional associations, see the reviews by Roby (1975) and Huber (1976). For a summary account of feminist movements, see Rowbotham (1974).

10
NATIONALITY

There is a fascinating passage in Margaret Atwood's *Surfacing* where four Canadians on their way up a river in the wilderness come upon a heron someone preceding them has killed and strung from a tree. Having surveyed its disgusting remains, the raconteuse asks herself "Why had they strung it up like a lynch victim, why didn't they just throw it away like the trash?" She then answers her own question:

> To prove they could do it, they had the power to kill. Otherwise it was valueless: beautiful from a distance but it couldn't be tamed or cooked or trained to talk, the only relation they could have to a thing like that was to destroy it.

The killers, therefore, are presumed to have definite characteristics: they are "power hungry" and bent upon proving their destructive capacities, particularly when the object has no narrowly utilitarian value. Having been so characterized, however, they are also presumed to have a specific *national* character, in that, the raconteuse continues to herself, "*It must have been the Americans . . .*" (my emphasis).

Now, as it happens our voyageurs subsequently meet up with the "killer Americans," and they certainly fit the stereotypes Canadians have of them: they are "quite large," they have "midwestern accents," they are very extrovertish, and so on. Yet at this point the story takes a most interesting turn, for, to the raconteuse's consternation, the killers prove *not* to be Americans, but *Canadians* like themselves!

In this chapter we shall try to answer two questions: (1) *do* Canadians have a distinct "national character"[1] — distinct especially from the national character of Britons and Americans, and (2) to the extent that some such modal personality differences exist, precisely where do they come from? However, before giving these answers it might be helpful to relate such questions to the theoretical debates which have underlain the previous chapters in Part 3.

A BRIEF REVIEW OF THE PLACE OF NATIONALITY AND NATIONALISM IN SOCIOLOGICAL THEORY

For Smith and deTocqueville, human nature is everywhere the same, but social conditions make for some national differences in personality. In the case of Americans as compared to Europeans, deTocqueville claimed, "equality of conditions" has produced a number of distinct characteristics. For example,

> In a foreign country two Americans are at once friends, simply because they are Americans. They are repulsed by no prejudice; they are attracted by their common country. For two Englishmen the same blood is not enough; they must be brought together by the same rank [deTocqueville, 1961:203].

As one would expect for those in the Comtean tradition, Functionalists such as Parsons have relied more upon cultural values than individual or group interests to account for national differences between peoples. Thus, just as Comte and Durkheim attributed French-English differences in individualism to differences in the dominant religions of the two countries, so Seymour Martin Lipset (1967; 1968), in one of the best-known comparisons of Canadians and Americans, attributes a portion of the differences between them to different religious traditions. In the view of such Functionalists as Eisenstadt and Smelser, nationalism is in turn "religion politicized," in that it is seen as a collective attempt to establish organic solidarity after the disruptive effects of modernization and anomie (Smith, 1971:42–45).

In the Marxian view, national unification is an important vehicle through which the bourgeoisie comes to power and expands and protects its business ventures. Nationalism, therefore, is largely a class-based ideology. Both national differences and nationalism, however, will eventually be subverted by the contradictory forces of capitalist development: on the one hand, the participation of more and more people in large-scale industry tends to break down national life-styles from within, and on the other, the expansion of large-scale industry beyond national boundaries tends to do so from without.

In their early writings Marx and Engels regarded these trends as progressive, having assumed that (1) the modernization accompanying imperialism would break down feudal traditions in the less-developed countries (they claimed that the national aspirations of the smaller, weaker nations were doomed to fail anyway), and that (2) the working classes of developed and undeveloped countries alike would ignore the nationalist appeals of their respective bourgeoisie and unite as workers on an international basis. In time, however, they observed that intervention in the less-developed countries led to much needless destruction, and that the working classes of the developed countries, far from always taking the side of their working-class counterparts, were often bought off by the spoils of imperialism, as in the case of English-Irish relations. As a consequence, Marx and Engels occasionally (but not consistently) called for anticolonialist revolutions in less developed nations (such as Ireland).[2]

The latter position, of course, is essentially that of Fanon and "Maoism." Perhaps the most important social-psychological phenomenon they added to this perspective is the national "inferiority complex," which is said to result from colonial domination, and may eventually be cured through nationalist revolt.

Weber's account differs from the Marxian and neo-Marxian in predictable ways. Thus, he suggested, the process of internal homogenization is increasingly carried out more through bureaucratization than capitalization; economic exploitation of one nation by another may well follow rather than precede political subjugation; enhancement of national prestige may itself be a sufficient basis for such expansions. Nor did he share Marx's faith in the eventual internationalization of workers, arguing instead they could be among the easiest to fall prey to the emotional appeals of nationalists (Weber, 1958b: 159–179).[3]

DO CANADIANS HAVE A DISTINCT NATIONAL CHARACTER?

As Coleman Romalis (1972) has suggested, the claims of Dennis Wrong, Martin Lipset, and others can, with some interpretive license, be construed as follows: Canadians in general are more "other-directed" than Americans, and less "self-directed."

Thus, so the argument goes, Canadians are more *collectively* and less *self*-oriented than Americans, as evidenced, for example, by the higher amounts of public ownership of industry and social welfare legislation in Canada. They are also more likely to relate to others in terms of their *"ascriptive"* characteristics—their age, sex, and family background, and less likely in terms of their individual *achievements;* more likely to relate to others in terms of their *particular* relationship to oneself than *universalistic* standards of justice, and so on. Finally, to these Parsonian distinctions Lipset adds a related one: Canadians are more *elitist* and less *egalitarian,* as indicated, for example, by the fact that a smaller proportion of Canadians than Americans attend university.

Emphasizing now the self side of the polarity, one would presumably expect Canadians to be less concerned with themselves as individuals, to be *less ambitious* and *less self-reflective.* One fact usually invoked to support the claim for a lesser achievement orientation among Canadians is their alleged tendency to avoid risky business ventures. They are also said to be *more cautious* than Americans in general, in that, for instance, they apparently take out more life insurance per capita than any other Western nation, and *more conservative,* as reflected not simply by the retention by Canadians of the British monarchy and its official religion, but the lower divorce and crime rates in Canada (Lipset, 1967; 1968).

Although the more popular reaction to this characterization has been to accept it, criticism has also been extensive.

As one might expect, one of the major counterarguments is that this characterization *exaggerates the differences* between Canadians and Americans. Indeed, in one of the most often-cited classics on the subject, Dennis Wrong (1955) himself cautioned that the differences between English and French Canadians are probably larger than those between English-speaking Canadians and Americans.

More recently, critics have argued the point in two other ways. Thus, in the first of these criticisms, Arthur Davis (1971), Romalis (1972), and Irving Louis Horowitz (1973) have all argued that the laudatory image of Americans in the characterization is in good part a function of Lipset's naive, American chauvinism (and, presumably, his Canadian sources' self-depreciation), in that Americans are far less egalitarian and liberal than Lipset claims. Alternatively, or in addition, Canadians are said to be far less elitist and conservative than the characterization suggests.[4]

Tom Truman (1971), for example, has pointed out that whereas a smaller proportion of Canadians attend university, a larger proportion of per capita income is spent on higher education in Canada. Romalis (1972:223) notes that

The Canadian elementary and secondary school system (as he

[Lipset] notes) fosters greater desires for individual creativity, "intellectuality," and scholarliness than does the American system, while the Americans are more concerned with "civic" values than are Canadians. To conclude on this basis, as Lipset does, that the Canadian educational system is more elitist seems to obscure the more important issue, which is that there is more of a tendency toward self-orientation.

Horowitz (1973) demonstrates that differential rates of college attendance, religious affiliation, divorce, and crime have all dramatically decreased since World War II. Finally, Gad Horowitz (1968) shows that Canada's greater conservative elitism has also been matched by a stronger tradition of socialism. (He suggests that Americans' extreme individualism lessens the likelihood of their thinking and acting in truly radical, collectivist, terms.)

This latter suggestion points to a second major criticism of the characterization of Canadians as more "other-" and less "self-directed": the *interpretations* Lipset and others have made of those national differences which exist.

Not surprisingly, one of these criticisms concerns Lipset's reliance upon *values*, culturally derived but believed in and voluntaristically acted upon by individual Canadians and Americans, as explanations for the differences. Thus, critics have argued, it is by no means clear that rates of educational attendance or crime reflect the values of individual Canadians and Americans, since the institutional structure is controlled by ruling elites rather than the majority of the population (Romalis, 1972; Shiry, cited in Horowitz, 1973).

Another is that Lipset and others have been too liberal in interpeting some national differences, and too narrow-minded in interpreting others. Of the first, for example, Romalis and Horowitz (1973) rightly question whether economic growth in fact reflects the achievement values of individuals, or whether a lower crime rate reflects less achievement motivation and more conservatism.

Of the second, Gad Horowitz (1968) argues that conservatism is not simply different from socialism, but contains certain elements in common with it (corporatism from feudal traditions). Thus Canadian traditions tend to involve an interesting dialectical process: their greater conservatism tends to provoke more anticonservative revolt, but the greater degree of corporatism among both left and right tends to provoke, or, in the case of the right, legitimate, more socialist responses. Romalis' (1972:22) argument, alluded to above, has much the same structure: in effect, he appears to argue, Canadians' greater dependence upon others also leads them to be less sure of themselves, and therefore more self-conscious as well. (Such a possibility follows from Symbolic Interaction theory, and receives some support in the male-female differences of the previous chapter.)

To recapitulate, many of the alleged differences between Canadians and Americans have been exaggerated and/or misconstrued. More seriously, however, we cannot be sure that the indicators of either the protagonists or antagonists in the debate actually measure "national character." Indeed, if the above critics are correct, they do not!

Shall we therefore answer our original question in the negative? While this must remain a distinct possibility, one might note that the absence of (English[5]) Canadian-American differences on more bona fide measures of personality has also yet to be demonstrated. In this regard, the reader might consider the findings of the following, more social psychologically oriented studies.

One is a comparative study by Paul Grayson (1973). Here English Canadians and Americans from two communities (one area of Toronto and Elmira, Illinois) were compared on a number of characteristics, including their tendency to interact or not interact with those of a different class, age, or sex. The results for occupational grouping, measured in this case by the occupations of those to whom respondents said they went for political advice during elections, are presented in Table 10.1.

TABLE 10.1

WHO CANADIANS AND AMERICANS SAY THEY GO TO FOR POLITICAL ADVICE (GRAYSON, 1973)

ADVISEE

ADVISOR	BROADVIEW RIDING (TORONTO)				ELMIRA, ILLINOIS			
	P/M	W.C.	SK.	S & U	P/M	W.C.	SK.	S & U
Professional/ managerial	38%	35%	25%	13%	68%	54%	34%	26%
White collar	21	31	25	11	14	31	14	22
Skilled	9	3	10	17	8	4	47	25
Semi- and unskilled	32	31	40	59	10	11	5	27

Note that Canadian blue-collar workers are less likely than their American counterparts to say that they consult their social "superiors," and that this could be construed to support deTocqueville's claim that the British societal structure and national character, and, by derivation, the Canadian to some extent as well, is more elitist and less egalitarian. However, note also that other results are less easily interpreted in these terms; that is, the allegedly greater egalitarianism of Americans does not extend to *upper-class* Americans, who in this case appear *more* rather than less likely to avoid their social "inferiors" than their English Canadian counterparts. On the other hand, one might also argue that the latter results themselves derive from a greater elitism on the part of Canadians—that it is precisely because the Canadian class structure is more firmly buttressed by institutional and ideological supports that upper-class Canadians feel secure enough to cross class barriers.[6]

In a second study, Milton Rokeach (1975) compared the value rankings of undergraduate students at the University of Western Ontario with those at Michigan State University. Table 10.2 contains

TABLE 10.2

VALUE RANKINGS OF CANADIAN AND AMERICAN UNDERGRADUATES (ROKEACH, 1975)

VALUES	MEN		WOMEN	
	AMERICAN	CANADIAN	AMERICAN	CANADIAN
SELF-DIRECTED				
LIST #1:				
1. Sense of accomplishment	7.1	9.2	8.2	10.5
2. Wisdom	6.8	8.3	6.0	5.9
3. Happiness	6.2	4.7	6.2	4.4
4. Inner harmony	8.8	7.4	7.4	3.3
LIST #2:				
5. Ambitious	6.4	9.4	8.2	11.4
6. Capable	7.5	9.9	10.8	10.9
7. Independent	7.7	6.9	9.1	9.7
8. Logical	8.3	10.5	12.1	12.3
9. Self-controlled	8.6	10.2	9.1	11.6
OTHER-DIRECTED				
LIST #1:				
1. Family security	8.1	7.5	8.8	8.8
2. Mature love	7.4	5.6	7.1	4.4
3. True friendship	8.7	7.3	7.0	5.5
LIST #2:				
4. Cheerful	12.0	8.8	10.3	7.5
5. Clean	14.1	15.4	14.4	13.9
6. Forgiving	10.5	9.1	8.7	6.5
7. Helpful	11.9	9.1	8.9	9.3
8. Honest	5.2	3.0	3.4	1.5
9. Obedient	15.0	16.6	15.6	16.0

the rankings of values (from two different lists of 17 values each) which might reasonably be construed to fit Kohn's self-versus-other distinction (see Chapter 8).[7]

Looking first at the *self*-oriented values, one can see that American men rank a "Sense of accomplishment", "Wisdom," and being "Ambitious," "Capable," "Logical," and "Self-controlled" higher than do Canadian men. However, in Kohn's operationalization of the self-other distinction "Happiness," "Inner harmony," and being "Independent" should show the same difference, but the differences are in the opposite direction. Much the same is true for the women, although now only four of the nine differences are in the predicted direction.

One way of summarizing these findings would be to say that there is a tendency for Canadians to be *less* self-directed along certain dimensions, but, as suggested by Romalis, they are actually *more* self-directed on others. (The interesting fact that these other dimensions are especially happiness and inner harmony will be taken up shortly.) The same tentativeness holds for the "other-directed" values. Thus, Canadian men do indicate a higher other-orientation on seven of the nine values, yet it may be significant that the two whose differences are in the opposite direction—"Clean" and "Obedient"— are central to Kohn's distinction. Canadian women show a greater other-orientation on six of the nine values, but they also rank "Obedient" somewhat lower.

Interestingly, a third study indicates both moderate-to-mixed results *and* suggests decreases between Canadians and Americans over time. Here Craig Crawford's (1975) conclusions seem particularly valid, since he first matched his Canadian and American communities on a number of relevant dimensions and then controlled for the effects of age, sex, occupation and other characteristics of individual respondents.

On the one hand, he found strong differences on Lipset's achievement versus elitism dimension, with Canadians being much less achievement oriented and much more elitist. On the other hand, Canadians were *less* collectively and *more* self-oriented in general, somewhat *less* conformist in particular, and significantly *less* traditionalistic and *more* modernistic in their general outlook on life.

In an attempt to determine changes in value-orientations over time, Crawford compared the values of Canadians and Americans of different ages, the assumption being that differences between the differences reflect such changes. After doing so, he discovered that whereas Canadians over 60 years of age were indeed very much less achievement-oriented and more elitist than their American counterparts, "Canadians under thirty years of age are approximately *equal* to Americans of the same age in achievement orientations but they are still significantly more elitist" (my emphasis). "The Canadian aged, as expected, tend to be slightly more traditional and socially conforming than the American aged, although, there do not appear to be any substantive differences in self-other orientations." Whereas older Canadians are less likely than their American cohort to participate in political and economic associations, "Canadian youth are slightly more involved in politics and markedly more involved in the economy than their American counterparts."

As Crawford himself concludes (1975:94), the latter trend in particular "is consistent with the notion that Canadians are becoming more accepting of American culture." This is the case for achievement-orientation more generally, and for social conformity. Interestingly, on the other hand, Canadians do not appear to be becoming less collectively oriented; rather, Americans are becoming more so. Similarly, there has actually been a large *increase* in differences in traditionalism, with Americans remaining relatively *highly* traditional and Canadians becoming much *less* so. Clearly, therefore, decreases in differences between Canadians and Americans over time do not simply reflect a trend toward Canadians becoming more like Americans.

It is not easy to summarize the results of these various studies, but it seems reasonable to conclude that while the differences are not great, and appear to have been decreasing, there *has* been something of a distinct English Canadian national character which can be documented in comparative-quantitative terms. It can in part be defined by its greater other- and lesser self-orientation, but considerable qualification is necessary. Specifically, whereas Canadians appear to have been less achievement oriented than Americans, they may also have been more self-reflective. Whereas they have been more deferential toward elites, they have not necessarily been more conservative or conformist in general.

One suspects, however, that this characterization omits our "inferiority complex," which, although poorly documented in any systematic manner, is one of our most distinctive and best-known character traits. Envy of the United States and self-depreciation have been recurrent themes in Canadian history.[8] For example, if Canadians have actually contributed at least their share of modern technical inventions, most Canadians have not sought out these facts, but instead lamented the alleged fact that "nothing interesting ever happens here." Whereas many Canadians justify American dominance of Canadian manufacturing by the supposed absence of Canadian personnel with expertise, the facts do not support such a supposition (Levitt, 1970). While Americans in the know have marvelled at the high quality of the C.B.C.'s dramas and documentaries, Canadians (the general public, that is) have paid little attention to the literature and art of other Canadians until, or unless, it has "made it in the States." As a consequence, generations of academics, writers, artists, actors, and musicians have trekked to the United States, or Europe, many of them never to return.[9]

It has long been contended in Canadian literary circles that this complex is reflected in the content of Canadian cultural works themselves. This idea appears to have gained influence largely through the teachings and writings of Northrop Frye, but has recently received wider recognition through Margaret Atwood's *Survival: A Thematic Guide to Canadian Literature* (1972).

According to Atwood, our national inferiority complex shows through our literature in a variety of different ways. Thus, she maintains, in contrast to the works of Britons and Americans, the central figures in Canadian pieces fail to control nature, and often die in the process. If in British literature animals are made into cultured humans with whom the writer and reader can pleasantly identify, and if in American literature animals are likely to be successfully hunted by the central figures, Canadian animal stories "are about animals *being* killed, as felt emotionally from inside the fur and feathers" (Atwood, 1972:74). If in other literatures heroes more generally die either for noble purposes (the dominant English theme) or while heroically defying authority (the American theme), in Canadian literature they are likely to die from such seemingly pointless circumstances as becoming lost in the snow.

Understandably, such a position has provoked cries of selectivity, and among such literary notables as Morley Callaghan and George Woodcock at that.[10] Interestingly, furthermore, some of the specific themes which Atwood is said to have left out are those which Lipset's critics have pointed out; that is, constructive introspection and revolt. However, that there has been a national inferiority complex among Canadians I take to be true, and it would not be particularly surprising if it has surfaced in our cultural products on occasion. Indeed, within the past year or so a Canadian cartoon strip which makes full use of the Canadian public's identification

Figure 10.1

with the complex has gained considerable popularity. As can be seen in the typical sequence in Figure 10.1, it is appropriately set on a desolate island ("nowhere"), and titled "The Outcasts."

HOW DID WE GET HERE?

The need to wrestle a livelihood from a cruel land has put a premium on some of the sterner virtues — frugality and caution, discipline and endurance. Geography even more than religion has made us puritans, although ours is a puritanism tempered by orgy. Outnumbered by the trees and unable to lick them, a lot of Canadians look as though they have joined them — having gone all faceless or a bit pulp-and-papery, and mournful as the evening jackpine round the edges of the voice, as if (in Priestley's phrase) something long lost and dear were being endlessly regretted. Or there are those who run — by car, train or plane (flying more air miles per capita than any other people), lickety-split as if the spirit of the northern woods, the Wendigo himself, were on their trails [Kilbourn, 1965:120].*

Shall we therefore consider the case settled? Certainly we would have no difficulty finding examples from various forms of Canadian culture which could be construed to support the link.[11] The problem, of course, is that proclaiming the link and buttressing it with this or that example hardly establishes it. Is there therefore better evidence available? Although there is precious little of it, two matters might be mentioned.

One is that it might make sense to determine whether societies in general which function close to the level of subsistence produce personality types which are conformist or otherwise "other-oriented." J. W. Berry of Queen's University (1967) has in fact made this argument in another connection and backed it up with a number of cross-cultural comparisons, but the results of a subsequent study (Munroe et al., 1973) do not consistently support those of the initial study. Nor, for that matter, have most Canadians ever lived in the nontemperate, severe areas of the country. Another interesting question is whether the people of Norway, Finland, Iceland, Mongolia, or Siberia, whose geography has been even less hospitable than our own, are even more cautious and conformist than Canadians are

---

*From The Making of the Nation by Wm. Kilbourn, reprinted by permission of the Canadian publisher McClelland & Stewart Ltd., Toronto.

alleged to be. Do they suffer from still stronger feelings of inferiority?

Clearly, these latter few suggestions are meant only half seriously, for it would seem to be stretching the point to argue that any greater physical hardships Canadian settlers may have had still account for much of their greater dependence upon others, cautiousness, and so on. Presumably, most of the latter must be attributed to other processes.

Ironically, however, it is just such a residue-from-the-past explanation which Lipset and his Parsonian-oriented account provides us. The difference is that the original events which are supposed to have produced the values of contemporary Canadians are not natural in the physical sense, but social structural. As I read Lipset, the principal ones are these:

(1) The transplanting of British values of elitism, and so on, to North America via the bodies of British emigrants.

(2) (Presumably) the modification of these values by frontier conditions (for example, it would have been difficult to closely control fur traders and settlers).

(3) Their further modification by Americans through their revolution. Not only did the latter not occur in Canada, but British values were reinforced there by the influx of Empire Loyalists.

(4) The threat which the U.S., as a model of democracy, posed to the British colonial authorities in Canada, who, in reaction, established a stronger central government and more controlled western expansion than occurred in the United States.[12]

As with his characterization of Canadian national character itself, criticism of Lipset's explanation was not long in coming.

One line of argument has been to criticise his choice and interpretation of historical events. Both Romalis (1972) and Horowitz (1973), for example, point out that Lipset's model-of-democracy argument is highly ethnocentric, for the United States has been heavily militaristic and vociferous about its alleged rights to the Western hemisphere at numerous points in history.[13] One cannot claim, therefore, as Lipset does, that Canadians' nationalism is mainly a reflection of their British conservatism. By the same token (and, strangely, this quote is cited by Lipset himself) it is not the case

> . . . that revolutionary forces developed no strength in Canada. We
> have had our revolutions but they have been largely unsuccessful, and
> being unsuccessful we try to forget them. Thus we have tended to
> dismiss our rebels of the past as misguided individuals out of accord
> with their fellow Canadians . . . [Clark, 1959:3].

If, therefore, the definitive Canadian tradition is one of counter-revolution, it and the values which are supposed to be embodied in it must have broken down on occasion. Indeed, according to some (Carl Cuneo, personal communication) Canadians *did* make a decisive break with Britain. It occurred when the merchants of Montreal clamoured for annexation to the United States in 1849 and were thereby successful in getting the British Parliament to repeal the Navigation Laws. (These required Canadian and American goods transported through Canada to be carried by British ships.)

An equally fundamental criticism concerns Lipset's very reliance upon values-as-residues as opposed to other sources. These critics usually turn to the theoretical position utilized earlier by Arthur Davis (1971) — the neo-Marxist model of neocolonialism. According to Horowitz (1973: 348–349), available evidence with regard to aspirations — for economic development, modernization, and so on — indicate few differences between Canadians and Americans, such that if there are differences in actual growth, or whatever, "the gulf arises in ways of achieving such modernization, and beyond that, the forms of parceling out wealth." To Romalis (1972:218–222), it is the colonial connection which makes sense of the aforementioned configuration of other- *and* self-orientations among Canadians:

> In many respects the Canadian elites are colonial fragments. They are unsure of their status relative to other national elites, and especially their reference elites in the United States and Great Britain; but they are very sure of their status with respect to the nonelite strata of Canadian society. This lends them the self-consciousness which characterizes most colonial elites, so that paradoxically they are simultaneously more autonomous and more conformist. . . . It is not that Canadians are more British, elitist, and particularistic, that is of primary importance here; it is that they are more colonial. . . .

In this account[14] the most important historical processes for understanding the social structure and national character of contemporary Canada are not those suggested by Lipset, but these (see especially Tom Naylor, 1972):

(1) The early molding of the Canadian political economy along "metropolis-hinterland" lines; that is, toward the extraction of such "staples" as fish, fur, timber, and grain for the colonizing country "in return for" finished goods.

(2) The various distortions and dependencies which (are alleged to) have arisen from this molding: the development of an indigenous Canadian bourgeoisie more along merchant, and subsequently financial, than industrial lines; the gearing of state policies toward the interests of the former more than the latter; the dependence of the Canadian economy upon first Britain's economy, and then the United States's, for industrially produced goods.

(3) As a consequence of the aforementioned distortions and dependencies, the weakness of indigenous Canadian industry: its late start, smaller size, and susceptibility to disruptions from without, and hence less favorable competitive position in comparison to foreign industry, either abroad, or in Canada as "branch plants" (wholly owned subsidiaries).

(4) On the one hand, the continuously dependent status of Canada as a nation (first vis-à-vis France, then Britain, and now the United States); on the other, the peculiar nature of its present dependency upon the U.S. (extremely high degrees of direct foreign investment and ownership).

The social-psychological implications of this account would then be, on the one hand, a "dependent" or other-directed and self-depreciating national character, and, on the other, movements for national independence.

This model also has its critics. For example, L. R. MacDonald (1975) argues that one can neither separate financial from industrial interests in Canadian economic development nor document their differential support for allegedly partisan government policies. Others (Moore and Wells, 1974) claim that the dependence of the Canadian bourgeoisie has been greatly exaggerated, such that its independent imperialist role has been vastly underplayed. Defenders of the model (Campbell, forthcoming; Warnock, 1976), on the other hand, have taken issue with each of these criticisms.

Given that these issues are neither completely resolved at present nor capable of being sufficiently investigated within the confines of the present work, I shall take the easy way out and simply make what I consider to be two reasonable suggestions.

One is that whether or not the above neocolonialist model is accurate enough in its historical details to explain Canada's present dependence upon the United States, the latter could still be explained on grounds consistent with a more general Marxist position. Specifically, even if one were to simply assume that the American industries which established branch plants in Canada were expanding from a larger market to begin with, and hence from a position of larger size and strength than their indigenous Canadian competitors, their early cornering of Canadian consumer goods, capital, and labor markets and, given Marxian theory, greater influence upon Canadian governmental industrial policies, would follow.

The other is that however we arrived at the present state, we have indeed been dependent. Until very recently, for example, *Time* and *Reader's Digest* were able to avoid paying taxes on their advertising revenue and thus have a great advantage over their Canadian competitors. Less well known are such matters as the ways in which the United States has been able to browbeat Canada into helping it solve its own balance of payment's crises:

> Washington demanded, and Canada agreed, to convert one billion dollars of her exchange reserves into U.S. securities. This represented over one-half of current holdings, which Canada will only be able to call on at the discretion of the U.S. Secretary of the Treasury [Levitt, 1970:13].

Given this dependence, it is not difficult to imagine some of the trends neocolonialist theorists have suggested, such as Canada's higher rates of unemployment as compared to the United States, Britain, and other OECD countries. However, such trends have yet to be unequivocally related to the factors postulated by the neo-colonialist model. Still less have they been related to the psychological alienation of Canadians. We know that Canadians have had a higher rate of job turnover (Whitestone, 1974), but we can hardly jump to the conclusion that American ownership of industries in Canada necessarily makes jobs more alienating. (It is even conceivable that a more rapidly expanding economy provides Canadians with more job opportunities.) We know that Canadian politicians make, and, certainly, administrate, policy decisions with much greater concern for the reactions of Washington than vice versa, but it is unclear that these decisions would be very much more in the "general public's" interest without this concern. We know that Canadians take out more life insurance, but we don't know that foreign control of their life chances is the source of the difference.

More typically, however, the social-psychological claims of adherents of the neocolonialist model have centred around the Canadian inferiority complex, and especially Canadians' alleged reactions to it. In the United States, they usually claim, nationalist ideologies only serve to justify imperialism. Since the spoils of the latter tend to buy off American workers, nationalism in the States is inherently regressive. In Canada, on the other hand, rebellion against foreign domination is said to be as progressive as it is rife. Thus, so the argument goes, since the bulk of Canadian industry is owned by the American bourgeoisie, and since those sectors of the economy which are indigeneous (for example, banking) also have strong interests in supporting foreign capitalist interests, the anti-American nationalism of Canadian workers will greatly increase the likelihood of their becoming anticapitalist (Davis, 1971).

The strongest argument for such a position is probably the example of the other Canadian nation — Quebec — for there, as argued in the previous chapter, a good case can be made that the "super-imposition" of national-ethnic upon class conflict has greatly advanced the latter. At the same time, it is easy to exaggerate the socialist potential in Quebec nationalism. Thus, as many Marxists (for example, Bourgue and Laurin-Frenette, 1972) as well as liberal federalists have pointed out, nationalism has appealed more to Quebec's middle than her working class, and it is by no means clear that the new Parti Quebecois government is going to be any more socialist than the NDP governments of the Western provinces have been.

These reservations appear to apply even more to English Canada, in that at least the most organized and vociferous, continuing nationalists have been the small-to-medium-sized businessmen and intellectuals of the Committee for an Independent Canada (CIC), and their underlying program appears to have been this: a bigger slice of the Canadian market for indigeneous Canadian businesses, professionals, artists, and intellectuals. That the "Waffle," the former left-wing opposition within the Ontario NDP, felt it necessary to appeal to these strata in its electoral campaigns is probably a sign of the weakness of nationalist sentiment among Canadian workers. (For harder evidence of the lesser appeal of nationalism to Canadian workers see especially the paper by Carl Cuneo (1976).)[15]

Some of the reasons for this are not difficult to surmise, for the English Canadian situation is far from analogous to that of Quebec. Rather, as Horowitz (1973) suggests, working for a multinational corporation in English Canada may well mean that one is more highly paid and has more fringe benefits than those working for indigeneous, and usually smaller, industries.[16] It also means, of course, that unlike the case of the Quebec worker, one's bosses will likely be of the same ethnicity and speak the same language. Finally, one's union is likely to have its headquarters in the United States, and its officers will speak the same language. (Cuneo, 1976, discovered that participation in most organizations increased the likelihood that Canadians would be nationalist — in this case, would not want political unification with the United States. However, the *opposite* was true for participation in unions; that is, members were more continentalist.)

I don't mean to argue here that nationalism among Canadian workers has not and will not become a source of progressive social change. One recent case is that of Canadian chemical workers. Here the refusal of Canadian officers of an American union to obey orders from their superiors which led to their expulsion, also led to the formation of a Canadian union whose structure may well turn out to be more internally democratic than that of the international. However, it is clear that nationalism is far from *necessarily* progressive. Thus, in a recent election in the United Steel Workers the choice was between a carry-over slate from the conservative administration of I. W. Abel and a reform slate headed by Ed Sadlowski. Lynn Williams ran for (and won) a position on the executive council, implicitly on a program of more autonomy for the Canadian section, but on the *conservative* slate.[17]

At the very least, however, Canadian nationalism has probably had a therapeutic effect upon the inferiority complex. This might be concluded from a study of Ontario high school students by Ted Harvey, Susan Hunter-Harvey and George Vance (1972), which indicates that those students who idealized the Canadian nation (as measured by their endorsement of such statements as "Canada is rightly one of the most respected countries in the world") and felt emotionally loyal to It ("I am a Canadian first, last, and always") had significantly higher self-esteem. Again, however, it is not clear that this particular trend (the raising of self-esteem by nationalistic feelings) necessarily has progressive political consequences.

These researchers conclude that *in general,* nationalism among the students they studied is a progressive force, in that students who express more nationalistic feelings are (1) more likely to move within a politicized environment (i.e., where their parents and peers are interested in politics), and (2) more knowledgeable about the official political process. However, if we distinguish between the two most important types of nationalism, a "traditionalist" outlook of high loyalty to, and idealization of, one's country and a "national liberationist" outlook of anti-Americanism and a desire for national independence, we find that the pattern is more complicated. Specifically, it is those whose self-esteem is apparently least likely to be raised by their nationalism (the "national liberationists") whose national sentiments are associated with (1) cynicism about the official political process, and (2) identification with the more progressive official parties (i.e., the NDP as opposed to the Conservatives).

I do not mean to imply here that the role attributed to the raising of national esteem in the neocolonialist model is therefore mistaken. Certainly an adequate test of the hypothesis would require us to actually correlate self-esteem with political stance and control for other sources of both nationalist sentiment and progressivism. Similarly, obviously a great deal hinges upon the relative strength of the various types of nationalist movements in existence at the time.

Rather, the point is that until such detailed analyses have been undertaken, one cannot simply assume, a priori, the validity of the neocolonialist model.

Notes

[1]This is Inkeles and Levinson's (1969) classic conception of national character. Note, however, that it differs from many more popular uses, where it often appears to refer simply to a society's culture.

[2]Their calls for international revolution were also tempered on occasion by the realization that given the reality of nation states under world capitalism, various proletariats would have to wage the class struggle within particular nations and seize control of their respective states.

[3]For the related, "mass society" explanations of Mannheim and William Kornhauser, see Smith (1971:57-60).

[4]Lipset himself (1968:31-63) moderated his earlier, laudatory characterization of the United States to include the free rein its political structure gave to its capitalist class and its "absorptive" tendencies vis-à-vis Canada.

[5]Obviously, the present account of nationality leaves out the other Canadian nation, Quebec. Although the focus upon the Quebecois in the previous chapter was mainly as a "minority group," some consideration was given there to their status as a nationality. See Rioux (1971), the articles by Bourque and Laurin-Frenette, and Ryerson, in Teeple (1972), and Milner and Milner (1973) for material pertinent to the issues discussed here with regard to English Canada.

[6]Grayson himself prefers this interpretation (see also Archibald, 1976c). However, see the latter source for the problems in unequivocally drawing such a conclusion from these data.

[7]I was unsure about excluding "Freedom" and "Pleasure" from the self-directed values. Also, since he regards "Considerate of others" as a *self*-directed value, Kohn (1969) might want to put "Polite" and "Responsible" in this category as well. However, the latter seem to me to be other-directed as well, so I have avoided placing them in either category.

[8]Which is not to say that this tendency is rife in all strata. For example, Craig McKie (personal communication) maintains that the complex is "markedly absent in some elite circles."

[9]This is clear for social scientists alone: Canadians who have gone and stayed south of the border include John Kenneth Galbraith, Erving Goffman, Dennis Wrong, Nathan Keyfitz, and others.

[10]See Thompson (1973) for a review of Atwood's critics. Note that whether a majority of Canadian works evidence the complex is not really relevant — the most important question is whether it is more in evidence in Canadian than British and American literature. Hopefully, someday someone will undertake a more systematic study of the matter.

[11]See, for example, Jock MacDonald's "The Secret of the Woods." Also, in a striking Quebecois example, a Laurence Gagnon painting (in the McMichael Collection) shows men cutting ice under a very forbidding sky, with a single ray of sunshine over the village in the distance.

[12]It is not meant to imply here that most of these ideas are original to Lipset.

[13]See Note 4 above.

[14]This tradition of Canadian scholarship begins with the "staples theory" of Harold Innis, Donald Creighton, and others (see Warnock, 1974; Easterbrook and Watkins, 1967), and continues into the present through the work of various left-wing nationalists (e.g., Levitt, 1970; Davis, 1971; Teeple et al., 1972).

[15]Just as the vast number of surveys Cuneo reviews indicate that Canadian blue-collar workers are much less nationalistic than other Canadians, so the vast bulk of the evidence strongly contradicts the claim that U.S. workers have been "bought off" by the "spoils" of imperialism (see Evansohn, 1977).

[16]Size rather than nationality of the corporation per se is undoubtedly the important characteristic here.

[17]For a more detailed evaluation of the role of nationalism among Canadian workers see the unpublished paper by Michael Ornstein, York University: "The Class Nature of Nationalistic Ideology in English Canada." See Laxer (1976) for a more optimistic account. For an in-depth assessment of Canadian nationalism more generally see Cuneo's dissertation (1973).

11

CHANGING WHAT WE DO

How might we best solve the "social problems" identified in Part 3? We might follow Adam Smith and attempt to educate and otherwise rehabilitate the individuals damaged by the system, or use deTocqueville's constitutional safeguards, not only as a means of rectifying the system's abuses, but as "preventative medicine." Alternatively, we might zero in on, and attempt to change, the "faulty communication" and unfortunate misunderstandings between individuals and small groups which Cooley and Mead, and later the Human Relationists, claimed are behind our social problems. Finally, were we to accept Marx's advice we should neither simply deal with the individual victims of the system, this or that relationship among them, nor tinker with the system itself, but collectively transform it through a socialist revolution. Let us consider each of these in turn.

BLAMING AND "REHABILITATING" THE VICTIM

As long ago as 1943, C. Wright Mills (1967:531, 534) succinctly pointed out that the approach of American social scientists to "social problems" has been to view "isolated and immediate problems as the 'real' problems." Related to this tendency to "slip past structure to focus on isolated situations" is "a tendency for problems to be considered as problems of individuals."

More recently, William Ryan (1971) has labelled the latter tendency "blaming the victim." We have in fact already encountered numerous cases of this in the preceding chapters, the most common being the "culture of poverty" explanation for class, racial-ethnic, sexual, and national inequality. As Ryan (1971:7–8) notes, this ideology differs from the older, more conservative social Darwinism in attributing the source of the problems to the victim's environment. However,

> The defect, the fatal difference—though derived in the past from environmental forces—is still located *within* the victim, inside his

skin. With such an elegant formulation, the humanitarian can have it both ways. He can, all at the same time, concentrate his charitable interest on the defects of the victim, condemn the vague social and environmental stresses that produced the defect (some time ago), and ignore the continuing effect of victimizing social forces (right now).

The perverse result of such analyses, Ryan continues, is that social change programs are "designed to change, not society, as one might expect, but rather society's victim."

> In education, we have programs of "compensatory education" to build up the skills and attitudes of the ghetto child, rather than structural changes in the schools. In race relations, we have social engineers who think up ways of "strengthening" the Negro family, rather than methods of eradicating racism.

The mental health problems of the poor are not treated as instances of structurally derived alienation from themselves, but as "intra-psychic problems that can only be corrected by therapeutic intervention in the psychic processes of the poor person himself" (Ryan, 1971:147).

To add insult to injury, many such programs — for example, many forms of compensatory education and psychotherapy — are both very costly and notoriously unsuccessful in changing even the victim.[1] Presumably, much of this derives from the failure of such programs to change the wider structural context to which the patient returns after treatment. Indeed, the internal structural features of the treatment process itself may neutralize treatment, or even exacerbate the "individual's" problems.

The process of being *labelled a deviant* is a case in point, although available research now suggests that the effects of labelling alone have probably been exaggerated.[2] But quite aside from this, incarceration in a boarding school if one is an Indian child or a mental hospital if one "has" mental problems is likely to increase the very powerlessness which, as we saw in Chapters 8 and 9, is a major source of learning and mental problems.

Goffman (1961) has provided a vivid picture of the process in his account of "total institutions." In such institutions as mental hospitals, he suggests, inmates tend to be treated under the same exigencies of mass production and control that they encounter in their everyday lives in the outside world. In the process they are not only cut off from the social support upon which their self-conception and mental stability is based, but stripped of the everyday material possessions and behavior patterns which are a source of individuality. Even worse, they are forced to undertake deference and other patterns of action which are blatantly incompatible with a sense of competence and dignity.

Given the overriding concern with efficiently controlling inmates, Goffman claims, rehabilitation is seldom even attempted. However, even if it were, the depersonalization and "mortification of the self" which presumably result from inmates' extreme powerlessness would probably neutralize any therapeutic value which isolated aspects of incarceration might have. Furthermore, given that the inmate is likely to be made totally psychologically dependent upon other inmates, the institution, or both, it would hardly be surprising if s/he comes to fear the outside world and actually takes steps to remain sheltered from it. (Chesler, 1973, suggests that this occurs particularly frequently among female mental patients.)

Although Goffman has perhaps exaggerated the "totalness" and rehabilitative uselessness of mental institutions in particular,[3] his account has nevertheless received some "harder" support in a study of a narcotics hospital by Charles Tittle (1972). Thus, self-evaluations were lowest among the inmates who were "in the middle phase of their institutional careers," which he interprets to mean that "self-esteem appears to be at its lowest ebb when inmates are farthest removed from the outside world." Also, those with the most exposure to purely custodial conditions had the lowest self-esteem.

Interestingly, however, there was a tendency for the opposite to be true for subjective feelings of powerlessness among the male inmates; that is, those who expressed more of a sense of deprivation of personal autonomy actually had *higher* self-esteem. Although Tittle himself simply takes this to contradict Goffman's hypothesis, it is highly possible, given the apparently high degree of objective powerlessness for most inmates, that reported deprivation is less an indication of actual individual differences in deprivation than of rebellion. Put otherwise, to admit that one is oppressed when others under the same objective circumstances do not may indicate that one is fighting back, and this may itself be a source of pride, as Ryan (1969) discovered in an outside setting.

HUMAN RELATIONING OFFENDER AND VICTIM

The approach of "Human Relationists," discussed briefly in Chapter 8, is considerably more sophisticated than that of traditional therapy or other forms of individualistic rehabilitation. Specifically, Human Relationists stress that intrinsic involvement in work and commitment to organizations require that individuals exercise control over their work and work cooperatively rather than competitively with others (see Katz and Kahn, 1966, Tannenbaum, 1966, and Blumberg, 1968, for reviews). Similarly, their recognition of the importance of cooperation more generally (e.g., see Johnson, 1973, and Deutsch, 1973) has led some of them to apply the same principles to racial-ethnic relations (see Allport, 1954:276, and Secord and Backman, 1974:187–195). Finally, Human Relationists are more likely than other social psychologists to have zeroed in on the *structure* of work and other organizations as well (e.g., see Katz and Kahn, 1966; Johnson, 1973:193–210). However, a major problem with their approach has already been identified in Chapter 8.

This is their failure to go beyond a concern with bureaucracy in general and recognize the basic conflicts of interest which are the *modus operandi* of capitalism. Indeed, like the "Utopian Socialists" of Marx and Engels' time, Human Relationists see their major mission as convincing Capital and Labor that (1) Management's traditional concern with "the job" or "production" is in workers' best interests, and that (2) Labor's traditional concern with "the employee" or "people" is not incompatible with it, and entire research programs (e.g., Rensis Likert, 1961, and Arnold Tannenbaum, 1968) are designed to show that if Management *were* to increase its concern with its employees, It would get higher productivity from them.

I, for one, am convinced that they have proven the *latter* point, but I am equally convinced that contrary to the assumptions they claim their research validates, (1) capitalism places severe limits on how much concern with employees' psychological welfare Management can, and especially *will*, have, and that for this reason, therefore, (2) Human Relations programs are objectively manipulative ("repressively tolerant," if you will).

The most popular programs to have come out of the Human Relations tradition are various forms of "*sensitivity training*," which is designed to have managers, employees (occasionally, both together), or people in general, interact, learn what makes themselves and others "tick," and therefore develop sympathetic understanding for each other. The training programs run all the way from structured exercises where, for example, participants become sensitized to being rejected and others' fears about it, to "T" or "encounter groups" where participants are simply encouraged to talk about themselves and each other. In this latter case the feelings and information which emerge are the material the group "works" on, and frank, in-depth "psychoanalyses" and strong in-group loyalties and antagonisms are typical outcomes (Back, 1972).

Predictably, given the degree to which we are alienated from others in our society, most find the intimate experiences with others pleasant and exhilarating, and come away with a feeling of euphoria and accomplishment. Indeed, as Kurt Back (1972) has documented, sensitivity training has become a full-fledged social movement with heavily religious overtones among a substantial number of middle-class Americans.

These "good vibrations" aside, the results of comparative-quantitative studies of the effectiveness of sensitivity training in changing the long term behavior and attitude patterns of individuals are rather sobering. After reviewing the effects of programs aimed specifically at managers, for example, John Campbell and Marvin Dunnette (1968:98) conclude that "the studies incorporating a measure of how well an individual can predict the attitudes and values of others before and after T-group training have yielded largely negative results." They conclude that training *does* tend to change individuals' behavior, yet, ironically,

> There remains the vexing problem of specifying the nature of these changes. Here the data are even less conclusive. . . . If this is true, . . . [it] makes it nearly impossible for anyone to spell out ahead of time the outcomes to be expected from any given development program.

After undertaking what is generally regarded as the most comprehensive and best-controlled evaluation of the effects of various types of sensitivity training upon college students, including their orientations toward others of a different race, Morton Lieberman and his associates (1973) were about equally as sober.

That sensitivity training produces few significant long-term changes in individuals should not surprise us, since, as Back (1972: 141) curtly puts it,

> The ominous problem comes after the session. People are led to believe that others care and want to help them to get a new look at their problems and maybe give some suggestions on how to deal with them. But here it ends. All the ideas discussed, the new ways found for one's life, were a good game within the rules of the encounter group.

Argyris (1964) provides a clear example from a real-life case: after finding that changes he had been able to induce in 20 top executives of a division of a large corporation were not having much effect in their actual behavior, he discovered that these executives "had to suppress some of this learning because the corporate president and the other divisional presidents, who were not participants in the laboratory, did not understand them."

If one does not change the *organizational* contexts within which individuals' everyday lives take place, therefore, one is unlikely to significantly change individuals through sensitivity training. However, it is rarely indeed that trainers attempt to do so. Furthermore, *at best, sensitivity training aims to change the structure of organizations by changing the individual members of particular organizations.* The assumption is that the problematic features of these organizations are simply part of a "vast misunderstanding" (Mills, 1970:19), and that if one can just get all of the individual members of the particular organizations in question to see this, the structure of the organization will change.

As argued earlier, however, the structure of our work and other organizations by no means simply relies upon the attitudes and intentions of individual members, high-level executives included, anyway. Rather, profit making requires some minimum degree of bureaucracy and insensitivity, which produces the alienation in the first place. It also leads top management to resist any significant organizational changes which training might otherwise produce. As Back (1972:162) notes, Management is most likely to use sensitivity training when It hopes it will give It a manipulative advantage: "Sensitivity training flourishes in nonunionized contexts and has been embraced sometimes by management as an alternative to unionization." "It is now generally conceded," Back concludes (1972:168), "that, while sensitivity training is used in hundreds of companies, there are hardly any in which the organization has been changed to conform to the principles implied in the training."

Human Relationists have had considerably more success when their programs have concentrated upon certain concrete aspects of the structure of work. For example, "job enrichment" programs, which increase the number of tasks workers perform, have been shown to reduce job dissatisfaction and increase productivity (Blumberg, 1968; Shepard, 1970). Similarly, "profit-sharing" schemes, where workers' pay is increased by such increases in productivity, have been still more successful in this regard. However, such programs are subject to many of the same failings as sensitivity training.

In the first place, such schemes by no means eradicate workers' alienation. We know, for example, that skilled workers, who by definition perform a larger number of tasks than unskilled workers, are *relatively less* (psychologically) alienated than unskilled workers, but they are still likely to be alienated in *absolute* terms. This is suggested by the results of a study by Argyris, who found that while skilled workers were more satisfied with their jobs, they did not differ from unskilled workers in their expressed desire

> . . . (1) to be left alone by management; (2) to be noninvolved, indifferent, and apathetic about the formal goals and problems of the organization; (3) to experience only surface interpersonal relationships; and (4) to earn fair wages and have secure jobs. These predispositions indicated apathy and alienation . . . [Johnson, 1973:204].

Fred Blum (1953:64–65) came to similar conclusions about the effects of a profit-sharing program: it produced more satisfaction with work and the company, but the "paucity of company identifications other than monetary ones shows clearly that workers are cut off from a larger community of work and labour."

Second, such programs are not all that much more fundamental, extensive, or durable than those associated with sensitivity training. Here, for example, is Goodwin Watson and David Johnson's (1972: 433) account of the fate of one such project:

> In a toy factory, a team of women sprayed paint on toys moving steadily along a carefully paced assembly line. A psychologist persuaded management to let the workers try regulating the speed of this moving belt to fit their preferred pace. The workers were paid on a piece-work basis. They liked the innovation because they could speed up when their energy was high and slow down when they were tired. The engineers were appalled by the irregular rates, but increasing output silenced their objections. Before long, production on this worker-regulated assembly line rose to uncomfortable heights. Workers in this department were taking home more pay than were supervisors in other parts of the factory. To cut their piece-rate would, of course, have demoralized these workers. Finally, despite the less efficient production, the uniform flow of work had to be resumed. Too much efficiency in one subsystem proved too upsetting to the balance of factors in the larger system of the plant. . . .

In closing, Human Relationism, for all its good theory and research, appears to be beset with serious internal contradictions. It holds it to be self-evident that interaction between offenders and victims is not enough to produce significant change; rather, the interaction must be free (between social equals) and open. In practice, however, Human Relationists seldom bring the two together, and when they do, the structural conflicts of interest which prevent unalienated interaction from materializing are not (indeed, *could* not be, under the circumstances) tampered with. They take it to be self-evident that people will only be fully involved in those programs in which they fully participate. On the other hand, rather than joining workers in the everyday struggles for cooperation and control *they* initiate, Human Relationists concoct their own schemes and sell them to Management, which then imposes them upon "its" workers.

SOCIOLEGAL REFORM: CARROTS, BUT MOSTLY STICKS

"You can't legislate attitudes."

This is the admonition one often hears about attempts to eliminate such phenomena as racism and sexism through legal and other governmentally introduced reforms. The element of truth in this dictum, to which I shall return shortly, is that coercing someone to do something will not necessarily make him/her like or believe in it. Note, however, that it is premised upon voluntaristic and idealistic assumptions which we have seen to be false within the context of our own society; that is, the more basic source of racism, sexism, and other manifestations of exploitation and competition is not the misguided attitudes and intentions of individuals abstracted from the structure of their everyday lives, but this very structure. Were sociolegal reform able to change this structure, one would therefore expect it to reduce these forms of alienation.

In fact, legal reform has undoubtedly been the proximate source of most of the changes we have seen in Management-Labour, race, and gender relations to date. The prevention of child labour and the shortening of the working day, the introduction of health-and-safety regulations and the minimum wage, legal protection to organize unions and unemployment insurance, have clearly done much more to humanize Management-Labour relations than any number of sensitivity training and other Human Relations' programs ever will within the present structure of our own society. The same can be said for antidiscrimination laws in employment, voting, housing, and education in race and sex relations.

The theoretical rationale behind such programs (but, as will be argued in a moment, usually not the political motivation) would seem to be much sounder than that behind Human Relations' programs. Specifically, it is presumably assumed, although implicitly (the official rationale is more likely to be that some people are too "old-fashioned" to change by themselves), that the employer, apartment-owner, school-supporter, or other offender has exploitative or competitive interests which will make him/her resistant to changing on his/her own, such that the threat of legal sanctions is necessary to effect humanitarian changes. Whether s/he happens to believe in the need for such changes is not totally ignored, in that there may be propaganda campaigns stressing the long term benefits of such programs to the offender, or more immediate "carrots" in the form of government compensation (for example, grants or tax reductions), but it is regarded as less important than actually getting the offender to stop exploiting, discriminating, or both.

The usual criticisms of such programs are two-fold: (1) as mentioned above, they are said to fail to change the attitudes and intentions of individual offenders, and (2) being coercive, they are also undemocratic and immoral.

As noted above, changing the attitudes of particular offending individuals would not solve these problems anyway. Nevertheless, it would not be correct to claim that legal reform cannot change attitudes.

One might first recall the Human Relationists' empirically supported contention that equal-status contact reduces prejudice, for to the extent that equal-opportunity laws force white and nonwhite people, men and women, to work, reside, and school together, their relationships should improve.

Indeed, whereas received opinion would have it that attitudes must change first before such programs can be successful, the evidence from studies of desegregation in the United States indicates that, if anything, the *reverse* is the case. Thus, after reviewing this evidence, Kenneth Clark concluded that "these data suggest that situationally determined behavioral changes generally *preceded* any observable attitudinal changes" (my emphasis). Furthermore, providing that people cannot simply avoid desegregation by, for example, moving out of their neighborhood when black people move in, the more *prejudiced* they are to begin with, the more *positive* toward blacks they are likely to become (see Brehm and Cohen, 1962: 274–276)!

Although a Human Relationist perspective would presumably lead us to expect that such changes would be greater if people were given the opportunity to "talk out" the reforms before they are implemented, Clark concluded that "neither time nor opportunity for preparing the public for change nor the gradualness of desegregation seem to be necessarily related to the 'effectiveness' of the desegregation process" (Brehm and Cohen, 1962:271). As proponents of psychological rationalizing theories,[4] Brehm and Cohen themselves stress that such changes should be greater when the external pressures to contradict one's true attitudes are not seen as so great that one does not need to modify one's attitudes toward blacks in order to justify one's behavior. However, remember that *social pressures* toward personal consistency are probably even greater than internal pressures (see Chapter 1), and being able to tell others that "I had no choice but to do it" could serve as a powerful neutralizer of social pressures to exploit and/or discriminate.[5]

The second criticism of legal reform — that it is undemocratic and immoral — can be most simply answered by a question: is it any *more* moral to leave employers with the "right" to exploit "their" workers, or apartment-owners with the "right" to deny "their" dwellings to nonwhites or women with children, than it is to force them not to exploit and/or discriminate? When considered in this light, it should be obvious that such seemingly abstract "rights" are in fact specific to a system based upon private property, and that we should clearly not respect them.

As the reader will have gathered, I am a strong advocate of legal measures to alleviate the problems with which we have been dealing. On the other hand, I don't believe that such measures, by themselves, can or will fully solve these problems.

One thing to note about most legal measures which have been applied to our problems is that they have tended to be piecemeal. For example, if one shortens the working day but permits employers to speed up production, one may permit employers to exploit workers to the same extent as before the change. There is little point to passing laws legislating rights to equal pay for equal work if employers can simply place women doing the same work as men into a different job classification — and get away with it.

That these programs are so lacking in foresight and comprehensiveness calls into question the intentions of their formulators and administrators. As suggested in Chapter 8, there is good reason to suspect that the State is more concerned with the best (collective) interests of Capital than those of the rest of us. It is not about to go beyond tinkering with the system to remove the fundamental conflicts of interest which make it tick. In this regard, it bears emphasizing that most of the major sociolegal reforms of bourgeois society have been introduced, much less through the humanitarian concern of politicians in power, than through the threat to the system of extraparliamentary collective behavior and social movements, and/or the need for the support of, or to prevent the coming to power of, left-wing third parties who have insisted upon such reforms.[6] For legal reform *within* the system alone, therefore, collective action *outside* the system is probably essential. However, it is also necessary because such reforms themselves tend to be piecemeal, if not downright puny, and thus ultimately inadequate. It is to this final strategy for change that we now turn.

REVOLUTIONARY SOCIAL MOVEMENTS

"Revolutionary" here refers to the fact that such collective action aims to change the basic *structure* of an entire society. To solve the problems which have concerned us here, eliminating private ownership of the means of production should be high on the agenda of such a movement. Contrary to popular conceptions, "violence" in the form of bloodshed and killing is not a *defining* characteristic of revolutionary action, since it is conceivable that a socialist revolution could be effected without it. However, it is unlikely that the ruling classes of most nations would give up their rule without violent resistance.

Were it to be effected, such action could well lead to "the disappearance of the colonized man" (Fanon, 1967:197). In China, for example, the momentum of events, and especially the visible support for rebelling against its quasifeudalistic structure, had remarkable effects upon hitherto highly submissive individuals, even in the more isolated villages (Hinton, 1966:131–134). Although the liberation of women was not initially on the agenda (China had had one of the most patriarchal of systems), this too was greatly stimulated by the upsurge in grass-roots participation (Hinton, 1966:157–189). Maurice Zeitlin (1967:73–77) reports somewhat similar findings for blacks in Cuba: having been discriminated against prior to the revolution, they were initially somewhat more likely than whites to be hostile to the revolution. However, actual participation and equal treatment in the aftermath subsequently led to their being among the most active and committed members of the new society.

Presumably, what makes revolutionary movements so effective in changing human relationships and "human nature" is that (1) they actually change a society's structure, and (2) there is much, much more participation in the process than is the case with individual rehabilitation, Human Relations programs, or legal reform within the structure of our own society. Needless to say, however, such movements are extremely difficult to launch, the process of structural change itself is anything but efficient, and, as is clear in the cases of Russia, China, and Cuba, it is difficult to maintain the momentum of the revolution and avoid unintended structural consequences.

Which strategies are best suited to effect structural change once a majority of the population are prepared to effect it, and how does one help bring a majority of the population to that point? I would argue that the major strategies of the most visible of the recent movements of the '60s and '70s — the black civil rights, peace and student, "counterculture," and feminist movements — have not been ideally suited to achieve either of these goals.

Looking first at the change programs of these movements, we see that the heaviest reliance has probably been upon legal reform, the most popular intermediate steps to achieve it being the election of reformist candidates and public demonstrations designed to change the positions of ruling elites through a combination of persuasion and threat. While these strategies have indeed effected many legal reforms and helped achieve other more limited objectives such as ending the war in Vietnam (Baker, 1974; Spates, 1976), such achievements have done little to alter the structure of capitalism. This also means that they have fallen far short of eliminating racism, sexism, imperialism, and other forms of exploitation and competition. Nor should one expect them ever to do so, since they leave most of the power of the class which rules the system intact.

Interestingly, the other major strategy — the alternative life-style of the counterculture movement — in many respects relies upon a version of Human Relationism to effect change. Thus, if for the Human Relationist in industry the problem is to get Management to relinquish Its outmoded view of workers and the work group, for counterculture proponents like Charles Reich (1971) the problem is to get willing workers and satisfied consumers to want and experience something more out of life. This something is basically a state of nonalienation — an (acted upon) consciousness of self and community with others.

According to Reich, affluence and unfulfilled aspirations for other things have already produced this "Consciousness III" among the middle-class youth of the counterculture. All that remains is that this life-style "spread" like a "yeast" (Reich, 1971:321):

> The Corporate State vanishes. It can no longer sell people things to satisfy any but real needs, which means that the consumer has regained power over what is produced. And it can no longer get anyone to work except for real satisfaction, which means that the status system is at an end, and people within organizations regain power over the organizations and structures of society. [Reich, 1971:329].

The kernel of truth in this position is that we cannot and should not wait to change our relationships with others and ourselves until after some future political-economic revolution, at which time we would somehow mechanically attempt to legislate less alienation into existence (see also B. Brown, 1973). Indeed, in this respect "consciousness-raising" encounter groups — that is, feminist and other groups whose members' self- and other-development efforts are directly linked with wider movements for social change — appear to be very effective. On the other hand, it is the height of *naiveté* (complicity?) to claim, as Reich (1971:331) does, that "should Consciousness III sweep the country, the federal government could simply be ignored until it became completely isolated from the people of the nation, and had no choice but to change."

In fact, of course, the state (any state, Reich's national chauvinism aside) is not neutral. It is not simply waiting to be persuaded by the demonstrated will of the majority. Nor would it be willing to stand aside if the majority were to proclaim that they now wanted to be ruled by "Consciousness III." Nor would the seizing of state power through whatever means be sufficient to permit the flowering of the new consciousness. Rather, as workers we will clearly have to take over our factories and other work organizations and organize ourselves as a class if we are to establish an egalitarian society where we shall be free to put the new life-style into practice.[7]

In other words, it is highly doubtful that strategies which do not seriously challenge the system (as attempts to persuade ruling elites and/or effect legal reforms within the system do not) and place control of its major institutions squarely in the hands of the majority (as a counterculture strategy does not) could effect structural change even if they were undertaken by a majority of the population. On the other hand, whether one chooses these more popular strategies or those centering around workers' control, the problem of persuading, nudging, provoking, or whatever, the majority of the population to demand and/or undertake structural change remains. The question of "minority influence" has in fact been systematically considered by a number of recent social scientists.

Ralph Turner (1969) begins by noting a paradox with regard to collective protest activities: whereas they are undertaken to draw attention to real grievances and thereby influence ruling elites and/or the general public to act on them, the public may not even *interpret* them as protests, let alone be persuaded by them. "Riots" in black ghettos, for example, are often seen simply as criminal actions; student demonstrations as simply the work of outside, self-interested agitators.

If protests are to have their intended effects, he suggests, their characteristics must be such that they resolve a dilemma. That is, the actions must be *provocative* enough to bring the protestors' appeal to the attention of the public (Moscovici and Nemeth, 1974, speak of the "distinctiveness" of the minority's position), yet not *so* provocative that they *threaten* the public to the point where its members "block out" the message of the appeal altogether. Presumably, there is also another dilemma; that is, whereas the actions must be provocative enough to attract attention, they must not be so provocative that they are not *credible* in terms of the appeal being made. Moscovici and Nemeth (1974), however, suggest that the position of the minority can be very extreme indeed and still be influential, providing that the "behavioral style" of the minority is *otherwise* credible enough.

Something of the importance of this balance among provocation, threat, and credibility can be gleaned from a study by Myron Rothbart (1970). Thus, it seems reasonable to conclude that students at McGill University in Montreal see the separation of Quebec from Canada as more likely, and its sources as lying more in "economic dissatisfactions," than do students at the University of Toronto because they are more personally threatened by the prospect of such an event. However, when one compares individuals within each of the two groups, one finds that the more a subject thought that s/he would be adversely affected by Quebec separation, the more opposed to it s/he was, and the more opposed to it s/he was, the less likely s/he saw it as being.[8] On the other hand, this "wishful thinking" or "head-in-the-sand" tendency was modified under conditions where one would expect the students to regard separatist protests as more credible; that is, the more students knew about the history of Quebec and separatism, the less likely they were to discount the possibility of separation's occurring.

Credibility therefore appears to be extremely important in determining the reaction to protest actions. Given that this is the case, when will such actions be regarded as credible?

According to Turner, members of the public who have already had experiences which would sensitize them to the protest nature of the action will be more likely to interpret it as such. This is born out in a study by Jefferies, Turner, and Morris (1971), where individuals who were already sympathetic to the black civil rights movement and/or had participated in related activities themselves were more likely to designate the Watts riots as protest actions. Presumably, it is also a partial explanation for the fact that the most highly educated are most likely to regard student protests as legitimate (Olsen, 1968; Ransford, 1972).

Turning now to the characteristics of the protest action itself rather than members of the public, we find analysts agreeing that the action will have more impact, if (1) a large proportion of the allegedly aggrieved persons are seen to have engaged in the action (Jefferies et al., 1971), and (2) if there is a large degree of consensus among the minority (Moscovici and Nemeth, 1974).

The latter researchers see the "shaking up" of the majority, by the minority's having confronted them with a counterposition too credible to dismiss, as the major intervening mechanism in the process of minority influence (Moscovici and Nemeth, 1974:223). The establishment of such a high degree of credibility, they suggest, does not even require a large and unanimous minority. Rather, even small minorities, and here they point to Freud and other lone scientists, can be influential if their behavioral style conveys certainty through other means: a great deal of personal effort to get their ideas across, the apparent absence of self-interest, and consistency over time, especially in the face of "insult, ostracism, or even persecution."

Moscovici and Nemeth's own research supports this reasoning to a remarkable extent, in that as long as it was consistent over time, the minority in their experiments (usually two unanimous members of a six-person group) succeeded in influencing the majority's judgments of *physical* stimuli, not simply more ambiguous social norms. However, it is not clear that the rational-persuasion process they suggest is the only or even the most important intervening mechanism in minority influence.

Although Moscovici and Nemeth (1974:220) claim that unlike the majority, the minority does not have the power to reward other dissenters from the majority with approval, this is not totally correct, for, as we saw in Chapter 8, a dissenting minority often seems to provide others with enough social support to at least *act* upon their attitudes when these attitudes already deviate from the majority. (Whether alternative means of support is sufficient to get one to *change* one's attitude, as occurred in Moscovici and Nemeth's experiments, is another matter.) However, in his classic work on the subject, Solomon Asch (1955) claimed to have demonstrated that uncertainty about the correctness of the majority position rather than social support for one's own position is what makes a dissenter woo group members from conforming to the majority.

Vernon Allen and John Levine (1968; 1969) conducted two experiments in an attempt to resolve this issue. In addition to a social support condition where a dissenter agreed with the subject's own attitude (which in turn deviated from that of the majority), they included one where the dissenter's judgments were even more incorrect than the majority's. When judging physical stimuli, as in the Moscovici and Nemeth experiments, the dissenter's having broken the group consensus, even when his position was very different from the naive subject's, significantly reduced conformity to the majority. However, when the stimuli were opinions (about other matters, and, one presumes, this would hold for political opinions), social support rather than simply "shaking up" subjects' faith in the majority position was required to decrease conformity. Furthermore, in the second experiment where they used a more refined measure of social support, Allen and Levine found that the latter variable significantly reduced conformity on visual and information as well as opinion items. They therefore conclude that "The results cast doubt on Asch's contention that breaking group consensus, per se, is responsible for the effectiveness of social support in reducing conformity" (Allen and Levine, 1969:389).

The implications of these various findings concerning minority influence would seem to be these: it is extremely important for dissenters to achieve credibility, but the rational-persuasion process implied by an exclusive concern with it is not in fact the only and perhaps not the most important means through which a minority can influence a majority. Rather, social support would seem to be at least equally as important. Assuming that our strategy for changing our political economy is to promote the basis for workers' control, how might we use this information about minority influence to better effect it?

One interesting if disconcerting fact about public reactions to collective protest actions such as ghetto riots and student demonstrations, is that blue-collar workers, at least in the United States, and presumably Canada as well, appear to be *less* likely than other sectors of the population to view such actions as protests and less likely to regard them as legitimate (Olsen, 1968; Jefferies et al., 1971; Ransford, 1972)! It is surprising because, like the protestors themselves, we would expect that those who *themselves* feel aggrieved by the System should be most sympathetic to the appeals of other aggrieved groups.

According to Turner (1969:819–820), however, such a "common cause" process is not the most potent. Rather, each class/sector of the public "tends to employ its own situation as the point of reference in assessing another group's claims of injustice." Since the socioeconomic position of ghetto blacks is so much more clearly *worse* than their own, middle-class people find the idea that riots are protests more credible; conversely, since the position of (most) college students is so much *better* than their own, blue-collar workers are *less* likely to regard student demonstrations as credible protests. The results of the Jefferies et al. study (1971:447) would seem to bear out this reasoning. However, there are probably other processes at work here as well.

A suggestive finding from an earlier study by Marvin Olsen (1968) is that the *stronger* were respondents' own feelings of cynicism and powerlessness about the official political process, the *less* likely they were to regard civil rights protests as legitimate. Furthermore, "It is the strong attitudes of political incapability and discontentment held by poorly educated persons, plus their advanced ages [although to a lesser extent], which primarily inhibit their acceptance of protest actions aimed at effecting social change" (Olsen, 1968:307). Ransford (1972:343) also reports something very similar.

This finding is open to a number of very different interpretations. Viewed from the angle of the credibility of these protests as rational-persuasive appeals, one might argue that blue-collar workers, feeling as they do personally powerless, do not believe that such actions will actually produce social change. If these actions are therefore seen as futile *as well as* existing to air grievances which appear to be no more (and, in the case of students, less) serious than their own, they may seem doubly illegitimate. On the other hand, a threat-social-support explanation such as that offered by Ransford (see also Chapters 8 and 9) would seem to be both simpler and more plausible: feeling politically powerless, blue-collar workers also feel (largely correctly) that changes to satisfy only certain sectors of the working class (blacks, native people, and women) will hurt their own interests.

This would seem to argue for a much more concertedly and explicitly working-*class*-oriented program than we have usually seen from recent social movements. More specifically, demands for equal rights for racial-ethnic minorities and women will probably be much less threatening to workers when they are integrated with demands that, for example, *all* working-class children receive extra help in attending college, and that any such programs be financed from corporate profits instead of workers' personal income taxes. More unanimity among protesters, of course, would also make for more credibility, since a common discrediting argument against the Left is that "they cannot even agree among themselves."

Yet, it would seem to argue for much more than this: demonstrations led by middle-class radicals to protest the actions of ruling elites, such as imperialistic intervention in the Third World, are surely not the best means for "making the revolution." It is not that such actions should not be undertaken. However, as Turner (1969: 826) suggests, a third party to a protest is unlikely to be swayed unless there are "shared membership group identities and circumstances that facilitate coalition formation."

Given that this is the case, much more effort should be focused upon action in and through the workplace, in rank-and-file caucuses as well as in unions. As long as radical action is, and is perceived to be, outside of and perhaps even opposed to the immediate interests of workers in general, it is likely to be misconstrued (or correctly construed, when the object is to push only sectional interests) and rejected by that sector of the population which must be mobilized if we are to slay Capitalism, the dragon-source of our alienation.[9]

Notes

[1]For evaluations of the success of various psychotherapy programs, see Eysenck (1966) and Bergin (1975).

[2]See Gove (1974) for empirical critiques of labelling theory, and Scheff (1974) for an answer to them.

[3]However, for an interesting subjective account of (false) incarceration in a mental hospital which seems to bear out many of Goffman's claims, see Rosenhan (1972).

[4]See Note 4, Chapter 1. Brehm and Cohen's particular brand is "dissonance theory."

[5]Robert Kennedy told an interesting anecdote about his experiences as Attorney General during the forced entry of James Meredith to the University of Mississippi as its first black student; that is, the local sheriff demanded more rather than fewer federal troops than Kennedy intended to send — so that he would have less difficulty justifying his acquiescence to his constituents!

[6]The "New Deal" is a good case in point, as are the old-age pensions, unemployment insurance, and other major reforms the NDP has formulated and its more mainline competitors have implemented to prevent it from coming to power. For other indications (and some frank admissions) that the ruling class has introduced reforms to get them in ahead of more left-wing proposals, see Domdoff (1971).

[7]The recent cases of Chile and Portugal are tragic examples of what is likely to happen when such actions are not the centrepieces of the revolution.

[8]A study of the reactions of London, Ontario, residents to the events of the "October Crisis" of 1970 indicates much the same thing (Sorrentino et al., 1974:215).

[9]This is not to suggest that workers can never be mobilized from the outside through the actions of students, as in France in May, 1968. However, not only were the conditions for mobilization exceptional (French workers are among the most organized and class conscious in Europe), but also, there was little fraternization between students and workers once the general strike was underway. That links between the two had not been established before the event probably goes a long way toward explaining its short duration.

BIBLIOGRAPHY

Abelson, Robert P. "Are attitudes necessary?" Pp. 19-32 in Bert T. King and E. McGinnies (eds.), Attitudes, Conflict, and Social Change. New York: Academic Press, 1972.

Adorno, Theodor, Else Frenkel-Brunswik, Daniel Levinson, and Nevitt Sanford. The Authoritarian Personality. New York: John Wiley & Sons, 1964.

Aellen, Carol and Wallace Lambert. "Ethnic identification and personality adjustments of Canadian adolescents of mixed English-French parentage". Pp. 173-192 in J. W. Berry and G. J. S. Wilde (eds.), Social Psychology: The Canadian Context. Toronto: McClelland and Stewart, 1972.

Agassi, Judith B. "The worker and the media," Archives Européennes de Sociologie 11:26-66, 1970.

Ajzen, I. and Martin Fishbein. "The prediction of behavior from attitudinal and normative variables," Journal of Experimental Social Psychology 6:466-487, 1970.

Alderman, Tom. " 'And what do you do for a living?' " The Canadian magazine October 12:2-13, 1974.

Alford, Robert. Party and Society. Chicago: Aldine, 1963.

Allen, Vernon and John Levine. "Social support, dissent and conformity," Sociometry 31 (June):138-149, 1968.

——— and ——— "Consensus and conformity," Journal of Experimental Social Psychology 5 (October):389-399, 1969.

Allport, Floyd H. Social Psychology. Boston: Houghton Mifflin, 1924.

Allport, Gordon. The Nature of Prejudice. Cambridge, Mass.: Addison-Wesley, 1954.

Antonevsky, Aaron. "Social class, life expectancy and overall mortality," Milbank Memorial Fund Quarterly 45 (April):31-73, 1967.

Archibald, W. Peter. "Symbolic interaction theory: a critical review and re-formulation," Zeitschrift fur Soziologie 1(July):193-208, 1972.

———. "Psychology, sociology and social psychology: bad fences make bad neighbours," British Journal of Sociology 27 (June):115-129, 1976a.

———. "Using Marx's theory of alienation empirically." Pp. 59-74 in R. Felix Geyer and David R. Schweitzer (eds.), Theories of Alienation. The Hague: Martinus Nijhoff, 1976b.

———. "Face-to-face: the alienating effects of class, status, and power divisions," American Sociological Review 41 (October):819-837, 1976c.

Aronoff, Joel and William D. Crano. "A re-examination of the cross-cultural principles of task segregation and sex role differentiation in the family," American Sociological Review 40(February):12-20, 1975.

Aronowitz, Stanley. False Promises. New York: McGraw-Hill, 1973.

Aronson, Elliot. The Social Animal. San Francisco: W. II. Freeman, 1976.

Argyris, Chris. "T-groups for organizational effectiveness," Harvard Business Review 42(March):60-74, 1964.

Arrow, Kenneth J. "Models of job discrimination." Pp. 83-102 in Anthony H. Pascal (ed.), Racial Discrimination in Economic Life. Lexington, Mass.: D. C. Heath, 1972.

Asch, Solomon E. "Opinions and social pressure," Scientific American 193 (November):31-35, 1955.

———. "Effects of group pressure upon the modification and distortion of judgments." Pp. 189-200 in Dorwin Cartwright and Alvin Zander (eds.), Group Dynamics. New York: Harper and Row, 1960.

Atwood, Margaret. Survival: A Thematic Guide to Canadian Literature. Toronto: Anansi, 1972.

Avery, Donald. "Continental European immigrant workers in Canada," *Canadian Review of Sociology and Anthropology* 12(February): 53-64, 1975.

Avineri, Shlomo. *The Social and Political Thought of Karl Marx.* Cambridge: Cambridge University Press, 1968.

Babchuk, Nicolas and Alan Bates. "The primary relations of middle-class couples: a study in male dominance," *American Sociological Review* 28 (March): 377-384, 1963.

Back, Kurt W. *Beyond Words: The Story of Sensitivity Training and the Encounter Movement.* New York: Russell Sage Foundation, 1972.

Bain, George S. *The Growth of White-Collar Unionism.* Oxford: Oxford University Press, 1970.

Baker, Norma J. "The nature of social change." Pp. 341-370 in Lawrence S. Wrightsman, *Social Psychology in the Seventies.* Belmont, Calif.: Wadsworth, 1972.

Bakke, E. Wight. *Citizens Without Work.* New Haven: Yale University Press, 1969.

Bales, Robert F. "Task roles and social roles in problem-solving groups." Pp. 437-447 in Eleanor E. Maccoby, T. M. Newcomb, and E. L. Hartley (eds.), *Readings in Social Psychology.* New York: Holt, Rinehart and Winston, 1958.

Banton, Michael, *Race Relations.* London: Tavistock Publications, 1967.

Baran, Paul A. and Paul M. Sweezy. *Monopoly Capital.* New York: Monthly Review Press, 1966.

Bardwick, Judith M. and Elizabeth Douvan. "Ambivalence: the socialization of women." Pp. 225-241 in Vivian Gornick and Barbara K. Moran (eds.), *Woman in Sexist Society.* New York: Signet (New American Library), 1972.

Bart, Pauline. "Depression in middle-aged women." Pp. 163-186 in Vivian Gornick and Barbara K. Moran (eds.), *Woman in Sexist Society.* New York: Signet (New American Library), 1972.

Barth, Fredrik. *Nomads of South Persia.* London: Allen and Unwin. New York: Humanities Press, 1965.

Bass, Bernard M., Judith Krusell, and Ralph A. Alexander. "Male managers' attitudes toward working women," *American Behavioral Scientist* 15 (2):221-236, 1971.

Bateson, Gregory. *Steps to an Ecology of Mind.* New York: Ballantine, 1972.

Battle, Esther S. and Julian B. Rotter. "Children's feelings of personal control as related to social class and ethnic group," *Journal of Personality* 31:482-490, 1963.

Beattie, Christopher. *Minority Men in a Majority Setting: Middle-level Francophones in the Canadian Public Service.* Toronto: McClelland and Stewart, 1975.

Becker, Ernest. "Mills' social psychology and the great historical convergence on the problem of alienation." Pp. 108-133 in Irving Louis Horowitz (ed.), *The New Sociology.* New York: Oxford University Press, 1964.

Bem, Daryl J. "Self-perception: an alternative interpretation of cognitive dissonance phenomena," *Psychological Review* 74(March): 183-200, 1967.

Benedict, Ruth. *Patterns of Culture.* New York: Mentor (New American Library), 1960.

Bentham, Jeremy. *The Principles of Morals and Legislation.* Darien, Conn.: Hafner, 1970.

Berger, Joseph, Bernard P. Cohen, and Morris Zelditch. "Status characteristics and social interaction," *American Sociological Review* 37 (June): 241-255, 1972.

Bergin, A. E. "Psychotherapy can be dangerous," *Psychology Today* 9 (November): 96-100; 104, 1975.

Berkman, Paul L. "Life stress and psychological well-being," *Journal of Health and Social Behavior* 12(March): 35-45, 1971.

Bernard, Jessie. *The Sex Game*. Englewood Cliffs, N.J.: Prentice-Hall, 1968.
———. *The Future of Marriage*. New York: Bantam, 1973.
Berne, Eric. *Games People Play*. New York: Dell, 1967.
Bernstein, Basil. *Class, Codes and Control, II: Applied Studies Towards a Sociology of Language*. London: Routledge and Kegan Paul, 1973.
Berry, J. W. "Independence and conformity in subsistence level societies," *Journal of Personality and Social Psychology* 7:415-418, 1967.
Beynon, Huw. *Working for Ford*. Harmondsworth, Eng.: Penguin, 1973.
Bianchi, Maria T. and Joyce S. Brodie. "Decision to work among Halifax women." Pp. 179-189 in Christopher Beattie and Stewart Crysdale (eds.), *Sociology Canada: Readings*. Toronto: Butterworth, 1974.
Bixenstine, V. E., H. M. Potash, and K. V. Wilson. "Effects of levels of cooperative choice by the other player in choices in a prisoner's dilemma game," *Journal of Abnormal and Social Psychology* 66/67:308-313; 139-148, 1963.
Blalock, Hubert M. *Toward a Theory of Minority-Group Relations*. New York: John Wiley & Sons, 1967.
Blau, Francine D. and Carol L. Jusenius. "Economists' approaches to sex segregation in the labor market: an appraisal." Pp. 181-199 in Martha Blaxall and Barbara Reagan (eds.), *Women and the Workplace*. Chicago: University of Chicago Press, 1976.
Blau, Peter M. "Co-operation and competition in a bureaucracy," *American Journal of Sociology* 49(May):530-535, 1954.
———. *Exchange and Power in Social Life*. New York: John Wiley & Sons, 1964.
Blauner, Robert. *Alienation and Freedom*. Chicago: University of Chicago Press, 1964.
———. "Internal colonialism and ghetto revolt," *Social Problems* 16(Spring):393-408, 1969.
Blum, Alan F. "Social structure, social class, and participation in primary relationships." Pp. 195-207 in Arthur B. Shostak and W. Gomberg (eds.), *Blue Collar World*. Englewood Cliffs, N.J.: Prentice-Hall, 1964.
Blum, Fred H. *Toward a Democratic Work Process*. New York: Harper and Row, 1953.
Blumberg, Paul. *Industrial Democracy: The Sociology of Participation*. London: Constable, 1968.
Blumer, Herbert. "Race prejudice as a sense of group position," *Pacific Sociological Review* 1(1):3-7, 1958.
Boas, Franz. *Contributions to the Ethnology of the Kwakiutl*. New York: AMS Press, 1969.
Bonavich, Edna. "Abolition, the extension of slavery, and the position of free Blacks: a study of split labor markets in the United States, 1830-1863," *American Journal of Sociology* 81(March):601-628, 1975.
Bonjean, C. "Mass, class and the industrial community," *American Journal of Sociology* 72:149-162, 1966.
Booth, Alan. "Sex and social participation," *American Sociological Review* 37(April):183-192, 1972.
Bott, Elizabeth. *Family and Social Network*. 2nd ed. London: Tavistock, 1971.
Bottomore, Thomas B. and M. Rubel (eds.). *Karl Marx: Selected Writings in Sociology and Social Philosophy*. New York: McGraw-Hill, 1964.
Bourque, Gilles and Nicole Laruin-Frenette. "Social classes and national ideologies in Quebec, 1960-1970." Pp. 185-210 in Gary Teeple (ed.), *Capitalism and the National Question in Canada*. Toronto: University of Toronto Press, 1972.
Boutlier, Marie. "Transformations of ideology surrounding the sexual division of labour: Canadian women during World War II." Paper presented at the Second Blue Collar Conference, University of Western Ontario, May, 1977.

Bradburn, Norman and David Caplovitz. *Reports on Happiness.* Chicago: Aldine, 1965.

Braverman, Harry. *Labor and Monopoly Capital: The Degradation of Work in the Twentieth Century.* New York: Monthly Review Press, 1974.

Brehm, Jack W. and Arthur R. Cohen. *Explorations in Cognitive Dissonance.* New York: John Wiley & Sons, 1962.

Brenner, Harvey. *Mental Illness and the Economy.* Cambridge, Mass: Harvard University Press, 1973.

Brewer, John. "Flow of communications, expert qualifications and organizational authority structures," *American Sociological Review* 36(June):475-484, 1971.

Broadfoot, Barry. *Ten Lost Years, 1929-1939.* Don Mills, Ont.: Paperjacks (General Publishing), 1975.

Brody, Hugh. *Indians on Skid Row.* Ottawa: Department of Indian Affairs and Northern Development, 1971.

Bronfenbrenner, Urie. "Socialization and social class through time and space." Pp. 400-425 in Eleanor E. Maccoby, Theodore M. Newcomb, and Eugene L. Hartley (eds.), *Readings in Social Psychology.* New York: Holt, Rinehart and Winston, 1958.

Broverman, Inge K., Donald M. Broverman, Frank E. Clarkson, Paul S. Rosenkrantz, and Susan R. Vogel. "Sex-role stereotypes and clinical judgments," *Journal of Consulting and Clinical Psychology* 34(January):1-7, 1970.

Brown, Bruce. *Marx, Freud and the Critique of Everyday Life.* New York: Monthly Review Press, 1973.

Brown, Roger. *Social Psychology.* New York: Free Press, 1965.

Brownmiller, Susan. *Against Our Will: Men, Women and Rape.* New York: Bantam, 1976.

Burstein, M., N. Tienhaara, P. Hewson, and B. Warrander. *Canadian Work Values: Findings of a Work Ethic Survey and a Job Satisfaction Survey.* Ottawa: Information Canada, 1975.

Butler, Juan. *Cabbagetown Diary: A Documentary.* Toronto: Peter Martin Associates, 1970.

Byrne, Donn E. *An Introduction to Personality: Research, Theory, and Applications.* 2nd ed. Englewood Cliffs, N.J.: Prentice-Hall, 1974.

Cameron, Ann and Thomas Storm. "Achievement motivation in Canadian Indian, middle- and working-class children," *Psychological Reports* 16:459-463, 1965.

Campbell, Donald T. "Social attitudes and other acquired behavioral dispositions." Pp. 94-172 in Sigmund Koch (ed.), *Psychology: A Study of a Science,* vol. 6. New York: McGraw-Hill, 1963.

Campbell, Jane. "Manufacturers, merchants and the tariff 1850-1879." In Carl Cuneo, Robert Gardner, and Norene Pupo (eds.), *The Social Production of Wealth: Critical Analyses of Class and Power in Canada.* Forthcoming.

Campbell, John P. and Marvin D. Dunnette. "Effectiveness of T-group experiences in managerial training and development," *Psychological Bulletin* 70(August):73-104, 1968.

Cantril, Hadley. *The Pattern of Human Concerns.* New Brunswick, N.J.: Rutgers University Press, 1965.

Chesler, Phyllis. *Women and Madness.* New York: Avon, 1973.

Chi, N. H. "Class voting in Canadian politics." Pp. 226-247 in Orest M. Kruhlak, Richard Schultz and Sidney I. Pobihushchy (eds.), *The Canadian Political Process.* Toronto: Holt, Rinehart and Winston, 1973.

Clark, Edmund, David Cook, and George Fallis. "Socialization, family background and the secondary school." Pp. 77-103 in Robert M. Pike and Elia Zureik (eds.), *Socialization and Values in Canadian Society.* Toronto: McClelland and Stewart, 1975.

Clark, S. D. Movements of Political Protest in Canada. Toronto: University of Toronto Press, 1959.

Clifton, Rodney A. "Self-concept and attitudes: a comparison of Canadian Indian and non-Indian students," Canadian Review of Sociology and Anthropology 12(November):577-584, 1975.

Clinard, Marshall B. (ed.). Anomie and Deviant Behavior. New York: Free Press, 1971.

Coburn, David. "Work and society: the social correlates of job control and job complexity." Unpublished Doctoral Dissertation, University of Toronto, 1973.

Coch, Lester and John R. P. French. "Overcoming resistance to change." Pp. 319-341 in Dorwin Cartwright and Alvin Zander (eds.), Group Dynamics. New York: Harper and Row, 1960.

⏤ Cohen, Albert K. and Harold M. Hodges. "Characteristics of the lower-blue-collar class," Social Problems 10(Spring):303-334, 1963.

Cole, Stephen and Hannelore Adamsons. "Determinants of faculty support for student demonstrations," Sociology of Education 42:315-329, 1969.

Coleman, James S. and Associates. Equality of Educational Opportunity. Washington, D.C.: Department of Health, Education and Welfare, 1966.

Comte, Auguste. The Crisis of Industrial Civilization: The Early Essays of Auguste Comte. Ronald Fletcher (ed.). London: Heinemann, 1974a.

⏤⏤⏤. The Positive Philosophy. Harriett Martineau (ed. and trans.). New York: AMS Press, 1974b.

Connerton, Paul. "Introduction" to Critical Sociology: Selected Readings. Harmondsworth, Eng.: Penguin, 1976.

Connolly, William E. "The challenge to Pluralist theory." Pp. 3-34 in The Bias of Pluralism. New York: Atherton, 1969.

Converse, Philip. "The nature of belief systems in mass publics." Pp. 206-261 in David E. Apter (ed.), Ideology and Discontent. New York: Free Press, 1964.

Cooley, Charles H. "Reflections on the sociology of Herbert Spencer," American Journal of Sociology 26(September): 129-145, 1920.

⏤⏤⏤. Social Organization. New York: Schocken, 1962.

⏤⏤⏤. Human Nature and the Social Order. New York: Charles Scribners' Sons, 1964.

Coutu, W. "Role-playing versus role-taking: an appeal for clarification," American Sociological Review 16:180-187, 1951.

Cox, Oliver C. Caste, Class, and Race. New York: Monthly Review Press, 1970.

Crawford, Craig A. "Social status, general personal orientations, and social participation: a comparison of Canadian and American survey data." Unpublished M.A. thesis, University of Waterloo, 1975.

Crooks, Roland C. "The effects of an interracial preschool program upon racial preference, knowledge of racial differences, and racial identification." Pp. 127-134 in David Koulack and Daniel Perlman (eds.), Readings in Social Psychology: Focus on Canada. Toronto: John Wiley & Sons, 1973.

Crowley, Joan E., Teresa E. Levitin, and Robert P. Quinn. "Seven deadly half-truths about women," Psychology Today 6(March):94-96, 1973.

Crysdale, Stewart. "Social effects of a factory relocation." Pp. 378-392 in William E. Mann (ed.), Canada: A Sociological Profile. Toronto: Copp Clark, 1971.

Culbertson, Frances M. "Modification of an emotionally held attitude through role playing," Journal of Abnormal and Social Psychology 54:230-233, 1957.

Cuneo, Carl. "Social class, language and the national question in Canada." Unpublished Ph.D. dissertation, University of Waterloo, 1973.

⏤⏤⏤. "The social basis of political continentalism in Canada," Canadian Review of Sociology and Anthropology 13(February):55-70, 1976.

Curtis, E. "The Kwakiutl". In vol. 10 of The North American Indian. Norwood, Mass.: Plimpton Press, 1915.

Curtis, James. "Voluntary association joining: a cross-national comparative note," *American Sociological Review* 36(October):872-880, 1971.

—— and Ronald D. Lambert. "Status dissatisfaction and outgroup rejection," *Canadian Review of Sociology and Anthropology* 12(May):178-192, 1975.

—— and ——. "Voting, election interest, and age: national findings for English and French Canadians," *Canadian Journal of Political Science* 9(June):293-307, 1976.

Cutler, Stephen J. "Voluntary association membership and the theory of mass society." Pp. 133-159 in Edward O. Laumann, *Bonds of Pluralism: The Form and Substance of Urban Social Networks.* New York: John Wiley & Sons, 1973.

Dahrendorf, Ralf. *Class and Class Conflict in Industrial Society.* Stanford: University Press, 1959.

Darley, John M. and Bibb Latané. "Bystander intervention in emergencies: diffusion of responsibility," *Journal of Personality and Social Psychology* 8(April):377-383, 1968.

Davis, Arthur K. "Canadian society and history as hinterland versus metropolis." Pp. 6-32 in Richard J. Ossenberg (ed.), *Canadian Society: Pluralism, Change, and Conflict.* Scarborough, Ont.: Prentice-Hall, 1971.

Davis, James A. "Communism, conformity, cohorts, and categories: American tolerance in 1954 and 1972-73," *American Journal of Sociology* 81(November):491-513, 1975.

Deaton, Rick. "The fiscal crisis of the state and the revolt of the public employee," *Our Generation* 8(4):11-51, 1968.

deBeauvoir, Simone. *The Second Sex.* H. M. Parshley (trans.). New York: Bantam (Jonathan Cape Ltd.), 1961.

Deci, Edward L. "Work — who does not like it and why," *Psychology Today* 6(August):57-58; 92, 1972.

Denton, Trevor. "Canadian Indian migrants and impression management of ethnic stigma," *Canadian Review of Sociology and Anthropology* 12(February):65-71, 1975.

deTocqueville, Alexis. *Democracy in America.* New York: Schocken, 1961.

Deutsch, Martin. *The Disadvantaged Child.* New York: Basic Books, 1967.

Deutsch, Morton. "A theory of cooperation and competition. An experimental study of the effects of cooperation and competition upon group process," *Human Relations* 2:129-152; 199-231, 1949.

——. "The effect of motivational orientation upon trust and suspicion," *Human Relations* 13:122-139, 1960.

——. "Cooperation and trust: some theoretical notes." Pp. 275-319 in M. R. Jones (ed.), *Nebraska Symposium on Motivation.* Lincoln: University of Nebraska Press, 1962.

—— and Robert M. Krauss. "The effect of threat on interpersonal bargaining," *Journal of Abnormal and Social Psychology* 61:181-189, 1960.

—— and ——. *Theories in Social Psychology.* New York: Basic Books, 1965.

Dobriner, William. *Class in Suburbia.* Englewood Cliffs, N.J.: Prentice-Hall, 1963.

Dohrenwend, Bruce P. and Barbara S. Dohrenwend. *Social Status and Psychological Disorder.* New York: John Wiley & Sons, 1969.

Dollard, John. *Caste and Class in a Southern Town.* Garden City, N.Y.: Doubleday (Anchor), 1957.

Domdoff, G. William. *The Higher Circles.* New York: Vintage (Random House), 1971.

Doob, Anthony N. and Alan E. Gross. "Status of frustrator as an inhibitor of horn-honking responses," *Journal of Social Psychology* 76:213-218, 1968.

Dorris, J. William. "Reactions to unconditional cooperation: a field study emphasizing variables neglected in laboratory research," *Journal of Personality and Social Psychology* 22(June):387-397, 1972.

Dosman, Edgar J. Indians: The Urban Dilemma. Toronto: McClelland and Stewart, 1972.
Doyle, Bertram W. The Etiquette of Race Relations in the South. Port Washington, N.Y.; Kennikat Press, 1968.
Dunning, Richard W. "Some problems of reserve Indian communities: a case study." Pp. 59-85 in James S. Frideres, Canada's Indians. Scarborough, Ont.: Prentice-Hall, 1974.
Durkheim, Emile. The Rules of Sociological Method. New York: Free Press, 1964a.
————. The Division of Labor in Society. New York: Free Press, 1964b.
————. Suicide. New York: Free Press, 1966.
————. Moral Education. New York: Free Press, 1973.
Easterbrook, W. T. and M. H. Watkins (eds.), Approaches to Canadian Economic History. Toronto: McClelland and Stewart, 1967.
Easton, Loyd D. "Alienation and empiricism in Marx's thought," Social Research 7(Autumn):402-427, 1970.
Edelman, Murray. "The conservative political consequences of labor conflict." Pp. 163-176 in Gerald G. Somers (ed.), Essays in Industrial Relations Democracy. Ames, Iowa: Iowa State University Press, 1969.
Ehrlich, Howard J. "Attitudes, behavior, and the intervening variables," American Sociologist 4:29-34, 1969.
Eichler, Margaret. "Women as personal dependents." Pp. 36-55 in M. Stephenson (ed.), Women in Canada. Toronto: New Press, 1973.
Eldridge, J. E. T. Sociology and Industrial Life. London: Nelson, 1973.
Elkins, Stanley M. Slavery. New York: Grosset and Dunlap, 1963.
Erlanger, Howard S. "Social class and corporal punishment in childrearing: a reassessment," American Sociological Review 39(February): 68-85, 1974.
Evansohn, John. "Workers and imperialism: where is the aristocracy of labor?" Insurgent Sociologist 7(Spring):54-63, 1977.
Eysenck, H. J. The Effects of Psychotherapy. New York: International Science Press, 1966.
Fanon, Frantz. The Wretched of the Earth. New York: Grove Press, 1966.
————. Black Skin, White Masks. New York: Grove Press, 1967.
Faunce, William. Problems of an Industrial Society. New York: McGraw-Hill, 1968.
Ferber, Marianne A. and Helen M. Lowry. "Women: the new reserve army of the unemployed." Pp. 213-232 in Martha Blaxall and Barbara Reagin (eds.), Women and the Workplace. Chicago: University of Chicago Press, 1976.
Ferree, Myra M. "Working-class jobs: housework and paid work as sources of satisfaction," Social Problems 23(April):431-441, 1976.
Fishbein, Martin and I. Ajzen. Beliefs, Attitudes, Intentions and Behavior. Reading, Mass.: Addison-Wesley, 1975.
Flora, Cornelia B. "The passive female: her comparative image by class and culture in women's magazine fiction," Journal of Marriage and the Family 33(August): 435-444, 1971.
Forde, C. Daryll. Habitat, Economy, and Society. New York: E. P. Dutton, 1963.
Form. William H. "Technology and social behavior of workers in four countries," American Sociological Review 37(December):727-738, 1972.
————. "Job vs. political unionism: a cross-national comparison," Industrial Relations 12(May): 224-238, 1973a.
————. "The internal stratification of the working class," American Sociological Review 38(December):697-711, 1973b.
———— and Joan Rytina. "Ideological beliefs in the distribution of power in the United States," American Sociological Review 34(February): 19-31, 1969.
Frideres, James S. Canada's Indians: Contemporary Conflicts. Scarborough, Ont.: Prentice-Hall, 1974.
Fried, Robert. The World of the Urban Working Class. Cambridge, Mass.: Harvard University Press, 1973.

Fromm, Eric. *The Sane Society*. Greenwich, Conn.: Fawcett, 1955.
——. *The Crisis of Psychoanalysis*. Greenwich, Conn.: Fawcett, 1971.
Fullan, Michael. "Industrial technology and worker integration in the organi-
zation," *American Sociological Review* 35(December): 1028-1039, 1970.
Fürstenberg, Friedrich. *Die Soziallage der Chemiearbeiter*. Neuwied and Berlin:
Luchterhand, 1969.
Galbraith, Kenneth. *The New Industrial State*. New York: Mentor (New Am-
erican Library), 1972.
Gamson, W. A. "An experimental test of a theory of coalition formation,"
Amercian Sociological Review 26:565-573, 1961.
——. "Experimental studies of coalition formation." Pp. 81-110 in Leonard
Berkowitz (ed.), *Advances in Experimental Social Psychology*. vol. 1. New
York: Academic Press, 1964.
Gans, Herbert J. *The Urban Villagers: Group and Class in the Life of Italian-
Americans*. New York: The Free Press, 1962.
Garfinkel, Harold. *Studies in Ethnomethodology*. Englewood Cliffs, N.J.: Pren-
tice-Hall, 1967.
Gartner, Alan, Colin Greer, and Frank Riessman (eds.), *The New Assault on
Equality: I.Q. and Social Stratification*. New York: Harper and Row, 1974.
Gavron, Hannah. *The Captive Wife: Conflicts of Housebound Mothers*. Har-
mondsworth, Eng.: Penguin, 1966.
Genovese, Eugene. *Roll, Jordon Roll*. New York: Random House (Vintage),
1976.
Geoffroy, Renee and Paule Sainte-Marie. *Attitude of Union Workers to Women
in Industry*. Ottawa: Information Canada. Royal Commission on the Status
of Women in Canada, Study No. 9, 1971.
Gerard, Harold B. "Some effects of status, role clarity, and group goal clarity
upon the individual's relations to group process," *Journal of Personality*
25: 475-488, 1957.
Geras, Norman. "Essence and appearance: aspects of fetishism in Marx's
capital," *New Left Review* 65:69-85, 1971.
Gergen, Kenneth. "Personal consistency and the presentation of self."Pp. 299-
308 in Chad Gordon and K. Gergen (eds.), *The Self in Social Interaction*.
New York: John Wiley & Sons, 1968.
Gerth, Hans and C. Wright Mills. *From Max Weber: Essays in Sociology*. New
York: Oxford University Press, 1958.
Giddens, Anthony. *Capitalism and Modern Social Theory*. Cambridge: Cam-
bridge University Press, 1971.
——. "Introduction" to *Emile Durkheim: Selected Writings*. Cambridge: Cam-
bridge University Press, 1972a.
——. *Politics and Sociology in the Thought of Max Weber*. London: Mac-
millan, 1972b.
Gillespie, Dair L. "Who has the power? The marital struggle," *Journal of Mar-
riage and the Family* 33(August): 445-458, 1971.
Gilmour, Robert S. and Robert B. Lamb. *Political Alienation in Contemporary
America*. New York: St. Martin's Press, 1975.
Godelier, Maurice. *Rationality and Irrationality in Economics*. London: New
Left Books, 1972.
Goffman, Erving. *The Presentation of Self in Everyday Life*. Garden City, N.Y.:
Doubleday-Anchor, 1959.
——. *Encounters*. Indianapolis: Bobbs-Merrill, 1961a.
——. *Asylums*. Garden City, N.Y.: Doubleday (Anchor), 1961b.
——. *Interaction Ritual*. Garden City, N.Y.: Doubleday-Anchor, 1967.
——. *Relations in Public*. New York: Harper and Row (Colophon), 1972.
Goldberg, Philip. "Are women prejudiced against women?" *Transaction* 5 (May):
28-30, 1968.
Goldthorpe, John H., David Lockwood, Frank Bechhofer, and Jennifer Platt.

The Affluent Worker in the Class Structure. Cambridge: Cambridge University Press, 1969.

Goodman, Mary E. Race Awareness in Young Children. New York: Collier, 1964.

Goodstadt, Barry and David Kipnis. "Situational influences on the use of power," Journal of Applied Psychology 54(June):201-207, 1970.

Gore, Pearl M. and Julian B. Rotter. "A personality correlate of social action," Journal of Personality 31:58-64, 1963.

Gough, Kathleen. "The origin of the family," Journal of Marriage and the Family 33(November): 760-771, 1971.

Gouldner, Alvin W. The Coming Crisis of Western Sociology. New York: Equinox (Avon), 1971.

Gove, Walter. "Individual resources and mental hospitalization: a comparison and evaluation of the societal reaction and psychiatric perspectives," American Sociological Review 39(February): 86-100, 1974.

―――― and Jeannette F. Tudor. "Adult sex roles and mental illness," American Journal of Sociology 78(January): 812-835, 1973.

Grabb, Edward G. "Subordinate group status and perceived opportunity: the French Canadian case." Unpublished paper, University of Western Ontario, 1977.

Grayson, Paul. "Comparative political networks." Unpublished paper, Atkinson College, York University, 1973.

Greenblum, Joseph and Leonard I. Pearlin. "Vertical mobility and prejudice: a socio-psychological analysis." Pp. 480-491 in Reinhard Bendix and S. M. Lipset (eds.), Class, Status and Power. New York: Free Press, 1953.

Greer, Germaine. The Female Eunich. New York: Bantam, 1972.

Griffin, John. Black Like Me. Boston: Houghton Mifflin, 1961.

Gurin, Gerald, Joseph Veroff, and Sheila Feld. Americans View Their Mental Health. New York: Basic Books, 1960.

Hacker, Helen M. "Women as a minority group," Social Forces 30 (October): 60-69, 1951.

Hall, Edward T. The Silent Language. New York: Fawcett, 1959.

Hamilton, Richard F. Affluence and the French Worker in the Fourth Republic. Princeton, N.J.: Princeton University Press, 1967.

Hamilton, Richard F. Class and Politics in the United States. New York: John Wiley & Sons, 1972.

Hamilton, Richard F. Restraining Myths: Critical Studies of U.S. Social Structure and Politics. New York: Halsted (Wiley), 1975.

Han, Wang San. "Two conflicting themes: common values versus class differential values," American Sociological Review 34 (October): 679-690, 1969.

Hansen, James E. "A dialectical critique of empiricism," Catalyst 3 (Summer): 1-19, 1967.

Harner, Michael J. "Population pressure and the social evolution of agriculturalists," Southwestern Journal of Anthropology 26:67-86, 1970.

Harvey, Ted G., Susan K. Hunter-Harvey, and W. George Vance. "Nationalist sentiment among Canadian adolescents." Unpublished paper, University of Western Ontario, 1972.

Henley, Nancy M. "Status and sex: some touching observations," Bulletin of the Psychonomic Society 2 (August):91-93, 1973.

Henry, Frances. Forgotten Canadians: The Blacks of Nova Scotia. Don Mills, Ont.: Longman, 1973.

Hess, Robert D. "The transmission of cognitive strategies in poor families: the socialization of apathy and under-achievement." pp. 73-92 in Vernon L. Allen (ed.), Psychological Factors in Poverty. Chicago: Markham, 1970.

Hewitt, John P. Self and Society: A Symbolic Interactionist Social Psychology. Boston: Allyn and Bacon, 1975.

Hinton, William. Fanshen: A Documentary of Revolution in a Chinese Village. New York: Vintage (Random House), 1968.

Hobhouse, L. T., G. C. Wheeler, and M. Ginsberg. *Material Culture and Social Institutions of Simpler Peoples.* London: Routledge and Kegan Paul, 1965.

Hochschild, Arlie Russell. "The sociology of feeling and emotion: selected possibilities." Pp. 280-307 in Marcia Millman and Rosabeth Kanter (eds.), *Another Voice: Feminist Perspectives on Social Life and Social Science.* Garden City, N.Y.: Doubleday (Anchor), 1975.

Hoggart, Richard. *The Uses of Literacy.* Harmondsworth, Eng.: Penguin, 1958.

Hollingshead, August B. and Frederick C. Redlich. *Social Class and Mental Illness.* New York: John Wiley & Sons, 1958.

Homans, George C. *Social Behavior: Its Elementary Forms.* Revised ed. New York: Harcourt, Brace, and Jovanovich, 1974.

Horner, Matina S. "Toward an understanding of achievement-related conflicts in women," *Journal of Social Issues* 28(2):157-175, 1972.

Horowitz, Gad. *Canadian Labour in Politics.* Toronto: University of Toronto Press, 1968.

Horowitz, Irving Louis. "The hemispheric connection: a critique and corrective to the entrepreneurial thesis of development with special emphasis on the Canadian case," *Queen's Quarterly* 80:327-359,1973.

Huber, Joan. "Toward a socio-technological theory of the women's movement," *Social Problems* 23 (April):371-388, 1976.

Hughes, David R. and Evelyn Kallen. *The Anatomy of Racism: Canadian Dimensions.* Montreal: Harvest House, 1974.

Hughes, Everett C. *French Canada in Transition.* Chicago: University of Chicago Press, 1943.

Hurst, Charles E. "Race, class, and consciousness," *American Sociological Review* 37(December):658-670, 1972.

Hurwitz, Jacob I., Alvin F. Zander, and Bernard Hymovitch. "Some effects of power on the relations among group members." Pp. 800-809 in Dorwin Cartwright and Alvin Zander (eds.), *Group Dynamics: Research and Theory.* New York: Harper and Row, 1960.

Hyman, Herbert H. "The value systems of different classes." Pp. 426-442 in Reinhard Bendix and Seymour M. Lipset (eds.), *Class, Status and Power.* Glencoe, Ill.: Free Press, 1953.

Hyman, Herbert H. and Paul B. Sheatsley. " 'The authoritarian personality': a methodological critique." Pp. 50-122 in Richard Christie and Marie Jahoda (eds.), *Studies in the Scope and Method of 'The Authoritarian Personality'.* Glencoe, Ill.: Free Press, 1954.

Inkeles, Alex. "Personality and social structure." Pp. 249-276 in Robert K. Merton, L. Broom, and L. S. Cottrell (eds.), *Sociology Today: Problems and Prospects.* New York: Basic Books, 1959.

Inkeles, Alex, and Daniel J. Levinson. "National character." Pp. 418-506 in Gardner Lindzey and Elliot Aronson (eds.), *Handbook of Social Psychology.* 2nd ed. vol. 4. Reading, Mass.: Addison-Wesley, 1969.

Israel, Joachim. *Alienation: From Marx to Modern Sociology.* Boston: Allyn and Bacon, 1971.

Jackman, Mary R. and Robert W. Jackman. "An interpretation of the relation between objective and subjective social status," *American Sociological Review* 38(October):569-582, 1973.

Jacobs, R. C. and Donald T. Campbell. "The perpetuation of an arbitrary tradition through several generations of a laboratory microculture," *Journal of Abnormal and Social Psychology* 62:649-658, 1961.

Jacoby, Russell. "Towards a critique of automatic Marxism: the politics of philosophy from Lukács to the Frankfurt School," *Telos* No. 10 (Winter): 119-146, 1971.

Jay, Martin. *The Dialectical Imagination: A History of the Frankfurt School and the Institute of Social Research, 1923-1950.* Boston: Little, Brown, 1973.

Jefferies, Vincent, Ralph H. Turner, and Richard T. Morris. "The public perception of the Watts riot as social protest," *American Sociological Review* 36(June):443-451, 1971.

Johnson, David W. (ed.). *Contemporary Social Psychology.* Philadelphia: Lippincott, 1973.

Johnson, Leo A. "The development of class in Canada in the twentieth century." Pp. 141-184 in Gary Teeple (ed.), *Capitalism and the National Question in Canada.* Toronto: University of Toronto Press, 1972.

————."The political economy of Ontario women in the nineteenth century." Pp. 13-32 in Women's Press Collective (eds.), *Women at Work: Ontario, 1850-1930.* Toronto: Canadian Women's Educational Press, 1974.

Johnstone, John C. *Young People's Images of Canadian Society.* Studies of the Royal Commission on Bilingualism and Biculturalism, No. 2. Ottawa: Queen's Printer, 1969.

Jones, Edward E. and Harold B. Gerard. *Foundations of Social Psychology.* New York: John Wiley & Sons, 1967.

Jones, James. *Racism and Prejudice.* Boston: Addison-Wesley, 1972.

Joy, Richard J. *Languages in Conflict.* Toronto: McClelland and Stewart, 1972.

Judek, Stanislaw. *Women in the Public Service.* Ottawa: The Queen's Printer, 1968.

Kagen, Spencer and Millard C. Madsen. "Rivalry in Anglo-American and Mexican children of two ages," *Journal of Personality and Social Psychology* 24(November):214-220, 1972.

Kahn, Robert L., David M. Wolfe, Robert P. Quinn, J. D. Snoek, and R. A. Rosenthal. *Organizational Stress: Studies in Role Conflict and Ambiguity.* New York: John Wiley & Sons, 1964.

Kamin, Leon J. *The Science and Politics of I.Q.* New York: Halsted (Wiley), 1974.

Kanter, Rosabeth M. "Women and the structure of organizations." Pp. 34-74 in Marcia Millman and Rosabeth M. Kanter (eds.), *Another Voice: Feminist Perspectives on Social Life and the Social Sciences.* Garden City, N.Y.: Doubleday (Anchor), 1975.

Kanter, Rosabeth M. "The impact of hierarchical structures on the work behavior of women and men," *Social Problems* 23(April):415-430, 1976.

Kaplan, Berton H., John C. Cassel, and Susan Gore. "Social support and health." Paper presented to the American Public Health Association Meetings, San Francisco. November, 1973.

Kaplan, Howard B. "Social class and self-derogation: a conditional relationship," *Sociometry* 34(March):41-64, 1971.

Katz, Daniel and Robert Kahn. *The Social Psychology of Organizations.* New York: John Wiley & Sons, 1966.

Katz, E. and P. R. Lazarsfeld. *Personal Influence: The Part Played by People in the Flow of Mass Communications.* New York: The Free Press, 1955.

Katz, Irwin. "A critique of personality approaches to Negro performance, with research suggestions," *Journal of Social Issues* 25(3):13-27, 1967.

Katz, Irwin and L. Benjamin. "Effects of white authoritarianism in biracial groups," *Journal of Abnormal and Social Psychology* 61:448-456, 1960.

Katz, Marlaine Lockheed. *Female Motive to Avoid Success: A Psychological Barrier or a Response to Deviancy?* Princeton, N. J.: Educational Testing Service, 1973.

Kelley, Harold H. "Communication in experimentally created hierarchies." Reprinted on pp. 781-799 of Dorwin Cartwright and Alvin Zander (eds.), *Group Dynamics.* New York: Harper and Row, 1960.

Kelley, Harold H. and Janusz Grzelak. "Conflict between individual and common interest in a N-person relationship," *Journal of Personality and Social Psychology* 21(February):190-197, 1972.

Kelman, Herbert C. "Attitude change as a function of response restriction," *Human Relations* 6:185-214, 1953.

Kern, H. and Michael Schumann. Industriearbeit und ArbeiterbewuBtsein: Eine Empirische Untersuchung uber den EinfluB der aktuellen technischen Entwicklung auf die industrielle Arbiet und das ArbeiterbewuBtsein. Frankfurt am Main: Europaische Verlagsanstalt, 1970.

Kilbourn, William. The Making of the Nation. Toronto: McClelland and Stewart, 1965.

Kimball, Meredith M. "Women and success: a basic conflict?" Pp. 119-135 in Marylee Stephenson (ed.), Women in Canada. Revised ed. Toronto: General Publishing Co., 1977.

King, B. T. and Irving L. Janis. "Comparison of the effectiveness of improvised versus non-improvised role-playing in producing attitude changes," Human Relations 9:177-186, 1956.

Kipnis, David and Joseph Cosentino. "Uses of leadership powers in industry," Journal of Applied Psychology 53(December):460-466, 1969.

Kirsch, Barbara A. and Joseph J. Lengermann. "An empirical test of Robert Blauner's ideas on alienation in work as applied to different type jobs in a white-collar setting," Sociology and Social Research 56(January):180-194, 1972.

Kohn, Melvin L. "Social class and schizophrenia: a critical review," Journal of Psychiatric Research 6(Supplement 1):155-173, 1968 (Pergamon Press Ltd.).

————. Class and Conformity. Homewood, Ill.: Dorsey, 1969.

————. "Class, family, and schizophrenia: a reformulation." Social Forces 50(March):295-309, 1972.

————. "Occupational structure and alienation." American Journal of Sociology 82(July):111-130, 1976.

———— and Carmi Schooler. "Occupational experience and psychological functioning: an assessment of reciprocal effects," American Sociological Review 38(February):97-118, 1973.

Komarovsky, Mirra. Blue-Collar Marriage. New York: Random House (Vintage), 1967.

————. Dilemmas of Masculinity: A Study of College Youth. New York: Norton, 1976.

Kon, Igor S. "The concept of alienation in modern sociology." Pp. 146-167 in Peter Berger (ed.), Marxism and Sociology: Views from Eastern Europe. New York: Appleton-Century-Crofts, 1969.

Kornhauser, Arthur. The Mental Health of the Industrial Worker. New York: John Wiley & Sons, 1965.

Koulack, David and David Cumming. "Acceptance and rejection as a function of ethnicity and belief intensity," Journal of Social Psychology 91(December):207-213, 1973.

Kuczynski, Jurgen. The Rise of the Working Class. New York: McGraw-Hill, 1967.

Kuhn, Manfred H. "Self attitudes by age, sex, and professional training," Sociological Quarterly 1(1):39-55, 1960.

Labov, William. Sociolinguistic Patterns. Philadelphia: University of Pennsylvania Press, 1972.

Laing, R. D. The Divided Self. Harmondsworth, Eng.: Pelican (Penguin), 1965 (Tavistock Publications Ltd.).

————. The Politics of Experience. Harmondsworth, Eng.: Penguin, 1967.

Lambert, Wallace E. "A social psychology of bilingualism," Journal of Social Issues 23(2):91-109, 1967.

Lane, R. E. Political Ideology. New York: The Free Press, 1962.

Langner, T. S. and S. T. Michael. Life Stress and Mental Health. New York: Free Press, 1963.

LaPiere, Richard T. "Attitudes versus actions," Social Forces 13:230-237, 1934.

Laski, Harold J. The Rise of European Liberalism. London: Allen and Unwin, 1958.

Latané, Bibb and John M. Darley. "Group inhibition of bystander intervention in emergencies," Journal of Personality and Social Psychology 10(November):215-221, 1968.
—— and Judith Rodin. "A lady in distress: inhibiting effects of friends and strangers on bystander emergency," Journal of Experimental Social Psychology 5(April):189-202, 1969.
Laurence, Margaret. The Diviners. New York: Bantam, 1975.
Lave, L. B. "Factors affecting cooperation in the prisoner's dilemma," Behavioral Science 10:26-38, 1965.
Lawler, Edward J. "An experimental study of factors affecting the mobilization of revolutionary coalitions," Sociometry 38(June):163-179, 1975.
Lawton, Dennis. Social Class, Language and Education. New York: Schocken, 1968.
Laxer, James and Doris Jantzi. "The de-industrialization of Ontario." Pp. 147-152 in Robert Laxer (ed.), (Canada) Ltd. Toronto: McClelland and Stewart, 1973.
Laxer, Robert M. Canada's Unions. Toronto: James Lorimer, 1976.
Lay, Clarry H. and David Cumming. "Ethnic origin, belief, and personality information in interpersonal attraction." Reprinted in pp. 67-75 of David Koulack and Daniel Perlman (eds.), Readings in Social Psychology. Toronto: John Wiley & Sons, 1973.
Leclair, Edward E. and Harold K. Schneider (eds.), Economic Anthropology: Readings in Theory and Analysis. New York: Holt, Rinehart and Winston, 1968.
Leggett, John C. Class, Race, and Labor: Working-Class Consciousness in Detroit. New York: Oxford University Press, 1968.
Lenzer, Gertrud (ed.), August Comte and Positivism: The Essential Writings. New York: Harper and Row (Torchbook), 1975.
Lepper, Mark R., David Greene, and Richard E. Nisbett. "Undermining children's intrinsic interest with extrinsic reward: a test of the 'overjustification' hypothesis," Journal of Personality and Social Psychology 28(January):129-137, 1973.
Levitt, Kari. Silent Surrender: The Multinational Corporation in Canada. Toronto: Macmillan, 1970.
Levitt, Morris. "The political role of American women," Journal of Human Relations 15(1):23-25, 1967.
Lewis, David. Louder Voices: The Corporate Welfare Bums. Toronto: James, Lewis, and Samuel, 1972.
Lewis, Lionel S. and Joseph Lopreato. "Functional importance and prestige of occupations," Pacific Sociological Review 6(Fall):55-59, 1963.
Lichtheim, George. Marxism: An Historical and Critical Study. New York: Praeger, 1965.
——. A Short History of Socialism. New York: Praeger, 1970.
Lieberman, Morton A., Irvin D. Yalom, and Matthew B. Miles. Encounter Groups: First Facts. New York: Basic Books, 1973.
Lieberman, Seymour. "The effects of changes in roles on the attitudes of role occupants," Human Relations 9:385-402, 1956.
Lieberson, Stanley. Language and Ethnic Relations in Canada. New York: John Wiley & Sons, 1970.
Likert, Rensis. New Patterns of Management. New York: McGraw-Hill, 1961.
Linn, L. S. "Verbal attitudes and overt behavior: a study of racial discrimination," Social Forces 43:353-364, 1965.
Lipset, Seymour Martin. Political Man. Garden City, N.Y.: Doubleday (Anchor), 1963.
——. The First New Nation. Garden City, N.Y.: Doubleday (Anchor), 1967.
——. Revolution and Counterrevolution. New York: Basic Books, 1968.
Lipsitz, Lewis. "Work life and political attitudes: a study of manual workers," American Political Science Review 58(June):951-962, 1964.

Lipsitz, Lewis. "Working-class authoritarianism: a re-evaluation," *American Sociological Review* 30(February):103-109, 1965.

Liska, Allen. "Emergent issues in the attitude-behavior consistency controversy," *American Sociological Review* 39(April):261-272, 1974.

Litwak, Eugene and Ivan Szelenyi. "Primary group structures and their functions: kin, neighbors, and friends," *American Sociological Review* 34 (August):465-481, 1969.

Lockheed, M. and K. Hall. "Conceptualizing sex as a status characteristic: applications to leadership training strategies," *Journal of Social Issues* 32(3):111-124, 1976.

Lockwood, David. "Sources of variation in working class images of society." Pp. 98-114 in Joseph A. Kahl (ed.), *Comparative Perspectives on Stratification*. Boston: Little, Brown, 1968.

Lopreato, Joseph and Lionel S. Lewis. "An analysis of variables in the functional theory of stratification," *Sociological Quarterly* 4(Autumn):301-310, 1963.

Lorimer, James and Myfanwy Phillips. *Working People*. Toronto: James, Lewis and Samuel, 1971.

Lucas, Rex A. *Minetown, Milltown, Railtown: Life in Canadian Communities of Single Industry*. Toronto: University of Toronto Press, 1971.

Luce, R. D. and H. Raiffa. *Games and Decisions: Introduction and Critical Survey*. New York: John Wiley & Sons, 1957.

Lukács, Georg. *History and Class Consciousness: Studies in Marxist Dialectics*. Cambridge, Mass.: MIT Press, 1971.

Maccoby, Eleanor and Carol Jacklin. *The Psychology of Sex Differences*. Stanford, Calif.: Stanford University Press, 1974.

MacDonald, L. R. "Merchants against industry: an idea and its origins," *Canadian Historical Review* 56(September):263-281, 1975.

MacLennan, Hugh. *Two Solitudes*. Toronto: Popular Library, 1945.

Mandel, Ernest. *Marxist Economic Theory*. New York: Monthly Review Press, 1970.

Mann, Michael. "The social cohesion of liberal democracy," *American Sociological Review* 35(June):423-439, 1970.

Mann, Michael. *Consciousness and Action in the Western Working Class*. London: Macmillan, 1973.

Manning, Peter K. "The decline of civility: Goffman's sociology," *Canadian Review of Sociology and Anthropology* 13(February):13-25, 1976.

Marchak, M. Patricia. "The Canadian labour force: jobs from women." Pp. 202-212 in Marylee Stephenson (ed.), *Women in Canada*. Toronto: New Press, 1973.

———. *Ideological Perspectives on Canada*. Toronto: McGraw-Hill Ryerson, 1974.

Marcuse, Herbert. *Eros and Civilization*. New York: Vintage (Random House), 1962.

———. *One-Dimensional Man*. Boston: Beacon Press, 1964.

Marglin, Stephen A. "What do bosses do? The origins and functions of hierarchy in capitalist production." Unpublished paper, Harvard University, 1971.

Martyn, Charles A. "Canadian Eskimo carving in historical perspective," *Anthropos* 59:546-596, 1964.

Marwell, Gerald and David R. Schmitt. "Cooperation in a three-person prisoner's dilemma," *Journal of Personality and Social Psychology* 21 (March):376-383, 1972.

Marx, Karl. *Capital*. Moscow: Progress Publishers, No Date.

———. *Grundrisse: Introduction to the Critique of Political Economy*. Martin Nicolaus (ed.), Harmondsworth, Eng.: Penguin-Pelican, 1973.

——— and Frederick Engels. *Selected Works*. Moscow: Progress Publishers, 1968.

—— and ——. *Ireland and the Irish Question.* Moscow: Progress Publishers, 1971.

—— and ——. *Collected Works.* vols. 3 and 4. New York: International Publishers, 1975.

—— and ——. *Collected Works.* vol. 5. New York: International Publishers, 1976.

Mason, Karen Oppenheim, John L. Czajka and Sara Arber. "Change in U.S. women's sex-role attitudes, 1964-1974," *American Sociological Review* 41(August):573-596, 1976.

Mathewson, Stanley B. *Restriction of Output Among Unorganized Workers.* Carbondale, Ill.: Southern Illinois University Press, 1969.

Matson, Floyd W. *The Broken Image: Man, Science and Society.* New York: George Braziller, 1964.

Mauss, Marcel. *The Gift: Forms and Functions of Exchange in Archaic Societies.* London: Routledge and Kegan Paul, 1970. (Published in the U.S. by Macmillan Publishing Co. Inc.)

Mayrl, William W. "Ethnomethodology: sociology without society," *Catalyst* No. 7(Winter):15-28, 1973.

McClosky, Herbert. "Consensus and ideology in American politics," *American Political Science Review* 58(December):361-382, 1964.

McConnell, James V. "Criminals can be brainwashed now," *Psychology Today* 3(April):14-18; 74, 1970.

McCord, William, Joan McCord, and Alan Howard. "Early family experiences and bigotry," *American Sociological Review* 25(October):717-722, 1960.

McCormick, Thelma. "Toward a non-sexist perspective on social and political change." Pp. 1-33 in Marcia Millman and Rosabeth Moss Kanter (eds.), *Another Voice: Feminist Perspectives on Social Life and Social Science.* Garden City, N.Y.: Doubleday (Anchor), 1975.

McWilliams, Carey. *A Mask for Privilege.* Boston: Little, Brown, 1948.

Mead, George H. *Movements of Thought in the Nineteenth Century.* Chicago: University of Chicago Press, 1936.

——. *Mind, Self, and Society.* Chicago: University of Chicago Press, 1962.

——. "Cooley's contribution to American social thought." Reprinted as forward to Cooley's *Human Nature and the Social Order.* New York: Schocken, 1964.

Mead, Margaret. *Cooperation and Competition Among Primitive Peoples.* New York: McGraw-Hill, 1937.

Meichenbaum, D. H., K. S. Bowers, and R. R. Ross. "A behavioral analysis of teacher expectancy effect," *Journal of Personality and Social Psychology* 13:306-316, 1969.

Meissner, Martin. "The long arm of the job: social participation and the constraints of industrial work," *Industrial Relations* 10(October): 239-260, 1970.

——, Elizabeth W. Humphreys, Scott M. Meis, and William J. Scheu. "No exit for wives: sexual division of labour," *Canadian Review of Sociology and Anthropology* 12(November):424-439, 1975.

Merton, Robert K. "Social structure and anomie," *American Sociological Review* 3(October):672-682, 1938.

——. *Social Theory and Social Structure.* New York: Free Press, 1957.

Meyers, Jerome K., Jacob J. Lindenthal, Max P. Pepper, and David R. Ostrander. "Life events and mental status: a longitudinal study," *Journal of Health and Social Behavior* 13(December):398-405, 1972.

Mézáros, Istvan. *Marx's Theory of Alienation.* New York: Harper and Row, 1970.

Michels, Robert. *Political Parties: A Sociological Study of the Oligarchical Tendencies in Modern Democracy.* New York: Collier, 1962.

Michener, H. Andrew and Morgan Lyons. "Perceived support and upward mobility as determinants of revolutionary coalitional behavior," *Journal of Experimental Social Psychology* 8(March):99-111, 1972.

Middleton, Chris. "Sexual inequality and stratification theory." Pp. 179-203 in Frank Parkin (ed.), *The Social Analysis of Class Structure*. London: Tavistock, 1974.

Milbraith, Lester. *Political Participation*. Chicago: Rand McNally, 1965.

Milgram, Stanley. "Behavioral study of obedience," *Journal of Abnormal and Social Psychology* 67(April):371-378, 1963.

———. "Some conditions of obedience and disobedience to authority," *Human Relations* 18:57-76, 1965a.

———. "Liberating effects of group pressure," *Journal of Personality and Social Psychology* 1(February):127-134, 1965b.

Miliband, Ralph. *The State in Capitalist Society*. London: Quartet Books, 1973.

Miller, S. M. and Frank Riessman. " 'Working-class authoritarianism': a critique of Lipset," *British Journal of Sociology* 12:263-281, 1961.

———, ———, and A. Seagull. "Poverty and self-indulgence: a critique of the non-deferred gratification pattern." Pp. 285-302 in Louis Ferman, J. Kornbluth and A. Haber (eds.), *Poverty in America*. Ann Arbor: University of Michigan Press, 1968.

Mills, C. Wright. "Situated actions and vocabularies of motive," *American Sociological Review* 5(June):904-913, 1940.

———. *White Collar: The American Middle Classes*. New York: Oxford University Press, 1956.

———. *The Power Elite*. New York: Oxford University Press, 1959.

———. *The Marxists*. New York: Dell, 1962.

———. *Power, Politics and People: The Collected Essays of C. Wright Mills*. New York: Oxford University Press, 1967.

———. "The contribution of sociology to studies in industrial relations," *Berkeley Journal of Sociology* 15:11-32, 1970.

Mills, Theodore M. "Power relations in three-person groups." Pp. 766-780 in Dorwin Cartwright and Alvin Zander (eds.), *Group Dynamics*. New York: Harper and Row, 1960.

Milner, Sheilagh Hodgins and Henry Milner. *The Decolonization of Quebec*. Toronto: McClelland and Stewart, 1973.

Mischel, Walter. "Consistency and specificity in behavior." Pp. 13-39 in *Personality and Assessment*. New York: John Wiley & Sons, 1968.

Misgivings. Title of a pamphlet released under the pseudonym "Memo from Turner," Toronto, 1972.

Monahan, Lynn, Deanna Kuhn, and Phillip Shaver. "Intrapsychic versus cultural explanations of the 'fear of success' motive," *Journal of Personality and Social Psychology* 29(January):60-64, 1974.

Moore, Steve and Debi Wells. *Imperialism and the National Question in Canada*. Toronto: Better Read Graphics, 1975.

Moscovici, Serge and Charlan Nemeth. "Social influence II: minority influence," Pp. 217-249 in Charlan Nemeth (ed.), *Social Psychology: Classic and Contemporary Integrations*. Chicago: Rand McNally, 1974.

———, E. Lage, and M. Naffrechoux. "Influence of a consistent minority on the responses of a majority in a color perception task," *Sociometry* 32(December):365-380, 1969.

Mott, Paul E., Floyd C. Mann, Quin McLoughlin, and Donald P. Warwick. *Shift Work: The Social, Psychological and Physical Consequences*. Ann Arbor: Institute for Social Research, 1965.

Munroe, Robert L., Ruth H. Munroe, and Robert E. Daniels. "Relation of subsistence economy to conformity in three East African societies," *Journal of Social Psychology* 89(February):149-150, 1973.

Naylor, R. Tom. "The rise and fall of the third commercial empire of the St. Lawrence." Pp. 1-41 in Gary Teeple (ed.), *Capitalism and the National Question in Canada*. Toronto: University of Toronto Press, 1972.

Nelson, J. I. "Participation and integration: the case of the small businessman," *American Sociological Review* 33:427-438, 1968.

Nelson, Linden L. and Spencer Kagan. "Competition: the star-spangled scramble," Psychology Today 6(September):53-56; 90-91, 1972.

Nobles, Wade W. "Psychological research and the Black self-concept: a critical review," Journal of Social Issues 29(1):11-31, 1973.

Nord, Walter R. "Social exchange theory: an integrative approach to social conformity," Psychological Bulletin 71(March):174-208, 1969.

Norman, Ross. "Cognitive-affective consistency and the attitude-behavior relation." Unpublished Ph.D. dissertation, University of Michigan, 1973.

Oakley, Ann. The Sociology of Housework. New York: Pantheon (Random House), 1974.

O'Connor, James. The Fiscal Crisis of the State. New York: St. Martin's Press, 1973.

Ogmundson, Rick. "Mass-elite linkages and class issues in Canada," Canadian Review of Sociology and Anthropology 13(February):1-12, 1976.

Ollman, Bertall. Alienation: Marx's Conception of Man in Capitalist Society. Cambridge: Cambridge University Press, 1971.

Olsen, Marvin. "Perceived legitimacy of social protest actions," Social Problems 15:297-309, 1968.

———. "Social and political participation of Blacks," American Sociological Review 35(August):682-696, 1970.

Orum, Anthony M., Roberta S. Cohen, Sherri Grasmuck, and Amy W. Orum. "Sex, socialization and politics," American Sociological Review 39(April): 197-209, 1974.

Parkin, Frank. Class Inequality and Political Order. Frogmore, Eng.: Paladin, 1972.

Parsons, Talcott. The Social System. New York: Free Press, 1964a.

———. Character and Social Structure. New York: Free Press, 1964b.

———. "Introduction" to Max Weber, The Theory of Economic and Social Organization. New York: Free Press, 1964c.

———. The Structure of Social Action. New York: Free Press, 1968.

Pateman, Carole. Participation and Democratic Theory. Cambridge: Cambridge University Press, 1970.

Pearson, Harry W. "The economy has no surplus: critique of a theory of development." Pp. 320-341 in Karl Polanyi, Conrad M. Arensberg, and Harry W. Pearson (eds.), Trade and Market in the Early Empires. New York: Free Press, 1957.

Petras, John W. and Bernard N. Meltzer. "Theoretical and ideological variations in contemporary interactionism," Catalyst No. 7(Winter):1-8, 1973.

Pettigrew, Thomas F. "Regional differences in anti-Negro prejudice," Journal of Abnormal and Social Psychology 59(July):28-36, 1959.

Phillips, Derek L. "Social class, social participation, and happiness," Sociological Quarterly 10(Winter):3-21, 1969.

——— and Bernard Segal. "Sexual status and psychiatric symptoms," American Sociological Review 34(February):58-72, 1969.

Piddocke, Stuart. "The potlach system of the southern Kwakiutl: a new perspective." Pp. 283-299 in Edward E. LeClair and Harold K. Schneider (eds.), Economic Anthropology: Readings in Theory and Analysis. New York: Holt, Rinehart and Winston, 1968.

Pineo, Peter and John Goyder. "Social class identification of national subgroups." Pp. 187-196 in James Curtis and William Scott (eds.), Social Stratification: Canada. Toronto: Prentice-Hall, 1973.

Polanyi, Karl. The Great Transformation. New York: Farrar and Rinehart, 1944.

Pope, Hallowell. "Economic deprivation and social participation," Social Problems 11(Winter):290-300, 1964.

Porter, John. The Vertical Mosaic. Toronto: University of Toronto Press, 1965.

Ransford, Edward. "Blue collar anger: reactions to student and Black protest," American Sociological Review 37(June):333-346, 1972.

Redfield, Robert. *Human Nature and the Study of Society*. Chicago: University of Chicago Press, 1962.

Reich, Charles A. *The Greening of America*. New York: Bantam Books (Random House), 1971.

Reich, Michael. "The economics of racism." Pp. 107-113 in David M. Gordon (ed.), *Problems in Political Economy*. Lexington, Mass.: D. C. Heath, 1971.

Reich, Wilhelm. *The Mass Psychology of Fascism*. New York: Simon and Schuster (Touchstone), 1970.

———. *Sex-Pol Essays, 1929-1934*. Lee Baxandall (ed.), New York: Random House, 1972.

Reimer, Everett W. *School is Dead: Alternatives in Education*. Garden City, N.Y.: Doubleday (Anchor), 1972.

Richer, Stephen and Pierre Laporte. "Culture, cognition and English-French competition." Pp. 49-58 in David Koulack and Daniel Perlman (eds.), *Readings in Social Psychology: Focus on Canada*. Toronto: John Wiley & Sons, 1973.

Richmond, Anthony H. *Post-War Immigrants in Canada*. Toronto: University of Toronto Press, 1967.

Riecken, Henry W. "The effect of talkativeness on ability to influence group solutions to problems," *Sociometry* 21:309-321, 1958.

Rinehart, James W. *The Tyranny of Work*. Don Mills, Ont.: Longman, 1975.

——— and Ishmael O. Okraku. "A study of class consciousness," *Canadian Review of Sociology and Anthropology* 11(December):197-213, 1974.

Rioux, Marcel. *Quebec in Question*. Toronto: James, Lewis and Samuel, 1971.

Robertson, Heather. *Reservations are for Indians*. Toronto: James, Lewis and Samuel, 1970.

Robinson, W. P. "The elaborated code in working-class language," *Language and Speech* 8:243-252, 1965.

Robson, R. A. H. "The effects of different group sex compositions on support rates and coalition formation." Monograph No. 1, Experimental Sociology Laboratory, University of British Columbia, 1971.

Roby, Pamela. "Sociology and women in working-class jobs." Pp. 203-239 in Marcia Millman and Rosabeth Moss Kanter (eds.), *Another Voice: Feminist Perspectives on Social Life and Social Science*. Garden City, N.Y.: Doubleday (Anchor), 1975.

Roethlisberger, F. J. and William J. Dickson. *Management and the Worker*. New York: John Wiley & Sons (Science Editions), 1964.

Rokeach, Milton. *Beliefs, Attitudes and Values*. San Francisco: Jossey-Bass, 1968.

———. "Some reflections about the place of values in Canadian social science." Pp. 152-190 in T. N. Guinsburg and G. L. Reuber (eds.), *Perspectives on the Social Sciences in Canada*. Toronto: University of Toronto Press, 1975.

Romalis, Coleman. "A man of his time and place: a selective appraisal of S. M. Lipset's comparative sociology," *Sociological Inquiry* 42(3-4):211-231, 1972.

Roman, Paul and Harrison M. Trice. *Schizophrenia and the Poor*. Ithaca: New York State School of Industrial and Labor Relations, 1967.

Roseman, Ellen. "Death on the job: the grim facts," *Toronto Star*, Saturday, December 14:A1, 14, 1974.

Rosen, Bernard C. "Race, ethnicity, and the achievement syndrome." Pp. 131-153 in B. C. Rosen, Harry J. Crockett and Clyde Z. Nunn (eds.), *Achievement and American Society*. Cambridge, Mass.: Schenkman, 1969.

Rosenbaum, James E. "The stratification of socialization processes," *American Sociological Review* 40(February):48-54, 1975.

Rosenhan, David L. "On being sane in insane places," *Science* 179:250-258, 1972.

Rosenkrantz, Paul, Susan Vogel, Helen Bee, Donald M. Broverman, and Inge Broverman. "Sex-role stereotypes and self-concepts in college students," *Journal of Consulting and Clinical Psychology* 32(March):287-295, 1968.

Rosenthal, Robert. On the Social Psychology of the Self-fulfilling Prophecy: Further Evidence for Pygmalion Effects and their Mediating Mechanisms. New York: MSS Modular Publications. Module 53:1-28, 1974.
——— and L. Jacobson. Pygmalion in the Classroom. New York: Holt, Rinehart and Winston, 1968.
Rothbart, M. "Assessing the likelihood of a threatening event: English Canadians' evaluation of the Quebec separatist movement," Journal of Personality and Social Psychology 15:109-117, 1970.
Rotter, Julian B. "Generalized expectancies for internal versus external control of reinforcement," Psychological Monographs 80(Whole No. 609): 1-28, 1966.
Rowbotham, Sheila. Women, Resistance and Revolution. New York: Random House (Vintage), 1974.
Roy, Donald. "Introduction" to Stanley Mathewson's Restriction of Output Among Unorganized Workers. Carbondale, Ill.: Southern Illinois University Press, 1969.
Roy, Patricia E. "The Oriental 'menace' in British Columbia." Pp. 287-297 in Michael Horn and Ronald Sabourin (eds.), Studies in Canadian Social History. Toronto: McClelland and Stewart, 1974.
Royal Commission on the Status of Women. "Poverty in relation to women." Pp. 209-220 in William E. Mann (ed.), Canada: A Sociological Profile. Toronto: Copp Clark, 1971.
Rubin, Zick. Liking and Loving: An Invitation to Social Psychology. New York: John Wiley & Sons, 1973.
Runciman, W. G. Relative Deprivation and Social Justice: A Study of Attitudes to Social Inequality in Twentieth-Century England. Berkeley: University of California Press, 1966.
Rushing, William A. "Class, power, and alienation: rural differences," Sociometry 33(June):166-177, 1970.
Ryan, William. "Preventive services in the social context: power, pathology, and prevention," Proceedings of the Mental Health Institute (May-June):49-58. Boulder, Col.: Western Interstate Commission for Higher Education, 1969.
———. Blaming the Victim. New York: Vintage (Random House), 1971.
Sahlins, Marshall D. "On the sociology of primitive exchange." Pp. 139-236 in The Relevance of Models for Social Anthropology. A.S.A. Monograph No. 1. London: Tavistock, 1965.
———. Stone-Age Economics. Chicago: Aldine, 1972.
Scheff, Thomas J. "The labelling theory of mental illness," American Sociological Review 39(June):444-452, 1974.
Schiller, Bradley R. The Economics of Poverty and Discrimination. Englewood Cliffs, N.J.: Prentice-Hall, 1976.
Schreiber, E. M. and G. T. Nygreen. "Subjective social class in America: 1945-68," Social Forces 48(March):348-356, 1970.
Schumann, Michael, Frank Gerlach, Albert Gschlössl, and Petra Milhoffer. Am Beispiel der Septemberstreiks — Anfang der Rekonstruktionsperiode der Arbeiterklasse? Frankfurt am Main: Europäische Verlagsanstalt, 1971.
Secord, Paul F. and Carl W. Backman. Social Psychology. 2nd ed. New York: McGraw-Hill, 1974.
Seeman, Melvin. "On the meaning of alienation," American Sociological Review 54(December):783-791, 1959.
———. "Alienation and engagement." Pp. 467-527 in Angus Campbell and Philip Converse (eds.), The Human Meaning of Social Change. New York: Russell Sage, 1972a.
———. "Alienation in pre-crisis France," American Sociological Review 37 (August):385-402, 1972b.
Seligman, Martin E. P. Helplessness: On Depression, Development, and Death. San Francisco: W. H. Freeman, 1975.

Sennett, Richard and Jonathan Cobb. The Hidden Injuries of Class. New York: Knopf, 1972.

Serrin, William. The Company and the Union: The 'Civilized Relationship' of the General Motors Corporation and the United Automobile Workers. New York: Random House (Vintage), 1973.

Shaw, Martin. Marxism and Social Science: The Roots of Social Knowledge. London: Pluto Press, 1975.

Shepard, Jon M. "Functional specialization, alienation, and job satisfaction," Industrial and Labor Relations Review 23(January):207-219, 1970.

———. Automation and Alienation: A Study of Office and Factory Workers. Cambridge, Mass.: MIT Press, 1971.

——— and Thomas R. Panko. "Alienation and social referents." Paper presented to the Ad Hoc Group on Alienation, International Sociological Association Meetings, Toronto, 1974.

Sheppard, Harold L. and Neal Q. Herrick. Where Have All the Robots Gone?: Worker Dissatisfaction in the '70s. New York: Free Press of Glencoe, 1972.

Sherif, Mustafer. "A study of some social factors in perception," Archives of Psychology No. 187, 1935.

Shiels, Howard D. "Agricultural Technology and Societal Evolution." Unpublished Doctoral Dissertation, University of Wisconsin, 1969.

———. "The importance of agriculture from the perspective of neoevolutionary theory," Rural Sociology 37(June):167-188, 1972.

Shostak, Arthur B. Blue-Collar Life. New York: Random House, 1969.

Siemiatycki, Jack. "The distribution of disease," Canadian Dimension 10(June): 15-25; 58, 1974.

Sigelman, Carol K. "Social-class and ethnic differences in language development." Pp. 227-254 in Lawrence S. Wrightsman, Social Psychology in the Seventies. Monterey, Calif.: Brooks/Cole (Wadsworth), 1972.

Simpson, George Eaton and J. Milton Yinger. Racial and Cultural Minorities. 3rd ed. New York: Harper and Row, 1965.

Skinner, B. F. Science and Human Behavior. New York: Macmillan, 1953.

———. Beyond Freedom and Dignity. New York: Knopf, 1971.

Smith, Adam. The Wealth of Nations. New York: Random House (Modern Library), 1937.

Smith, Anthony D. Theories of Nationalism. London: Duckworth, 1971.

Smith, Dorothy E. "An analysis of ideological structures and how women are excluded: considerations for academic women," Canadian Review of Sociology and Anthropology 12(November):353-369, 1975.

Smith, M. Brewster. "Competence and socialization." Pp. 270-320 in John A. Clausen (ed.), Socialization and Society. Boston: Little, Brown, 1968.

Snyder, David and Paula M. Hudis. "Occupational income and the effects of minority competition and segregation," American Sociological Review 41 (April):209-234, 1976.

Sorrentino, Richard M. and Judith-Ann Short. "Effects of fear of success on women's performance at masculine versus feminine tasks," Journal of Research in Personality 8:277-290, 1974.

———, Neil Vidmar, and Michael Goodstadt. "Opinion change in a crisis: effects of the 1970 Canadian kidnapping crisis on political and ethnic attitudes," Canadian Journal of Behavioural Science 6(3):199-219, 1974.

Spates, James L. "Counterculture and dominant culture values: a cross-national analysis of the underground press and dominant culture magazines," American Sociological Review 41(December):868-883, 1976.

Spencer, Herbert. The Principles of Sociology. New York: D. Appleton, 1884.

Stein, D. D. "The influence of belief systems on interpersonal preference: a validation study of Rokeach's theory of prejudice," Psychological Monographs 80(Whole No. 616), 1966.

Stember, Charles H. *Education and Attitude Change*. New York: Institute of Human Relations Press, 1961.

Stoll, Clarice Stasz. *Female and Male: Socialization, Social Roles, and Social Structure*. Dubuque, Iowa: W. C. Brown, 1974.

Strauss, Murray A. "Communication, creativity, and problem-solving ability of middle- and working-class families in three societies," *American Journal of Sociology* 73(January):417-430, 1968.

Stryker, Sheldon. "Role-taking accuracy and adjustment," *Sociometry* 20:286-296, 1957.

Sullerot, Evelyne. *Women, Society, and Change*. New York: McGraw-Hill, 1971.

Swados, Harvey. "The myth of the happy worker." Pp. 105-113 in Eric and Mary Josephson (eds.), *Man Alone: Alienation in Modern Society*. New York: Dell (Laurel), 1962.

Swanson, Guy. "Mead and Freud: their relevance for social psychology." Pp. 25-45 in Jerome G. Manis and B. N. Meltzer (eds.), *Symbolic Interaction: A Reader in Social Psychology*. Boston: Allyn and Bacon, 1967.

Swingle, Paul G. and Angelo Santi. "Communication in non-zero-sum games," *Journal of Personality and Social Psychology* 23(July):54-63, 1972.

Sydiaha, D. and J. Rempel. "Motivational and attitudinal characteristics of Indian school children as measured by the Thematic Apperception Test." Pp. 278-287 in J. W. Berry and G. J. S. Wilde (eds.), *Social Psychology: The Canadian Context*. Toronto: McClelland and Stewart, 1972.

Szymanski, Albert. "Racial discrimination and White gain," *American Sociological Review* 41(June):403-413, 1976.

Tallman, Irving and Gary Miller. "Class differences in family problem solving: the effects verbal ability, hierarchical structure and role expectations," *Sociometry* 37(March):13-37, 1974.

Tannenbaum, Arnold S. *Social Psychology of the Work Organization*. Belmont, Calif.: Wadsworth, 1966.

————. *Control in Organizations*. New York: McGraw-Hill, 1968.

Taylor, Donald M. and Lise M. Simard. "The role of bilingualism in cross-cultural communications." Pp. 139-148 in J. W. Berry and G. J. S. Wilde (eds.), *Social Psychology: The Canadian Context*. Toronto: McClelland and Stewart, 1972.

Taylor, Laurie and Paul Walton. "Industrial sabotage: motives and meanings." Pp. 219-245 in Stanley Cohen (ed.), *Images of Deviance*. Harmondsworth, Eng.: Penguin, 1972.

Taylor, Norman W. "The French-Canadian industrial entrepreneur and his social environment." Pp. 271-295 in Marcel Rioux and Yves Martin (eds.), *French-Canadian Society*. vol. I. Toronto: McClelland and Stewart, 1964.

Teeple, Gary (ed.). *Capitalism and the National Question in Canada*. Toronto: University of Toronto Press, 1972.

Terkel, Studs. *Working: People Talk About What They Do All Day and How They Feel About What They Do*. New York: Pantheon (Random House), 1972 (Wildwood House Ltd.).

Thibaut, John. "An experimental study of the cohesiveness of underprivileged groups," *Human Relations* 3:251-278, 1950.

———— and Claude Faucheux. "The development of contractual norms in a bargaining situation under two types of stress," *Journal of Experimental Social Psychology* 1:89-102, 1965.

———— and Harold H. Kelley. *The Social Psychology of Groups*. New York: John Wiley & Sons, 1959.

Thomas, Darwin L., David D. Franks, and James M. Calonico. "Role-taking and power in social psychology," *American Sociological Review* 37(October):605-614, 1972.

Thompson, E. P. "Time, work-discipline, and industrial Capitalism," *Past and Present* No. 38(December):56-98, 1967.

Thompson, J. Lee. "Can Canada survive Survival? An article on Survival: A Thematic Guide to Canadian Literature," American Review of Canadian Studies 3:101-107, 1973.

Tittle, Charles R. "Institutional living and self-esteem," Social Problems 20 (Summer):65-77, 1972.

―― and Richard J. Hill. "Attitude measurement and prediction of behavior," Sociometry 30:199-213, 1967.

Tomeh, Aida K. "Informal participation in a metropolitan community," Sociological Quarterly 8(Winter):85-102, 1967.

Tresemer, David. "Fear of success: popular, but unproven," Psychology Today 7(March):82-85, 1974.

Truman, Tom. "A critique of Seymour M. Lipset's article: 'Value differences, absolute or relative: the English-speaking democracies'," Canadian Journal of Political Science 4(December):497-525, 1971.

Tudor, Bill. "A specification of relationships between job complexity and powerlessness," American Sociological Review 37(October):596-604, 1972.

Turner, R. Jay. "Occupational inadequacy and psychiatric disorder." Paper presented at the meetings of the Society for the Study of Social Issues, New York, 1973.

Turner, Ralph B. "The public perception of protest," American Sociological Review 34(December):815-831, 1969.

Turner, Roy (ed.). Ethnomethodology: Selected Readings. Harmondsworth, Eng.: Penguin, 1974.

Udy, Stanley H. Work in Traditional and Modern Society. Englewood Cliffs, N.J.: Prentice-Hall, 1970.

Upjohn Institute. Work in America. Cambridge: MIT Press, 1973.

VanLoon, Rick. "Political participation in Canada: the 1965 election," Canadian Journal of Political Science 3(March):376-399, 1970.

Vener, Arthur M. and Clinton A. Snyder. "The pre-school child's awareness and anticipation of adult sex-roles," Sociometry 29:159-168, 1966.

Verba, Sidney and Norman H. Nie. Participation in America: Political Democracy and Social Equality. New York: Harper and Row, 1972.

Vinacke, W. Edgar. "Variables in experimental games: toward a field theory," Psychological Bulletin 71(April):293-318, 1969.

Warner, Lyle G. and Melvin L. DeFleur. "Attitude as an interactional concept: social constraint and social distance as intervening variables between attitudes and action," American Sociological Review 34(April):153-169, 1969.

Warnock, John W. "Metropolis/hinterland: the lost theme in Canadian letters," Canadian Dimension 10(June):42-46, 1974.

――. "Imperialism and the Canadian left," Canadian Dimension 11(March): 15-25, 1976.

Watson, Goodwin and David Johnson. Social Psychology: Issues and Insights. Philadelphia: Lippincott, 1972.

Weber, Max. The Protestant Ethic and the Spirit of Capitalism. New York: Scribner, 1958a.

――. From Max Weber. Hans Gerth and C. Wright Mills (eds.), New York: Oxford University Press, 1958b.

――. The Theory of Social and Economic Organization. Talcott Parsons (ed.), New York: Free Press, 1964.

Wellman, Barry, Paul Craven, Marilyn Whitaker, Sheila Du Toit, and Harvey Stevens. "The uses of community: community ties and support systems." Centre for Urban and Community Studies and Department of Sociology, University of Toronto, Research paper No. 47, 1971.

Westergaard, J. H. "The rediscovery of the cash nexus: some recent interpretations of trends in British class structure." Pp. 111-138 in The Socialist Register. London: Merlin Press, 1970.

White, Ralph and Ronald Lippitt. "Leader behavior and member reaction in three 'social climates'." Pp. 527-553 in Dorwin Cartwright and Alvin Zander (eds.), *Group Dynamics*. New York: Harper and Row, 1960.

White, Terrence H. "Autonomy in work: are women any different?" Pp. 213-226 in Marylee Stephenson (ed.), *Women in Canada*. Toronto: New Press, 1973.

Whitestone, Bruce. "Shedding false images," *London Free Press*, March 11, 1974.

Whyte, William H. *The Organization Man*. Garden City, N.Y.: Doubleday (Anchor), 1957.

Wicker, Allan W. "Attitudes versus actions: the relationship of verbal and overt behavioral responses to attitude objects," *Journal of Social Issues* 25(4):41-78, 1969.

Wiley, Mary Glenn. "Sex roles in games," *Sociometry* 36(December):526-541, 1973.

Wilkening, E. A. and Richard D. Rodefeld. "Job satisfaction of owner-managers, hired managers, and hired workers as related to farm, social, and job characteristics." Paper read at Rural Sociological Society, Baton Rouge, Louisiana, August, 1972.

Williams, Robin. *Strangers Next Door*. Englewood Cliffs, N.J.: Prentice-Hall, 1964.

Wilmott, Peter and Michael Young. *Family and Class in a London Suburb*. Harmondsworth, Eng.: Penguin, 1968.

Winchel, Ronny, Diane Fenner and Phillip Shaver. "Impact of coeducation on 'fear of success' imagery expressed by male and female high school students," *Journal of Educational Psychology* 66(May):726-730, 1974.

Winks, Robin W. *The Blacks in Canada: A History*. Montreal: McGill-Queen's University Press, 1971.

Women's Press Collective. *Women at Work: Ontario, 1850-1930*. Toronto: Canadian Women's Educational Press, 1974.

Women's Studies Group. "Relations of production, relations of reproduction." University of Birmingham, *Working Studies in Cultural Studies*, vol. 9:95-118, 1976.

Yackley, Andrew and Wallace E. Lambert. "Inter-ethnic group competition and levels of aspiration." Pp. 214-228 in J. W. Berry and G. J. S. Wilde (eds.), *Social Psychology: The Canadian Context*. Toronto: McClelland and Stewart, 1972.

Young, Michael and Peter Willmott. *Family and Kinship in East London*. London: Routledge and Kegan Paul, 1960.

Zajonc, Robert B. "The process of cognitive tuning in communication," *Journal of Abnormal and Social Psychology* 61:159-167, 1960.

────── and David M. Wolfe. "Cognitive consequences of a person's position in a formal organization," *Human Relations* 19(February):139-150, 1966.

Zander, Alvin, Arthur R. Cohen, and Ezra Stotland. "Power and the relations among professions." Pp. 15-34 in Dorwin Cartwright (ed.), *Studies in Social Power*. Ann Arbor, Mich.: Institute for Social Research, 1959.

Zaretsky, Eli. "Capitalism, the family, and personal life," *Socialist Revolution* 3:1-108, 1973.

Zdravomyslov, A. G., V. P. Rozhin, and V. A. Iadov. *Man and His Work*. White Plains, N.Y.: International Arts and Sciences Press, 1970.

Zeitlin, Irving. *Marxism: A Re-examination*. New York: Van Nostrand, 1967.

──────. *Ideology and the Development of Sociological Theory*. Englewood Cliffs, N.J.: Prentice-Hall, 1968.

Zeitlin, Maurice. *Revolutionary Politics and the Cuban Working Class*. Princeton, N.J.: Princeton University Press, 1967.

──────. "Corporate ownership and control: the large corporation and the Capitalist class," *American Journal of Sociology* 79(March):1073-1119, 1974.

Zweig, Ferdynand. *The Worker in an Affluent Society*. London: Heinemann, 1961.

INDEX

Deutsch, Morton, 101, 104-5
Dialectical relationships, 35, 44
Discrimination see Racial-ethnic conflicts
Distributive justice, 25
Division of labor: Adam Smith's view of, 21; Marx on, 33, 34, 70, 114, 118; as arising from "human nature", 40; Durkheim on, 58, 59, 115; related to exchange, cooperation, and competition, 115, 118, 120, 121; and alienation, 130, 133, 163
Dohrenwend, B., 182
Doob, Anthony N., 150
Dorris, William, 102-3
Dosman, Edgar, 208, 219
Douvan, Elizabeth, 211
Doyle, Bertram, 198
Dramaturgy, 93-95
Dunnette, Marvin, 252
Dunning, Richard, 219
Durkheim, Emile, 55-61, 62, 63

"Economic anthropologists," 108
Ego defenses, 176-77
Elites, 78, 79, 141
Empathy, 84-85
Encounter groups, 260.
see also Sensitivity training
Engels, Friedrich: on the Reformation, 68; on racism and sexism, 186, 187; on nationalism, 230, 231
Equality of opportunity, 22
Ethnomethodology, 95
Exchange relationships: in Marxian theory, 33, 114-15, 118, 120; in primitive societies, 108-114; technological development, 114, 116-18, 120-21; related to population size and density, 114-15, 120, 121; Durkheim on, 115, 119, 120; Malthus on, 115
Exchange Theory, 24-30; view of interpersonal relationships, 25-28; account of social organization, 28-29, 30; and Marxian theory, 47, 48; Cooley on, 82-83; and experiments on cooperation and competition, 100, 104-112 passim, 117
Exploitation: as source of racial-ethnic and sexual antagonism, 186, 187, 188, 191

"False consciousness," 17, 37, 40
Family, 54-55, 186-87
Fanon, Frantz, 46, 231
Faucheux, Claude, 9, 10, 21, 25

Faunce, William, 176
Ferree, Myra, 223-24
"Fetishism of commodities", 40-41, 42, 43
see also Commodity treatment of workers
Flora, Cornelia, 193
Form, William H., 156
"Frankfurt School", 44, 45, 46, 47, 142, 143
French, John, 127
French Canadians: discrimination against, 190, 195, 198-99, 209; other-orientedness of, 205; characteristics of, 209-10; work orientations, 220-21; class consciousness of, 220-21; nationalism of, 244
Freud, Sigmund, 44, 45, 46, 62
Freudo-Marxists, 44-47
Fried, Robert, 156, 157, 159
Fromm, Erich, 46-47, 203
Functional Theory of Stratification, 28, 54, 56, 153
Functionalism, 50-64, 82, 83, 91, 115

Galbraith, John Kenneth, 75
Gans, Herbert, 156, 157-58, 166
Garfinkel, Harold, 95
Gartrell, John, 121, 129
"Generalized other", 89, 90
Gerard, Harold, 8, 9, 10, 99, 101, 152
Gergen, Kenneth, 7, 8, 9
Gilmour, Robert S., 147
Ginsberg, M., 116-18
Goffman, Erving, 8, 93-95, 150, 151-52, 153, 162, 249-50
Goldthorpe, John H., 155
Graburn, Nelson, 131
Grayson, Paul, 234
Greer, Germaine, 204
Griffin, John, 198
Gross, Alan E., 150

Hall, Edward, 103
Hamilton, Richard, 192, 193
Harner, Michael, 118
Harvey, Ted, 245
Henry, Frances, 205
Hess, Robert, 169, 171
Hobbes, Thomas, 9, 51, 53
Hobhouse, L. T., 116-18
Hodges, Harold M., 158, 172
Hoggart, Richard, 156, 157, 165, 166
Hollingshead, A. B., 182
Homans, George, 25, 28, 29, 30, 154
Horner, Matina, 211-12
Horowitz, Gad, 233, 240, 241, 244
Housework, 217, 223-25

Managers: Weber on, 74
Mandel, Ernest, 117
Manipulation: Mills on, 77, 78
Maoism, 231
Marcuse, Herbert, 45, 46, 47, 52, 142, 153, 165, 166
Marglin, Stephen, 132
Market exchange conception of society, 30
see also Exchange Theory
"Market value": in Exchange Theory view of interpersonal relationships, 25-26, 27.
see also Value and labor
Marriage: and mental health, 217-18; alienating effects for women, 217-19
Marwell, Gerald, 120
Marx, Karl, 33-44: critique of classical political economy, 33-34, 47, 71; conception of human nature, 34-35, 57; on alienation, 35-37, 38, 40, 58, 61, 76, 128, 134, 135, 159, 160, 174; on class consciousness, 42-43, 48, 143, 160; on competition, 63, 108, 119; on capitalism, 67, 70; on rationality, 81; on racism and sexism, 186-87; on nationalism, 230, 231
Marxism: and Exchange Theory, 47, 48; Weber on, 68, 71
Maryl, William, 95
Mass media, 165-66
Materialism, 2; of Bentham, 17; of Marxists, 43
Mathewson, Stanley, 137
Mauss, Marcel, 108, 109, 112
McCormick, Thelma, 226
Mead, George Herbert, 88-92, 248
Mead, Margaret, 108
"Means-ends" orientation, 36, 139, 142, 149, 154, 155, 173, 193.
see also Alienation, Commodity treatment of workers
Meichenbaum, D. H., 170
Meissner, Martin, 163
Mental hospitals, 249-50
Mental illness: and alienation, 177-83 passim, 215; causes, 178-79, 180-81; relationship with class, 179, 181-83; and employment status, 179-80; among women, 215-19
Mercantilism, 16
Merton, Robert, 56, 62: contributions to theory of anomie, 60-61; on bureaucrats, 75
Mézáros, Isvan, 35
Michael, S. T., 182

Michener, Andrew, 167
Middle class, rise of, 16
Milgram, Stanley, 3, 4, 5, 6, 30, 47, 63, 167
Mills, C. Wright, 76-79: on alienation, 77, 140, 148; on power elite, 78, 79, 141; on labor elite, 79, 138; on social problems, 248
Mills, Theodore, 101-102
Minority influence, 260-63
Monopoly, 47
Morris, Richard T., 261
Moscovici, Serge, 261, 262

National character, 229
National characteristics of Canadians, 231-38; self-directedness or other-directedness, 231-3, 235-6, 237; achievement motivation, 232, 233, 236, 237; conservativism, 232, 233, 237; elitism, 232, 233, 234-5, 236, 237; "inferiority complex", 237-38, 243, 245; historical processes producing, 238-46
Nationalism, 230-31; in Quebec, 244; in English Canada, 244-45
Native people: discrimination against, 189-90, 195, 198; class consciousness of, 220; personality characteristics, 207, 208-9; attitudes towards work, 219-20
Nelson, J. I., 147
Nemeth, Charlan, 261, 262
"Neo-interactionists", 91-92
New Democratic Party, 145
Nord, Walter, 27
Norms: establishment of group, 12, 29; Durkheim on, 57, 58, 59, 61; Merton on, 60, 61; and "bystander emergencies", 63; Cooley on, 87; Garfinkel on, 95; related to exchange, cooperation, and competition, 119, 120

Oakley, Ann, 224-25
Okraku, Ishmael, 141, 146
Ollman, Bertell, 37
Olsen, Marvin, 264
"Open system theory", 62-63
Oppression: effects on working-class people, 173, 174, 175; effects on minority groups, 207-10; effects on women, 210-19
"Organic solidarity", (Durkheim's theory of) 58, 59
Organicism, 53, 55-57, 62-63
Organization of workers (Marx), 42